a

sociology of

sociology

a sociology of sociology

by
Robert W.
Friedrichs

Fp

THE FREE PRESS
A Division of Macmillan Publishing Co., Inc.
New York

Collier Macmillan Publishers
London

Printed in the United States of America

The Free Press
A Division of Macmillan Publishing Co., Inc.
866 Third Avenue, New York, N.Y. 10022

Collier Macmillan Canada, Ltd.

First Free Press Paperback Edition 1972

Library of Congress Catalog Card Number: 77-91882

printing number
2 3 4 5 6 7 8 9 10

For Kenneth Underwood,
who stood, even at a distance,
as model for the academician
in dialogue with the world

Contents

Foreword

SOMETHING has changed in American sociology, and Robert Friedrichs' book attests the fact. It examines the claims of a scientific sociology by criteria other than those found in such self-criticism as American sociology did undertake in the post-war period now ending. That self-criticism developed within a set of assumptions which are now themselves matters for debate. Anticipating the author's argument by recapitulating it would be no service to the reader; Professor Friedrichs, in any case, is quite competent to speak for himself. He has documented the way in which a discussion of the scientific status of sociology at first revolved upon itself (and served, at the same time, as a legitimation of the prevailing distribution of power and influence in academic sociology) and then—precisely when its curious admixture of involution and self-congratulation was at its height (or its nadir)—moved beyond the boundaries set for it.

Many colleagues are cited in this work; none will be able to claim that they have been dealt with unfairly. The author's conclusions are his own, and are no less authentic for having been advanced in a tentative way. Professor Friedrichs' conception of the development of thought is historical; he understands his work as an element in a situation which in itself inevitably will be transcended. The book, however, is a contribution to a new balance of intellectual forces in the social sciences. Perhaps the most useful procedure, in this preface, would be to sketch something of its international context.

At first sight, the effort seems gratuitous. Professor Friedrichs has documented amply, if documentation were required, the vertiginous domestic post-war ascent of American sociology. As the United States became a dominant world power, American sociology's international fortunes rose correspondingly. Where Talcott Parsons, and entire generations before him, had made scholarly pilgrimages to Europe, did not now younger Europeans (and many older ones, too) take the opposite path? Despite rear-guard actions fought by some of the established figures—incorrigible, or more accurately, it would seem, unteachable—what were once the great metropolitan centers of sociology fell under American influence. Industrial sociology at Paris, opinion studies at Frankfurt, and mobility studies at the London School of Economics—such was the measure of empiricism's influence.

Appearances of this sort, however, were deceptive. For some elements in the European universities, American sociology seemed to offer a broom with which to sweep away a century's accumulated metaphysical dust. Comte was a European, no doubt, but Comte's program for a science of society was being put into effect by Yankee pioneers—no less Comtean for their failure to have read the master. This view overlooked the European origins of empirical sociology. To historical ignorance, however, it added sociological blindness: the post-war emphasis on research technique in Europe reflected many of the social imperatives that accounted for similar emphases in America. A society dominated by large-scale organization, a political system manipulated to produce consensus, a culture that had lost a sense of transcendence (whether in traditional religious or revolutionary humanist form)—these had no use for a critical or reflective sociology. What was needed, apart from political legitimation and moral reassurance, was concrete information on the actual functioning of men within social settings deemed immutable. Alternatively, guidance was sought on the way to reinforce or, if necessary, engender that immutability.

An empirical sociology of the kind celebrated in the late 1940's and 1950's in the United States and imitated by some in Europe was quite unable to offer that guidance. Not the least impressive aspect of the moral and intellectual scandal represented by Project Camelot was, as Robert Nisbet has seen, its intellectual fraudulence: Rarely has so much been promised by those able to deliver so little. To the credit of scholars like Robert Merton, they abstained from absurd claims as to what sociology could do in its present state. They insisted that they were laboring to construct an intellectual edifice which by its nature would remain forever incomplete, and that in any case, they were far in the rear of the natural sciences. The very comparison, however, implied hopes about what sociology might accomplish at some future date if sufficient resources were put at the disposal of those who subscribed to the belief in a natural science model for social science. The moral asceticism of the scholars who developed this position is beyond question. It may be suggested, nevertheless, that the response they obtained for their programatic conception of sociology was due to a political climate in which the potential uses of an empirical sociology and its actual capacities were hardly distinguished by eager clients.

We touch, here, upon a fundamental characteristic of empirical sociology. There is a very real sense in which its findings may be used for quite divergent political ends. Much depends upon the extrapolations from data, the interpretations to which they are subjected. A good deal of the empirical work done in post-war Europe, even in a period that seemed to be one of unequivocal American influence, embodied the reformist or radical political traditions never quite missing from European sociologies. The work of Georges Friedmann and his group on the condition of the working class in French factories, the enquiries by the *Institut für Sozialforschung* into the structure of German popular "authoritarianism," the work by David Glass and his colleagues at London on the mechanisms (particularly selection through education) of the British class system were not dictated by a conception of a cumulative and pure sociology. Rather, they sought to explore social institutions in a critical manner, with a view toward accumulating the sort of knowledge that would enable men to construct a more rational, a more just, polity. Briefly, it may be suggested that a semblance of intellectual convergence, upon examination, did not quite conceal basic differences as to the uses of sociology. The European practitioners of a committed sociology, moreover, worked in an intellectual atmosphere still charged with philosophical meaning. They differed, in this respect, from Americans, whose political sense of the uses of sociology was no less acute than theirs, but whose larger intellectual horizon was far flatter.

I have said that the political meaning or utilization of an empirical sociology is open; the same findings may well be incorporated in differing visions of the polity. This openness is also a characteristic of the dimensions of sociology bearing upon our view of human nature, of the course of human history. The limits of the autonomy of empirical sociology, of course, vary from case to case. Ordinary public-opinion surveys, for instance, generally rest upon liberal conceptions of the efficacy of public opinion which suppress some fundamental aspects of political process in industrial societies. Notions of "reference groups" often assume an innate provincialism as a human characteristic (despite the fact that many who promulgate these notions pride themselves on their own cosmopolitanism). Professor Friedrichs' work concerns sociological interpretation in this open area, where political predisposition and philosophical idea are at least as efficacious as empirical data in shaping the conclusions of sociologists.

It is common enough to assert that a pragmatic philosophy constitutes the philosophical background of American sociology. It is frequently forgotten, however, that pragmatism was a systematic sort of philosophic discourse—developed in an encounter with philosophical tradition. The vulgarized derivatives of pragmatism and, afterward, the same sort of derivatives of neo-positivism, must be distinguished from the serious philosophical efforts represented by the original doctrines. The absence of metaphysics vaunted by British thinkers, after all, is a consequence of a highly developed philosophical tradition: The association of the teaching of philosophy and sociology at the London School of Economics (and sociology's belated incorporation in the Honors School of Philosophy, Politics and Economics at Oxford) attest the philosophical nature of the British position. In this country, however, we have been confronted by conceptual tradition distinguished precisely by its separation from philosophy. In Europe, a substantial education in philosophy has been a consistent component of the education of sociologists: The attendant contention of doctrines has in the long run contributed to a very considerable self-awareness on the part of sociologists.

The epistemological positions taken by sociologists in Europe have been many: neo-Kantianism, neo-positivism, phenomenology, a Hegelian Marxism and a positivistic Marxism, existentialism, and several sorts of theologically induced ontology, not the least, Thomism. These positions each have generated a number of variants, and the elements have been combined with an entire range of political options. The emergence of a Catholic Left strongly influenced by Marxism suggests that the intrinsic possibilities for doctrinal combinations in this situation have been many, if by no means infinite. At the same time, the recent promulgation of structuralism in its many Parisian versions shows that reflection on method in the social sciences, at a certain point, must inevitably transform itself into philosophical discourse.

For our immediate purposes, the point is to see that Professor Friedrichs' effort to re-think the office and import of empirical sociology is part of a larger movement of thought, which may well constitute a general response to separate national versions of the same felt imperatives. A sociology conceived in rigorously empirical terms has turned out to be so restricted that it could not meet its stated functions; particularly, an empirical sociology has been overtaken by new trends in industrial social structure. (The announcement of the "end of ideology" was followed in short order by the students' revolt, and the analysis of consensual integration in America preceded the decomposition of our polity in the mid-60's.) In addition to questions of this sort, addressed to perplexities as to our historical direction, there have been others, tuned to the recurring moral dilemma of man in society: How shall we live?

Let us consider, in very brief compass, two instances of recent European sociological debate. The first, appropriately enough, is taking place in western man's common spiritual capital, Paris. The reformed curriculum for instruction in sociology, proposed to the Ministry of Education by the French University teachers of sociology in 1966 as part of the Fouchet reforms in higher education, seemed to mark the end of an epoch. Philosophy was all but eliminated from the sociology curriculum; the discipline was conceived in terms remarkably similar to those prevailing in America. Yet, outside the lecture halls (and, often enough, inside them) a different sort of debate went on. Were the social sciences, and *pari passu* sociology, to be treated as part of a large effort to de-code and demystify human history? Structuralism in the version propounded by Lévi-Strauss insisted on the fundamentally limited and recurrent nature of the forms of society and culture, on the applicability of the techniques of a general analytic language to history. A Marxist counter-attack, of sorts, was mounted from the *École Normale Superieur*: Althusser and his disciples opposed to this version of structuralism a Marxism purified—if that is the word—of its humanistic content. To a Marxism concerned with the realization of a human potential, they opposed a Marxism defined by the analysis of objective (primarily economic) structures. Meanwhile, the Marxist humanists insisted on the primacy of a sociology rooted in the conception of potential human purpose, a sociology critical of the oppressiveness of institutions. Henri Lefebvre, who at Strasbourg and Nanterre was the teacher closest to the leaders of the May, 1968, revolution, may be considered the most significant spokesman in sociology of this group. Its affiliation with the work of Jean-Paul Sartre is clear. Meanwhile, among some of the younger sociologists, like Pierre Bourdieu, the assimilation of a developed research methodology gave rise to a more open interpretation of the practical operations of enquiry—in effect, a revolt against undue schematization and formalization, by those at home in the new language of sociological discourse. Some of these tendencies have found a rather unique expression in the work of Alain Touraine, who is at home in both traditions. Touraine has insisted on the limits of an analysis confined to predictable constraints. His own sociology encompasses the transcending of constraint. A similar analysis of the overcoming of institutional definitions and boundaries can be found—if in a different language—in the work on religion by Henri Desroche. Desroche, a former Dominican influenced by Marxism, has joined the theologians in the effort to locate in religious experience a type of human experience which can generate new sorts of communities.

It will be seen that the emphasis on much of French sociology, then, is on the social possibilities for transforming human existence rather than on the simple description of that existence. Much of this work, in turn, reflects the influence of the late George Gurvitch, himself an exceedingly vigorous polemicist. Gurvitch insisted on sociology's status as the study of society's self-transformation, and repudiated a preoccupation with technical method in favor of an analysis of social reality. Combining the influences of Marxism, of a French national tradition in sociology from Saint-Simon and Proudhon to Durkheim, and phenomenology, Gurvitch may now be seen to have led a successful defense against the technical trivialization of French sociology.

These tendencies, of course, exist in fruitful if uneasy co-existence with rather different ones. Uniting a rather broadly conceived positive and historical method with a sceptical liberalism, Raymond Aron has set himself the task of persuading his contemporaries that the world being what it is, it is not likely to change very much. He regards most of the methodological debate among his colleagues much as its critics regarded late medieval scholasticism. Yet he, too, would acknowledge the irreducible element of interpretation in sociological analysis.

It would appear that the Germans have lost their philosophical pre-eminence in European sociology to the French. It is true that the French, for years avid students of German thought, have now become again exporters of ideas across the Rhine. Nonetheless, the very particular post-war condition of German society—combined with the recovery of a profound national tradition in sociology—has imparted an intensity to sociological controversy in Germany which is instructive for the rest of us. The situation, if not manifesting quite so many facets as the one in France, is complex enough. I shall content myself here (as I did in the French case) with a summary statement of some of its major tendencies. German sociology, in the immediate post-war epoch, was notable for its practically mechanical (and often uncritical) reception of American social research technique. However, major philosophical tendencies did combine with this trend.

The post-war history of the relationship of the *Institut für Sozialforschung* in Frankfurt to empirical research is illuminating. Returned from the U.S. after the war, Theodor Adorno and Max Horkheimer insisted—in opposition to the representatives of a more or less unashamedly speculative tradition in sociology—that the delineation of an objective reality was a primary task of sociology. As post-war society consolidated itself in the Federal German Republic, the delineation of objective reality assumed an ever more constricted function. Social research technique, in effect, was fused with a political consecration of the institutions of the Federal Republic. Adorno and Horkheimer shifted their emphasis to a reinstitution of a critical dimension in sociology—if, to be sure, in highly abstract fashion.

Their intellectual origins lay in a highly academicized Marxist tradition. Quite another tradition inspired Helmut Schelsky, practically untranslated but surely one of the most significant of European post-war sociologists. A student of Hans Freyer, he subscribed to the belief that the dreadful immanence of industrial society, if it entailed a closure of man's previous metaphysical horizons, brought as compensation a great increment in man's collective capacity to master nature and society. "A Scientific Civilisation," as he termed it, demanded an empirical sociology as an instrument of self-observation and self-regulation. The empirical status of sociology reflected the limitations on man's capacity to transcend the immediate historical situation: Sociology mapped the world he was constrained to live in. Briefly, Schelsky's defense of empiricism in sociology rests on a metahistorical diagnosis of the course of civilization.

The work of Dahrendorf differs, again, from these emphases. He has translated his own writings, but the context of German debate in which they were conceived is not always easy to follow. Dahrendorf's endorsement of empiricism in sociology follows from his acceptance of Popper's doctrines *re* method in general. To this he has allied a political program closely resembling Popper's celebrated prescriptions for "piece-meal social engineering." Practically, it would seem, the position is close enough to Schelsky's. In fact, Dahrendorf distinguishes rather more sharply between the historical situation of western society and the representation of it in sociology. The latter, he supposes, depends upon relatively universal criteria of method.

A thorough attempt to ground sociology in historical experience, while legitimating the discipline's claims to give a critical rendering of what men have made of history, has now come from Frankfurt. Horkheimer's successor in the chair of sociology and philosophy there, Jürgen Habermas, in a notable series of works, has combined a critical sociology with a philosophical analysis of the process of social knowlege. He has depicted sociology, and in particular, empirical sociology, as part of a human effort to master the environment and has criticized the view that it can be understood as a mute recording device for social process. Sociology, and intellectual activity generally, as part of that process has a liberating function.

It will be seen, even from so cursory and schematic a treatment of France and Germany as this, that the kinds of debate now occurring in European sociology raise issues of the kind treated in this book. The recent increase in activity amongst sociologists in the state socialist regimes of eastern Europe suggests that debate of this sort cannot be far off there—if the minimal political conditions for its emergence exist. Discussion in Yugoslavia, and at other times in Czechoslovakia, Poland and, upon occasion, in the German Democratic Republic, allows us to envisage the inner structure of a Marxist critique of a reified Marxist sociology. Many of the problems of the self-definition of the sociologist *re* the institutions of power would appear to be similar to those we face.

That, however, is running ahead of the current argument. For the moment, let it be said that in concentrating on the American scene, Professor Friedrichs has not shown a limited and provincial viewpoint. Rather, by bringing to bear on that scene an array of arguments rooted in other traditions, he has contributed to the future attainment of a goal much to be desired: the reduction of our provincialism and the internationalization of scholarly debate in sociology.

NORMAN BIRNBAUM

Amherst College

Preface

ROBERT MERTON has recently—and quite appropriately—called for a sociologically sophisticated rendering of sociology's own biography. Pointing out that historians of science have themselves turned of late to the logical framework of the sociology of science as they seek to unravel the tangled skein of development of the natural sciences, he would have sociology begin the even more demanding task of analyzing its own history in terms of the social context that enveloped and nurtured it. Attention, he argues, should be granted such features as the "filiation" of paradigms and the differential status of their advocates, their diffusion and subsequent modification, the impact of a given socio-cultural milieu and a given time.

The volume before you is an effort to do just that, modified only by the insistence that, contrary to Merton's view that a "history" offers no instruction regarding the substantive viability of a "theoretical" posture, such an enterprise may be justified by the light it sheds on today's internecine battles over the discipline's paradigmatic base. History may have little or no adjudicative role when confronted by conflicting theoretical claims in the natural sciences. But the same should not be claimed of the social sciences, for cognitive activity in the latter realm is of necessity social and thus must be seen as interactive with the substantive concerns of such disciplines. Still, the issue I would seem to take with Merton may be more apparent than real when it is noted that the present exercise is not offered as a "history," but rather as a "sociology" of sociology. The epistemologies then become commensurate, the potential interaction more self-evident. Those who would demand justification for the latter need but turn to the body of the text itself.

The book was quite self-consciously *not* titled "*The* Sociology of Sociology" for it does not claim to have discovered the only defensible paradigm for a sociological analysis of the discipline. But it does indeed claim to be examining sociology as it is and has been advanced over the past generation or two in the United States. The empirical data necessary to support that claim—as with Parsons' assertion that *The Structure of Social Action* was essentially an empirical exercise—must of necessity involve concrete reference to the sociological product of others if it is to avoid being seen simply as "A Sociology of *a* Sociology." The author must take lone responsibility for the former "sociology." But I would evidence our communal responsibility for the second "sociology." This I would have been unable to do without breaking into the argument time and again with empirical evidence: with chapter and verse drawn from the corpus of sociology itself.

I am burdened as well by a decision to direct the volume not simply to the fully trained sociologist well-attuned to the subtle features of his chosen profession and broadly informed of the drama's cast of characters. Although it is not written as a textbook *per se*, it would include the student, the academician in a related discipline, and the informed layman within its circle of readers. Thus, much evidence it will bring to bear may appear common knowledge to the enjoined sociologist.

Although the volume represents a new substantive thrust in American sociology and risks a radically new frame within which the discipline might seek self-understanding, it stands indebted to a host of those, both within and outside the field, who have sought to comprehend the interaction of science and society. I was fortunate to have come to sociology relatively late in my personal odyssey and so brought to it earlier ventures in history, philosophy, economics, and political science. These were capped, in sociology, by the skeptical empiricism of T. C. McCormick, the passionate historical engagement of Hans Gerth, and the fluent theoretical and epistemological sophistication of Howard Becker. To them I owe especial gratitude. With a move from Wisconsin to Columbia, the inspiration of Paul Lazarsfeld was added to that of McCormick, C. Wright Mills to that of Gerth, and Robert Merton to the foundation in Becker. The conceptual doors opened by each will be readily apparent in the work before the reader.

Although the seeds of the present work were planted more than a decade ago in seminars at Chapel Hill which focussed upon the presuppositions undergirding theory and model-building in the behavioral sciences, it was not until a sabbatical afforded a full year (1963–64) to extensive reading and intensive writing that the present volume began to take shape. Still, it was the stimulation of a continuing series of joint seminars in the sociology of science with John Ollom, a colleague in physics, that was to provide the point of departure and the sustaining logic that frames the effort, for it was through Professor Ollom that I was introduced to Thomas Kuhn's demonstrably exciting monograph, *The Structure of Scientific Revolutions*. And that has made all the difference. My indebtedness to Kuhn's insight into the life cycles of scientific paradigms will become so apparent in the pages ahead that I need do little more here than express my profound admiration for him. From that point on the jigsaw puzzle fell into place. All that remained was the burden of rhetoric and style. That the latter may have suffered is, I believe, no less apparent to the writer than to the reader. For the text may appear inordinately burdened with reference to the work of others. Had such reference been eliminated, the volume might have been considerably more modest in length. But if I had indeed taken such a step, the work would have then had to be retitled "A Sociology of *a* Sociology."

There are a number of other acknowledgments that must be offered even more explicitly. The section of Chapter 12 headed "Phenomenological Options" is a revision and extension of a paper entitled "Phenomenology as a General Theory of Social Action" published in *The Journal of Value Inquiry* (Spring, 1968), 2(1): 1–8; Chapters 7 and 8 represent a major expansion of an essay titled "Choice and Commitment in Social Research," *The American Sociologist* (February, 1968), 3(1): 8–11. It is quite clear that the work would still be in mid-passage if it were not for the sabbatical leave provided by Drew University, together with the post-doctoral grants made available by the Lilly Endowment and the Hazen Foundation. It was the Danforth Foundation that underwrote the epistemological probing at the University of North Carolina.

I would be remiss as well if I failed to express appreciation for the resources made available during the sabbatical year by the International House of Japan and I.C.U., both within range of the delightful semi-rural Japanese community which provided the setting for the larger portion of the work of that year. Indeed, if it had not been for the many manifestations of gracious concern on the part of our Japanese neighbors for the *gaijin* settled so unceremoniously in their midst, much of that leave might have been lost in the effort to acclimate a not atypical American family of four to the complex simplicity of the Japanese countryside. Thanks, too, must go to John Marsh, Principal of Mansfield College, Oxford, for making available the facilities of his Hall and for extending the very real privilege of working in the Bodleian.

Important, too, has been the feedback provided by the opportunity to present portions of the argument at the 1966 meetings of the International Sociological Association at Evian, the 1967 meetings of the American Sociological Association in San Francisco, and the graduate colloquia at both Columbia and Drew. More particularly I would acknowledge indebtedness to Norman Birnbaum and Robin Williams for the assessment each made of the manuscript or portions thereof, and to Peter Berger, Dwight Culver, Allan Eister, Joseph Elder, Charles Estus, Robert Herman, William L. Kolb, Alfred McClung Lee, Charles Loomis, Morton King, Arnold Nash, Robert Nisbet, Adam Schaff, and Edward Tiryakian—together with a host of others in related disciplines—in whose work the dialogical calling of social science has been made manifest. A special note of appreciation must be added for the manner in which the more perspicacious undergraduates at Drew and the graduate students at Brooklyn College pushed me towards a clarification of both the thesis developed herein and the rhetoric by which I sought to communicate it. Appreciation also is due to Miss Mary Lou Hahn, who assisted in compiling the bibliography, and to Mrs. Ruth Demaree and her associates, who carried the major typing burden.

Finally, I would be completely unrealistic if I were to overlook the profound contribution made by a wife whose latent talent for colloquial Japanese and imperviousness to cultural shock and sheer material deprivation enabled the sabbatical year at Tokyo's rural fringe to be a successful one. For this and all that every scholar who seeks to be productive owes his spouse, I thank her.

R. W. F.

Preface to the Paperback Edition

It has been three years since the galleys of the original edition left the author's desk. By the time this paperback edition appears, nearly nine years will have passed since the inception of this unsolicited and, in many ways, over-ambitious first attempt to examine, at some length, the sub-community that identifies itself as "sociology." There would be every reason to assume, therefore, that subsequent developments within the discipline, within the society in which it is rooted, and within the author's own perspective (through the critiques of his students and his peers) may have seriously dated the volume and the projections it risked.

The fact is that the central thesis has held up startlingly well and may, in fact, command even more "face validity" than when initially set forth.

This is particularly true of the volume's readiness to ignore —for heuristic purposes—Thomas Kuhn's clear admonition in the first edition (1962) of *The Structure of Scientific Revolutions* that his thesis could be applied with profit only to the "mature," that is, *natural,* sciences. For, shortly after the appearance of *A Sociology of Sociology,* the Postscript to Kuhn's second edition (1970a)—reinforced by an essay published in response to his early British critics (1970b)—indicated not only that he had come 'round to the view that "the members of all scientific communities, including the schools of the 'pre-paradigm' period, share the sorts of elements which I have collectively labelled 'a paradigm' " (1970a, p. 179), but also that he wished to underscore "the need for similar and, above all, for comparative study of the corresponding communities in other fields" (1970a, p. 209). That I was far from alone within the social sciences in ignoring his initial claim of exclusivity may be illustrated by the attention granted Kuhn's thesis in the recent work of Douglas (1971) and of Lodahl and Gordon (1972) in sociology; by Coats (1969), Loasby (1971), Bronfenbrenner (1971), and Kunin and Weaver (1971) in economics; by Wolin (1968, 1969), Almond (1969), Easton (1969), and Truman (1965) in political science; by Scholte (1966) in anthropology; and by the N.S.F.-funded Program in the History of the Social Sciences at Duke University which has largely focused about the extrapolation of paradigm revolutions to the "less mature" sciences.

This is not to say that he would share *all* the features he had associated with the paradigmatic life-style of a "mature" science. *Symbolic generalizations* (within sociology the characterization, for instance, of its subject matter as fundamentally "systematic," as at root "conflict-ridden," or in terms of a "dialectical interaction" of the two); *metaphysical models* (sociologically, perhaps, when societies are viewed as cybernetically equilibrating and/or evolving in some linear fashion —or the opposite); *shared values* (illustrated herein by the particular self-image assumed by the sociologist): these, he was now ready to grant, are types of paradigms to which natural science had no exclusive claim. What he would reserve to the "mature" scientific community would be the role of the *exemplar:* "the concrete puzzle–solutions which, employed as models or examples, can replace explicit rules as a basis for the solution of the remaining puzzles of normal science" (1970a, p. 175).

Though I am tempted to agree with Kuhn at this point, the heuristic fruitfulness I have discovered to date in the application of his general thesis to sociology impels me to risk his approbation again. I have never claimed that there was complete symmetry between the biography of a social science such as sociology and any of the natural sciences; indeed, the nature of their fundamental disparity is the central message of my book. Paradoxically, however, I have found it necessary to *posit* their identity in order to establish the conditions under which their distinctive epistemological features may be precipitated.

Exemplars *do* play a major role in the life cycle of sociological paradigms. It is just that they take on a different character within our discipline. This is not the place in which to present the evidence; I have detailed it elsewhere for those who are epistemologically inclined (Friedrichs, 1972b). All I find myself forced to say is that the *nature* of the "puzzle solutions" and of "normal" science in the social sphere differs substantially between the natural sciences and a fully social science. When one begins to perceive sociology as concerned fundamentally with the "puzzles" centered about the compulsive hold of given social constructions and "normal" social science (and thus sociology) wed immutably to a dialectical epistemology, then Kuhn's exclusively natural scientific claim to the crucial role of "exemplars" also dissolves.

Of more general interest, I suspect, was my conclusion that the sociology of the 1970s would evidence an increase in paradigmatic options, and that we would begin to tolerate that pluralism as a measure of our social scientific maturity. Certainly there are few who would deny that the theoretical and epistemological marketplace is more crowded than ever with prospective paradigms—symbolic, metaphysical, valuational, and exemplary. The phrase "orthodox sociology" is rapidly disappearing from our seminars and learned papers, except when offered within an historically descriptive context. Both undergraduate and graduate students are reading Goffman, Skinner, Levi–Strauss, the Marx of the "Grundrisse," "West Coast" and "East Coast" phenomenology, classic and contemporary Anarchism, Merleau–Ponty, Sartre, and Hegel, whether or not they have been assigned. A new Black Ibn Khaldun has been rediscovered.

There may be, however, less unanimity over a concomitant growth in pluralistic "tolerance" on the part of those on either side of the lectern. Still, if the publishing houses stand, as I believe they do, as indicators of a discipline's consumptive tolerance range, they offer an encouraging sign. And to discover the American Sociological Association honoring Oliver Cox, Harrison White, and the present author with its highest purely symbolic honors has at least convinced the latter that *his* projection of the likely extension of the profession's (to be distinguished from the discipline's) pluralistic tolerance had been considerably underestimated both in speed and in breadth.

But what of the suggestion that a "dialectical" image of our subject matter was likely to gain in prominence? Certainly the strategic location (in the *American Sociological Review*) and supportive tenor of Louis Schneider's recent essay (1971), together with a distillation of my own views in the most prominent of the British journals (Friedrichs, 1972a), grant some credence to the projection. Other direct evidence may be found in the recent work of Schermerhorn (1970), in the introductory text by Coulson and Riddell (1970), and in the use made of the term in the inaugural lecture celebrating the first professorship in sociology at that bastion of the natural sciences and the humanities, Cambridge University (Barnes, 1970). And, recalling that I argue that it is the perspective rather than the term itself that is apt to gain in initial prominence, Alvin Gouldner's (1970) best-selling advocacy of a "reflexive" sociology is strongly suggestive. The appearance of Gurvitch (1971) in English translation and the recent, essentially sociological, "primer" by Boulding (1970) characterizing history as "dialectics and development" in its subtitle, and the "excursion" into the "dialectics of social life" by the Chairman of Columbia University's anthropology department (Murphy, 1971), however, confront the concept and its historical roots head on and cannot help but assist in relocating it within the sociological vocabulary of the West. Finally, the startling openness of the profession to the present volume stands as preliminary vindication.

All of which is not to say that the author has been unmoved by his critics, unaware that his grasp of the field was quite finite, or blind to developments in the discipline that he had not expected. Gouldner's *The Coming Crisis of Western Sociology,* though strikingly congruent with the present volume (see Friedrichs, 1971), convinced me that *I* was wrong in arguing that those who criticize Parsons's emphasis on equilibrium theory as reflecting relative conservatism (vis-à-vis the ideological "norm" within sociology) were heading in the *wrong* direction—that the tree's epistemological roots were the culprit, not its ideological fruit. The seeds from which the Parsonian orchard has grown, along with the pruning and replanting since, reflect the hand of a horticulturist consistently dedicated to the essential suitability of American institutional development. The epistemological trail which I would have my reader follow must be viewed simply as an unraveling of the genetic code which Parsons consciously or unconsciously selected as a vocabulary and grammar that would serve that end.

In placing before the reader the array of paradigmatic alternatives to the image offered by "system" as the presumptive subject matter of the discipline, I had been insufficiently aware of the distinctive flavor and potential impact of the "West Coast" phenomenological version of "everyday reality" that typically centers about the name of Harold Garfinkel—a major oversight, but perhaps one that many had made who stood geographically distant from the circle of southern California institutions which has harbored most of the "invisible college" involved, and who were not privy to the informal media of communication typically used.

Much the same must be admitted relative to my discussion of the "young" versus the "mature" Marx. The appearance in English of portions of his unpublished "Grundrisse" (McLellan, 1971) suggests that there was more coherence to Marx's intellectual biography than his published works led one to believe. At the same time, the potential corporate integrity of his work in no way disturbs the argument set forth herein: that sociology in the socialist world is facing the same essential split into "system" and "conflict," "priestly" and "prophetic" polarities we witness within Western, essentially American, sociology. Indeed, one is heartened by the potential impact of the newly available manuscripts, for they cannot help but serve as additional building blocks by means of which a truly international sociology may ultimately be constructed.

But by far the most portentous development—at least for the paradigmatic options available to the discipline—has been the unexpected (at least to the present author) revival of Comtean positivism. The seeds that I had taken note of lay in Homans's regression to Skinnerian categories and William Catton's more sophisticated extrapolation of the deceased Lundberg's infatuation with man as "mechanism"—a posture that led Catton to conclude, via analogy with Newton's first "Law of Motion," that sociology need concern itself *only* with change. Upon this base has burst B. F. Skinner's extremely provocative *Beyond Freedom and Dignity* (1971). Combined as it can readily be with the new thrust within the upper echelon of sociology's professional elite toward social policy-making roles, it promises to offer, when transformed in vocabulary from biological and psychological to *social* "reinforcement," a new paradigmatic point of departure for all those who would continue to identify the epistemology of sociology with that of the natural sciences.

The strenuous efforts I have taken in this volume to clarify the "metaphysical model" of social man that lies at the base of any completely and consistently applied *natural* science epistemology (culminating in Chapter 10: "Sociological Man as Natural Man") are completely vindicated in Skinner's treatise. It is a realm in which notions of freedom, dignity, and autonomy are fictions framed only for the innocent, and Skinner has the courage (and professional security) to finally let this be known. "Control," the key to the *method* of science, is projected upon man as his universal and inescapable condition; the fundamental criterion left to differentiate his behavior is relative *efficiency,* the very yardstick that serves as final adjudicator between alternative resolutions to the puzzles of natural science.

If a new breed of sociological Skinnerians were to pick up the paradigmatic burdens currently slipping from the shoulders of the Parsonians (as I suspect may turn out to be the case), it would be altogether within the Western—and particularly the American—tradition. Both Skinner and Parsons appear to have been the products of essentially Calvinist households and inherited from them the weight of the latter's predestinarian assumption, expressed in the mature Skinner's rejection of any "freedom" or "autonomy" to man and, in Parsons, through the conceptual priority and presumptive status his later work has granted to "system." Both have responded to the tension which history has all too often documented as the posture's concomitant, by preaching a startlingly similar "innerworldly asceticism"—Parsons in his "voluntaristic" insistence upon "effort" and "the exercise of will," Skinner by his commandment that thou shalt "control." And the end result of both projections is, as with Weber, a rationized, impersonal world devoid of conflict or autonomy. Theirs is not the harsh imagery of a *1984;* rather, it reflects the paternalistic transposition of a Calvinist communitarianism into a cybernetic secularism, with program-bearing behavioral scientists standing as "functional equivalents" to scripture-bearing men of the cloth.

This is not, of course, altogether fair to either. My acknowledgment of Parsons's numerous lasting contributions to sociology's self-understanding are evident throughout this volume. And, there is a demonstrably humane voice behind the overt positivism in Skinner that is trying to say something more, just as the vision of a secularized holy Roman Church lay behind the manic pretensions of the prophet of Paris. Skinner comes closest to identifying its authenticity when he characterizes the course of evolution as "sensitizing" an organism to the "consequences of its actions." Translated into human social terms, this is the classic legal and philosophic definition of "responsibility"—and identical to the empirical referent that I, following Weber, identify herein as a central product of the sociologist's craft. But Skinner remains caught in the equally classic dilemma of providing no existentially convincing motivational basis for furthering one's "sensitivity to the consequences of one's actions," since he can grant no empirical referents to "freedom" or "autonomy"—as is the case with all those who model their image of social man exclusively upon the presumptive logic of the natural sciences. Yet it is precisely this dilemma to which the *dialectical* nature of the logic of *social* research would speak.

One final note of warning: For those who would reduce sociology to the sociology of knowledge, the present volume has been—and cannot help but continue to be—a disappointment, for the author is among that overwhelming majority within the discipline who presume it to be a science, however dialectical in nature. This means that it must assume that there *is* something "out there," accessible to public verification which, though socially constructed, cannot be reduced at any given moment to mere phenomena projected by a prior, though "bracketed," perceptual "reality," and rooted in a completely relativized substratum that is "social class," "vested interest," or some other form of "false consciousness." Thus, the present venture is in the tradition of the sociology of science, not in that of the sociology of knowledge, as the latter developed upon the classic foundations laid by Karl Mannheim. Science condemns itself to normative as well as descriptive criteria, as Thomas Kuhn has been among the latest of a lengthy lineage to testify. There is "good" scientific practice and "bad" scientific practice—to put the issue in its most simplistic terms—and this exercise must be judged accordingly. It must not be judged on the assumption that all that is of concern to sociology—or to a sociology of sociology—simply reflects the relativized interests of a given stratum or biography.

This is not to say that *sociologists* are not prone to intrude their own class, professional, or personal interests upon their work. Indeed, Chapters 7 and 8 are perhaps the fullest expression of the manifold ways in which they are *forced* to do so. And, very conscious efforts are made to illustrate the precise way in which those dominating the direction taken by sociology over the past generation have unwittingly subordinated themselves to such interests. For those who wish to explore our history in this regard, in more detail, no guide currently available is more provocative than Alvin Gouldner's *The Coming Crisis of Western Sociology.*

Yet to acknowledge a firm and crucial place to a sociology of knowledge that roots itself in a Mannheimian relativism is not to reduce sociology itself or this exercise in the sociology of science, in solipsistic fashion, to it. Exceedingly persistent "order" in human action over time is available to public verification by the perceptive and trained craftsman, as is the opportunity to contribute to its dialectical denial as awareness of that order is bent back upon the site from which it was precipitated to permit and encourage its transcendence.

Thus, the relative empirical validity of the present effort is to be judged not only by its public verifiability, but also by the degree to which its audience is capable of denying it as a descriptively accurate account of their future activity as sociologists.

Bibliography

Almond, Gabriel, "Political Theory and Political Science," *American Political Science Review,* 63 (December 1969): 869–79.

Barnes, J. A., *Sociology in Cambridge, An Inaugural Lecture,* New York: Cambridge University Press, 1970.

Boulding, Kenneth E., *A Primer on Social Dynamics: History as Dialectics and Development,* New York: Free Press, 1970.

Bronfenbrenner, Martin, "The 'Structure of Revolutions' in Economic Thought," *History of Political Economy,* 3 (Spring 1971): 136–51.

Coats, A. W., "Is There a 'Structure of Scientific Revolutions' in Economics?", *Kyklos,* 22 (1969): 289–95.

Coulson, Margaret A. and David S. Riddell, *Approaching Sociology: A Critical Introduction,* New York: Humanities Press, 1970.

Douglas, Jack, "The Rhetoric of Science and the Origins of Statistical Social Thought: The Case of Durkheim's Suicide," in E. A. Tiryakian, ed., *The Phenomenon of Sociology,* New York: Appleton–Century–Crofts, 1971, pp. 44–57.

Easton, David, "The New Revolution in Political Science," *American Political Science Review,* 63 (December 1969): 1051–61.

Friedrichs, Robert W., "Friedrichs on Gouldner: The Case for a Plurality of Sociologies of Sociology," *LSU Journal of Sociology,* 2 (October 1971): 100–106.

______, "Dialectical Sociology: Toward a Resolution of the Current 'Crisis' in Western Sociology," *British Journal of Sociology,* 23 (March 1972).

______, "Dialectical Sociology: An Exemplar for the 1970s" *Social Forces,* 50 (June 1972).

Gouldner, Alvin W., *The Coming Crisis of Western Sociology,* New York: Basic Books, 1970.

Gurvitch, Georges, *The Social Frameworks of Knowledge,* Oxford: Blackwell, 1971.

Kuhn, Thomas S., *The Structure of Scientific Revolutions,* Second Ed., Enlarged, Chicago: University of Chicago Press, 1970.

______, "Reflections on My Critics," in Imre Lakatos and Alan Musgrave, eds., *Criticism and the Growth of Knowledge,* New York: Cambridge University Press, 1970.

Kunin, Leonard and F. Stirton Weaver, "On the Structure of Scientific Revolutions in Economics," *History of Political Economy,* 3 (Fall 1971).

Loasby, Brian J., "Hypothesis and Paradigm in the Theory of the Firm," *Economic Journal,* 81 (December 1971).

Lodahl, Janice B. and Gerald Gordon, "The Structure of Scientific Fields and the Functioning of University Graduate Departments," *American Sociological Review,* 37 (February 1972): 57–72.

McLellan, David, *Marx's Grundrisse,* London: Macmillan, 1971.

Murphy, Robert F., *The Dialectics of Social Life: Alarms*

and Excursions in the Anthropological Theory, New York: Basic Books, 1971.

Schermerhorn, R. A., *Comparative Ethnic Relations: A Framework for Theory and Research,* New York: Random House, 1970.

Schneider, Louis, "Dialectic in Sociology," *American Sociological Review,* 36 (August 1971): 667–78.

Scholte, Bob, "Epistemic Paradigms: Some Problems in Cross-Cultural Research in Social Anthropological History and Theory," *American Anthropologist,* 68 (1966): 1192–1201.

Skinner, B. F., *Beyond Freedom and Dignity,* New York: Knopf, 1971.

Truman, David, "Disillusion and Regeneration: The Quest For a Discipline," *American Political Science Review,* 59 (December 1965): 865–73.

Wolin, Sheldon, "Paradigms and Political Theories," in P. King and B. C. Parekh, eds., *Politics and Experience,* New York: Cambridge University Press, 1968, pp. 125–52.

———, "Political Theory as a Vocation," *American Political Science Review,* 63 (December 1969): 1062–82.

1 The Structure of Social Scientific Revolutions

It can be said that the first wisdom of sociology is this—things are not what they seem.

Peter Berger

IN 1962 Thomas Kuhn, one among a new breed of historians of science who are tutored in the ways of the behavioral as well as the natural sciences, published a slim volume entitled *The Structure of Scientific Revolutions*. Whatever one's judgment may be of its central thesis, one thing was soon made abundantly clear: The essay itself has stirred a revolutionary reappraisal of the life history of a science among both historians and sociologists.

Completed under the stimulus of a year at the Center for Advanced Studies in the Behavioral Sciences, it offered a completely new perspective by which one might come to understand the maturation and growth of a scientific discipline. Its central thesis is that the communal life of science, rather than being dictated by the formal logic that justifies its methods of verification, demonstrates considerable affinity to the life-cycle of the political community. Indeed, Kuhn's posture is quite literally a "radical" one, for the political community that he offers as a pattern is not the constitutional community that fits the ideological proclivities of the contemporary West but rather—as the title of the volume would indicate—the *revolutionary* community.

Kuhn rejects as insufficient the traditional image that

portrays a science as but the linear accumulation of one verified hypothesis after another, broken simply by periods of greater or lesser growth in specific sub-disciplines. Even a notion as fundamental to the orthodox discourse of scientists as "progress" is questioned, for the revolutions of which he would speak are seen to alter the fundamental images of reality that provide a science with its stable base—thus disallowing any easy assessment in scalar terms. Kuhn would argue, in fact, that major shifts in empirical and/or theoretical models are grounded in what are essentially *conversion* experiences in which a new "world view" competes almost ideologically with an older frame of reference. There is no simple, clean-cut movement from "error" to "truth." What appears is a competing *gestalt* that redefines crucial problems, introduces new methods, and establishes uniquely new standards for solutions. At the moment of polarization the devices and procedures that mediate differences in perspective and evidence in "normal," non-crisis science fail. Advocates of alternative models talk past one another, for there is—at least for that moment—no fully institutionalized framework of substantive assumptions that both accept. Personal factors, aesthetic predilections, the age, role, and private interests of individuals, and sub-specializations all are involved. Persuasion rather than proof is king.

For those intimately acquainted with the family squabbles that have erupted among sociologists over the past generation or two, a number of tempting illustrations may have already come to mind. If so, I would like to shift the blame from Kuhn to myself. For Kuhn draws his case from evidence provided by the natural sciences—largely, in fact, from physics and chemistry. Indeed, he is quite explicit in contending that a science must have reached a level of maturation beyond the mere eclectic assemblage of competing "schools" to qualify for inclusion beneath the umbrella he raises. But if one were to apply Kuhn's posture to the behavioral sciences, it would be possible to conceive of the divisive struggle currently being waged within sociology not as humiliating proof of the discipline's relative immaturity but as evidence of its coming of age. It might enable us to begin safely to ignore the incessant demand that we profess ourselves worthy of the label "scientific" and instead get on with both the routines and the revolutions that are thereby our nature. Rather than running in embarrassment from evidence of fundamentally competitive models, we might find we were justified by them.

The thesis developed in *The Structure of Scientific Revolutions* need not be expected to apply in detail to sociology—or to any of the behavioral or social sciences. Kuhn would be the last to profess that it did. Indeed, he suggests a number of potential disparities quite explicitly. Nor would it be correct to infer that I have found the match a complete one, for it should be quite obvious to even the most single-minded devotee of sociology that her history is much more attenuated than that of her neighbors in the physical and biological sciences. Still, the argument Kuhn has fabricated has not only captured the imagination of sociologists of science, but has moved beyond into the realm of general speculation concerning our professional nature and destiny. The issue, then, is no longer whether the thesis warrants application to sociology, but how long we should entertain it as a reasonable hypothesis without attempting to assess its plausibility in terms of the facts at hand.

I have been forced to the conclusion that Kuhn's thesis is far too intriguing to allow it to remain but an engaging possibility. If through systematic confrontation with the empirical evidence presently available its applicability to the biography of sociology can be denied, a burgeoning range of speculative hypotheses can be laid to rest. If, on the other hand, it were sustained, the self-understanding achieved might be enormous. As with all social research, the exercise would not claim finality—simply the responsible and imaginative testing of an hypothesis through the application of pertinent, publicly documented experience. Indeed, the first portion of the volume is even more modest. It does not purport to have initiated a series of case studies in depth or to have been responsible for gathering original data. As suggested above, it seeks only to assay its viability "in terms of the facts at hand." Later segments of the volume, however, are less reticent. Rather than merely applying Kuhn's stencil to "the empirical evidence available," they attempt to spell out the potential implications of the Kuhn thesis for sociology's future and for its relationship with the humanities. If it is deemed in the process to step beyond the confines of a sociology of sociology, so be it. Still, it would seem wise not to judge even the latter sections prematurely, for the definition of the scope of the first term in the phrase "sociology of sociology" is of course contingent upon a resolution of the last term.

Much the larger portion of the activity we have come to designate as scientific, Kuhn acknowledges, falls under the rubric "normal"; that is, the participants share a common "paradigm." The latter term has become particularly popular among sociologists of late because it communicates the notion expressed by the term "model" without invoking that word's physical imagery. A paradigm is an "example," but one that is typically linguistic in base rather than physical, a conceptual reference rather than a perceptual one. But it is a *prime* example that serves as a common frame of reference, a "definition of the situation" that provides a basic focus of orientation. "Normal science" proceeds within the confines of a single paradigm, a relatively "classic" study or experiment that has been sufficiently compelling to shape a discipline's sense of where its problems lie, what its appropriate tools and methods are, and the kinds of solutions for which it might settle. It is grasped before a conceptual schema, a "law," a theory, or a set of methodological postulates are articulated and communicates a "sense of the real" that elicits commitment and out of which further commitments are then drawn. Without such a paradigmatic foundation, all problems, all methods and tools, all "facts," and all criteria for identifying solutions are likely to appear equally relevant. With it one is possessed of map and compass; the gradual linkage of percept to concept becomes cumulative and relatively routine. Although such "normal science" demands skill, imagination, and perseverance, it is similar to solving a complex jigsaw puzzle. That is, the rules are known; one is assured that the pieces will eventually fit with another and that there are both enough and yet not too many. That this may not be the case—indeed, is not—is never a major burden while gradual headway in ordering the bits and pieces within the frame is clearly being made.

The initial consolidation of a discipline about a single

paradigm is typically accompanied, Kuhn suggests, by its acquiring a recognized place in the larger scientific community and curriculum, developing its own journals, and elaborating into specialized sub-disciplines. The individual scientist need no longer begin each empirical or theoretical venture anew, creating his own first principles, his own language, methods, and standards. Rather, the common base is made clear in textbooks, with the history of the substantive area appearing to have led inevitably to the present paradigm. Those few who are unable to accept the consensus thus achieved are written off as beyond the scientific pale or returned to the problematic realm of philosophy which an empirical science would seek to leave behind.

With the paradigmatic base thus secured, the group or community turns its attention to what is essentially mop-up work. Members focus on those facts and theories that are seen as most relevant in the paradigm's terms. The more imaginative extend them to related areas through analogy and prediction. Constants are identified and quantitative laws are drawn. The few who would still operate in terms of other paradigms are simply ignored, for the discipline has concluded that there is no other scientifically justified stance for the given area. That the product of such normal science sacrifices novelty for precision and new departures for detailed explanations is to be expected and is, indeed, its strength. Such science progresses rapidly because it is not distracted by alternate frames. It narrows the range of meaningful problems sufficiently so that only the limited ingenuity of the particular scientist involved should inhibit their successful solution. Socially important problems that are not easily contained within the paradigm are simply put aside.

A scientist perceives little of this process self-consciously. His professional education takes place, typically, within the confines of a single paradigm. The structures that guide him are simply the way his science *is*. He learns them as he learns his mother language and the norms of his personal life: by internalizing as "real" the "reality" of those about him. The "rules" he lives by are raised to the level of consciousness only if and when the paradigm itself is shaken. Only then does he begin to subject them to critical examination and admit debate about them. And all this would appear to be to the good, for it protects normal science from being distracted by novelty that fails to penetrate to the heart of its paradigm. Normal science is rigid; it does not readily countenance threats to its foundation. Since that initial consensus—or, if the discipline has changed its paradigm before, its new "constitution"—had been paid for at such a high price, there is understandable reluctance to exchange it for another without extreme provocation. Normal science is continually burdened by inconsistency and uncertainty; they are its everyday fare and provide the puzzles for which it seeks answers. Only when they take the form of persistent anomalies may their base be legitimately questioned.

But even when anomalies of major dimensions do arise, they are treated initially as "counterinstances" that demand adjustment on the part of the earlier frame. *Ad hoc* modifications are brought into play that enable the established paradigm to cover the instance. Evidence *per se* is never by itself sufficient to light the fuse of revolution, scientific or political, for evidence has never been all neatly stacked in one direction. A scientist is by nature continually pushing against the frontier of the inexplicable; it does not startle him. He sees it simply as one more challenge to his ingenuity. And furthermore, he did not originally accept the paradigm on the basis of evidence but rather on the authority of text and teacher. If the anomaly persists, however, it will attract increasing attention—and from the discipline's more prominent figures. If it still resists resolution, the field will be defined increasingly in its terms. That is, the subject matter of the discipline will begin to center about the problem. More *ad hoc* arrangements will be suggested from increasingly disparate directions. In the process the routines of normal science will become blurred and quarrels will break out over how to interpret the common paradigm. But the reason the paradigm itself has remained relatively unsuspect is that there is no generally acceptable alternative. And science cannot proceed without a paradigm, for it by definition represents a scientist's fundamental frame of reference. The destruction of the old must await the candidacy of the new; the two must occur simultaneously. To have it otherwise would be to reject science itself.

The effort to fill the hiatus is likely to force some within the community involved to apply what had been the largely implicit assumptions of the older paradigm in an increasingly conscious fashion, focusing upon its elemental structure perhaps for the first time since its original acceptance. Such conscious attention to fundamentals has as one of its features an increased interest in philosophical analysis. Normally, Kuhn contends, the practicing scientist finds the speculative nature of philosophy of little interest. Those who have dabbled in it and whose projections are highly marketable because of their personal scientific prominence almost invariably lose status among their peers in the process. Yet a significant minority appear forced, when faced with a persistent anomaly, to re-examine the roots of their scientific assumptions—some to reassess the implications of the epistemological path they had chosen to tread.

Not unexpectedly, those who contribute most centrally to the fabrication of the new paradigm are apt to be relatively young and/or new to the discipline, men whose training and careers to that date had escaped the rigidities that were normal to socialization within the traditional paradigmatic framework. The more mature—although they may contribute significantly to the discovery of the anomalies that set the revolutionary process in motion—have been wed much too successfully and long to the earlier model. Indeed, the brightest minds of the generation dominant at the moment are apt to prove the most intransigent; they are the ones who will marshall the rearguard action and stand most stubbornly against the new claimant. Some will not be converted; they will simply be by-passed. Indeed, the revolution does not so much seek any direct conversion of the mass membership of the community but rather tries to capture those key figures who are the "gatekeepers" to the texts that guide the younger generation through the discipline's rites of passage and on into full responsibility in the field. A key to the maturity of a science, Kuhn points out, lies in the degree of dependence upon textbooks throughout the apprenticeship period. In the most fully developed sciences a student is not likely to be pushed beyond acquiring textbook knowledge until he moves on to his own creative research. Thus the text plays a role much more equivalent to "holy writ" in the natural sciences than it does in the social and behavioral sciences or in the humanities.

"Extraordinary science" entails, then, a sharp break from the cumulative march of "normal science," a temporary return to a situation much like that confronting the discipline prior to its original consolidation. There is no longer a clear-cut and secure path to guide one's choice of method. Hypotheses that might have been rejected at other times as extravagant are condoned; the air—professional meetings, the journals—is filled with dissent and rancor; philosophical forays are launched. The actual "revolution" occurs, however, only when an alternate paradigm and its advocates and supporters are primed and ready.

The term "revolution" is appropriate, Kuhn argues, not only because the new paradigm is incompatible with its predecessor, but also because there is no institutionalized conceptual framework that will encompass and mediate between the two—at least at the time. If there were, it would in fact be the reigning paradigm. This is not to say that there are no *commitments*, no implicit "rules" of the highest order, that frame one's identification with the larger community of science. Kuhn is quite clear about this, although he does little more than to suggest that they have to do with an obligation to extend the scope and precision with which the world is ordered. Normal science fails just as, in times of revolution, the normal channels of political discourse fail. Simple "proof" is insufficient because those adhering to the traditional paradigm and those supporting the new one use their separate paradigms in that paradigm's defense and because neither, at the time one is confronted with the choice, can claim to have integrated all empirical phenomena confronting the discipline. One must first step into one frame or the other—remain in faith or risk the new faith—before evidence for or against the new paradigm is sought. Nor can one argue that the successful new claimant to orthodoxy is able eventually to include the earlier; the earlier would have been changed in the process. What *may* be included is the capacity to order the phenomena that had been ordered successfully by the former. The retention of the earlier paradigm as in fact but a special, restricted case of the later one denies the earlier its original integrity and would threaten the integrity of the new.

The acceptance of the new frame is apt to call forth a new definition of the discipline itself. Certain old issues will be discarded as "unscientific" or relegated to the gray zone of applied science. Others that had been peripheral at best will now take the center of the stage, may perhaps be viewed as archetypical of that entire branch of science. Methods and tools will change, as will the standards or criteria for identifying solutions. Theory that had appeared earlier to have been developed inductively and around which specialized sub-disciplinary concerns had come to be centered will be recast, as will the boundary lines of the sub-disciplines themselves.

The "world" that engages a scientist, Kuhn argues, is not simply an environment acted upon by a denatured epistemology mediated by a neutral language. Rather it is the joint product of a particular normal scientific tradition, with its associated vocabulary and grammar, and an environment. This means that after a revolutionary episode, the scientist must be re-educated in terms of a new image of the world. The shift in perception is analogous to a switch in visual *gestalt*—the pieces may be the same but the totality now takes on an entirely new order. Although scientists and philosophers have long sought a set of symbols and a logical frame that would emancipate them from the "subjectivity" of an implicit context, they have made little or no headway. The presumptive base remains. And when the *gestalt* that is imbedded in that base changes, a scientist finds himself confronted with a new world.

It might appear strange that such all-pervasive revolutions have not been routinely acknowledged as an inherent aspect of the life history of a science. But there is a very good reason for their relative "invisibility." We pointed earlier to the integral part played by textbooks in a mature science and the crucial role their "capture" plays in the transition to the new paradigm. The key to such lack of awareness lies in the fact that when the textbooks are re-written in terms of the new *gestalt*, the "history" of the discipline—insofar as it appears in the texts at all—is rewritten as well. There is no partisan intent involved. The writers themselves now see the discipline's history *through* the new paradigm, and in all good faith select, rephrase, and emphasize as the main current of the discipline that thread of research and theory, among the many threads that had been spun, which indeed led most directly to the new *gestalt*. The rest, like forms of pre-hominid man-ape that succumbed to the vicissitudes of geological change and biological competition, are simply dropped from the lineage, although their ancestries and successes were, to a crucial moment, just as significant as those that survived in the new paradigm. A science that hesitates to forget its fathers, Whitehead warned us, is lost. No wonder, then, that science appears even to those most intimately involved as linear and cumulative. With each revolution the discipline re-draws its family tree.

"Progress" in the achievement of "truth," however, is not guaranteed by the succession of one paradigm after another. The frames are too limited—too culturally relative, the sociologist would put it—to provide a firm basis for applying either term. Within a single *gestalt*—that is, within a given phase of "normal" science—the former may well be quite appropriate. But "truth" would apply to neither. We know only the route we have taken, not the goal to be attained. Within the context of that lineage we may be in a position to claim only that one paradigm is more satisfactory than another. The ultimate paradigm stands inviolate.

The general thesis that Kuhn proffers, then, stands in the highest tradition of the sociology of knowledge and its more youthful progeny, the sociology of science. What we seek to discern in the venture ahead is the degree to which it may justifiably serve as a stencil for a sociology of sociology as well.

"Normal" and "Revolutionary" Sociology

2

> ... normal science repeatedly goes astray. And when it does—when, that is, the profession can no longer evade anomalies that subvert the existing tradition of scientific practice—then begin the extraordinary investigations that lead the profession at last to a new set of commitments, a new basis for the practice of science.
>
> Thomas Kuhn

Paradigmatic Consolidation

MANY sociologists, so personally involved in the disputes over theory that mark the cutting edge of any science, might be tempted to maintain that sociology has never in fact projected a common paradigm. Certainly it would be difficult to argue that there was any broad consensus regarding the fundamental nature of sociology's subject matter either in Europe or in America during the period leading up to the Second World War. No single theoretical posture or piece of research stood as a self-evident key to orthodoxy. Perhaps the closest approximation to a common point of departure in America lay in the notion expressed by the term "institution" as redefined by Sumner in conjunction with his coinage of the words "folkways" and "mores." Some introductory texts were organized around the particular position of the author or authors involved (as, for example, Ogburn's "cultural lag" thesis). Others, after introducing the student to an eclectic vocabulary drawn from a miscellany of the discipline's founding fathers, were likely simply to cluster a wide array of "social problems" within a series of relatively independent "institutions." No larger conceptual scheme existed other than the vertical dimension provided by social "dynamics" and the horizontal cut

Notes to this chapter will be found on pages 329–331.

supplied by social "statics." The entire package would then be labeled "society." When a volume was published on social theory *per se*, it would usually turn out to be either a translation of a classic from the German or French, or a survey of "schools" of thought traced from their origins to their contemporary disciples.

Bid by "action"

On the other hand, it would be equally difficult to deny that by the late 'thirties and early 'forties a singular image had begun to emerge. No single volume on sociological theory to appear in Europe or America over the middle third of the present century served more nearly as a common point of reference than did *The Structure of Social Action* (1937). In it Talcott Parsons claimed to have drawn together the viable threads from the positivistic warp and the idealistic woof woven by the discipline's fathers. The cellular unit of the paradigm was the "act," a term chosen quite self-consciously by Parsons to emphasize the contrast he would draw with the word "behavior" as it had come to be used in the positivist tradition. Whereas "behavior" reflected the sheer empirical phenomenon of movement, an "act" presumed, above all, an active, creative, evaluating "actor"; it was "voluntaristic," that is, it was directed toward a subjectively determined end through the choice of one among a number of alternative means. The general posture containing the paradigm Parsons labeled "analytical realism." It presumed both the appropriateness and the possibility of constituting "action" within a "system" that was logically closed. Indeed "systems" and "theory" were used interchangeably in the 1937 volume.

The relatively dormant state into which developments in theory fell during World War II served the position's interest, for it provided time for the new seed to germinate. Ten years later the action image had dug its roots deeply into the graduate curriculum in sociology at Harvard and had begun to attract allies in anthropology and psychology from what was to become Harvard's interdisciplinary Department of Social Relations. Harvard's graduates had in the meantime transplanted action seedlings into major sociology departments across the country.

The massive impact Parsons was to have upon American sociology, however, had to await the publication in 1951 of *Toward a General Theory of Action* and *The Social System* and, two years later, *Working Papers in the Theory of Action*. Together with *The Structure of Social Action*, these books represented a body of theory unique in American sociology in terms of its consistently rarefied level of abstraction, its systematic development, and, indeed, its sheer length and weight. To graduate students seeking the doctorate in the post-war period, it was almost as vital to know Parsons as it was to know statistics and to have a reading knowledge of German and French.

But an interesting and not-too-subtle change had taken place between the late 'thirties and the early 'fifties in the emphasis Parsons chose to give his posture and in the selective focus his audience chose to grant it. John Finley Scott (1963) documents this shift in his insightful paper, "The Changing Foundations of the Parsonian Action Scheme," drawing heavily upon a generally overlooked essay by Parsons written prior to the publication of *The Structure of Social Action*, titled "The Place of Ultimate Values in Sociology Theory" (1935). Scott concluded that whereas both the early essay and the *Structure* volume represented essentially philosophical attacks upon a stereotyped "behaviorism" in the name of a creative, fundamentally indeterminate, and subjective "action," his post-war publications masked the earlier polemic in equivocal language and that this represented a return to a cautious naturalism that could expect a more congenial response from his audience. Scott suggested, quite reasonably, that the shift in language and emphasis might well have come about in part through Parsons' quite practical effort to extend the action image to include those sociologists within his own department who had been unwilling to accept his philosophical predilections as well as others in the neighboring disciplines encompassed by the "Social Relations" context of the interdisciplinary department he chaired at Harvard. However, Parsons (1951b:52n) has come to speak quite openly of his later work as a very real "revision and extension" of his pre-war posture. He argues, in fact, that the earlier volume, unlike his later works, did not reflect the insights provided by psychoanalytic theory and the more recent developments in behavior psychology and in the anthropological analysis of culture.

Shift to "system"

There was, however, something considerably more self-evident in the new dispensation that caught Scott's inquiring eye. *Toward a General Theory of Action*—a volume directed at the social and behavioral sciences as a whole—continued to focus upon the term *action*. The *Working Papers*—aimed primarily at the social psychologist—also highlighted the word in its title. But the volume that sought to speak directly to sociologists—*The Social System*—permitted action to slip into the background and promoted *system* to the seat of honor. In *The Structure of Social Action*, system was merely an assumption; in *The Social System* it suddenly took on a substantive quality. No longer was system but the property of any logically consistent venture. Now it stood as surrogate for social reality, for the "stuff" of sociological inquiry. Here, at least for the sociologist *per se*, was a striking candidate for paradigmatic status. Indeed, one need not have looked as far as *The Social System* volume itself. The motif was plainly exhibited in the sub-sections and contents of the *General Theory* and *Working Paper* volumes themselves. Whenever one turns therein from the philosophical and semantic context to the substantive concern of sociologists, one is confronted not by action but by system. And whereas action—well motivated though its coinage may have been—had failed to touch a vital nerve in more than that small minority of sociologists who were philosophically sensitive, system somehow spoke in timely fashion to a much wider assemblage.

Link with functionalism

The mutual reinforcement supplied by the system image on the one hand and the proclivity of sociologists to accept it on the other was due to the impact on both of a common posture—*functionalist theory*. Although the fuctionalist stance runs through Comte's *consensus universalis* and Spencer's contention that integrative forces continually offset societal pressures for differentiation, its main lines were developed largely by anthropologists. Moving from William Robertson Smith and Franz Boas to Durkheim's analysis of primitive religion, it was made fully explicit in the work of Malinowski and Radcliffe-Brown and channeled back into sociology largely through the reception granted Ruth Benedict's minor classic, *Patterns of Culture*. The text of Parsons' *Structure of Social Action*, however, remained untouched; the word "function" did not even appear in its index. By 1945, however, Parsons (1945:48) had been thoroughly infected by the new strain. In detailing "The Present Position and Prospects of Systematic Theory in Sociology" for Gurvitch and Moore's *Twentieth Century Sociology*, he italicized the term, characterizing it as "the all-important concept," and distinguishing his new posture from his earlier "analytical" stance by terming it quite explicitly a "structural-functional system." That a change had indeed occurred in his perspective he admitted most explicitly in the prefaces to the succeeding editions of *The Structure of Social Action*. The 1949 edition, he wrote, represented "a shift in theoretical level from the analysis of social action as such to the structural-functional analysis of social systems" (1949:D). The 1968 preface states that "the theory had become more Durkheimian than Weberian"—particularly the relevance of the former "to the theory of an integrated sociocultural system, as this had come to be emphasized in the 'functional' school of British anthropology" (1968: xi).

But it would be inaccurate to imply that Parsons was the single channel through which functionalism was injected into the veins of post-war American sociology. Znaniecki, with *The Method of Sociology* in 1934, had preceded Parsons' diagnosis and prescription by a generation, while the larger discipline's courtship of functionalism had manifested itself widely enough by 1949 to have elicited Robert Merton's classic critique as the introductory essay in his *Social Theory and Social Structure*. The first text organized in functionalist terms, Kingsley Davis' *Human Society*, appeared the same year, followed a year later by George Homan's influential re-interpretation of a wide array of prior sociological studies in similar functionalist fashion in *The Human Group*. Of those works that set the tone for what was to become the sociological orthodoxy of the 'fifties, only Marion Levy's *The Structure of Society* appeared after Parsons' dual offering in 1951.

What Parsons did, then, that was so crucial was to offer a maturing discipline the image of *system* as its focal conceptual referent. Here was a single word that not only summed up the essential common denominator that ran through the wide array of functionalist positions, but made implicit functionalists of that broad band of non-theoretically oriented sociologists who were simply searching for a common semantic base to which they might anchor their professional vocabulary. "System" had an obviously attractive ring, in other words, to the many who found their discipline entirely too "unsystematic"; it anointed their work with the clarity of logic, blessed it with a conceptual rigor that they associated with the more firmly established sciences. Although the "ism" attached to "functional" served to remind the cautious that the forest of functionalism was cluttered with snares to catch the unwary, system stood forth as a relatively neutral alternative devoid of apparent substantive content and ready to serve the varied bidding of her diverse sociological masters.

Re-enforcement

But *system* would not in all probability have achieved the paradigmatic stature that it did had it not been for two other factors. The first was the sudden hand-in-glove development of cybernetics and the electronic computer. Forced into being by the technical demands of World War II, the clumsy electro-mechanical calculating devices harnessed to such developments as radar and sonar were granted a new civilian life when Norbert Wiener was astute enough to view them as potential self-regulating systems when articulated internally through feedback mechanisms. As one generation of computers replaced another, social theorists and methodologists began to see their system qualities as grist for sociological model-building. Since such simulation was unavoidably conditioned by the system-nature of the electronic computers themselves, the theoretical product inevitably took on a system cast. One of the by-products—"game theory"—was doubly attractive, for it enabled sociologists and cyberneticians to link two or more sub-systems into larger contextual systems in a manner analogous to the way in which human agents adjusted their responses to the action—or presumed intended action—of others. Suddenly sociologists seemed to possess conceptual and technical tools as precise as the neat models economists had been using for so long. And the paradigm that underwrote the bright new day was "system."

But perhaps an even more important factor supporting the new system edifice was to be found in the climate of the times. A combination of factors—the startlingly smooth transition from a wartime economy to the material reconstruction of Europe and the retooling demanded by the new electronic age, reinforced at a strategic moment by the demands of the Korean episode; de-Stalinization in Russia and the resistance of the Eastern European peoples to militant Marxism together with the collapse of McCarthyism in America; open-ended prosperity and the return to the homilies of family, education, and Eisenhower—all united to underwrite an era of unparalleled conformity and commitment to the *status quo*. David Riesman noted the trend at the beginning of the 'fifties when he coined the term "other-directedness." Essentially the same feature was elaborated thereafter in William Whyte's "organization man" syndrome at the conclusion of the decade, and capped by Daniel Bell's pronouncement of "the end of ideology." It was a period in the life history of the American intellectual that provided every kind of subtle support the system advocate might wish for a paradigm whose point of return was dictated by the relative equilibrium that was the image's unstated premise. An increasingly prosperous stability—professional as well as civic—conditioned the sociological as well as the lay mind, tempting the former to perceive in system and its operative theoretical model, functionalism, an image and a posture that might justify the new faith in an ordered transition from one equilibrium to another.

This is not to say, of course, that either system or "functionalism," its theoretical derivative, monopolized the paradigmatic life of sociology even in the 'fifties. Eclecticism was still being widely sold—particularly in the undergraduate marketplace which is so heavily conditioned by textbook style and by course syllabi set in graduate schools the generation before. Methodology, spurred by advances made during the military's sponsorship of survey research during World War II, seemed beholden to no master paradigm—until the model-building and game-playing made available to it by the digital computer linked it surreptitiously with the system presumption. Although psychoanalytic theory had been one of the factors that enabled Parsons to classify the surface contradictions of personality and society within a larger systemic whole, its role as a competing paradigm never began to approximate the impact it had made upon cultural anthropology in the 'forties.[1] Sociologists had been inoculated against it by the interactionist stance derived from George Herbert Mead. And the latter's emphasis upon role-expectations and the continual feed-back the latter presumed left the "interactionist school" unwitting allies of the more self-conscious system theorists. Dennis Wrong's (1961) plea for a sociology rooted in Freudian theory was eloquent testimony to the latter's relative absence.

C. Wright Mills was, of course, at the zenith of his productivity—but one of the reasons his voice stood out so clearly was that it seemed so out of tune with the over-all harmony. The University of Chicago, although failing in the post-war period to regain the predominant role it played in the 'twenties and 'thirties, seemed to maintain, both in its graduates and through the influence of the *American Journal of Sociology*, a self-conscious distance from the new orthodoxy preached in the eastern citadels of Harvard, Columbia, Princeton, and Yale. Although Mead's interactionism seemed no real barrier, the muck-raking tradition associated with Park and Ogburn's insistent focus upon social change served to insulate her and guarantee that she would be among the last to leave the skeptics' corner into which her pragmatic tradition had led her the generation before. Still, even Chicago's leading theorist was a Parsonian emissary. Edward Shils co-authored and co-edited a number of the more crucial Parsonian testaments, the two having maintained close intellectual rapport since the period before the publication of *The Structure of Social Action*.

Yet the degree of paradigmatic dominance that Kuhn perceives in histories of the natural sciences was not to be discovered even in American sociology in the 'fifties. Perhaps both the complexity of the social sciences and their inextricable involvement with human values will never allow such a level of near unanimity. Or, it may be that the logic of the social sciences is in some significant fashion out of key with that of the natural sciences, possessed, in the longer run, of a dynamic that short-circuits the "natural" order that stands as a paradigm's ultimate criterion.

Still, sociologists are well trained in the art of accepting half a loaf when the full loaf—precision, certitude, closure—is unavailable. Kuhn would be the first to admit that a paradigm is never completely unchallenged even at the height of its dominance in any given natural science. Skepticism is, after all, the life blood of the scientific mind. Excommunication, although figuratively appropriate at times in describing the response of the scientifically orthodox to those who would challenge the ruling paradigm, is unavailable to the open community of science. And if paradigmatic unity is but the approximate condition of a natural science even at the zenith of a "normal science" phase, then the utility of Kuhn's model for sociologists of sociology may yet be defended. Although the consolidation about the system paradigm in the decade and a half following World War II was far from total, the field of force that the image exerted was remarkable in light of the eclectic state of the discipline before the war. Furthermore, the *actually* operative images may be less crucial for our analysis than the image that was *thought* at the time to be dominant. Thus, although any sociologist active during this period could easily recall many a limited battle that continued to rage, the fact that stands out in retrospect is that system and its attendant notion, functionalism, was *deemed* by the well-informed professional to represent sociological orthodoxy in the 'fifties.

Maturation

Looking back from the vantage point of the mid-'sixties Don Martindale (1965 : 144) could characterize the rise of the paradigm's major theoretical implication—functionalism—as ". . . the most dramatic development in sociological theory since World War II." Of the two most recent texts available at the time of this writing that sought simply to draw together the major alternatives projected by the dominant theorists of the period, one—

Loomis' *Modern Social Theories* (1961)—enclosed them all within a scheme that had been developed in a volume titled, significantly, *Social Systems: Essays on Their Persistence and Change* (Loomis, 1960), while the other—Sorokin's *Sociological Theories of Today* (1966)—classified eleven of thirteen strains in system terms. A third volume (Demerath and Peterson, 1967) described in its sub-title as *A Reader on Contemporary Sociological Theory* . . . , granted the word "system" top billing in its main title.

There is considerable justification in concluding, then, that with the conceptual and theoretical withdrawal and return occasioned by World War II, sociology's pre-paradigmatic period of adolescence as a science was drawing to an end. A core vocabulary and a common theoretical posture were beginning to emerge. With them sociology seemed finally on the point of moving from the ordering of its own house to cumulative research. With its subject matter conceived in terms of system analysis, sociologists might confidently set out to piece together the functional imperatives that now appeared all about them, nesting one sub-system within another and enveloping all within a dynamic equilibrium.

Although the "Harvard School" dominated the first published version of the paradigm, the system image was not simply the product of a single mind or academic center. It appeared in varying format from the pens of a wide variety of social theorists scattered across the country. Although the encyclical-like nature of the "General Statement" that introduced Parsons and Shils' *Toward a General Theory of Action* in 1951 may have suggested the handiwork of a *Curia Romana*—signed as it was by nine of the most prominent theorists in the behavioral sciences—the many who lived and worked and had their sociological being within the paradigm bowed to no Pope, possessed no elaborate catechism in common. Although "convergence" became a popular term to apply to the theoretical currents of the day,[2] and use of the term "social system" was a sign of at least minimal sophistication among graduate students, orthodoxy, true to the American tradition, was plural. But equally true to that tradition, it would claim a core vocabulary and a simple credo that transcended sectarian boundaries. From its central conceptual reference—

system (the notion if not always the term)—all that identified the invisible fellowship of the true church flowed. For almost all the fundamental "stuff" that was the discipline's peculiar subject matter came to be spelled out in its terms. No longer was sociology to perceive the "group"—or the "individual" in the "group"—as its common starting point. Rather its vocabulary was to be reconstructed around relationships abstracted from the layman's world of persons, from the functional interrelationships that are presumed by system. Instead of the individual the sociologist now saw "role"; in the place of the group or the society, a nested sequence of interactive systems. Assuming the equilibrating order that is system over time, his attention turned from the disjunctive to dwell upon the reciprocal responses and countervailing forces that would be expected to maintain the integrity of the system in the face of strains introduced by external factors or through internally induced differentiation.

It was a posture that seemed to justify extrapolating the electronic computer beyond its function as a high-speed calculation instrument to simulating the actual structures of society. Parsons' interest in cybernetics was by no means accidental. The social had been set down as sharing the systemic nature of the digital computer. Thus the sociologist's focus shifted from relatively discrete "social problems" to an examination of the *functional* prerequisites of social systems and the dynamics involved in boundary maintenance.

Although no single keystone secured the paradigm's arch, Homan's analysis of the observations and experiments of Roethlisberger and Dickson in the Western Electric researches played a key role, similar to the one played by Malinowski's delineation of the "kula ring" in the functionalist revolution in anthropology the generation before. Indeed, even though Homans continued to speak in the earlier idiom of "individual" and "group," he extrapolated an image drawn from the examination of the small group to encompass the entirety of civilization in a virtuoso display of system analysis. That the pivotal research (the Hawthorne experiments), could remain so long unquestioned even though it was in fact startlingly weak in both method and interpretation suggests the paradigmatic need they seemed to have fulfilled.[3]

Sociology, of course, already had developed its own journals and acquired a recognized place in the academic firmament the generation before. Indeed, it had divided into a dozen or more easily recognized sub-disciplines. Meanwhile the last of the major universities had succumbed to the new vision, while the half dozen elite eastern colleges that had disdained her immodest adolescence yielded one by one in turn. Societies affiliated with the parent American Sociological Association multiplied, as did the journals they spawned. The dominant texts and authors of the pre-war period, which emphasized the institutional and problem (and/or cultural lag) approaches, were quickly overshadowed by those that rewrote the discipline's history in terms of the system assumption together with an explicit dedication to value-neutrality. Indeed, more young people were exposed to the new dispensation in the 'forties and 'fifties than had confronted sociology throughout its entire pre-paradigmatic history.

The new Ph.D. had no need, during this period, to underpin each empirical or theoretical venture with his own first principles, his own language, methods, and standards. The system paradigm was set down for him in lecture and text as "given." Those who proved to be ideologically or psychologically immune to the frame were apt to be written off as idiosyncratic and consigned to the speculative arena of philosophy or to the deserted halls of political activism. With its paradigmatic base assured, the discipline simply sought to get on with the normal tasks of any science—applying its paradigm to those facts and theories that appeared most amenable to its terms. The more imaginative were encouraged to extrapolate them in related areas through analogy and model construction. Structural categories were identified and theorems drawn up that could be assessed in quantitative terms. Sacrificing the dysfunctional for the functional, the dynamic for the static, did not at the time seem too great a price to pay for clarity of focus. Sociology was making rapid progress because it was not being distracted by fundamentally competing frames. By narrowing the range of meaningful problems, it assured itself that only the limited ingenuity of the particular sociologists involved would inhibit their solution. Such issues as power and irreducible conflict, not easily contained by the paradigm, were simply put aside.

It would be asking too much to expect sociologists—or any scientific community at an equivalent period—to have been self-consciously aware of the dynamics of the situation through which they were moving. The system paradigm was simply the way sociology "was." The substantive nature of the sociologist's commitment would be raised to the level of consciousness only if and when the paradigm itself were to be shaken. Only then would he begin to subject it to critical examination. And this would appear to be all to the good, for it protected his "normal" scientific activity from being distracted by novelty. Because the consensus that surrounded the paradigm had been paid for at such a high price but a short time before, sociologists should indeed have been reluctant to return to the barricades without extreme provocation. Thus, although sociology maintained a much more tentative and open posture *vis à vis* the revolutions that might yet await her than would be expected in the case of one of the more established natural sciences, she did seem, in the decade or two following the Second World War, securely tied to a systemic view of social reality. Though far from satisfied with her accomplishments, her practitioners had begun, by the end of the 'fifties, to taste the heady wine of self-conscious maturity. Who then would have predicted that such productive and hard-won consensus would shortly have been destroyed, that the discipline would find itself immersed again in the throes of paradigmatic revolution?

Division in the Ranks

Kuhn contends in *The Structure of Scientific Revolutions* that paradigms in the natural sciences are shattered as fundamental anomalies between hard, raw, empirical data and paradigm-derived theories, rules, and procedures appear and persist. Although he acknowledges that subjective consideration may lead any single scientist to withdraw his support for the reigning *gestalt* in favor of another, at no time does he suggest that any given revolution in paradigm might be a function of a wider shift in ethos occurring within the society involved. In other words, although he perceives cyclical periods of relative equilibrium alternating with periods of paradigmatic revolution, he fails to inquire into the possibility that the revolution might have been prepared by, indeed might be the product of, a more thoroughgoing shift in perspective within the socio-cultural setting.

Shift toward activism

Few would contest the widely acknowledged fact that the ethos dominating post-war America through the 1950's was indeed conservative. We have already pointed out the features of the national and international scene that contributed to it, as well as a few of the many sociologists who sought to analyze it in the language of their discipline. Bell's "end of ideology" thesis, fortified by the publication the same year—1960—of Seymour Lipset's persuasive *Political Man*, was a remarkably perspicacious summary of the historical and technological factors underlying the ideological *détente* that had dominated the intellectual climate of the 1950's. That the sociological perspective has typically proven more fruitful in ordering the past than it has been in projecting the future, however, was to be dramatically exemplified in Bell's case. For the revolutionary events of the 1960's, and the re-emergence of ideological factors that accompanied them, dated Bell's volume almost immediately. Although he had been aware of the renaissance of "socialism" in the emerging Asian and African states, Bell—together with almost the entire sociological community in America—was completely unprepared for both the impact of the domestic civil rights revolution and the manner in which it in turn served to link American youth with the new ventures in the name of Marx among the underdeveloped peoples and to pipe its ideological springs back into the mainstream of American intellectual life. Nor could he predict the manner in which the United States would replace the Good Neighbor Policy with a new, more militant version of the Monroe Doctrine and seek to extend the *Pax Americana* to Southeast Asia as the French and British withdrew. Furthermore, Bell had little reason to be aware of the impact the "rediscovery" of the young, humanistic Marx would have upon a generation tutored in the subjective strains of existentialism, for the "early

Marx" had only begun to be made available in English in the late 1950's. Add to all this the wholly unexpected rise of "Black Power," the manner in which the intellectual community withdrew its support of the national political leadership because of the escalation of the Vietnam struggle, and revelations of the role of the military and the intelligence services in the body politic, and one begins to see why an imagery focused about notions of "system maintenance" and "functional integration" began to yield before sustained inquiry.[4]

That sociology had entered a "time of troubles" there was no doubt. Indeed, it possessed a marked resemblance to that period of crisis that Kuhn saw as a necessary prologue to the emergence of a new paradigm. Such periods, Kuhn argued, were never immediately apparent, for even "normal" research within a freshly stamped and internalized *gestalt* confronts an ever-renewed range of unknowns. The key lies in their persistence.

Although answers will be fashioned within the dominant frame that may satisfy those who sponsor them, those without a proprietary interest in the parent paradigm or in the specific articulations offered are not apt to be won over. If the doubt is not allayed and the skeptic not converted, the seeds of heresy begin to germinate. But could sociology, as it moved from the 'fifties into the 'sixties, admit to any pervasive discontent with the paradigm that was the "social system"? Did any claim challenging its fruitfulness not only persist but grow? The evidence would appear to be overwhelmingly in the affirmative.

Challenge of change

Disaffection with the dominant paradigm took from the first a quasi-ideological form. System theory, particularly the Parsonian variety, was seen simply as providing justification for the conservative impulse dominating the post-war period. The stubborn anomaly that resisted solution in system's terms was "change"—*fundamental social change*. The first of what was to become a torrent of critiques may have been Wayne Hield's essay titled "The Study of Change in Social Science," published in 1954 in Britain, a setting that was both a step removed from the American sociological scene and less resistant ideologically to the prospect of radical change. Focusing upon the works of Parsons and Merton, although extending his charge to a broad array of small-group theorists and social psychologists, Hield contended that sociological theorists had taken the lead in directing the attention of social scientists toward social *control* rather than social *change*, and that they functioned self-evidently to emphasize processes of adjustment to the *status quo*. Indeed it was not an observation that was original with Hield. Another European, Gunnar Myrdal, had spoken directly to the concept of function in similar fashion in the theoretical section of his *An American Dilemma* as early as 1944.[5]

Concern over the presumption of stability that seemed to adhere to system theory was largely confined during the 'fifties, however, to the more historically oriented European. David Lockwood (1956), Dorothy Emmett (1958), and Norman Birnbaum[6] developed the theme further in Britain, although Ralf Dahrendorf's influential "Out of Utopias: Toward a Reorientation of Sociological Analysis" (1958) and his English version of his study of *soziale Klassen* (1959) were exported to the United States. It was not until Barrington Moore's *Political Power and Social Theory* (1958) appeared that American sociology was itself enjoined.

The issue, however, was not fully exposed to the sociological community at large in this country until C. Wright Mills directed the full fire of his passion and intellect, in *The Sociological Imagination* (1959), against what he held to be the conservative implications of the "grand theorist" and an associated "abstracted empiricism" and "bureaucratic ethos." The timidity of the many before the evident prowess of the acknowledged spokesman for system analysis—Talcott Parsons—thereafter rapidly disappeared.

In its place one found, as the 'fifties gave way to the 'sixties, a broadly mounted attack upon the system paradigm's implicit commitment to social equilibrium. In the forefront was Dennis Wrong's (1959; 1961) lively post mortems over the "failure" of American sociology and its "over-socialized" view of man. Off to one side was William Kolb's (1961; 1962) contention that the functional posture adhering to system theory clashed head-on with Judaic-Christian assumptions about man upon which the institutional life of Western man had been built. A wide array of criticisms drawn from a variety of disciplinary perspectives were brought together under the aegis of Max Black (1961) at Cornell. Wilbert Moore (1963) broke open the anomaly that was fundamental social change in a slim but penetrating study. Two of Parsons' closest associates, Kaspar Naegele and Edward Shils, used their introductory and concluding essays in his *Theories of Society* (1961)—Parsons' massive reconstruction of the historical roots of the dominant paradigm —to set forth their explicit reservations. The year 1963 elicited John Finley Scott's delineation of the distance Parsons had come from his early voluntarism. The profession had cause to be startled in 1964 when George Homans used his presidential address before the American Sociological Association to repudiate the functionalist position he had been such a central agent in espousing. Don Martindale (1965) then summed up the larger case in his recitation of "The Limits of and Alternatives of Functionalism in Sociology," while the new critique was evidenced at the introductory text level with the appearance of Alfred McClung Lee's *Multivalent Man* in 1966.

The significance of the flood of critical pieces—only a few of which have been noted—is impossible to deny. Seen within the framework of Kuhn's image of the development of a scientific discipline over time, they signaled the breakup of the consolidation that had been occurring since World War II around the system paradigm and an almost random search for an alternative. Nor could there be any doubt over the nature of the anomaly that persistently escaped the articulations fashioned by the apologists of the system paradigm in response to the growing unease. Mihailo Popovich (1966) reported that only six of the thirty eminent American sociologists to whom he spoke over the 1963–64 academic year thought that the discipline could by that time claim a single over-arching theoretical posture; when asked to identify the most important problem facing the field, the dominant response was "social change."

In his classic formulation of the paradigm in *The Social System*, Parsons had openly acknowledged, with remarkable foresight, that a theory of fundamental social change simply could not be derived from his conceptual scheme—either in the form then laid down or in the forseeable future.[7] However, goaded perhaps by the manner in which the admission was used by his critics to attack system theory itself, he, with his students and collaborators, began to focus increasingly upon the problem until, at the time of this writing, their work would seem almost entirely focused on the issue. Indeed Kuhn's delineation of the typical route leading to a "scientific revolution" would have us expect precisely that. Those committed to the paradigm projected a lengthy series of modifications of the functional implications of system analysis that would serve, in their minds, as a means for articulating "system" with the nettlesome dimension of "change." Some of those who have sought to interpret this period in Parsons' development claim to have distinguished a "late analytic" phase that superseded the "early" period represented by *The Social System*, *Toward a General Theory of Action*, and the *Working Papers*. Parsons himself has most recently distinguished two stages in the development of his theory beyond the point it had reached at the beginning of the 'fifties. The first coincided with the publication of *Economy and Society* in 1956 when the "social system" was extended to include the "economy"—and its cousin "polity"—as precisely definable *sub*-systems within the larger paradigm. The second, appearing in the middle and late 'sixties, involved his attempted rehabilitation of social evolutionism. The former was clearly the more modest attempt, basically but an effort to broaden the boundaries of system to embrace those political and economic factors that so many in the discipline had come to feel had eluded his functionalist net. The latter, however, was spurred by Parsons' admission that "legitimate objections could also be raised about the same [i.e., the early 'fifties] phase with reference to the problems of accounting for the change in societies and in their related cultural and psychological systems," and seemed to fly directly in the face of his earlier position regarding the inability of system theory to encompass fundamental change.[8] Here was a radical effort at articulation, one that bordered indeed on "counter-revolution."

Among the many who offered more modest routes to

the articulation of function and change were Barber, Bredemier, Buckley, Cancian, Dore, Fallding, Hempel, Simpson, and Smelser. Some, following the lead of Lewis Coser (1956), took the tack that conflict itself might be seen as functional. Others looked wistfully to synthesis or complementarity. Fallding (1961) was ambitious enough to project a *modus vivendi* for reconciling Parsons and Mills; Pierre van den Berghe (1963) saw the contending parties as incompatible but mutually fruitful. S. N. Eisenstadt, although supporting the evolutionary departure taken by Parsons, cautioned against any ready identification of change—even institutionalized change—with adaptation.[9] Wilbert Moore, however, may have captured the nature of the challenge most succinctly when he titled a collection of essays *Order and Change* (1967). Clearly, both the *ad hoc* adjustments and the stubborn resistance that Kuhn sets forth as characteristic of the early stages of a scientific revolution were abundantly evident as sociology moved from the consensus of the 'fifties to the division of the 'sixties.

Introspection

As frustration over a fundamental anomaly lengthens into crisis, the scientific discipline involved, Kuhn notes, becomes archly self-conscious. It begins to perceive *itself* as a problem, turning introspectively to a conscious concern over those habits, rules of thumb, and assumptions that are, during the routines of normal scientific activity, quite foreign to its taste.

That sociology, as it moved from the 'fifties to the 'sixties, stood as a case in point would be difficult to deny. Although it had immersed itself in the task of unraveling the norms—manifest and latent, conscious and subconscious—that dictated the social idiosyncrasies of the clergy and the medical profession, the professional soldier and the managerial elite, those who bought and sold in the academic marketplace and those who sold only their bodies, the "black bourgeoisie" and the professional thief, only sporadically had it directed a disciplined and skeptical eye at the myths and realities that governed its own communal existence. As long ago as 1946, Kurt Wolff had thrust a few "Notes Toward a Sociocultural Interpretation of American Sociology" before his colleagues, reminding them that the discipline, in addition to being a science, was also an outlook, orientation, or culture. Perhaps the notes were lost or the lecturer chided for lack of tact. In any case, Wolff's lead was not followed. Robert Merton, singularly able student of the sociology of science, has been among the handful who have exclaimed in print over the void, but even he appeared to dismiss the failure as simply evidence of our busyness elsewhere.

Seeds

And yet there was a grain of truth in Merton's apology, for the scientist caught up fully in the routines of "normal," non-revolutionary science feels little need to look within. Even though sociology had nurtured a sociology of science at the breast of a sociology of knowledge whose genealogy in turn extended well back into the early nineteenth century, it resolved the issue to its own satisfaction, during the heyday of the system paradigm, by shifting the burden to the philosopher and historian of science. That the former rejected the undertaking even more casually as beyond his present concern with the logic of symbolic categories and the latter focused almost exclusively upon the natural sciences appeared to move very few. It was clear, furthermore, that sociologists were of no mind during this period to be completely frank about their domestic life in public. The manifest function of playing one's cards close to the chest had been apparent at least since the time Lester Ward's *Dynamic Sociology* had been banned by Czarist censors whose questionable grasp of English had confused the title with "dynamite" and "socialism." The sociology of the 'forties and 'fifties had only just achieved academic and scientific respectability. To encourage second thoughts regarding its hard-won status as a natural science or reward through publication sociological analyses of the ideological struggles that teemed just below the discipline's public surface appeared quite irresponsible. Talcott Parsons (1961:9) might in his massive tomes declare in passing that scientific investigation is itself a form of social action, replete with its own implicit moral and ethical standards, but this was safely catalogued as theory.

Finally, the development of a sociology of sociology was inhibited by its apparent paradoxical nature. Sociologists, probably due to the struggle they faced in convincing both the larger academic community and themselves that they were indeed scientists, have become the most self-consciously "scientific" among the behavioral and social disciplines. And the *logic* of science would appear to grant only the most grudging and temporary place to paradox. Science has been seen as the epitome of logic in its application to the empirical scene; paradox, thus, is irrational. Therefore a sociology of sociology is foreign coinage, not currency of the realm. As much as it honors the essentially sociological stance of Marx, the discipline—at least in America—had remained pre-Hegelian. Dialectical logic may be permitted occasionally in game theory, but sociology is not regarded as a game among other games. It is viewed rather as a science whose very logical structure evolved to lift the film of paradox from the eyes of man. And since the position had borne much attractive fruit, the pragmatic context of the American scene dictated abstinence.

Emergence of a sociology of sociology

Thus, only as the discipline discovered its consolidating paradigm—system—in grave difficulty was it tempted to open the pandora's box that was the sociology of sociology. Indeed, it took the explosive impact of C. Wright Mills's *The Sociological Imagination* in 1959 for a sociology of sociology to intrude upon the sociologist's *conscience collective*. Although the book stood uncomfortably close to Sorokin's *Fads and Foibles* as a heated polemic fired too often by the feuds and fuels that have their place in the Faculty Club at the end of a long and trying day rather than published works that seek seriously to enlighten and inform, it did open the way for sociology's inevitable confrontation with itself.

Meanwhile a solid empirical base was beginning to be laid down in Podell's summary of the changes that had taken place in undergraduate sociological curricula and Matilda White Riley's and Richard Simpson's analyses of shifts within the make-up, professional interests, and substantive output of members of the American Sociological Association. A dimension of depth was later added with the publication of a series of volumes focusing upon the impact of researcher upon subjects and subjects upon researcher: Vidich, Bensman, and Stein's *Reflections on Community Studies*; Schwitzgabel's *Street-Corner Research*; Philip Hammond's *Sociologists at Work*; Arthur Shostak's *Sociology in Action*; and, most recently, those essays in John Seeley's *The Americanization of the Unconscious* which reflect the apparent trauma elicited by his earlier *Crestwood Heights* investigation.

The most strategic contribution to the new mode was the presidential address given by the discipline's ranking methodologist before the American Sociological Association in the autumn of 1962. Although Lazarsfeld's paper, "The Sociology of Empirical Research," focused only upon the impact of the research bureau on the larger profession, there was no more appropriate person to crack the cake of sociological custom than one of the discipline's elder statesmen. He added at about the same time an intriguing examination of "International Sociology as a Sociological Problem." At the very least the sociology of sociology could no longer be ruled in poor professional taste.

Professionalization

Of more importance to the perspective's long-run development, however, was the decision, taken by the Council of the ASA, to expand a "Section on the Profession" that had been added to the discipline's official journal as recently as 1958 into an independent publication. Begun in 1965 under the editorship of Talcott Parsons, *The American Sociologist* suddenly offered the budding sociologist of sociology a receptive medium through which his investigations and speculations could be communicated to his peers. It afforded ample room as well for feedback through a generous allotment of space for letters from its readers. A steady stream of papers already have been published in the journal, reflecting a wide range of empirical and theoretical concern with the social nature of sociology itself and no doubt encouraging many within the discipline to perceive the sociology of sociology for the first time as a focus for research.

The journal was itself as much a product of the increased interest in the nature of the sub-community of sociology as it has been a stimulus to further inquiry. Its immediate roots lay almost certainly within that nexus of concerns that had led but a little earlier to the appointment of a committee of the Council of the American Sociological Association to draft a "Code of Ethics" for the profession in response to the growing impact of the discipline upon the world at large and the response of that larger society to that impact. William Goode had sensed the mood somewhat earlier and addressed himself to it in an influential presidential address before the Eastern Sociological Society entitled "Encroachment, Charlatanism, and the Emerging Profession: Psychology, Sociology, and Medicine." Although the product of this initial committee—a draft code—was tabled by the Council, the interest that its proponents and opponents engendered led in turn to further debate and publication. Parsons, capitalizing on his editorship of *The American Sociologist*, elaborated a "professional" image of the discipline that he had outlined earlier in a widely read essay entitled "Some Problems Confronting Sociology as a Profession." And when "Project Camelot"—that painful object-lesson in the international implications of Pentagon-sponsored social research on the roots of insurgency—humiliated the sociologist before his fellows in the behavioral sciences and led to sharp restrictions on his research initiative, he turned with a very real sense of urgency to a re-examination of the assumptions that guided his work. Not even the foundation-stone upon which American sociology had come to rest—its "value-free" presumption—remained inviolate. Sociologists suddenly found themselves struggling with the ethical roots of their *own* endeavors. Gideon Sjoberg's *Ethics, Politics, and Social Research* joined Irving Horowitz' *The Rise and Fall of Project Camelot* and his most recent *Professing Sociology: Studies in the Life Cycle of Social Science* on the sociological reading lists, while Vollmer and Mills' *Professionalization* collection took on a more personal tone. The Council of the ASA sought to redress the damage done to the discipline's public image by recharging a committee to formulate a code of ethics, only to find itself almost immediately embroiled in an embarrassing battle over a resolution that would commit the Association's name to a public condemnation of the Vietnam war. Indeed, sociology's domestic affairs took on such a lively cast that the anthropologists began to direct attention to it as a sub-culture worthy of serious investigation.[10]

A community of scholars that had begun to evidence through the 1950's a remarkable period of relative consensus found itself toward the end of the 'sixties in imminent danger of breaking into hostile camps. Having just projected its own sense of stable well-being and unity upon the larger cultural and intercultural scene by heralding "the end of ideology," it discovered that the generation moving through the graduate schools in the 'sixties had rediscovered Marx. Led by a phalanx of established sociologists who had never completely despaired of the activist stance, the graduate generation of the 'sixties tended to see itself in humanistic terms rather than simply in the value-free garments that had come to be associated with the behavioral sciences. Some who had earlier sensitized the public to the dangers of stereotyping were themselves tempted to invent categories that might be used as subtle weapons in the increasingly divided discipline.[11] That the discipline had in fact split by this time into at least two contentious "parties" was evidenced in the responses drawn from a 50% sample of the ASA membership to a 14-page questionnaire that sought, in 1964, to elicit opinion on a wide variety of theoretical, methodological, and professional issues.

Thus, both the raw material and the necessary motivation for a systematic and disciplined venture into the sociology of sociology appeared available by the mid-'sixties. Indeed by 1967 the profession seemed to grant its official blessing to those who were ready to launch such an inquiry by providing sessions on "The Sociology of Sociology" for the first time at an annual meeting. All that seemed missing was a sustaining frame, a scaffold of theory that, even if it were found wanting, would support a provisional venture.

Return to philosophy

The breakthrough into a sociology of sociology was accompanied by a complementary burst of activity in the philosophy and logic of the social and behavioral sciences.

Indeed, Kuhn is quite explicit in pointing out that scientists are little given under normal conditions to philosophical speculation, but seem almost compulsively drawn to examine their epistemological roots when their paradigms are seriously threatened. An entire generation of sociologists had been operating up to this time within a methodological context that assumed that the logic of science was unitary. Some few granted lip service to Weber's *verstehen* perspective—the empathetic appropriation of the meaning granted a situation by the subjects. It was treated in practice, however, simply as a method that provided insightful hypotheses that would then be dropped into a logic that was in no way different in principle from the logic underlying the experimental method in the physical and biological sciences. The fabrication of "ideal" or "constructed" typologies might have seemed to some to be a unique feature of the social sciences as they sought to grasp the data of history in terms amenable to the essential logic of the experiment. To the larger discipline, however, such conceptual invention was in no fundamental way different from a physicist inventing categories capable of structuring his pointer readings. There seemed, then, no reason to concern oneself with a distinctly *social* scientific logic. Felix Kaufman's *Methodology of the Social Sciences*, published as early as 1944, appeared quite sufficient to meet the needs of the occasional philosophically inclined student. The ideologically saturated volumes by Friedrich Hayek (*The Counter-Revolution of Science*) and Karl Popper (*The Poverty of Historicism*) were regarded simply as anti-Marxist tracts, whereas Michael Polanyi's *Personal Knowledge* concerned itself with the logic of science in general. Furthermore, all were infected by a continental image of the term "science" that ran against the grain of Anglo-American usage.

The first crack in the ice appeared with the publication of Peter Winch's *The Idea of Social Science and Its Relation to Philosophy* in 1958. Both it and a second volume in 1960 (Quentin Gibson's *The Logic of Social Inquiry*) were handicapped, however, by the British context from which they drew, a context that has classified much of what American practice views as sociology under the category of social anthropology and relegates the remainder to a very minor role within the academic community. Even Edward Tiryakian's *Sociologism and Existentialism*, published in 1962 in this country, could be viewed as essentially continental, for Tiryakian had written it as the direct result of exposure to the Durkheimian and existentialist positions during a year's leave in France. The flood-tide broke through with a vengeance, however, in 1963: Robert Brown's *Explanation in Social Science*, Carlo Lastrucci's *The Scientific Approach: Basic Principles of the Scientific Method*, William McEwen's *The Problem of Social-Scientific Knowledge*, and Maurice Natanson's *Philosophy of the Social Sciences, A Reader* all appeared the same year. Abraham Kaplan's *The Conduct of Inquiry: Methodology for Behavioral Science* followed hard upon their heels in 1964. Significantly, none was brought out by major publishing houses in the behavioral or social sciences; only in 1965 did one of the latter—Macmillan, in its release of David Baybrooke's slim paperback reader *Philosophical Problems of the Social Sciences*—deem the venture worthwhile. Nevertheless, the handwriting on the wall—etched as it was to coincide with the appearance of a sociology of sociology—marked an important moment in the life cycle of the dominant paradigm. It was both a symptom of the mounting crisis and a condition for its ultimate resolution.

Search for an Alternative

Kuhn would remind us, however, that a paradigm is not rejected simply through the slow accretion of evidence that denies its full utility. This is because the paradigm is not just a theory among theories but rather a fundamental image of the nature of one's subject matter. Most of the overt debate hovered during this period about the issue of functionalism. Unfortunately, functional theory was itself but a derivative of the more fundamental notion of society as a social *system*. Thus, theorists could tinker with the former, reject it in fact altogether, without resolving their problem—without, indeed, uncovering it. There was and is no more astute analysis of functionalism *per se*—ways in which it could be protected from a simplistic identification of *what exists* with *utility*—than Merton's essays in *Social Theory and Social Structure* published initially in the 'forties. The paradigm upon which functionalism rested, however, lay beyond the critique undisturbed. And although an increasing portion of the profession is becoming aware of the true culprit, the system assumption remains at the heart of almost all the basic texts in the field.

But even more important to an understanding of sociology in the 'sixties was the recognition, with Kuhn, that a paradigm is not to be denied until another is ready to take its place. We are not able to operate as cognitive beings unless we have some point of conceptual reference. It is not a theory but an image, an image that we grasp as at least one face of "reality." Nor can it be a congeries of bits and pieces. Rather, as it settles into place it takes on the nature of a *gestalt*, transforming the entire manner in which we perceive our subject matter. The destruction of the old must await the candidacy of the new. The two processes must occur simultaneously. To have it otherwise would be to reject science itself, perhaps the entire range of man's attempts to order his world. The "revolution" is achieved only when an alternate paradigm has been issued, the intellectual shock troops deployed, and the institutionalized forces of the *ancien régime* fully engaged. What, then, was the repertory offered by the sociological theater in the 1960's?

"*Evolution*"

We have already pointed out how Parsons himself sought to extend the system stance to encompass permanent structural change by setting social systems within the larger embrace of social *evolution*. But in so doing he was not abandoning the system motif. Instead, as he introduced the dimension of history he enclosed it within the system imagery of biology. System was still the basic unit, but now it was seen over broad expanses of time in terms immediately analogous to those developed to trace the life-cycles and lineages of living organisms. Indeed it was a timely enunciation, for it was supported by a recurrence of interest in cultural universals and evolution by anthropologists. And there is no doubt that the new latitude provided change was considerably broader than that granted in the earlier dispensation. There could be equally little doubt that system remained the master paradigm. What had occurred was simply a shift in linguistic base from the terminology of cybernetics and Newton's "laws of motion" to a neo-Darwinian grasp of history. The new "system" saw organic continuity, differentiation, mutation, and competition writ large, all encompassed by the circular assumption that the survival of societal forms attested to their evolutionary utility and, *vice versa*, that such utility would guarantee their survival. This is not, however, to deny its attractiveness. There was good reason to expect that the evolutionary frame would appear most congenial to the sociologist conditioned to the system image. But if it settled there the flurry of discontent evidenced in sociology during the 'sixties would appear in retrospect as but a minor civil disturbance rather than the potential paradigmatic revolution of which Kuhn speaks.

Re-emergence of "action"

A more ambitious effort to restructure the controlling paradigm has come most recently from Amitai Etzioni. Both his professional activity and major elements of his theoretical position—his accentuation of power and the political dimension in general, the assumption of social entropy rather than social order as point of departure, and of "transformability" rather than homeostatic stability as his goal—have led and promise to continue to lead many of the younger generation within the discipline to perceive him as the rightful heir to C. Wright Mills's mantle at Columbia and within the larger profession. Yet both his paradigmatic image and the manner in which he develops it reveal a remarkable kinship with the Parsonian corpus. *Action*, the paradigm that is offered, is basically the same image that Parsons projected in *The Structure of Social Action* in the 'thirties, reissued in the diluted and ambiguous form demanded by the search for theoretical consensus in the early 'fifties, and overshadowed thereafter by the attractiveness of the system frame. Both view human behavior in fundamentally voluntaristic terms, although Etzioni treats it not primarily as a constant but as a variable function of particular social structures.

Etzioni's aim, thus, is spelled out by the title of his most recent work: *The Active Society* (1968). The image conjured is a most attractive one—particularly congenial, one can hardly doubt, to those caught up in the activist orientation that swept through the graduate schools during the mid and late 'sixties.

Its indebtedness to Parsons' earlier work and to much of his later work as well is striking. Citations to Parsons outnumber those to any other figure: some 42 as over against 18 to Marx and 13 to C. Wright Mills; Merton follows more closely with 23, Weber with 22. Indeed, there is some evidence that Etzioni himself is not consciously aware of the full dimensions of his debt to Parsons. He speaks approvingly at one point of the "voluntaristic element" *added* by Parsons in several of his *later* essays as if he might not be fully aware of the central role it played in the latter's *Structure of Social Action* and in the essay on "The Place of Ultimate Values in Sociological Theory" that preceded it in 1935. Like Parsons, Etzioni claims quite explicitly to move between the polar temptations of idealism and realism and views his posture as the end-product of the convergence of the individualistic and collectivistic traditions in social thought. He, too, would veer from any reification of the "individual" and move instead toward such terms as "role" and "social unit." Both Parsons and Etzioni link respect for functional analysis with a benevolent image of society and emphasize the significance of consensus, Etzioni going so far as to endow collectivities with "selves" and to speak of the "general" or "shared will." And each is enamored of cybernetic models. Although Etzioni would reject Parsons' latter-day evolutionism, he proffers a faith in "emergence" that would seem to share many of the former's qualities. Each find "detachment" on the part of sociologists a mixed blessing. And although Etzioni would appear to stand somewhat to the left of Parsons ideologically, he denies the utility of such a notion as that of a "power elite" in analyzing social stratification, consigning it instead to the realm of role-analysis.

No interpretation of the action paradigm as reconstructed by Etzioni in the nearly 700 pages of *The Active Society* could do it justice in the space available here. Indeed, the parallel between the early (and portions of the more recent) Parsons that has been drawn may appear too selective. It was done, however, out of the conviction that the self-evident magnitude of the overlap is apt to enhance the survival power of the new action paradigm in the battles that await it. Revolutionary movements, to succeed, may have to demonstrate the capacity to elicit wholesale desertions among loyalist troops. To do so they may have to appeal to imagery already imbedded within the orthodox frame. The apparent capacity of Etzioni's reincarnation of the action frame to do just that suggests that it may have to be taken quite seriously indeed.

Freudian imagery

There was also evidence, during the 1960's, that "counter-revolution" could not be completely ruled out. Dennis Wrong's diagnosis of the "failure" of American sociology contained a prescription as well. He would have the discipline turn back to perceive the discontents bred by civilization in psychoanalytic terms so that the Hobbesian inclination to view force as the final adjudicator between the conflicting interests of the individual and his society might be addressed once again. The oversocialized view of man was simply the result of an overintegrated image of society. Man the social animal need not be transformed into an entirely *socialized* animal. The key, rather, lay in a return to a psycho-physiological conception of man: "*in the beginning there is the body*" (1961:191). The paradigm sees society as the product of discrete ids wrestling with superegos that only partly overlap, all potentially reducible to issues of biology and demography.

Return to "behavior"

The general thrust would be easier to deny as naïvely pre-Durkheimian if it were not supported from the very throne of contemporary small-group theory. For George Homans, at one point a central spokesman for the functionalist position, has recently taken a position remarkable in its similarity, but with Skinner replacing Freud. We must *bring men back in*, Homans insisted in his 1964 presidential address to the American Sociological Association. Structural-functionalism, dominant for a generation, had run its course; indeed it "now positively gets in the way of our understanding . . . to show the interrelationships of institutions is not the same thing as explaining why the interrelationships are what they are" (Homans, 1964b:809, 811). Neither equilibrium nor survival, concepts at the heart of the system paradigm, could fill the bill. Although they might help in formulating statements about relationships, they were deductively derived; no empirical evidence drawn from an existing society could deny—and thus serve to test—either. The theory, then, although not wrong, simply was no theory. But in seeking to fill the gap, Homans turned back to the individual man of behavioral psychology—to learning theory with a hedonist flavor. The paradigm he would project need not even include other individuals, simply the physical environment. He would expect in the final analysis that the fundamental variables involved would be derived from biology (Homans, 1964a:225). The call was not simply to the barricades but to counter-revolution. Harvard's Department of Social Relations would return under Homans quite literally to the womb.

Society as "mechanism"

Although George Lundberg's death in 1966 might have suggested to some that the ultimate reductionist stance in sociology—the image of society as a matrix of mechanical forces—would now slip from sight, the claim may prove to be somewhat premature. For the very same year saw a more sophisticated restatement of the positivist credo set forth by one of Lundberg's disciples, William Catton, under the universally appealing title, *From Animistic to Naturalistic Sociology*. The physical vocabulary (mass, force, field, space, acceleration, gravitation) and thus the paradigm of society as *mechanism* remained, but its exposition took a strategic new tack. Whereas Lundberg had claimed the "mature" Parsons as a brother-in-arms when the latter paraphrased what he interpreted as Newton's "laws of motion" in the *Working Papers* as fundamental laws of social equilibrium, Catton argued quite persuasively that the Parsons-Bales version was permeated by a homeostatic assumption entirely foreign to Newton's axiomatic posture. Catton pointed out that Newton projected the three "laws" in fact as *axioms*: that the first—the axiom of inertia—simply claimed that the uniform flow of time and motion required no explanation as such. Parsons transformed this claim into a homeostatic principle, arguing that there was a tendency *toward* stability in social system analysis. Catton took quite the opposite point of view, holding with Newton that stability, continuity, and equilibrium are precisely those things that mechanics—and thus sociology—need not concern themselves about; indeed, *their only concern should be with change*.

The dilemma posed by system theory's confrontation with fundamental change simply dissolves. System, insofar as it retains utility as a concept, becomes but a plank in one's epistemological platform. Change is king, for it is all that should interest us. And when the posture is wrapped neatly in a "naturalistic" package, the whole may indeed appear a welcome gift. With the electronic computer serving analogically as its epistemology and Fortran as its mechanistic code, society as mechanism might indeed be granted a second life.

Responsible man

Another candidate for paradigmatic office—considerably more influential than the exposure granted it by the discipline's gatekeepers might suggest—meanwhile had been nominated from the opposite end of the epistemological pole. William Kolb, in a scattering of articles, reviews, and papers delivered at professional meetings, offered what he characterized as an essentially *Judaic-Christian* image of social man. One of its prime features was a "conditional freedom" that served to guarantee that man's volition would not be completely absorbed within the conceptual vice of system analysis, for it would provide a source of social change that lay beyond a system's internal tensions and its larger environment. An essentially neo-orthodox image in the tradition of the Niebuhrs, it deemed that which the Biblican tradition has identified as sin and guilt and the finite quality of man's comprehension to be of sociological significance. In addition, such universal aspects of the existential predicament as the threat of meaninglessness, the forced choice between others as ends or as means, and one's ultimate rootedness in the non-empirical were viewed as inherent qualities of man's personal and social existence that inevitably impinge upon his empirical activity. By excluding such dimensions from one's image of social man—as generally appeared to be the case in social research—the task of ordering man's social behavior, Kolb argued, would be severely handicapped.

Phenomena of everyday reality

A more elaborately developed option than any of the foregoing appeared with the publication by Peter Berger and Thomas Luckman of *The Social Construction of Reality* in 1966. Drawing directly from the late Alfred Schütz' amalgam of Husserl's phenomenological method with Weber's *verstehen* sociology and George Herbert Mead's symbolic interactionism, it offered a typified *everyday reality* as its fundamental paradigm. Husserl's stance, although at odds with the classic existentialist position through its focus on phenomenological "essences," appealed, as did existentialism, to modern man's search for an alternative to the traditional polarity of realism and idealism. Schütz concentrated upon demonstrating the viability of the "common sense world" as both point of departure and point of return for man's forays into the problems of social existence. Berger and Luckmann go on to illustrate the manner in which that world of everyday life is socially constructed on man's initiative through the processes of objectivation, institutionalization, and legitimation, the product in turn internalized as subjective reality and fed dialectically back into the matrix that precipitated the original objectivation.

But this was by no means all. Berger and Luckmann are moved by a larger dialectical urge: to free sociologists —and ultimately, laymen—from the fetters of a social "reality" that is after all but man's own creation. This would permit him to escape the more indirect manipulation that results from the internalization of that "reality" as the "really real" through an "ecstatic" act of apprehension which affords man insight into the social source of his compulsiveness. Through such a phenomenologically informed extension of the posture of the sociologist of knowledge, they are able to project a "sociological consciousness" whose air of debunking relativism cuts through our tendency to reify our social product and thus alienate ourselves from our existence as fundamentally creative and responsible beings. Man, then, in those occasional moments of ecstasy—literally, when "standing outside one-self"—is a potential agent of change and not simply its prisoner or puppet. He is not simply enclosed in an ordered "system." Rather, "system" itself is man's creation—"functional" perhaps in man's effort to stabilize his conceptual and empirical worlds, but subject always to man's capacity to comprehend that *he* is the one who in the final analysis constructed, objectified, and internalized it and that he is always potentially capable of stepping outside both it and its empirical referents. "Everyday life," thus, was thrust into the paradigmatic mix by an image of the sociologist as engaged.

Subjective reality

That there is more than one path to phenomenology has been evidenced by Edward Tiryakian's recent proposal that sociologists ground themselves in a "subjective realism." Turning from an earlier effort to complement Durkheim with the dimension of depth offered by existentialism, Tiryakian (1965, 1966) would have an existentially-informed phenomenology provide sociology with its general conceptual base and a "transobjectivity" with its fundamental methodology. Neither concept has as yet been systematically developed, and thus the paradigm is not completely clear. Still, the springs within the sociological tradition that would feed the new plant were evident. They lay in the "holistic" tradition, Scheler's intentionality, Parsons' early voluntarism, Weber's *verstehen*, and a dialectical relationship between the qualitative and the quantitative that would appear akin to that found in Marxist theory. Although Tiryakian's implicit critique of the objectivist stance of many contemporary sociologists and his inclination to humanize it through recourse to developments in phenomenology suggest that there are broad areas of agreement between Tiryakian and Berger, the tone and texture of their two positions are sharply at odds. Whereas Berger views the structures projected by sociology through the images of prison and puppeteer, Tiryakian finds them—when viewed through the prism that is "subjective realism"—as not simply "real" but implicitly "good" as well. Berger, in other words, would see the relativizing motif as a permanent charge to the sociologist whereas Tiryakian would dispense with it when sociology's paradigmatic base has shifted to "subjective realism." Indeed, there is much in the Tiryakian posture that recalls Parsons' original "analytical realism," particularly as it was expressed in the latter's early essay on the place of ultimate values in sociological theory.

Polarization

The "conflict" image

But as intriguing as this assortment of candidates for paradigmatic status may have appeared, there could be no doubt whatsoever that the most popular pretender to the throne was *conflict*. Indeed, if the issue were to be decided by a simple head-count, a conflict paradigm seemed to have claimed by the early 'sixties an allegiance at least the equal of the system stance. Thirty-nine per cent of the professional membership who responded to the questionnaire (some 3500 sociologists) framed and distributed by Alvin Gouldner in 1964 (Gouldner and Sprehe, 1965) agreed with the statement that "the underlying reality in all groups is a series of more-or-less powerful tensions and conflicts." Only 38 per cent disagreed; the remainder were undecided. When spelled out in less all-encompassing terms ("Many modern social institutions are deeply unstable and tensionful"), the affirmative response shot up to 78 per cent. Although it might continue as titular monarch for some time, the system image could thus no longer lay claim to serve as the fundamental organizing frame for the discipline as a whole. There is good reason to suspect, in fact, that "conflict" has made even further headway among sociologists since the survey was conducted—may indeed be the dominant paradigm today in terms of comparative numerical support within the discipline.

Conflict theory

Conflict theory is, of course, neither new to the Western mind nor a novelty to sociology *per se*. Heraclitus is typically credited as its first proponent in the West, while Hobbes's "war of all against all" set the tone for its development in the modern period. Marx had but to recognize the significance of the division of labor to translate such conflict into class war, Adam Smith having presumed conflicting interest to be the foundation of classical economics the century before. In addition, the Darwinian thesis offered a grim model of conflict among the species. Among those nineteenth-century social theorists who were wed to the paradigm were Bagehot, Gumplowicz, Ratzenhofer, Novicow, and Kidd, while turn-of-the-century spokesmen were Georg Simmel and Franz Oppenheimer in Germany and Albion Small in the United States. Unless one were to view Ogburn's cultural-lag thesis as simply one of its mutant forms, however, the period between the two World Wars was singularly free from major sociological ventures in the genre. George Vold's efforts to rekindle interest in the model were almost entirely limited to the sub-discipline of criminology.

But with the publication in 1959 of *The Sociological Imagination*, C. Wright Mills nailed a thesis to the door of the profession that acted as a catalyst in precipitating a reappraisal. Sociologists, Mills argues, should seek first of all to situate themselves within the conflicting eddies that coursed through the particular historical setting of which they were a part. Then, using the most sophisticated tools of empirical analysis available (which would include biography and comparative historical studies), they should direct their sociological imaginations to the task of unraveling the subtle and not-so-subtle dynamics of power and privilege therein. Only then might one be in a position to fully appraise the conflicting alternatives among which human reason and human freedom must choose in order to create a viable future.

In speaking thus, Mills claimed the inspiration and perspective of Karl Marx. Yet Mills was equally convinced that Marx should be transcended both as a model for a science of society and as an ideological base. Although he was later to conclude that the Soviet system would provide a more reliable structural foundation for the future than the direction taken at mid-century by the American "power elite," he did so from a pragmatic vantage point rather than from within the circle of dialectical materialism. Indeed, Mills (1963:575) took a posture so far from the mainstream of Marxist-Leninism as to commend Toynbee's *A Study of History* as worthy of the attention of sociologists "for years to come" and to include Paul Tillich's *The Protestant Era* and *The Courage to Be* within a list of recommended readings for students of society. Socialism he seemed to regard in much the same fashion as Durkheim described it: "not a science, a sociology in miniature . . . [but] a cry of pain, sometimes of anger, uttered by men who feel most keenly our collective malaise" (Durkheim, 1958:7). One should not have been surprised, then, that a commemorative article by a Soviet writer on the anniversary of Mills's untimely death pictured him as a "tragic hero" who yet remained a "victim of bourgeois ideology" (Kassoff, 1965:117).

Although most of what he wrote concerning the "sociological imagination" lay implicit within Mills's personal and professional history from the time he began contributing to the *New Republic* as a graduate student, the indictment he offered of the orthodox paradigm dominating the profession in the 'fifties was reinforced by the mark he had made among his colleagues with his incisive studies of organized labor, "white collar" America, and the "power elite." There was, furthermore, something charismatic about the man. He evidenced a rough-hewn Old Testament bluntness and verve that transformed staid and perfunctory professional meetings into vivid and energetic debates.

The Sociological Imagination provided a ready-made script for the many within the discipline who, although gratified by the new stature that the prevailing paradigm had guaranteed them, began—in their new-found security—to relish the risk of conflict once again. "Grand theory," "abstracted empiricism," and the "bureaucratic ethos" projected an image of complacency and withdrawal—the very qualities that many sociologists had begun to see as seductive and therefore dangerous in the larger temper of their times. In "grand theory" structures of domination had no place. Equilibrium rather than tension, system rather than conflict, were to provide the point of departure and of return. Thus sin, by the stroke of a general theory, was no longer original. Nor might any of its more contemporary metaphors—class conflict, national and international domination, the libidinal discontents of civilization—serve in its place. They must of necessity be seen as but temporary states of disequilibrium within a functionally balanced network of social interaction. Sociology's narcissistic focus upon methodology—its "abstracted empiricism"—was equally debilitating, for it sought to limit a sociologist's attention to the minutiae within man's larger cultural and historical experience that could be grasped through quantification. The distortions of "grand theory" and "abstracted empiricism" are then compounded by the bureaucratized setting in which most social research is now carried out. For the instinct for survival of the research institute, bureau, or team further compromised and routinized the sociological imagination, leaving it maimed and incapable of confronting the realities of conflict, power, and interest. The imaginative, the tangentially-inclined, the socially disturbed are weeded out of the research machinery, for they hamper and embarrass a structure that has come to have an impersonal appetite of its own.

The paradigmatic fire that Mills kindled clearly warmed the sociological imaginations of many of his confreres. It may, however, have served to consume him as well. The polemical nature of his later works, the squandering of his sociological talents on ideological outbursts, his readiness to condone the naked use of power all bespoke an intensity that saw force as the ultimate arbiter among men. As he wrote in an especially revealing passage in *The Sociological Imagination*: "We cannot deduce—Hume's celebrated dictum runs—how we ought to act from what we believe is. Neither can we deduce how anyone else ought to act from how we believe we ought to act. In the end, if the end comes, we just have to beat those who disagree with us over the head" (1959:77).

Although Mills was certainly the prime catalytic agent in the reintroduction of the "conflict" posture within sociology, it may have been sparked as well by Kurt Wolff's translation of Simmel's *Conflict* volume in 1955. Lewis Coser addressed himself to *The Functions of Social Conflict* the following year, although—as we have already noted—he did so within an essentially system frame. Focus by the International Sociological Association upon "Conflict Groups and Their Mediation" at Liége in 1953 and on "Problems of Social Change" at Amsterdam in 1956 had by 1957 culminated in the publication by UNESCO of a collection of papers brought together under the title *The Nature of Conflict*. *The Journal of Conflict*

Resolution had by this time begun publication at Ann Arbor, while James Coleman added fuel when he shaped diverse community case studies into a natural history of conflict at that level in the volume *Community Conflict*. And by 1959 Ralf Dahrendorf's influential *Class and Class Conflict in Industrial Society* had been published in an English edition.

Converts to the paradigm found—or founded—a new range of journals in which the concept was accepted as central. In addition to the *Journal of Conflict Resolution*, there appeared the *Sociological Quarterly*, the *International Journal of Comparative Sociology*, *History and Theory*, and *Revista Brasileira de Ciecias Sociais*—underwriting in the process the development of a whole new sub-discipline on the sociology of international conflict. Amitai Etzioni, although returning later to the action image emphasized in Parsons' earliest works, dramatized the new thrust through his early work with the Institute of War and Peace Studies at Columbia. Meanwhile Thomas Schelling had published *The Strategy of Conflict* in 1960; Kenneth Boulding, the sociologically informed economist, *Conflict and Defense* in 1960; and the "Craigville Papers" (*International Conflict and Behavioral Science*) appeared in 1964. More recently Jesse Bernard (1965) has sought to catalogue the multiple approaches that have been made to the concept; Wilbert Moore (1964) has explored the possibilities of predicting a variety of its forms; Elton MacNeil (1965) has brought together, in summary form, the resources that the disparate disciplines within the behavioral sciences have been able to apply to it; and Lewis Coser (1967) has followed his earlier volume on conflict's functional features with a second.

The new mode also was underwritten by the many who found direct inspiration in the works and life of C. Wright Mills. Although here the key words were apt to be "history," "power," and "politics," the disjunctive nature of social reality ran as an assumption throughout. Barrington Moore's *Political Power and Social Theory*, published four years before Mills's death, was a perfect case in point, although the full range of Mills's influence had to await the memorial volumes put together in '63 and '64 by Maurice Stein and Arthur Vidich (*Sociology on Trial*) and Louis Horowitz (*The New Sociology*). In addition, the founding of the glossy periodical *Trans-action* in late 1963 at Washington University added substantially to the paradigm's audience.

In an analogous vein were the dozens, perhaps hundreds, of papers, articles, and volumes that began to flood the scene on the issue of "alienation." Although he had not made any extensive use of the term himself, Mills had seen it as symbolizing the default of contemporary social science. Appearing as the central theme of the recently recovered early manuscripts of Marx, it served as the social-psychological side of the coin that had been engraved on its sociological face with "conflict." Its most compelling spokesman in terms of the response engendered from the "New Left" both in America and in Western Europe has been the now-aged member of the "Frankfurt School" of socialist sociology, Herbert Marcuse. In volumes and essays beginning with *Reason and Revolution* in 1941 and highlighted by *One Dimensional Man* in 1964, Marcuse set forth to justify—via a latter-day and pessimistic reading of Marx and an optimistic reassessment of Freud—active social conflict which would have modern man include intolerance and subversion among the necessary and appropriate weapons for social change. That the posture may have already begun to affect the direction of sociology in America is suggested by Barrington Moore, Jr.'s, collaboration with Marcuse in *A Critique of Pure Tolerance* (Robert Wolff, 1968); his sponsorship, with Kurt Wolff, of a collection of essays in Marcuse's honor (*The Critical Spirit*, 1968); and Moore's recent essay, "Revolution in America" (1969). Perhaps even more compelling evidence is furnished by Norman Birnbaum's *The Crisis of Industrial Society* (1969), which combines the philosophical and psychological insights of Marcuse with the comparative historical sensitivities of C. Wright Mills. Although a full assessment of Marcuse's impact upon the discipline may have to await the ascension to professional power of the generation of graduate students trained in the 1960's, Marcuse does indeed appear the most likely candidate for the role of polar spokesman for the conflict paradigm in the years lying immediately ahead. Indeed, if the political activism that began to evidence itself with the American Sociological Association's 1967 meetings and the emergence of both "black" and "radical" caucuses at the 1968 convention, together with the appearance of a spate of "underground" sociological periodicals, are more than momentary manifestations of the larger temper of the times, the conflict image has yet to reach its apogee.

As the revolutionary struggle between conflict and system moves toward its peak, we would do well to recall that the criteria brought to bear and the weapons introduced by the contending parties have more in common with one's assumptions regarding the political scene than they do with the stereotypical image of a scientific community. Thus, one is not surprised to find Parsons succumbing to the temptation to characterize the competing paradigm as "neo-Marxism."[12] This is unfortunate, for the springs that nourish the contest are much more widely scattered across the ideological and philosophical terrain than the system advocate could be expected to perceive or its most aggressive opponents to demonstrate. A more judicious summary identification of the contending postures, replete with reference to the anomally that spurred the creation of the new claimant, was the title given by Demerath and Peterson to their 1967 "Reader on Contemporary Sociological Theory . . ." noted earlier: *System, Change, and Conflict.*

Dialectical Cease-fire?

One final candidate for paradigmatic office must be introduced. It had in a very real sense to await the division of the house of sociology, for its historic role has been to merge system and conflict into a single image. This is the notion of social reality as *dialectical.* Although social scientists in the West have found the strident tone in which it has been proclaimed by an institutionalized Marxism and its failure to shed substantial light on the problems of the natural sciences sufficient reason to reject it, the recent renewal of interest in the early Marx has led an increasing number of sociologists to reassess its viability.

The dialectical frame had its European roots among the pre-Socratics, saw its initial formulation at the hands of Plato, and then moved on, through Plotinus and the neo-Platonists, to such early Church Fathers as Clement of Alexandria, Origen, and Saint Augustine. Denied within the medieval synthesis when it was rejected by Aquinas, it survived in the concepts of complementarity and polarity utilized by such scholastics as Albertus Magnus and in Eckhart's mysticism. Revived in the "*docta ignorantia*" of Nicholas of Cusa and in the writings of St. John of the Cross and Boehme, it found brief expression in Kant's "dialectic of a radical negation of dialectic" and in the works of Fichte prior to its classic elaboration at the hands of Hegel.

Re-emergence of "dialectical" image

By the mid 1960's all serious discussion of the dialectical *motif* in sociology had to refer not simply to classic Hegelian and Marxist models but also to a posture set forth by Georges Gurvitch. Three years before his death in 1965, Gurvitch brought together the methodological and substantive thoughts that had been the culmination of a lifetime of vigorous theoretical and empirical work in sociology in the volume *Dialectique et Sociologie*. For Gurvitch the dialectic served not only as a descriptive paradigm for social reality but also as a method of study and as a way of conceptualizing the relationship between that method and the social reality it sought to grasp. Although he saw it in broader terms than that suggested by the classic Hegelian and Marxist thesis-antithesis-synthesis trinity, his claims regarding its explanatory power were more modest. It was a *pathway* rather than a point of arrival, a "description" rather than an "explanation." Gurvitch meant that, contrary to Marx' contention, the dialectic cannot be used inductively or deductively in the ordinary sense for precipitating empirical social "laws." Such explanatory law may be available in the social sciences as it is in the natural sciences but only through the traditional canons that undergird "causal" analyses. In the social sphere, however, the dialectic mitigates against any easy or complete predictive scheme. System theory, presuming conceptual closure, violates the openness of dialectical theory and so is quite inappropriate as the sociologist's fundamental conceptual reference.

A comparable position is taken by the most prominent of German sociologists, especially Schelsky, Adorno, and Dahrendorf, although they would appear to restrict their application of the dialectic to an examination of the relationship between the scientific subject and the scientific object. The interaction of the two in a fashion analogous to that characterized by quantum mechanics demands, in some of their minds, a re-examination of the discipline's assumptions and their revision in the direction of a social transcendentalism. Otto Kuhne (1958) views the subject matter of sociology in system terms, but then goes on to perceive those systems as products of the interaction of polar opposites, a stance that has had a lengthy and honored place in the development of the social sciences without reference to a larger dialectical format. It should not be surprising, then, to find that American sociologists, when proposing a "dialectical" posture within sociological theory, have tended to restrict their image of that frame to an emphasis upon such conceptual polarity. This would appear to be the case with Reinhard Bendix and Bennett Berger's (1959) advocacy of the "perspective of dual tendencies," Wilbert Moore's (1960) emphasis upon "dichotomous classification," Llewellyn Gross's (1961) focus on "neodialectical instances," and Clement Jedrzejewski's "dialectics of complementarity."

The work of Alfred Schütz leads one from this relatively static apprehension of conceptual polarity back toward Gurvitch's concern for the relationship between social reality and the sociologist as subject. As long as one remains within the conceptual world of the social scientist, he argued, one is able to avoid the dialectical problems posed by "everyday reality," for the former replaces the intimate dialectic between Mead's subjective "I" and objective "me" with *types*, with the artificial images of puppetry. Direct phenomenological comprehension of that everyday reality, dialectical in nature, is then transformed and made available to the syllogistic logic of science. When Berger adds a Sartrean Marx to the mix, however, the dialectic remains at the center of the sociologist's workbench. For man not only created his everyday world (the process of objectivation), but it turns round and produces him in turn. Socialization is no longer conceived as the internalization of the institutionalized values and norms of the culture or sub-culture. Rather it is dialectically linked with alienation, the two working together as a single interactive process. What might have been but an exercise in the sociology of knowledge, then, is transformed into the sociologist's central task—setting forth in empirical terms that dialectical process in concrete historical situations. What Berger has been unwilling to suggest, however, is that the potential product of the sociologist's insight—the ability to stand outside oneself and respond to the dialectical image projected—might itself be conceived as part of the very same dialectical matrix.

This last possibility was one of the features of a second product of post-war dialectical thought in France—the wedding of Marxian social philosophy with an existentialist epistemology, attempted by Jean-Paul Sartre in his *Critique de la Raison Dialectique* in 1960. Calling for the displacement of the quasi-dialectic available in orthodox Marxism and the analytical logic dominating American sociology with a full-fledged and open-ended commitment to dialectical reasoning, Sartre projected a social science that would be capable of generating and regenerating its own "laws." The product was a sociology and a social philosophy that regarded any attempt, linguistic or otherwise, to encapsule man and his society within the bounds of system to be a form of alienation. Thus, in the name of a new and fully dialectical Marxism, Sartre sought to provide a foundation for a new sociology that would transcend the orthodoxies of the left and of the right.

Although relatively few American sociologists appeared by the mid-'sixties to be taken by the potentials of a negotiated peace between the system and conflict paradigms that a dialectical framework seemed to promise, there was reason to suspect that it was an image from which considerably more might be heard in the future. Not until 1963 had the official journal of the profession seen fit to clear and publish its first article treating in sympathy and some detail with the classic dialectical stance, and even then the paper in question was framed in such a manner as to be equally sympathetic to the system model.[13] The full impact of the recovery of the early Marx would not be felt until the graduate students of the early 'sixties had moved into the academic and publication marketplaces. Only a small portion of Jean-

Paul Sartre's *Critique de la Raison Dialectique* was available in English, and that not until 1963. Gurvitch's *Dialectique et Sociologie* had yet to be translated, although an elaborate analysis of it was made available by Phillip Bosserman in 1967. Berger and Luckmann's extension of a dialectical sociology of knowledge into the heart of sociological theory had been published only as late as 1966, while the bridging of the ideological chasm between the West and the Marxist East had only been formally pledged by the election of Jan Szczepanski of Poland as President of the International Sociological Association that fall. The sociologist of sociology, therefore, began to suspect that the dialectic, unencumbered by a special ideological cast, might provide a strikingly "functional" alternative to a choice between system and conflict as the 'sixties moved into the 'seventies. Certainly the fact that one of the discipline's leading exponents of the system paradigm chose to title his presidential address before the 1967 meetings of the American Sociological Association "In Praise of Conflict and Its Negation" was a propitious sign.[14]

First- and second-order paradigms

But the fundamental reason why a dialectical posture is likely to gain a respectable hearing in the decade ahead lies in an altogether different consideration. A crucial factor—largely irrelevant to revolutions in the physical and biological sciences—has been overlooked. Kuhn did not claim, you will remember, that his thesis could in fact be applied neatly and surely to the social sciences. The burden of attempting to do so is entirely my own. But in carrying that burden I have discovered that the paradigms of which I have spoken up to this point may not in fact represent that paradigmatic dimension which is most controlling.

Kuhn finds that natural scientific revolutions hinge upon shifts in the fundamental image a discipline has of its *subject matter*. A social science may have to confront a more fundamental paradigmatic dimension if it is to comprehend or extrapolate radical changes in the former, a level that addresses itself to the grounding image the social scientist has of *himself as scientific agent*. The reason this may be necessary is quite simple. Social scientists interact with their subject matter in a much more intimate manner than do scientists dealing with biological and physical phenomena. And whereas atoms and cells are not in any consequential way influenced by the image the physicist and the biologist hold of themselves as scientists, social phenomena may be immediately and profoundly conditioned by the image the social scientist has internalized regarding the nature of his activity. The paradigms that order a sociologist's conception of his subject matter, in other words, may themselves be a reflection, or function, of a more fundamental image: the paradigm *in terms of which he sees himself*.

When the evidence begins to suggest that sociology began to consolidate about the system paradigm in conjunction with an even more evident consolidation on the part of sociologists' self-images, the potential of the new paradigmatic dimension becomes evident. When one discovers in addition that the recent mass disaffection with the system *gestalt* appears to have been accompanied, perhaps preceded, by a comparable desertion of the prevailing self-image, further exploration seems called for.

Sociology: The Prophetic Mode

One prophesies . . . because persuading others to anticipate the future which he foretells furthers his present designs.

E. A. Ross

Lay Sociology

The reluctance of sociologists until relatively recently to undertake the kind of self-examination implied by a "sociology of sociology" may well be due in part to the conviction that the field is already inordinately burdened by a politically inconvenient public image. Confessions may cleanse the soul, but if our priest—in this case the lay public—listens to the encyclicals of an age well past, we may be tempted to settle for the drug cabinet instead. A little group therapy perhaps, but within the discipline itself.

Indeed, the public image is a curious one. Sociologists are regarded as rebellious adolescents, kicking over the facts and fables laid down by the hard-headed adults of this world. If they are not condemning their elders for conformity, they portray them as normless. Sociologists are the age's professional critics, castigating it for its enthronement of the art of manipulation at the unholy price of alienation. Laymen typically conceive of sociologists as institutionalized muckrakers, dredging deep for the day's cultural contradictions. Scientists? Hardly, for science doesn't read that easily, and "sociology" appears in the home almost monthly through one or another of the book clubs.

Notes to this chapter will be found on pages 331–333.

The image is hard to displace, for it has been etched deeply by scores of people who have addressed the general public in the discipline's name. A few have written from formal chairs of sociology in our great universities. More are, in fact, laymen themselves—energetic and imaginative laymen who often have read more widely in select areas of the discipline than has the average sociologist himself. Many of those responsible for the public's characterization are professionals trained in related disciplines who have succumbed to the temptation in the last decade or two to extend their inquiries to areas hitherto monopolized by sociologists. A small but colorful group are journalists, with or without causes, who may be tempted to shift their vocabularies with the prevailing trade-book winds.

Normlessness

Although one might have expected that a discipline so heavily indebted to Durkheim might see the contemporary situation in "anomic" terms, *normlessness* itself has not been heavily emphasized in sociological materials dispensed to the public at large over the last decade or two.[1] Robert Merton had seen *anomie* as the ultimate product of a culture whose institutionalized means were inconsistent with its accepted goals—in clear reference to the American scene—but he did so in technical essays for professional sociologists and within the context of the 1930's when traditional ends and means appeared less sustaining than they have since become. The term has not played a major role in his later essays, even those addressed to his fellow sociologists. It continues to enter into discussions at the social-psychological level and into the assessment of such deviant behavioral patterns as delinquency, crime, suicide, and radicalism, but it is clear that the larger sociological heart is not in the task. The banner that has led the parade to the sociologist's book shelves has been, by and large, its very opposite.

Conformity

Conformity clearly has been the more honored concept. The tradition-, inner-, and other-directed trinity of David Riesman's *The Lonely Crowd* has become part of the ritualized language of our secular day. Certainly the general cry of "conformity" was taken up by literally scores of other students of the social scene and echoed from institution to institution down through the nineteen-fifties. The country's business elite saw it imaginatively detailed in the bureaucracy of big business through William Whyte, Jr.'s, glossy *Fortune* series, while the larger public saw it elaborated and popularized in *The Organization Man*.

Community studies whose prototypes appeared in the Lynds' *Middletown* volumes in the late 'twenties and 'thirties saw "Yankee City," "Plainville," "Elmtown," "Southerntown," "Prairietown," "Jonesville," "Crestwood Heights," and a dozen or so others that did not carry fictitious names as breeding grounds for the stratified rigidities of class and caste. Vidich and Bensman's *Small Town in Mass Society* is but one of the more recent in a lengthy lineage.

The image of political man as rational arbiter of his separate interests was, meanwhile, being shattered by studies depicting educational and political interest as correlated with one-party conformity, while the crucial "independent" swing vote found its clues in such items as the nuances in the voice of the local bartender, the re-enforcement of an ethnic or religious identification, or the practiced sincerity that registers on a 24-inch television screen. Documented initially in public opinion studies run by Berelson and Lazarsfeld (*The Peoples' Choice* and *Voting*) and by Campbell, Gurin, and Miller (*The Voter Decides*), and parlayed in thousands of classrooms across America via the texts of V. O. Key, Jr., and Burdick and Brodbeck, and, more recently, those by Lipset and by Kornhauser, the sociological fall-out finally settles upon the general public in the "background" political analyses made available through the mass media. Those who strayed from the lists of best sellers or read the book reviews of those who had may also have seen the impact of conformity in the more subtle area of civil liberties through Grodzins' *The Loyal and the Disloyal*, Stouffer's *Communism, Conformity, and Civil Liberties*, J. W. Aldridge's *In Search of Heresy*, Lazarsfeld and Thielens' *The Academic Mind*, and Daniel Bell's *The New American Right*.

Will Herberg's delineation of a third generation's

search for social identification in *Protestant, Catholic, Jew* set off a whole series of flagellations of men of the cloth. T. S. Matthews illustrated the drugging effects that are dispensed through the American press in *The Sugar Pill*. More recent landscapes of the scope of Riesman's effort have included Walker and Heyns' *An Anatomy for Conformity*, the Hausers' *The Fraternal Society*, and Robert Prestus' *The Organizational Society*. Peter Viereck's *The Unadjusted Man* picked up essentially where *The Lonely Crowd's* brief introduction to "autonomous man" had left off, while Winston White's *Beyond Conformity* took to task the very ideologues whom he argued had been at base responsible for the contemporary critique. And, we have already pointed out how C. Wright Mills depicted the sociological community itself, in *The Sociological Imagination*, as but a reflection of the larger mood of conformity dominating the day.

Manipulation

Inspired perhaps by the imagery of Orwell's *1984* and Aldous Huxley's *Brave New World*, the analysis included not only the state of the victim but also the nature of the villain. Here the act of *manipulation* was given top billing, with the culprit shifted from performance to performance according to the sentiments of the playwright. Mills portrayed *The Power Elite* as an interlaced and interchangeable network within the highest echelons of industry, government, and the military. The metaphorically inclined among the lay public could easily have filled in the frame provided by Mills by leafing through the dust jackets on the non-fiction shelves of the neighborhood lending library during the 'fifties. A "nation of sheep" was pictured attaching a "white collar" to an otherwise "naked society" and being led by a Judas-goat social structure down a path marking "the causes of World War III." The "waste makers'" way was paved by "image merchants," "hidden persuaders," "the fourth branch of government," and "the fictions of American capitalism." There was some infighting between "the operators" and "the vested interests" as "the quest for wealth" was pursued by "the pyramid climbers," but "power and morality in business society" was largely a chorus sung before a backdrop of "power without property." Even "the academic marketplace" fitted neatly into a minor role. Although Orwell might grant us another generation in transit, the lay public, once the "brave new world" was "revisited," was confronted by the suggestion that "tomorrow is already here."

Contradiction

But a school of thought with more influence among sociologists was not satisfied to stop with this "devil theory" of society. Coming to the fore with the growth and domination of functional analysis, it focused upon elements in a social or cultural system that appeared to be *contradictory*. Merton's early analysis of "Social Structure and Anomie" was, in fact, more truly consistent with system analysis than it was an exercise in the application of a Durkheimian concept. Normlessness was by no means the most likely product of his paradigm. Rather, it more clearly mapped the routes by which normatively oriented sub-cultures might appear as derivatives of a larger system with inconsistent means-ends relationships. The analysis has gone considerably beyond where Merton left it in 1938 and has led to countless substantive studies of sub-cultures whose goals or whose means are at odds with those of other sub-cultures or with those of the larger systems of which they are a part. Some social theorists have argued that an examination of contradictory goals within the over-all social scene in America has been hindered by the structural-functional school's initial and central commitment to the system concept, but even system analysis at the macrocosmic level has proved productive.

Within the larger American cultural scene, a belief in God and the sacrificial love ethic of the Biblical religions is counterposed by the norms of a competitive, materialistic, *laissez-faire* economic ideology. The commercial exploitation of sexual imagery is poised over against the inhibitions of a Puritan conception of the body and its functions. Merle Curti argues that the "American paradox" is posed by an unrivaled support for education linked with an ever-present anti-intellectualism, whereas Richard Hofstadter formulates essentially the same posture in terms of the perennial conflict between the intellectual and the common man. A renewal of interest in de Tocqueville's *Democracy in America* once again drew attention to our improbable dedication to both freedom and egalitarianism and stimulated such efforts as that by Seymour Lipset to view "the first new nation" as the product of the contending polarities of equality and achievement. Meanwhile Gunnar Myrdal—along with a sizeable company of young scholars who were to make their individual marks upon the development of sociology over the decades following World War II—had delineated what was "an American dilemma" of major proportions some ten years before the full dimensions of the contradiction between our democratic code and our legal and educational standards were set forth by the Supreme Court. And Margaret Mead is but the most prolific of a large band who have recorded the American female's pursuit of equality while holding tight to her highly valued privileges of femininity.

Such cultural and/or sub-cultural contradiction and conflict has been but one of many foci of sociological interest over the last two decades. It has, however, claimed a disproportionate amount of attention from the lay public. It not only offers the popularizer the built-in guarantee of controversy, but its very nature leads to its inclusion in those courses that dominate enrollments in undergraduate sociology curricula: "American Society," "Social Problems," "Cultural and Racial Minorities," "Marriage and the Family." Its link with the larger conscious concerns of sociological theorists may indeed have been less manifest than has been inferred. Functional analysis does not necessarily lead to a concern with *dys*functionality, though fortunately there were many on hand to point out the tautological nature of a functionalist theory that did not do so. It might be worth adding, however, that from the point of view of a sociology of sociology the quite evident and admitted effort over the last decade or two to order sociological thinking within the frame of the system concept may itself have been a latent function of the strongly felt need on the part of social theorists for conceptual closure in response to the impact on them of a peculiarly unsystematic social and cultural milieu. Analogously, other-directedness and other manifestations of conformity might be regarded—at least by many sociologists—as an expression of the larger public's need for social identification and security in a highly contradictory cultural environment.

Alienation

The layman finds himself depicted, then, as the product of a manipulated conformity that blunts the cutting edge of the contradictions that threaten to cleave his culture. At the social psychological level the image has been shifting from Durkheim's "anomie" to the *alienation* proffered by the young Marx and contemporary psychotherapists. Foremost among those shaping the concept for the public at large has been Erich Fromm, fluent analyst of the private and public psyche. Although his talents as social theorist were evident with the publication in 1941 of *Escape from Freedom*, it was not until almost fifteen years later that he attempted, in *The Sane Society*, a systematic examination of what Freud had called "civilization and its discontents." Alienation becomes the link between contemporary character and culture, the key to the diagnosis of an insane society. Drawing upon a synthesis of late Freud and early Marx, Fromm saw modern man as blocked by a dehumanized social structure from satisfying his true needs and realizing his humane nature. He attempted to document his case more recently by abstracting the twenty-six-year-old Karl from the Marx who lived and wrote until the age of sixty-five (*Marx's Concept of Man*, 1961) and then went on to synthesize the precipitant with the Freud of the "discontents" (*Beyond the Chains of Illusion*, 1962).

Fritz Pappenheim's more scholarly exercise, *The Alienation of Modern Man: an Interpretation Based on Marx and Tönnies*, preceded Fromm's Marx volume by two years and joins Fromm, Herbert Marcuse, Raya Dunayevskaya, and others in assuming that *Die oekonomischphilosophischen Manuskripte* of 1844 undergirded all of Marx's later works. The publication of all of the 1844 and 1845 essays for the first time in English in 1959 and the availability of T. B. Bottomore's translation of approximately two-thirds of them in Fromm's *Marx's Concept of Man*, as well as other selections translated and published in 1956 and 1963, however, presaged a widespread examination of the early Marx and a reinforcement of the inroads that the alienation concept had already made upon serious discussions of the condition of social man.[2] For alienation has, in fact, already become common currency among sociologists.[3]

The term, along with its synonyms and antonyms, has carried the general outline of Fromm's diagnosis to the educated layman as well, with Helen Lynd, Hannah Arendt, Lewis Mumford, and Orrin Klapp standing high among those registering its broader implications. Joost Meerloo (*Suicide and Mass Suicide*) and Bruno Bettelheim (*The Informed Heart*) draw up the traumas of the Nazi period to delineate the ultimate impact of alienation, while Robert Nisbet has examined one of the responses man has made in his *Quest for Community*. A broad array of pertinent descriptive materials have been brought together most recently by Eric and Mary Josephson in *Man Alone: Alienation in Modern Society*, and, in two volumes, by Gerald Sykes in *Alienation: The Cultural Climate of Our Time*. The pictures painted are almost uniformly grim.

But of special significance to a sociologist of sociology is the revealing manner in which the notion of alienation has been turned back upon the very sociologists who would characterize contemporary society in its terms. It is *they* who in fact are held to be the alienated, not the structures of the social system itself. "Much of the resistance against the theory of action (that is, against the predominant theoretical scheme that has come to be associated largely with the writings of Talcott Parsons) comes," argues Edward Shils, "from . . . obstinately alienated sociology . . ."—the product of those who contend "that the main and inescapable function of sociology is to be the critic of its society."[4] That C. Wright Mills was wont to wield the term with even greater vigor in precisely the opposite direction may suggest how the routines and revolutions within our discipline may intrigue and challenge students of the sociology of sociology.

The Hebraic Analogue

But the fact of the matter is that the layman *believes* that the image of the modern world projected by sociologists *is* a harshly critical one, one that emphasizes conformity and manipulation, cultural contradiction and alienation, while playing down balancing and adjustive mechanisms. Shils's argument does apply to those who have spoken and written for the lay public. To them sociology does appear as "an outlook that radically distrusts the inherited order of society." Recent American sociology may have been burdened, as many have suggested, with a theoretical structure that granted but a secondary place to man's dissentious activity, but if so it has been a game played but intramurally. The sociologists and social theorists who have flexed their muscles for the larger public have been engaged in an entirely different sport.

The exercise, however, is not a new one. Its public record stretches back nearly three millennia, although the equipment and credentials of the players have changed to fit the symbols and styles of a new and secularized day. A hint is found in Fromm (1955:69) when, after depicting the age as one of narcissism, destructiveness, incest, conformity, and irrationality, he counters with the assertion that their opposite "coincides essentially with the norms postulated by the great spiritual leaders of the human race." Clues are dropped in the title and throughout the body of Peter Berger's *The Noise of Solemn Assemblies* and when Berger is characterized by his biblically versed friends as an "angry young prophet." Although Berger is clearly unhappy about the appellation, nevertheless he has affirmed that "Amos has something to say to our present situation."[5]

"Prophets" versus "seers"

The alienation to which Amos and the other Biblical prophets testify is, of course, an estrangement from the Lord God of Israel. The alienation of which the sociologist appears to the layman to speak is an alienation from one's untapped creative resources and an estrangement from the bonds of community with one's fellows. Although the product of differing frames of commitment, the diagnoses have similar empirical references. Neither is simply descriptive; both are acts of judgment that project consequences while offering hope to the responsive "remnant." The Hebraic scriptures are quite explicit in distinguishing between the *roeh*, who acted simply as "seers" in foretelling the future, and the *nabi*—the "prophets"—who sought, through their projections of past behavior into the future, to *alter* that future. On the sociological side "one prophesies" argued E. A. Ross (1943:10) "because persuading others to anticipate the future which he foretells furthers his present designs."

Commitment is imperative to both prophetic modes, commitment that shakes man loose from a position of neutrality as he faces the choice of treating his fellow as an end in himself or as but a means to one's own ends. Abraham Heschel (1962:284) reminds us that "the knowledge of evil is something which the first man acquired; it was not something that the prophets had to discover. Their great contribution to humanity was the discovery of the evil of indifference." The seventh- and eighth-century B.C. prophets of Israel were the antithesis of cool cataloguers of social norms. They were engaged—and in public.

But there are those who are tempted to draw the analogy even more tightly. E. W. Heaton (1961:106–10) falls among those contemporary Biblical scholars who see the Old Testament prophets as looking back to the common life of a desert community for the social dimensions of the judgment they voiced upon an Israel which had clothed itself with the relatively new garments of urbanization:

> . . . the people of God had accepted the debased standards of a competitive society and had lost the personal integrity which their forefathers had learnt in the days of Moses. (The covenant tradition of equality and brotherhood learned in the desert had been smashed by the new "civilized" standards of the kingdom.) . . . The eighth century B.C. in its earlier phase had been enjoying a post-war boom almost without precedent. . . . The period from about 785 to 745 B.C. was therefore a veritable gala-time for the ambitious and the unprincipled *nouveaux riches*. . . . What they found in society was not only cruelty, but cruelty masquerading under the cloak of piety.

Narrowly conceived it has the ring of a C. Wright Mills, a Vance Packard, or an Erich Fromm; viewed broadly it reflects the classical sociological contrast between *Gemeinschaft* and *Gesellschaft*, that juxtaposition of a personal and communal traditionalism over against the routinized rationality of impersonally structured associations examined at such length by Tönnies and Max Weber, elaborated by Howard Becker in his "sacred" and "secular" polarities, and dissected in the varying editions of Parson's pattern-variables.

If one were to choose from a secularized and ideal-typical version of the "offices" of Christ delineated in the classical fashion of a Calvin—that is, from the image of Christ as Priest, Prophet, and King, one would have to acknowledge that the role that comes closest to the *layman's* image of the contemporary sociologist is that of *prophet.* A "priestly" office concerns itself more nearly with the effort to bring man into touch with an image of the "real" through the mediation of the community's tradition in symbol and ritual; the office of "king" speaks to the responsibility for day-to-day leadership in the city of man. The "prophet" speaks in the Biblical tradition for Him who

> . . . shall not judge by what his eyes see,
> or decide by what his ears hear;
> but with righteousness he shall judge the poor,
> and decide with equity for the meek of the earth,
> and he shall smite the earth with the rod of his mouth,
> and with the breath of his lips he shall slay the wicked.[6]

In secular language, the sociologist as prophet does indeed contend, as Shils suggests, "that the main and inescapable function of sociology is to be the critic of its society."

Peter Berger would argue, in fact, that the critical stance is inherent even in the simple descriptive tasks that confront him:

> To ask sociological questions . . . presupposes . . . a measure of suspicion about the way in which human events are officially interpreted by the authorities, be they political, juridical or religious in character. . . . We will not be far off if we see sociological thought as part of what Nietzsche called "the art of mistrust." . . . The social mysteries lie behind the façades (1963: 29–31).

Berger himself appears as a particularly striking example of the prophetic mode when his devastating denial of the possibility of the renewal of today's church in *The*

Precarious Vision and *The Noise of Solemn Assemblies* is joined to the constructive role he portrayed as available to sociologists in his later *Invitation to Sociology*. One must emphasize the word "available," however, for Berger sees the discipline burdened today with an inordinate number of younger sociologists "who find themselves driven to radical diagnoses of society . . . with no place to go except to a sort of masochistic cult of debunkers who reassure each other that things could not possibly be worse" (1963:162).

Some may be tempted to dismiss the analogy of sociologist as prophet with the observation that not many sociologists over the past generation fall within the general type. But this is not the same as denying that *laymen* have regarded sociologists primarily as institutionalized social critics. "A few sociologists," acknowledges Shils (1961:1408), "have become public figures in America. . . ." And how does he go on? By adding the pertinent phrase, "prophets of the same order as famous scientists and publicists." C. Wright Mills was a perfect example. Although he has been characterized as "a loner not a leader," Shils pointed out that he had been over the decade and a half following World War II the most widely read sociologist in the world. And, although Mills was often dismissed as social philosopher and/or ideologist within the discipline, one review of introductory texts published in the five years preceding his death in 1962 found that only Merton and Parsons took precedence in the number of citations made to the works of sociologists, classic or contemporary. As his obituary notice in the *ASR* brought out, "He rarely indulged in pure analysis; he demanded that we judge each situation morally as well as objectively. . . . He felt a moral responsibility to set things aright in the world . . . though he had no 'circle' of disciplines, wherever people felt oppressed by the world, they heeded his voice. . . . Mills was a prophet . . ." (Goode, 1962:580). Indeed, in donning the prophet's mantle, Mills, along with the many others who have been responsible for the public's image of sociologists as social critics, wore a garment woven by the founders of the profession and worn over the ensuing century and a half by many of her most creative practitioners.

Sociology, in fact, was born from the loins of prophecy. Frank Manuel's delightful volume, *The Prophets of Paris*, documents all too thoroughly her origins in the almost manic utopianism of a little band of Frenchmen over the last decades of the eighteenth century and the first half dozen of the nineteenth. Focused about the prodigious publications, parlor-room lectures, and coffee-house dialogues of Turgot, Condorcet, Saint-Simon, Fourier, and Auguste Comte, along with peripatetic converts who streamed from one to the other, the vision of a science of social man was born. It differed radically from the prophecy of the Biblical tradition and many of the critiques of our day in that it was energized by an image of science that denied the tragic dimension to history, even though, paradoxically, the lives of its mentors were themselves classic tragedies. Manuel locates its points of critical mass in two lectures delivered in 1750 at the Sorbonne by a youthful scion of an illustrious Norman family; a last testament written under sentence to the guillotine of an age of reason gone mad; tracts copied by hand by a penniless and consumptive count; thoughts that formed in the mind of a traveling salesman as he contemplated discrepancies in the price of apples; and seventy-two lectures held in the apartment of an unemployed mathematician, which had to be interrupted temporarily after the thirteenth when the lecturer was committed to an insane asylum.

And what was this vision that they sought to grant life and power? A conception of world history as moving act by act to the perfection of man; the transformation of the social order through methods that had brought about a revolution in the physical sciences and in the technical arts; an understanding of man's search for knowledge in all its relevant dimensions as a movement from a theological through a metaphysical to a positivistic stage; an image of the *status quo* as chained to the irrational moralities and institutions of a bygone day; and the hierarchic interlocking of the sciences with sociology enthroned as queen.

Comte appears to have been the most imaginative publicist of the group and, as a reward for inventing and popularizing the term "sociology," is generally designated as the father of the new discipline. But the honor may be tarnished by the fact that he would hardly have been satisfied with the designation "sociologist" himself and looked upon the discipline as a synthesizing science that was to order all of what we have come to call the social and behavioral sciences. Furthermore, neither the *Philosophie positive* nor the *Polity* were at base his own creations. He himself listed Hume, Kant, Condorcet, de Maistre, Gall, and Bichat as his "spiritual antecedents," while others have seen in his works the influence of Pascal, Montesquieu, Bossuet, Vico, Bourdin, and Saint-Pierre. A contemporary Comtean—and they are very hard to find—might wish to counter with the fact that Comte determined, upon recovering from the serious mental breakdown that overtook him at the age of 28, never again to read the works of another. But even if he did carry out his pledge, the systematic theses that came from his quill would seem to speak more eloquently of the common intellectual atmosphere that intoxicated the "prophets of Paris" than they do of Comte's own foresight.

A note may be in order regarding the apparent paradox that confronts us when we join with Manuel in including within the category "prophet" a man who foresaw sociologists in the role of "priests" of a new religion of positivism. There is no doubt that priests they were to be, with Comte assuming the prerogatives of high priest as soon as the political masters of Europe were to come to their senses. Plans were elaborately drawn: 20,000 priests would be provided for western Europe, one to each 10,000 families; the High Priest would, it hardly needs saying, be located in Paris, the new Jerusalem of the scientific religion of humanity; seven would be selected as subordinate national chief priests and the whole organized in an authoritarian, hierarchic manner modeled after the organization of the Roman Church. Comte had projected the role with such thoroughness that a list of positivist saints had already been drawn up, one designated for each day of the year. The point pertinent to this discussion, however, is the role Comte was actually playing. Comte did indeed elaborate an image of the sociologist as priest *in his writings*, but he witnessed *with his life* to the image of sociologist as prophet. Manuel's analogical language makes the point most clearly (1962:7, 299):

Like the great Prodromos, they appeared in the wilderness of a corrupt Paris to announce the coming. In a confusion of roles they sometimes imagined that in their person the Messiah himself had already arrived. Saint-Simon thought that he was the reincarnation of Socrates and of Charlemagne; the disciples evoked the analogy with Jesus. . . . Auguste Comte . . . preferred to relate himself to Saint Paul. . . .

Unlike their German counterparts, none of the prophets of Paris were closeted academic philosophers, and for them action was always bound up with theory. They were all committed men; they knew what they wanted the future world to be like, often down to the minutest social arrangement. They were of the dawn, not the twilight. Philosophical history was for them a prerequisite for sound prophecy, and prophecy was necessary for right conduct.

But like most of the prophets of Israel, those of early nineteenth-century Paris exerted little tangible influence during their lifetimes beyond the small and feuding cults each left behind. Comte wasn't even read in France while he lived, for his writings fell between the activists of the Revolution of 1848 and the expansive humanitarianism of many of the leaders of the Second Empire. Positivism did gain a foothold in England through the interest John Stuart Mill took in the *Philosophie positive*, but it faded with the publication of the manic flights of imagination of the *Polity* and the appearance of the more congenial individualism of Herbert Spencer. Comte was read by many of the alienated intellectuals of late nineteenth-century Russia, influencing the work of Kovalevsky in particular, and positivism was kept alive by small circles in Holland, Italy, Sweden, and the United States. What limited influence Comte's thought exerted on Durkheim appeared to be mediated through the response to Comte of one or more German writers who had, in turn, been introduced to the *Philosophie positive* through England and Mill. The prophet was, however, honored in South America where the intellectual elite of the last century found in the *Polity* a means by which they could abandon the claims of the Roman Church without disturbing the social framework for which the Church, almost alone, had stood. Brazil, in fact, accepted Comte as its official philosopher and emblazoned the motto of the Positivist Church, "*Ordem e Progresso*," on its national flag. It was the latter term—"progress"—standing as it did at the base of positivism, that was to nurture the prophetic stance in intellectual climes that rejected Comte's specific formulations.

The Prophetic Lineage

Shils has argued rather persuasively that the alienative strain was, in fact, planted by Hobbes as early as the seventeenth century. After its meteoric rise—and fall—at the hands of the prophets of Paris, it was nurtured back to life in the late nineteenth century through German social philosophy in general and the writings of Karl Marx in particular, both drawing from the springs of continental Romanticism and Hegelian notions of alienation. The "dreams of reason" of the seventeenth and eighteenth centuries delineated recently by René Dubos were providing the motor and motive power for social scientific developments of the nineteenth and twentieth. The prophetic strain even found a vehicle in the qualified optimism of English utilitarianism. John Stuart Mill could express a belief "that the general tendency is, and will continue to be, saving occasional and temporary exceptions, one of improvement—a tendency towards a happier and better state. This . . . is . . . a theorem of science" (Popper, 1957:118–119). And the dreams were tested—for perhaps the first time—by surveys undertaken in the urban areas of England during the first period of the Reform Parliament. Their larger significance was heralded by Jeremy Bentham, while the lessons learned contributed to Le Play's *Les Ouvriers Européens* (1855) and Charles Booth's encyclopedic *Life and Labor of the People in London* (1892–7).

The image of science as an instrument of social reform, however, had to await passage to America to see its full fruition. Her first systematic sociologist, Lester Ward, set the stage with his contention that "the true guide, the Moses that is to lead man out of the wilderness, is science." Indeed, "the real object of science is to benefit man. A science which fails to do this, however agreeable its study, is lifeless" (Rumney and Maier, 1953:167). Even Ward's *bête noire*, William Graham Sumner, was on an essentially preaching mission, convinced as he was that his Spencerian sociology would assist mankind to avoid much of the useless travail its leaders so often prepared for it. He had, indeed, trained for the ministry and served for a time as an Episcopal curate.

The American Social Science Association, parent of the American Sociological Society, appears to have been founded upon a concern for the underprivileged stratum of society that the industrialization of the nation had made increasingly visible. The very first formal teaching of methods of social research in an American university was done at the University of Chicago by a former minister (Charles R. Henderson) after Albion Small's appointment to the chair of sociology there during the last decade of the nineteenth century. In a paper delivered at the first official meeting of the American Sociological Society in 1906, Small stated emphatically that the study of social behavior was not to be considered an end in itself, that its rationale could only be the improvement of society. Most of the discipline's first- (and many of its second-) generation leadership had close ties to the Christian church. One of Ward's grandfathers and Giddings' and W. I. Thomas' fathers had been ministers. In addition to Sumner and Henderson, Small, Vincent, Hayes, Lichtenberger, Weatherly, and John L. Gillin were former clergymen, and Ellsworth Faris served as a missionary.

Furthermore, the case has been made that the dominant role played by midwestern universities—particularly the University of Chicago—during the first decades of this century directed the discipline toward a concern with the manifest and latent social effects of industrialization and urbanization, to which those having come to maturity within the ethos of an agrarian Protestantism were particularly sensitive. Park's background in journalism opened the doors of Chicago's graduate department to the muckraking prose of such monographs as *The Unadjusted Girl*, *The Gang*, *The Ghetto*, *The Jack-Roller*, and *The Gold Coast and the Slum*. This ameliorative strain culminated in *The Polish Peasant in Europe and America*, a monumental five-volume integration of sociological theory and data drawn from personal documents. Even students under the methodology-oriented Giddings at Columbia found that the required curriculum included course work in criminology and penology, pauperism and the poor laws. University departments were likely to combine sociology with what later came to be designated as social work. The first of the great community studies in the United States—*Middletown*—was financed as a project of an Institute of Social and Religious Research and, together with *Middletown in Transition*, read like episodes from Lincoln Steffen's autobiography.

Don Martindale (1957) has detailed the manner in which the conceptual framework of American sociology accented, during the period, the phrase "social problems" and the manner in which the terms "social pathology" and "social disorganization" came later to the fore. An examination of the political ideologies of sociologists looked upon today as the founders of the discipline (Palmore, 1962) offers additional evidence of this activist stance: more than twice as many could be characterized as on the political left than those falling on the right. The findings are supported by the elaborate if not completely dispassionate survey by A. H. Hobbs (1951) of textbooks published in the United States between 1926 and 1945 covering the areas of introductory sociology, social problems, and the family. The author reports a distinctly critical diagnosis of existing social institutions combined with a highly optimistic image of the contribution that sociology might make to a more intelligent reordering of human affairs.[7]

In the decades preceding the 'sixties the prophetic stance came to center about the persons and writings of Karl Mannheim, Pitirim Sorokin, Robert Lynd, Robert MacIver and Louis Wirth. C. Wright Mills, as we have suggested, stood as archetype for a somewhat younger generation. Lynd's classic essay, *Knowledge for What?* (1939:125–26), spoke for almost all within the larger circle by declaring that the task of sociologists was to discover "what kinds of order actually do exist . . . and what functionally more useful kinds of order can be created. . . ." Lynd went on to contend, in fact, that "it is precisely the role of the social sciences to be troublesome, to disconcert the habitual arrangements by which we manage to live along, and to demonstrate the possibilities of change in more adequate directions. Their role, like that of the skilled surgeon, is to get us into immediate trouble in order to prevent our chronic present troubles from becoming even more dangerous."[8]

We have already pointed out in Chapter 2 that sociology had not, in this pre–World War II period, achieved the level of consensus regarding the fundamental nature of her subject matter that a Kuhn would recognize as characteristic of a mature science. What agreement that did exist appeared to lie at a more primordial paradigmatic level: in the implicit assumption that the sociological role was to be justified ultimately by the stance that is characterized here as "prophetic." Indeed, the predominance of the prophetic approach might help to explain the absence of consolidation about a common substantive paradigm. "Prophecy" in the Hebraic tradition was paired with *iconoclasm*—the *breaking* of icons. The stance it represented then and in its sociological garb more recently, thus, would seem to grant priority to the destruction of false images. A paradigm may well lie behind the action of the prophet, but the emphasis is upon breaking false images rather than putting forth more adequate ones. Simply put, it means only that those enamored of the prophetic posture find their special forte to be criticism rather than construction. If this is true, one would have expected that consolidation about a common image of social "reality" might have had to await the demise of prophecy.

The most pertinent observation to be made in conclusion, however, is that—with the exception of Mills—every one of the secular prophets who had once dominated the main stream of American sociology was by the mid 1950's either retired or dead.

The Cloak of Neutrality

There ain't no sin and there ain't no virtue. There's just stuff people do.

Jim Casy in Steinbeck's *The Grapes of Wrath*

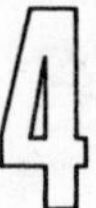

The Death of Prophecy

JACQUES BARZUN could hardly have been more mistaken when he suggested that the term "behavioral sciences" has replaced "social sciences" because of what he saw as the sociologist's "desperate conviction that man does not behave and should be made to with the help of science." What actually had happened was that in the decade and a half following World War II, the prophetic strain in American sociology had been dying out as the first-generation products of the graduate programs at Columbia and the great universities of the Midwest passed from the scene. In their place appeared a younger generation carefully trained in the methods of empirical research and dedicated to the gospel that value judgments were to be described and not made. Howard Becker (1950:213, 247) could write that "the sociologist is resigned to the fact that the age of prophecy is over. . . . In the scientific role, prophecy has no place; prediction must be our guide."

Many students may have been drawn to the field initially because they felt that it offered them a prime opportunity to articulate programs of social reform. Instead, they found themselves struggling with graduate courses in contemporary methodology, sampling design,

---

Notes to this chapter will be found on pages 333–335.

advanced statistics, computer programming and structure-functional theory. Although Paul Lazarsfeld may still cherish the radical socialist tradition he was heir to in central Europe during the 'twenties and 'thirties, he grudgingly acknowledges that the kind of empirical research that has come to dominate sociology is inimical to radical social change. In fact, the shift at Columbia from Lynd to Lazarsfeld and from MacIver to Merton goes far towards symbolizing the profound change that had been abuilding in American sociology for some time but which had failed to engulf the positions of power in the profession until the immediate post–World War II period.

Put most concisely by Everett Hughes (1962:81) while president-elect of the American Sociological Association, it meant that, "In his capacity as a student of reality, the sociologist is presumed to be neutral." His is *not* the reformer's role but rather a dedication to the chaste pursuit of what *is*. Epistemologically, the new dispensation demanded the sharp differentiation of the empirical from the existential, the public from the private, the indicative mood from the imperative. Only thus might the sociologist achieve full membership in the community to which he had aspired so long—the brotherhood of science.[1]

With the demise of prophecy and their own reduced sense of personal and professional responsibility for the impact of their research, sociologists after World War II predictably began turning to models of human social behavior that were themselves free of apparent ideological content. Awaiting their call was that most neutral handmaiden, the electronic computer, which was developed initially as a supremely efficient device for processing vast amounts of data, but sociologists soon became aware that its feedback capacity could be utilized to emulate social interaction. Freed by its youth from the chains of tradition, the Department of Social Relations at Johns Hopkins sought in fact to focus its graduate curriculum about the new technique. The Department's early promotional fliers claimed that "by programming on a digital computer models of basic social processes, combined as they are in actual social systems, it becomes possible to *simulate* the behavior of a social system functioning through time." Moreover, the electronic genie could recreate the "dynamics of community controversy" and "rebellion generating systems." The growing list of publications on computer simulation indicated that the Johns Hopkins department was not the only one smitten.

A paradox was shaping up. On the one hand sociologists were admonished to ignore the applied implications of their work. Yet at the same time more and more of them were becoming involved in full- or part-time applied activity. In other words, at the very time that the profession identified its role as no longer responsible for the social consequences of its activities we find, paradoxically, that its membership rushed headlong into activities which *had* practical consequence as their common end. Somehow irresponsibility in theory had been accompanied by responsibility in fact—though the question of just what it is sociologists had chosen to be responsible for had as yet to be answered. Reinhard Bendix (1951: 191–92) suggested that the new emphasis on the applied function meant that sociologists had abandoned their efforts to develop a science of society and thereby any hopes of making man a more rational creature. In its place they had substituted the view that sociology simply was a tool for those fortunate enough to have been trained in its methods. Freed from the restraints of social responsibility, sociologists could apply their specialized skills in any manner that might further their own or their sub-culture's interests.

Roots

The rejection of what we have called the prophetic mode in sociology had an impressive pedigree. Kant had early identified natural experience as the criterion of what existed rather than what ought to exist. Poincaré had said the same thing but in the language of the logician: "If the premises of a syllogism are both in the indicative, the conclusion will be equally in the indicative . . . the principles of science . . . can only be in the indicative; experimental truths are also in this same mode, and at the foundations of the sciences there is not, cannot be, anything else." Some authorities attribute some of the credit to Durkheim and to first Marx and then Freud later on for undermining the optimistic rationalism of the Parisian visionaries.

Actually it was Max Weber who translated the articles of faith of nineteenth-century science into the scriptures of the mid-twentieth-century sociologist.[2] "An empirical science," wrote Weber (1949:54), "cannot tell anyone what he *should* do—but rather what he *can* do." In a short essay entitled "Science as a Vocation" (Gerth and Mills, 1946:146, 152) he specifically renounced the prophetic within the social-scientific tradition, stating that ". . . [it] is not the gift of grace of seers and prophets dispensing sacred values and revelations . . . [for] whenever the man of science introduces his personal value judgment, a full understanding of the facts ceases." Weber was sophisticated enough to realize that scientific endeavor itself rested on a very real commitment and that the scientist was making but one of a number of choices that were ultimately grounded in the non-empirical. But his proposed solution to the value dilemma, after the decision to follow the scientific path had been made and a problem area had been staked out, was simply to advise sociologists to take on the concepts and values of the particular social and cultural milieu they were examining—i.e., the *verstehen* approach.[3]

Kurt Wolff suggests that the new stance began making its influence felt in America as early as the 1920's. Cooley's *Social Process* (1918) bore no traces of the new approach, whereas Lundberg, Anderson, and Bain's *Trends in American Sociology*, published at the end of the decade, contained a lusty statement of the new creed. Lundberg declaimed the gospel with considerable clarity and verve until his death.

The key to Lundberg's thinking lay in his conviction that the sciences were to be "the point of reference with respect to which validity of all knowledge is gauged. . . ." Moreover, scientists should in no way be any more responsible for judging the *value* of an activity than should a cow for making an unbiased judgment about the value of grass. Lundberg then argued that social scientists should limit themselves to three tasks: (1) delineate the alternatives that exist under given circumstances and point out the consequences of each; (2) discover what men want under such circumstances; and (3) develop those administrative or engineering techniques that will satisfy those desires in the most efficient and economical manner, ". . . regardless of what they may be at any given time, regardless of how they may change from time to time and regardless of the scientist's own preferences" (Lundberg, 1947: 36, 50). Perhaps the latter helps to unravel the apparent contradiction between Lundberg's commitment to the radical separation of fact and value on the one hand and the almost evangelistic fervor with which he responds affirmatively to the question posed in the title of his little volume, *Can Science Save Us?* There are few sociologists whose works bristle more openly with value-judgments than Lundberg's; even his introductory sociology takes on the quality of a sacred text, with each paragraph numbered in chapter and verse style. All this Lundberg communicates with his left hand while the right declares that a value-free sociology cannot afford the "luxury of indignation," "personalistic and moralistic interpretations," or "deeply cherished ideologies resembling in form if not in content their theological predecessor."

Although Lundberg's positivism was atypical of the profession at large, his identification of objectivity with ethical neutrality was unusual only because he spoke to and for the position a decade or two earlier than most of his contemporaries. But it was integral to the image of the sociologist projected by that instrument of professional socialization—the introductory text—almost without exception over the two decades following World War II. Students entering the field during that period had every reason to accept the commandment that sociologists should say nothing about the "goodness" or "evil" of human social behavior. Their task, like the natural scientists', was to discover empirical uniformities that could be used to predict and control other empirical phenomena. Woe to the doctoral candidate who dared question the union of objectivity with neutrality.

Some sociologists, along with a number of natural scientists and philosophers and logicians of science, however, were beginning to have some second thoughts about their presumed neutrality. Still, the struggle to become accredited members of the scientific fraternity had been long and so often frustrating that few sociologists were willing to suggest that they had simply exchanged one priestly garment for another. The majority position was understandable, for it presented a reaction against Comte's utopianism and the bourgeois ethic that had nurtured a reformist sociology in America during the latter part of the nineteenth and first half of the twentieth centuries. It might also have appeared as a healthy counter to a Marxism that identified social science with economic determinism or to those religious traditions that prejudged the nature and destiny of empirical man.

Impact upon Substantive Concerns

The movement away from the prophetic mode can be traced clearly in a number of empirical studies that have examined the changes that have occurred in the substantive interests and research activity of sociologists over the past generation or so. Indeed, these studies do more than simply support the thesis. They suggest, paradoxically, that their self-conscious dedication to value-neutrality during the 'forties and 'fifties may have led sociologists not to a passivity in the face of the value-laden decisions that confronted them in their professional activity, but to a relatively consistent set of responses that reflected a very real—if relatively new—hierarchy of sociological values whose nature may have had an impact far beyond the confines of their own professional sub-community.

Perhaps the most elaborate of the studies was carried out by Richard Simpson. Simpson (1961:458–66) drew upon a tabulation of (1) fields of interest listed by American Sociological Association members in their official directory, (2) papers read at the Association's annual meetings and those published in its official journal, and (3) courses listed in college catalogues. Data from periods extending as far back as 1935 were contrasted with comparable data as recent as 1959. What hard evidence did Simpson uncover concerning the shift in professional direction, or its effects, over that period? Considerable.

First, let us look at *fields of speciality* as set forth in ASA directory listings. During the 'thirties and 'forties, when Europe was racked by ethnic conflict, and the American black, stirred by economic gains and the migration to urban areas that accompanied World War II, intensified his agitation for equality, sociologists were paying less and less attention to race and ethnic relations. The period of *least* apparent interest coincided, strangely enough, with the five years immediately following the Supreme Court's decision outlawing segregated education in 1954, which dramatically thrust the issue before the American people. Simpson's data also showed that training in demography fell off just as the issue of over-population was identified nationally and internationally as perhaps one of the most pressing problems of the age. Adult and juvenile crime in rural America was beginning to match the inflated rates in urban areas—and preparation in criminology went down.

In paying obeisance to value-neutrality, sociologists during the 'thirties and 'forties were turning their backs on critical questions of social disorganization and seeking islands of non-involvement. Research methods and system analysis became the fashion, along with such unsystematic and substantive-oriented fields as medical and industrial sociology and communications and opinion, where the financial rewards were attractive and subsidized research easier to come by, and judgments of value could be left to others.[4]

Simpson's analysis of *papers read* at annual meetings of the A.S.A. between 1946 and 1959 reveals almost exactly the same pattern and adds striking evidence of the kind of latent commitment that often lurks beneath a manifest dedication to a value-free stance. He found military sociology among the four fields that clearly had expanded and international relations among the four that clearly had contracted. International relations was also among those substantive areas showing a decrease in *articles published* in the A.S.R. over the same period. The rest of the data, with the exception of a fall-off in publication of articles on work and industry, were in line with the directory and papers-presented findings. In a somewhat similar vein Hans Zetterberg (1956:18), comparing research projects reported by sociologists in 1953–54 with those of 1946–47, found a 75 per cent decline in the social theory–history of ideas category (from 132 projects to 34).

"Producers" versus "consumers"

Perhaps special mention should be made of the evidence that the Simpson study provides of a conflict of interest between the "producers" and "consumers" of sociological information, at least if we define the directory listings, papers presented, and articles published as more indicative of the interests of sociologists as "productive participants" and course offerings as more nearly indicative of the demand of student "consumers." Comparing studies of course offerings conducted in 1942 and 1957 with his own data, Simpson found that "producer interest" went down in a number of problem-oriented areas (race and ethnic relations, demography, and criminology) even in the face of an increase in "consumer demand," that "producer interest" had decreased in two "neutral" areas in which "consumer interest" had diminished, and that "consumer demand" was non-existent in two others (military and medical sociology) in which "producer interest" had increased sharply. The 1957 study, associating graduate courses with "producer interest" and undergraduate courses with "consumer interest," linked the value-free stance to graduate curricula and the value-laden to undergraduate offerings. We must be cautious in attempting any neat correlation, however, because one of the producers' expanding interests was *military* sociology. A person could argue that the increased interest in such value-laden areas as military sociology did not reflect the concerns of sociologists as "producers," but rather the interests of another "consumer"—the military arm of the federal government. This is indeed a more appropriate reading of the situation. Almost no one would contend that sociologists in and of themselves have become more intrigued by military matters than by affairs that have to do with the international community in general. The point, however, is that their increased involvement with military questions—relative to other substantive areas—may be a *latent* function of their self-conscious shift to a code of value-neutrality. Value judgments are going to be made somewhere by someone. When sociologists abdicated responsibility for some of them they customarily had made, it simply was to make their services available to the highest bidder, as most men do.

To describe this stance as "value-neutral" would be naïve. It is the kind of façade that sociologists are the first to see through when they examine the folkways of such professions as law, medicine, or higher education in general. For what they traded was one value for another—the personal value that they assigned to the solution of certain problems for the delightfully impersonal value of financial support. Forty per cent of the research published by six leading sociological journals in a recent year was subsidized—and 40 per cent of that by the federal government (Tibbitts, 1962:892).

Flight from "social problems"

We might add here a few words about the impact of all this upon the study of "social problems" *per se*. Simpson's study revealed that interest in social problems had diminished in terms of each of the criteria examined (directory listings, A.S.A. papers, *A.S.R.* articles, and course offerings). *Sociological Abstracts* (begun as recently as 1953), though it subdivided sociology into more than thirty sub-sections, made no reference at all to the term, providing in its stead one category that lumped together "criminology" and "social disorganization." Courses in "social problems" or "social disorganization" began to disappear from graduate programs. The chairman of one of the country's largest departments acknowledged to me that at least in the case of his school the change was being made simply because sociology has been redefined as a descriptive rather than as a normative discipline. Indeed, those sociologists who continued to center their interest around action research felt forced to organize a separate Society for the Study of Social Problems and to develop their own journal, *Social Problems*, as an outlet for their research.

One recent survey of the history and current status of sociologists' concern with social problems focused upon what it termed "the conflict of normative and empirical approaches." Its author (Martindale, 1957:367) concluded that because theories of social problems were normative in nature rather than empirical they thus were outside the province of the scientist. The effort to construct such theories merely reflected a misguided effort ". . . to seek scientific objectivity under conditions where it was in principle impossible." Some in the discipline argued that social problems were a legitimate area for research but should be turned over to the professionals in social welfare—an ideal solution, perhaps, from the point of view of a sociologist. The trouble was that many social workers also had lined up on the side of "scientific objectivity" and had become increasingly reluctant to identify themselves with any particular normative stance. At least one sociologist, Hans Zetterberg (1962), went so far as to admonish welfare practitioners to legitimatize group work theory by adhering to the canons of science rather than to normative standards.

One clue that suggests that the issue may not have been resolved successfully is that although sociologists had been trying to demonstrate why social problems were no longer one of their legitimate concerns, many in the larger intellectual community came to view science itself, along with its awesome implications, as *the* social problem of our day. One might wonder, in fact, if the flagging interest in the sociology of social problems may not have been accompanied in many a sociological psyche by a compensating increased interest in the sociology of science.

Status and Power

In 1945 Leo Crispi could title an article addressed to his fellow academicians "Social Science—a Stepchild" with little fear of contradiction. If there were any doubters they may have been convinced the following year when the Senate voted an amendment to a bill seeking to establish a National Science Foundation that eliminated any reference to a proposed division for the social sciences. In commenting on the vote at the time, Lundberg (1947:399) was led to observe that it was simply "a reflection of the common feeling that the social and physical sciences have nothing in common and that at best the social sciences are a propagandist, reformist, evangelical sort of cult."

And yet by the end of 1960 a Division of Social Sciences had been established within the National Science Foundation on a formal level of equality with the Divisions of Natural and Biological Sciences. It was provided, during its first year of operation, with a budget of nearly three-and-a-half million dollars to underwrite approximately 130 grants. The tenor of congressional comment had by this time swung around a full 180° from that prevailing but a decade and a half before. One of the managers of the 1962 Independent Offices Appropriations Bill now stated before Congress that he couldn't ". . . escape the belief that the vast amount appropriated for this agency—and for that matter, for all the agencies of our Government—is disproportionately small for the social sciences . . ." (Alpert, 1961:785).

This turnabout did not happen overnight nor without dedicated lobbying by sociologists and other social scientists. And it did not occur until ethical neutrality had become the accepted mode of self-identification throughout sociology. One candid review (*N.Y. Times*, 12/5/60) of the events leading to the remarkable reversal in congressional attitude pointed out, however, that the cause had received a setback with the publicity given the role that behavioral research played in the 1954 Supreme Court decision regarding segregated public education. The first NSF grants to the social sciences had in fact been made as early as 1955, although they were then typically camouflaged within larger projects initiated by the Division of Biological Sciences. Three years later an "office" of social sciences had been established in the NSF with a budget of somewhat over $850,000. Moreover, a variety of federal government offices had supported research in the social sciences in general and in sociology in particular both prior to and since the establishment of the National Science Foundation. What tends to distinguish the NSF from other federal sources of funds, however, is the relative independence the Foundation claims from the utilitarian and applied concerns of the federal establishment.

The lobbying activity that went into the successful effort to cut the social sciences in on the NSF pie was an ingenious juggling act, if the booklet "National Support for Behavioral Science," published in 1958 over the names of such sociologists as Robert Merton and Samuel Stouffer and 13 other social scientists, is any indication. Merton and Stouffer had been among the most sophisticated exponents of ethical neutrality. But in this instance they were willing to go far beyond a simple denial of the prophetic stance to sell the behavioral sciences as guardians of American might in the confrontation with international communism. Under the topic, "Nature of Behavioral Science," one discovered the following:

> The United States finds itself today in a world situation which demands assessment of every resource of physical, intellectual, and moral power. [But] . . . we could be surpassed by a country which concentrated serious effort to that purpose, if we do not intensify our own efforts.
>
> We must assume the probability of a breakthrough in the control of the attitudes and beliefs of human beings. . . . This could be a weapon of great power in Communist hands, unless comparable advances in the West produce effective counter-measures (1958:5, 6).

The authors go on to include sections on "Contributions of Behavioral Science to Fostering the Peace," "The Place of Behavioral Science in National Defense" (the latter discussed at greater length than the former), and "Contributions of Behavioral Science to the National Strength and Spirit"—among a number of others. Merton's participation in the authorship of this pamphlet is perhaps especially telling. In striving to build the case for his—and sociology's—new "detachment," a *New Yorker* "portrait" of Merton (Hunt, 1961:63) reported him mumbling, "That damned popular image again!" in response to a congressman's jab of "Why don't you sociologists get to work and contribute something useful?" It's apparently as difficult to have one's cake and eat it in sociology as it is in any other area.

It would appear that Merton and Stouffer were willing, when they saw that the professional stakes were high enough, to accept partial responsibility for an essentially evangelical tract. Except for the anxiety caused by the congressional investigation of the National Science Foundation in 1963–64 (and the potential vulnerability of most sociological research to the utilitarian interests of the taxpayer), the evidence suggests that the gamble paid off handsomely. A single mailing from the American Sociological Association to its 7000 plus membership in 1966 included more than seven full pages listing research funds available from branches of the federal government alone. The profession of sociology seemed to have succeeded in dissociating itself from the remnants of its prophetic lineage and shifted, following the lead of the larger community of science, from "sectarian" opposition to "churchly" affiliation with the larger culture.

There certainly was no Machiavellian plot to achieve status and power by the shift from social critic to public and private servant, even though some might argue that many of the discipline's leaders were by this time men of the world who had learned well the ways of both Madison and Constitution Avenues. As Goode (1960:902) admitted in his insightful presidential address before the Eastern Sociological Society, "No occupation . . . becomes a profession without a struggle. . . . The emotion-laden identification of men with their occupation, their dependence on it for much of the daily meaning of their lives, causes them to defend it vigorously and to advance its cause where possible." And although Goode opposed the professionalization of sociology, he saw further movement in that direction as inevitable, admitting the half-truth in Shaw's observation that every profession was a conspiracy against the laity. Such half-truths are nurtured, however, when Merton (1962:28) can be discovered stating, perhaps in an unguarded moment, that ". . . as long as the locus of social power resides in any one institution other than science, and as long as scientists themselves are uncertain of their primary loyalty, their position becomes tenuous and uncertain."

In much less dramatic terms, sociologists gradually became aware that identification with an image before which the public had already come to defer—that of the natural scientist—was much the more profitable step to take. And since the prophetic role had never been a tempting alternative to the physical or biological scientist, it seemed equally inappropriate and dispensable to the sociologist. As training in sociology served increasingly as a tried and true vocational ladder for sons and daughters of the lower middle classes, it has become increasingly difficult for sociologists not to feel pressed by the immediacy of their professional interest. Prophecy will pay some few quite handsomely—but only a few, and typically at the apparent expense of the larger mass of less charismatic personalities.

Conclusion

Reviewing the posthumously published essays of C. Wright Mills, Bennett Berger (1963:3) described Mills's "sin" as being "a political activist and a polemicist in a period when professional sociologists were more concerned with establishing their discipline as an objective science and institutionalizing it in the universities than they were with saying something important about the world and making what they said effective in the arenas of political combat." Mills's *The Sociological Imagination* had indeed been a bitter characterization of a discipline which he felt had succumbed to the disengaged exercises of the "grand theorist" and the "abstract empiricist": sociology had become "less a creative ethos and manner of orientation than a set of Science Machines operated by technicians" (Mills, 1959:16).

But the anguished cries of the few were muffled by a generation characterized in its broader political dimensions by "the end of ideology"—by a decline of passion and the rise of indifference within and beyond the intellectual community. Shils (1961:1434) perceived that ". . . the program of 'ethical neutrality' involved not simply abstention from the belief that recommendations for policy could be based exclusively on statements of fact. It involved, for many social scientists, a belief that an utter detachment in matters of policy was incumbent on a social scientist, beyond even the boundaries of his scientific role. For such social scientists—and there were certainly sociologists among them—it involved renunciation of the role of responsible citizen."[5]

The intellectual community's retreat from responsibility may have part of its source, paradoxically, in the way in which "democracy" has become a substitute for religion in the formal acculturation process. Counting heads has taken on the nature of a sacred obligation, with even preordained decisions being solemnized by formal vote, whether of a PTA committee, a session of a faculty senate, a board of directors, or a nominating convention. The ritual somehow lends rationality and an aura of justice to the most irrational expression of vested interest. Thus, when a social scientist resolves the problem of direction by taking into consideration everyone's opinions but his own, he is acting in a fashion that he perceives, perhaps but semi-consciously, as "democratic" and thus in and of itself justifiable.[6] The result is not to make scientists more rational in the traditional sense of the term. Rather the product is the kind of single-mindedness that has so many times in the past accompanied the rise of a new priesthood, a single-mindedness that encourages either withdrawal from the world of responsible choice into the cloistered neutrality of science or a hedonistic pursuit of the perquisites that may be gained through status and power in a new episcopacy.

Sociology: The Priestly Mode

Men live by myths, scientists as much as other men. . . .

Herbert Shephard

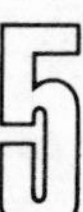

The Separation of Knowledge from Valuation

BENEATH the aura of neutrality with which sociologists had cloaked themselves by the middle of the present century was a new version of the age-old search for an elixir that would transform base metals into gold. This latter-day "philosopher's stone" was to take the form of an epistemology that would rescue knowledge from contamination by subjective valuation.

Modern versions stem from David Hume's eighteenth-century characterization of valuation as but passion and passion as but a sentiment that varied according to an individual's perceptions. "Vice and virtue, therefor, may be compar'd to sounds, colours, heat and cold, which . . . are not qualities in objects, but perceptions in the mind" (Hume, in Couch, 1960:26–27). This was the position that animated Comte's claim that any proposition which could not be reduced to a simple statement of fact was therefore devoid of sense. The logical positivism of the Vienna Circle in the 1920's was merely a restatement of the same predisposition within the context of an Einsteinian science and a logic informed by the reductionism of Russell and the early Wittgenstein, although the force of the stance may have been strengthened by the Circle's claim that not only were the classic issues of

---

Notes to this chapter will be found on pages 335–337.

metaphysics "non-sense," but that one couldn't even raise such questions about them.

The classic linguistic traditions cultivated at Oxford and Cambridge shifted the focus of the movement in England toward the analysis of linguistic forms. In this version the metaphysician is treated as a "patient" rather than as the "criminal" he appeared to be to the Vienna Circle. Although it came to monopolize the attention of the philosophical community in America, the exodus from the Continent of the Circle members before the threat of Nazism and the re-establishment of key members in chairs of the philosophy of science in leading American graduate schools largely guaranteed the predominance of logical positivism in the philosophical thinking of natural and social scientists in America during the 'forties and 'fifties.

Those sociologists who interested themselves in the philosophy of science during this period, then, were confronted by a posture that held that all *significant* propositions either were empirically verifiable or redundant. The "meaning" of a proposition became its method of verification. Ethical statements either were to be included somehow within the compass of social science or failed to be descriptive of anything whatsoever.

The Derivation of Value from Cognition

Paradoxically enough, however, what started with Hume's dictum that valuation cannot follow from cognition has led a number of those influenced by it round full circle to the contention that intelligible valuation must be *derived* from the empirical. Because statements were held to be either empirically logical or "non-sense," the only way to render valuation intelligible was to see "oughts," too, in terms of the logic of science.

Thus it was that a George Lundberg (in Odum, 1951: 208), though professing at one point to distinguish "ought" from "is" in the radical manner of Hume, went on to re-interpret the imperative statements grounded in social experience in such a way that they were themselves transformed into indicative statements.

I am now prepared to argue that the whole preoccupation of mankind throughout the centuries with the word "ought" has been merely another semantic confusion. Such a statement as "we ought not to steal" *and any other "ought" statement whatsoever*, can be shown to owe its peculiarity and its apparent difference from any other ordinary scientific statement of fact to certain unspoken premises which are always implied in "ought" statements. Actually, it amounts to this: If we steal, then we are likely to suffer retribution; then don't steal. When "ought" statements are thus fully stated they become identical with other scientific statements, all of which are of the "if . . . then" type. That is, *they are predictions of what will probably occur under stated conditions*, and in this respect differ not at all from scientific statements except that the probability and conditions of the former have not as yet been so fully worked out, on account of the lack of development of the social sciences.

Those "experiences" that link behavior to its reward can then, hypothetically at least, be examined empirically for their truth value. All one needs is a broad enough sample.[1] The circle is complete. Valuation, which earlier had been packed off as irrational, is now accepted back in cognition's own guise.

"Needs" or "purposes"

One of the most popular versions practiced by sociologists of the priestly mode involves the appointment of "need" to the pulpit of the defrocked "ought"; a closely related alternative is the empirical identification of "purpose."[2] The failure of either version to transcend the indicative mood should, however, be obvious. Proponents simply assume that because man has exhibited certain kinds of behavior in the past, that behavior must have reflected certain "purposes" and/or "needs." The difficulty is that *all* past behavior may be so labeled. Because this grants the terms no power of discrimination, advocates are forced to introduce additional criteria laden with implicit value-judgments, the most typical of which is sheer quantitative presence and/or "universality." The latter has, in fact, been taken up quite explicitly by a growing number of young anthropologists in their effort to free themselves from their discipline's traditional commitment to "cultural relativity"—men and women who find it difficult to resist attendance at the wedding of

Murdock's massive and cross-indexed Human Relations Area Files to the electronic computer.

Sociology itself has not been able to remain completely immune. Alvin Gouldner (1960:171) has confronted it with the temptation to establish a "norm of reciprocity" as a "Principal Component" universally present in "moral codes." The sociologist's role in interpreting the norm, he says, "parallels that of the physicist who seeks to identify the basic particles of matter, the condition under which they vary, and their relations to one another."[3] He thus not only felt compelled to inflate the hypothesis by likening it to the building blocks of subatomic physics, but by capitalizing "Principal Component" endowed it with an almost transempirical status reminiscent of the Natural Law tradition. The implication is that if indeed a norm were discovered to be universal, then the need or purpose it meets *should* in fact be met universally in the future. Whether such a universal norm will emerge depends to a considerable extent on the criteria used to segment "moral codes" from other implicit and explicit norms exhibited by particular cultures. Murder may exist in all cultures; this does not suggest that it should be *fundamental* to explaining the nature of past or present human behavior, to say nothing of guaranteeing its significance for the future. Gouldner no doubt is well aware of all this. The problem lies in the temptation he places before his audience.

"Health" and "Adaptive capacity"

The secular magic of "need" and "purpose" have tended to shade over in the attitudes that many persons have towards the concept of mental health. Or, when the focus is more clearly in terms of the social fabric, the criteria shifts toward communal health, as with Moreno.[4] Unfortunately, therapeutic criteria—whether founded upon individual or communal "health"—assume that continuity of human life is the ultimate standard against which ethical systems must be judged. That this, in fact, need not be the case is evidenced by the creeds of many theologies still extant. A third form taken by neo-positivism is one that has been out of favor for some time in the social sciences. Still it appears to have been nourished faithfully by biologists and now seems sturdy enough to seek re-entry into the sociological marketplace. Indeed, the route has been temptingly laid out by the discipline's foremost theorist, Talcott Parsons (1964, 1966). Although Parsons himself would reject any conscious effort to grant cognition precedence over evaluation, the enthusiasm with which he has turned of late to identifying specific "evolutionary universals," such as "democratic association," is apt to encourage many who would identify the process and products of evolution as overriding "oughts." What is defined in terms of its *adaptive capacity* by Parsons is translated by students of evolutionary history into the survival of the fittest. But *anything* that survives may be defined as "fittest," as possessing "adaptive capacity," for it *did* survive. And if one goes beyond such a simplistic interpretation of the Darwinian paradigm, one is forced right back into the waiting arms of other value-ridden criteria for that which is to be deemed the "good."

Pragmatic criteria

A fourth strain has been uniquely American, having been first conceived by Charles Peirce and William James and brought to rational fruition by John Dewey. This strain is pragmatism, whose ultimate criterion of "works" is a secular version of the utilitarian moralism that Calvin failed to wrest from the brethren he led forth from the Mother Church. The romantic element that the cold rationalism of pragmatism in fact so often conceals is exemplified by a recent paper, "Proposal for an Experiment to Test Religious Claims to Produce Altruistic Men and the Possible Effects of Such Testing upon Education."[5] The advocate would enroll a multi-disciplinary behavioral science team as relatively long-term novices in a Zen Buddhist temple; this would then enable them to determine whether or not the process of self-immolation actually worked. The fact that Zen is committed to the eradication of the very distinction between means and ends that is so critical to the scientific community, that the author betrayed utterly no awareness of the incompatibility of the epistemologies involved or of the simple logic of the experimental process *per se*, seemed to confuse the issue not one whit.

Correlation with postulates of science

But the most ingenious recent effort to squeeze the blood of norms from the turnip of empiricism has come from the fertile imagination and prolific pen of F. S. C. Northrop. Northrop's (1950:124) paraphrase of John Steinbeck's Jim Casy ("There ain't no sin and there ain't no virtue—there's just stuff people do") is startlingly congruent: "There are no purely ethical facts as there are no purely ethical meanings. There is only the nature of things and one's basic theory concerning what is." His thesis appears quite conventional in its initial stages, for he projects an empirically derived theory of natural science (physical and biological) and a similar body of theory built up from factual social science. *Normative* social theory is something quite different from both, for he rightly insists that one must maintain "the distinction between what is actually the case in society and what ought to be the case." But he early gives away the ultimately reductionist nature of his scheme: "I would like to suggest that the word 'value' really means nothing but the hierarchy of concepts . . . that the top reverberating circuts of your cortex have trapped as the primitive ones . . ." (1953:330). He would then apply this posture to escape from cultural relativism in ethics:

If we can make the additional assumption that all the concepts used to conceptualize the raw data of experience refer to the data of nature, then . . . nature is common to different cultures, and we have a factor to appeal to outside culture . . . before there was culture, there were only nature and natural man with his nervous system; so that the initial reference for his concepts was nature. . . . If this be true and value is nothing but a conceptual system, then one culture is better than another to the extent that its conceptual system takes care of more raw data which hit the sensory end-organs of the human nervous system (1953:331).

The issue, thus, is made to hang upon *conceptual efficiency* interpreted solely in *empirical* terms. What does this mean? It means that Northrop grants the criterion role to the logic of science. All other approaches to experience are to be judged in its image.

The verification of normative social theory (i.e., any ethic) is to be obtained . . . by checking its basic philosophical postulates . . . with the postulates of the philosophy of natural science prescribed by the facts of nature. . . . The philosophy defining a particular normative social theory (thus) has the two apparently paradoxical properties of designating both an "ought" for culture which introduces choices, moral values and ideals, and an "is" for nature which permits verification . . . (1959:338).

Thus he is willing to conclude that "that normative social theory is the scientifically verified and correct one in which the basic philosophical primitive ideas and postulates are identical with the primitive ideas and postulates of the philosophy of natural science . . ." (1950:124). "In other words, the word 'good' is but a name for the deductively formulatable system of empirically verifiable basic common denominator concepts of natural science" (1959:342).

As David Bidney (1953:171) observes, Northrop's scheme is a monism, comparable in grand design to the monistic theories of Freud and Marx. But whereas the proletariat and man's libido are a bit tarnished and old hat, Northrop waves a banner to which the growing multitude of the community of science may be sorely tempted to rally. Here is reductionism in the grand manner presented at a most timely juncture in the heady growth of the behavioral sciences.

The Dependence of Cognition upon Valuation

When Jeremy Bentham observed that the word "ought" ought never to be used except in saying it ought never to be used, he posed the value dilemma confronting today's social scientists. For although impaled on one side by the horn which would completely separate cognition from man's affective and valuational modes and run through on the other by the effort to erect a system of valuation upon an exclusively cognitive base, the community of science has become aware gradually that cognition itself rests necessarily upon a foundation of commitment. And, although we live in a philosophical climate that is largely anti-Kantian, the priority that he gave to "Practical" over "Pure" reason has echoed and re-echoed down through the generations to remind us that, though nature was prior to man, man was prior to science. The concerns and categories of the scientific community are the product of man's interest and the commitment by him of his energies: he has *valued* the ends of which the methods of science are but the means and has poured his limited energies into their pursuit. As one interested observer has put it, "Science requires of the scientist a sort of marriage ceremony in which the man says to science, . . . 'I commit myself to you; leaving all other attractions I will cleave to you.' . . . no matter how impersonal all the objects and ends of science, the scientist himself remains even in science a person of whom the moral act of devotion to a cause is required."[6]

In an intriguing paper entitled "The Masks of Society: the Grounds of Obligation in the Scientific Enterprise," John F. A. Taylor describes the nature of that commitment: "It is not merely behavior, but normative behavior, a behavior in obedience to rule . . . that . . . it is . . . neutral in what it prescribes is precisely what is *not* true of it. On the contrary, it is a mask, a mask which both disciplines and blinds, which must inevitably blind because it disciplines the vision that complies with it. . . . The rule which guarantees the disinterestedness of inquiry is not itself neutral with respect to the matter of disinterestedness." Taylor argues, in fact, that it is immediately analogous to the obligation a man has as *homo civitas*: "The society of scientists is bound together by common commitment to a rule of evidence in precisely the same way that the citizens of a political community are bound together by common commitment to the principle of a legal order."[7]

The central point at issue has been expressed by a broad array of natural scientists and philosophers.[8] But none has put it—along with its implication—better than has Michael Polanyi (1958:266–67):

> We must recognize belief once more as the source of all knowledge. Tacit assent and intellectual passions, the sharing of an idiom and of a cultural heritage, affiliation to a like-minded community: such are the impulses which shape our vision of the nature of things on which we rely for our mastery of things. No intelligence, however critical or original, can operate outside such a fiduciary framework. . . . While our acceptance of this framework is the condition of having any knowledge, this matrix can claim no self-evidence. . . . This then is our liberation from objectivism: to realize that

we can voice our ultimate convictions only from within our convictions. . . .

All this should hardly be news to the informed sociologist, even if he failed to take any interest in the epistemic foundations of science, for a goodly array of voices has been saying much the same from within his own discipline at least since the contemporary image of social science was molded at the hands of Max Weber. Weber it was who made abundantly clear not only that science was just one of a number of possible ways of addressing oneself to the universe of experience, but that it was a route which, when chosen, involved a commitment which was directly at odds with alternative commitments. Indeed, it demands a passion that is the product of exclusiveness and is supported by a built-in cognitive bias. For no science, Weber pointed out, is absolutely free from presuppositions, and no science can prove its fundamental value to the man who rejects those presuppositions.[9]

Unfortunately, few sociologists since Weber's time have seen fit to grant it the attention the latter felt it deserved. Robert Merton did so somewhat indirectly and relatively early in his career through his study of the manner in which the values clustering about seventeenth-century English Puritanism acted to stimulate the commitments integral to natural science; and later, in the context of a series of essays on the sociology of science, he argued quite explicitly that scientific activity of necessity involved "emotional adherence to certain values" (1962:27). These in turn are spelled out as including the obligations of universalism, disciplinary "communism," disinterestedness, and organized skepticism (1962:550–61). Bernard Barber takes up the same theme in his exploration into the sociology of science, characterizing science as "a moral enterprise . . . subject to clear ethical standards."[10]

Though Talcott Parsons has made clear that he views the community of science as but one social system among many—and one that operates in any given case within the value nexus of a larger social structure—he has shied from any direct statement about the precise nature of the commitments involved. Inferentially, however, it is clear he believes it entails a preference for "neutrality," "universalism," "performance," and "specificity" in contrast to "affectivity," "particularism," "quality," and "diffuseness"—the former set distinguishing an ethos he characterizes by the term *rationality*, the latter by an ethos he labels *traditional*. Thus, though he has argued that cognitive activity is coterminous with, rather than subordinate to, evaluative and/or "cathectic" activity, participation in scientific activity would first entail an evaluative or "cathectic" *predisposition* in favor of the former set. In other words, though Parsons has been unwilling to announce the fact in the dramatic tones of a Weber, he stands with the latter in acknowledging that scientific cognition rests upon precedent evaluation (or cathexis).

I think it would be hard to dispute the view, however, that among those standing in the forefront of American sociological theory over the last decade or two, Howard Becker has dealt with the issue most incisively (1957: 141):

> In the case of the predictively oriented social scientist *qua* scientist, his norms lead to the exclusion of esthetic, playful, religious and like considerations, except as they promise to yield greater predictive power. He consistently makes judgments to the following effect: "All value-judgments, other than the supreme value-judgment that prediction is in and of itself worthwhile, are to be set aside by the social scientist in his strictly scientific role." If the predictive statements resulting from the social scientist's activity are verified, he still has no warrant for assuming he possesses Truth in any final sense of the word; he has merely selected and properly handled those kinds of evidence that have a crucial bearing on the achievement of the sophisticated social scientist's supreme value. The difference between the observer and the persons he observes is in essence the difference between the adherent of a predictive value system and persons yielding allegiance to other kinds.

In other words, objectivity itself is rooted in selective valuation.

Sociologies of Knowledge and of Science

Sociologists need not be steeped in the somewhat esoteric language of the epistemologist nor even be familiar with the loftier ranges of sociological theory to appreciate the fact that science is a function of a peculiar and selective complex of cultural values. For one entire substantive branch of their discipline—the sociology of knowledge—takes its nature from this very assumption. Following hard upon the impact of Marx's historicism, Emile Durkheim, Max Scheler, and Karl Mannheim left the discipline with a framework of theory and a body of case studies that, regardless of their differences, should encourage sociologists to view cognitive structures as products of a larger value-laden cultural context. Weber's interest in the historical origins of modern capitalism had in the meantime led him to concern himself with the cultural nexus that nourished the rebirth of scientific activity in the seventeenth century, the stimulus in turn for Merton's early work on the role played by Calvinists in the founding of the British Royal Society, as well as for those studies illustrating the different attitudes of Protestants and Catholics toward careers in the natural sciences. Lewis Feuer's (1963) attempt to replace worldly asceticism with an individualistic hedonism as the key to that renascence simply serves to alter the cast of characters while leaving the inherent plot undisturbed. Even Gunter Remmling's suggestion (1967) that the sociology of knowledge itself is a product of a more general "age of suspicion" does nothing to destroy the underlying perspective, for it uses the very logic of the sociology of knowledge it sought to deny.

Unfortunately, sociologists have been somewhat reluctant to accept the full implications of the framework they would apply to the views of others, for it would leave them in the awkward position of relativizing themselves as well. Just as Marx and Lukacs would exempt the exact sciences and a detached portion of the bourgeoisie and class-conscious proletariat, and Mannheim would at one point grant cognitive clairvoyance to a free-floating intelligentsia, so contemporary sociologists are tempted to follow the path of Durkheim and the later Mannheim in somehow excluding the scientist. And yet at the very time they do this, more and more sociologists are moving in force into the sub-discipline of the sociology of science, revealing implicitly—even if many are not as yet secure enough to admit in theory—their acknowledgment that science stands within and not outside the circle of culturally patterned values. Only gradually will studies such as Bramson's *The Political Context of Sociology*, Mills's *The Sociological Imagination*, Berger's *Invitation to Sociology*, and Horowitz' *Professing Sociology*—which place sociology itself squarely within the circle—settle into the sociologist's consciousness and encourage him to an explicit acknowledgment of his cultural relativity. The day will then have come when sociologists will be able to paraphrase the historian who has evidenced his sense of security through the admonition, "Before you study history, study the historian. . . . Before you study the historian, study his historical and social environment." And those who have examined the valuational context that encompassed sociologists in the decade and a half following World War II will discover that the self-image that came to assert itself was one startlingly consistent with a secular version of the priesthood.

Sociologist as Priest

Although our generation has witnessed a spate of declarations to the effect that "God is dead," as early as 1907 Henry Adams had delineated the end of the age and the *entré* of the new tellingly and vividly in that portion of his autobiography in which he wrote of "The Dynamo and the Virgin." Reflecting Bacon's dictum that "*scientia potentia est*," Adams recounted how he was overwhelmed with awe—an essentially religious awe—upon confronting for the first time the magnificently cold power of a huge dynamo. It was a symbol that could, Adams felt, usurp the throne of the Virgin in a new era. "Religion," said Saint-Simon, "cannot disappear; it can only be transformed."[11] And although sociologists are amused today by the priestly functions Comte set for his *homo sociologus*, there is much in the ethos of the scientist in general and the sociologist in particular which makes one wonder if that amusement is not in some slight degree the response of men who are in fact just a little nervously embarrassed over the suggestiveness of the analogy.

If, as has often been claimed, the scripture of science is in its most canonical form embodied in physics, one may be excused for turning first to the domain of the head priest for one's operative imagery. For Einstein wrote of the role of the physicist in terms that were superempirical indeed: ". . . whoever has undergone the intense experience of successful advances made in this domain is moved by profound reverence for the rationality made manifest in existence. By way of this understanding he achieves a far-reaching emancipation from the shackles of personal hopes and desires, and thereby attains that humble attitude of mind towards the grandeur of reason incarnate in existence, and which, in its profoundest depths, is inaccessible to man. This attitude . . . appears to me to be religious, in the highest sense of the word."[12] The sociologist has added of late a Durkheimian inclination to identify the social system with the godhead —to translate the traditional statement of faith into Albion Small's, "We live and move and have our being as parts of each other."

Moreover, if we were to follow Lewis Feuer's account of the rebirth of science in the West, science is decked out with an ethic that is analogous to a traditional conception of the churchly ethic—except that it stands it on its head: "Not asceticism, but satisfaction; not guilt, but joy in the human status; not self-abnegation, but self-affirmation; not original sin, but original merit and worth; not gloom, but merriment; not contempt for one's body and one's senses, but delight in one's physical being, not the exaltation of pain, but the hymn to pleasure. . . . So far from regarding it a sin, the scientific intellectuals took frank delight in pride" (1963:7, 15). Nor is Bernard Barber or Robert Merton completely unaware of the priestly elements in the church of science. "A pattern of thought and writing had developed," they have written, "which would be appropriate, perhaps, for a religious group where changeless tradition is the thing and ancient revelation must remain intact."[13]

Prediction and control

I would again, however, have the reader turn to Howard Becker for the keenest appreciation for, and sharpest expression of, what some have termed "the myth of the anti-myth." Becker begins with an acknowledgment that John Stuart Mill, Ernst Mach, Albert Einstein, and most of those who have sought to conceptualize in instrumental terms the ends and means of science are quite correct in viewing predictive efficiency as the essential focus of the scientific enterprise. He then argues that to predict the recurrence of phenomena is, in a very real sense, to develop the capacity to control that recurrence—at least hypothetically. Whether or not one actually seeks to control that recurrence, the scientist commits himself to control *per se* through the necessity of applying a logic in which control plays the central role—the logic of the experiment. Becker goes on to contend, in fact, that

> . . . mere preference for control cannot account for the persistence of scientific enterprise. Such preference necessarily transmutes itself into ultimate value; the scientist becomes a priest of the faith in the possibility and supreme desirability of control. The secular society in which he has grown up and which sanctions his preference-system is endowed with sacred values by his enterprise; the quest for control becomes a quest for the Holy Grail. Nonrational? Yes! What ultimate values have ever been rational? Impartial? No! What priest was ever impartial? . . . The Church of Science, moreover, applies "pressures." If a scientist strays off the straight and narrow path by injecting other preferences and ultimate values into his supposedly scientific work, he will soon find that his books are no longer in the Holy Canon, his articles can be published only in journals which lack the Imprimatur and Nihil Obstat, and eventually he may discover that all his writings are in the Index Expurgatorius or even the Index Librorum Prohibitorum. Worse still, the institution with which he is identified may suffer Interdict, and he himself may be visited with Excommunication.[14]

Faith in order

The natural scientist is clearly a committed member of a dedicated community. Though I would not wish to argue with Becker, or with Weber from whom Becker derived the notion, that his faith centers about a consecration of "control," still, a priestly scent is very much in the air. Natural scientists seek to "understand" experience in a rather special way, one which differentiates them from artists, philosophers, historians, or theologians. Their approach to knowledge would, above all, honor reliability in the perception of order. Historians, although dedicated equally to the reliable reclamation of "fact," need be concerned with order only in the sense that they would place those "facts" in appropriate sequence. Philosophers and theologians, although traditionally dedicated to ordering the totality of man's experience, may jeopardize reliability to the end. An artist would order his own perceptions but need feel no obligation to extend his responsibility to the perceptions of others; indeed, he would focus upon the uniqueness of his own prism. A natural scientist would join the historian—indeed, surpass him—in the standards he sets for reliability. He is driven beyond the latter, however, in his quest for order. For he seeks evidence of order that is *stable* over time, recurrent patterns, "laws" that securely frame man's world. His aim is to sift through the flux that is experience to recover—and state in the most spare and precise fashion—those aspects of nature and man that enable him to project, with measured reliability, such evidence of order into the future. His is a priesthood that dedicates itself abstemiously to the prediction of order over time. Whatever fails to contribute to that end must, in his catechism, be renounced.

The community of faith of which natural scientists are a part may—indeed, ideally does—provide the broadest of freedom in the pursuit of such order; but *order* it must be. Disorder, like heresy or unbelief, is seen simply as challenging the orthodox to more faithful witness. The scientist as priest would address his professional and communal life to confronting, ever more intimately, the reliably ordered core of nature and natural man and would seek to mediate between it and the flux that is the evident world of the layman. His is not the priesthood of all believers; the initiation rites are much too exacting, the preparatory rituals too demanding, the language of communion too specialized. Ordination, furthermore, demands renunciation. Anything that would threaten reliability in the precipitation of order—the unique, the private, the absolute—must be relinquished as heresy. Indeed, from this point of view the "prophetic" mode is the focal threat, for it is dedicated to change, not order; risk, not reliability; "subjective" standards, not "objective" perception. The prophet would destroy the priestly edifice that is the Church. The prediction to which the scientific priesthood is dedicated is the antithesis of prophecy; the priest would project the order of the past into the future, honoring both as revelation of the continuity that is nature's core; the prophet would *use* short-term projections of order as a weapon to destroy the actual fulfillment of that projected future. "One prophesies," Ross reminded us, ". . . because persuading others to anticipate the future furthers his [the prophet's] present designs." And those designs are directed toward change, not simply the perception of order.

Nor would the analogy appear idiosyncratic. Ralph Lapp titles a recent volume on scientists *The New Priesthood*, Spencer Klaw chooses *The New Brahmins*, while Fitch, in an article headed "The Scientist as Priest and Savior" (1958), finds scientists constituting themselves an "order" apart from the larger world through the appropriation of a special language (mathematics rather than Latin), discipline (a long novitiate in research rather than in a monastery), and attitude (commitment to the revelations of the empirical rather than the trans-empirical world). Even Bernard Barber speaks approvingly of the "ministry of science to mankind."[15] Science does not merely supplement the ethic of ordinary existence: ". . . its critical rationality challenges the traditional moralities of other social activities . . . it is not really science and morality that are in conflict but the morality of science and the morality of ordinary behavior." For although truth is a value common to both, the truth of the one is not the truth of the other. "This conflict exists . . . and cannot be explained away by mere good will."[16] The question revolves, of course, around one's choice of a larger frame.

The scientist as "priest" is committed to an end that he defines as both a truth and a good in and of itself. The truth and the good are, as with all faiths that have moved our world, institutionalized within a highly dedicated culture or sub-culture and involve a specialized frame of discourse, common symbols, an elaborate communal ethic, a complex hierarchical organization, and a variety of other features commonly found in the established "churches" of our day. Physicist Harold Schilling (1958) has argued that science also has its creeds and that "the way they came into being, and the role they have played in science subsequently, are essentially the same as those of religious creeds." Reinhard Bendix (1951: 190) even would seem to suggest that as priestly groups have been wont down through the millennia, so too have social scientists assigned themselves the exclusive function of mediating and interpreting truth for the layman. That truth is no longer revealed to the latter; the layman may approach it only through the priestly office:

> Modern social scientists . . . no longer believe that men can rid their minds of . . . impediments to lucid thought: *only scientists can*. . . . They assert that there is only one escape from the consequences of irrationality: that is by the application of scientific method. And this method can be used effectively only by the expert few. . . . Instead of attempting to make people more rational, contemporary social scientists often content themselves with asking of them that they place their trust in social science and accept its findings.

The priestly office is an exclusive office, for only through its rites may the layman confront the underlying order from which his essential humanity springs.

Recovery of the Prophetic Mode

> **Precisely because scientific research is not conducted in a social vacuum, its effects ramify into other spheres of value and interest. Insofar as these effects are deemed socially undesirable, science is charged with responsibility. The goods of science are no longer considered an unqualified blessing. Examined from this perspective, the tenet of pure science and disinterestedness has helped to prepare its own epitaph.**
>
> **Robert K. Merton**

6

The Multiplication of Roles (and Wishes): A Latter-day Myth?

HOW was it possible for as rigidly abstemious a posture as the "priestly" to dominate a sociology whose province was a sprawling, pluralistic culture? How could sociologists reconcile the lip-service they had given the value-free stance with the multiplicity of value postures that even the most single-minded American had to assume throughout his twenty-four-hour day, his seven-day week? In fact, the answer offered was simplicity itself. Sociologists found their key in the term "role." Introduced into sociological usage in the 1920's through the influential lectures of George Herbert Mead at the University of Chicago and seconded by Ralph Linton in anthropology, it served to cap the divorce of valuation from the vocation of the social scientist filed earlier in Europe by Max Weber.

Value "polytheism"

Weber had found himself forced into what Howard Becker later termed a "polytheistic" position: a conviction that the Gods of this world were irreconcilably multiple, that therefore one simply had to make one's choice. The generation that followed Weber, however, softened the harsh exclusiveness of science's demands

---

Notes to this chapter will be found on pages 337–340.

when it appropriated the role concept. With it the severity of choice was muted by the suggestion that one might play a scientific role part of a day or week or lifetime without jeopardizing the integrity of contradictory roles assumed at other times. Conscious guilt for what might appear to be chameleon-like behavior could be expiated, for hypocrisy or ambivalence was dissolved in the solvent of shifting roles. The case has been argued, in fact, that hypocrisy itself might be an untenable term for the social scientists: that such behavior should rather be seen as but a manifestation of "role conflict."

High among those who argued the case for role-hopping was Howard Becker, himself trained at Chicago and in a Germany still stirred by the memory of Weber's brilliance. He perceived *homo sociologus* as governed by value-judgments relevant to prediction and control, while the same man as non-scientist might shift his allegiance to other more appropriate norms. "It is entirely possible," he argued, "to be both humanitarian and scientist. There is danger, of course, that one preference-system will block out the other, that one ultimate value-loyalty will stifle the other, or that there will be a fateful mixture of both roles which will vouchsafe no opportunity of playing either well. Yet I should hesitate to say that the dangers of value-polytheism are greater than the dangers of value-monotheism. . . . I would even say that they are less" (1950:302). Becker—and sociologists at large—felt that "role-playing," although itself a concept which reflected the assumptions of science, would in turn provide a prescription that would mediate between the demands of objectivity and the claims of the personal. Faust's lament—"Two souls, alas, within my breast abide"—had been superseded by the turn of a Meadian phrase.

"*Value-monotheism*"

Undoubtedly the dangers of "value-monotheism" are greater than those of "value-polytheism." When reinforced by a larger pluralistic ethos, the introjection of the notion of role-playing would appear both pragmatically and ideologically attractive. An occasional savant may stir the larger intellectual world by decrying the chasm that it perpetuates between "the two cultures," but safe is safe. Sociology had gained a place of stature and a share of power in the world at large; it would be professionally irresponsible for sociologists to risk the fruits of ethical neutrality by thrusting themselves into the arms of the value-laden.[1] However, a sociologist who resolves the issue through recourse to the multiplication of roles not only fails to see how he thus reduces other frames to the exclusively sociological, but also leaves the question of when one should move in and out of the varying and potentially conflicting roles completely unanswered. Not merely unanswered, but unanswerable—unless, of course, he once again smuggles in concepts that remain within or are derived from his original epistemological stance. Yes, "value-monism" is risky; but to suggest that risk should be a crucial factor in the contest of ideas would appear strikingly at odds with the larger tradition of rationality that we all share. We are not and cannot be assured that those whose professional prerogative it is to seek order in the social maze must somehow be guaranteed immunity from the "fear and trembling" that appears to be the burden of other men. Although role theory has proven exceptionally fruitful *within* the intellectual frame that sociology shares with the sciences in general, this provides no argument whatsoever for limiting ourselves when engaged in cross-epistemological discussions to the symbolic inventions of one discipline. It might even behoove sociologists not to *assume* simply that there is something innately inappropriate or abnormal in accepting more than one role at a time.

Fortunately for us—though perhaps disastrously for himself—Weber had not been all of a piece. Although he quite self-consciously chose the route of science for himself, the rationalized and bureaucratized world he projected for the future was clearly a horrendous spectacle in the recessive eyes of that other self which crept incessantly back into his existence to direct it and judge it in humanitarian terms immediately reconcilable to the tradition of faith that he thought he had left behind. At one point we find Weber (1949:38) acknowledging, perhaps as much to himself as to his readers, that "behind the particular 'action' stands the human being. An increase in the subjective rationality and in the objective technical 'correctness' of an individual's conduct can, beyond a certain limit—or even quite generally from a certain standpoint—threaten goods of the greatest (ethical or religious) importance to his value-system." Merton (1962: 24–25) would seem to have transposed this sense of uneasiness in Weber from the personal mode into the societal in his observation that

> precisely because scientific research is not conducted in a social vacuum, its effects ramify into other spheres of value and interest. Insofar as these effects are deemed socially undesirable, science is charged with responsibility. The goods of science are no longer considered an unqualified blessing. Examined from this perspective, the tenet of pure science and disinterestedness has helped to prepare its own epitaph.

In other words, even if a scientist might himself have found role-playing an adequate solution to conflicts in his own life-space, his society is much less likely to find the same solution appropriate to its larger concern. For, from the perspective of the enveloping culture, science is not deemed an alternative mode of orientation but merely a sub-community that alternately reflects and contributes to the direction and pattern of the overall society. And even if society does conditionally permit a scientist to divorce himself from the overall set of values, this neutralist stance may "spill over" into its wider concerns.[2]

Professional Uneasiness

Indeed natural scientists, whose neutrality stance had inspired the value-free posture among sociologists, have begun of late to suspect that their own claim may in fact be untenable. The new mood was initiated perhaps by the dramatic manner in which a small group of physicists and mathematicians took upon themselves the responsibility of urging the American government to protect itself from the possibility that the Nazi government might achieve a breakthrough in the use of atomic fission. It has been continued by such groups as the Federation of American Scientists, organized by those involved in the Manhattan Project; by those represented in the founding of and audience for the *Bulletin of the Atomic Scientists*; by the Pugwash movement; and by the

Society for Social Responsibility in Science, a group whose membership has included such figures as Einstein, Pauli, Born, and Yukawa.

The new attitude moved into the very heart of American science only as recently as the summer of 1960 with the wide publicity granted a report, four years in the making, of a Committee on Science and Promotion of Human Welfare of the two-million-strong American Association for the Advancement of Science. Its chairman observed that he felt that the earlier faith which scientists had held in their capacity to remain master of their creations could no longer be wholly justified by the facts; that the examination, criticism, and refinement of evidence relevant to the great public issues of the day had now to be acknowledged as a basic responsibility of scientists; and that this duty could not be met if scientists imprisoned themselves within the confines of their research roles, oblivious of the potential impact of their work.[3] The AAAS followed its statement of principles by highlighting an address titled "The Moral Un-neutrality of Science" by C. P. Snow, whose "two cultures" thesis had begun to stir widespread debate. Speaking directly and bluntly of the professed value-free character of the discipline, he stated: "I can't accept it for an instant. I don't believe any scientist of serious feeling can accept it. It is hard, some think, to provide the precise statements which will prove it wrong. Yet we nearly all feel intuitively that the invention of comfortable categories is a moral trap. It is one of the easier methods of letting the conscience rust."[4]

Social and behavioral scientists were, of course, not entirely immune to the reassessment that natural scientists were making. By and large, however, the opportunity for direct and dramatic confrontation over the issue had been blunted by the branching off, some years earlier, of those behavioral scientists who had felt ill-at-ease with the priestly norm of neutrality. The first defectors were psychologists, whose clinical links may have made them relatively responsive to the norms of the parent culture. Organized as early as 1935, the Society for the Psychological Study of Social Issues, although maintaining an integral relationship with the American Psychological Association (it is the latter's Division 9), has stretched its self-image broadly enough to have at one point petitioned the White House for the cessation of atmospheric nuclear testing. Its newsletter has dealt with such subjects as "Roles for Psychologists in Promoting Peace" and "On Being Politically Effective," while a recent presidential address was entitled "The Image of Man." Its *Journal of Social Issues* had earlier published a supplementary series that included titles such as *Social Responsibility* and *Research for What?*

Although a small handful of sociologists had likewise bestirred themselves as early as the late 1940's—Nathan Glazer, Kurt Wolff, and Robert Lynd among them[5]—a comparable organization from the sociological side, the Society for the Study of Social Problems, was not formed until 1951. Its *Journal of Social Problems* provided an alternative publication route for those studies in social deviation that the official journal of their professional association had begun to reject as the latter moved self-consciously toward the neutralist stance. Although it exhibits an active interest in questions of professional ethics and academic freedom, the SSSP and the editors of its journal have been more reluctant to jettison the tidy concept of role-separation than has the SPSSI.

An analogous outlet for the anthropologist was founded in 1941 as the Society for Applied Anthropology. It claims to have been the first behavioral science organization to commit itself formally to an explicit code of ethics. In introducing the code a contextual statement indicates that members of the Society recognize their responsibility for the effects of their acts and recommendations and notes their obligation to assist a culture to regain its stability if they inadvertently create a crisis for it. Observing that the end should never be used to justify unethical means, they admit their obligation to protect the anonymity of informants and to prevent irreversible damage to health or the physical environment. In concluding, the statement shifts from "recognizing" the validity of such norms to an explicit pledge:

> To advance those forms of human relationships which contribute to the integrity of the individual human being; to maintain scientific and professional integrity and responsibility without fear or favor to the limit of the foreseeable

effects of their actions; to respect both human personality and cultural values; to publish and share new discoveries and methods with colleagues: those are the principles which should be accepted and which should be known to be accepted *by all those who work in the disciplines affecting human relationships.*[6]

The implication of the final clause went unheeded by the parent American Anthropological Association until the latter decided, in 1966, to work toward a set of "ethical guidelines."

Meanwhile the post–World War II years saw psychologists transformed from a university-based community of research scholars and teachers to an association dominated numerically by the explosion of clinical psychology into diagnostic and therapeutic activities largely independent of an academic milieu. This one-sided growth—along with the efforts of the clinicians to establish and protect their professional standing *vis-à-vis* the medical profession—led the American Psychological Associaton to frame and ratify a set of "Ethical Standards" whose opening sentence contended that "the psychologist is committed to a belief in the dignity and worth of the individual human being."[7] The effort was not without cost, however; a minority resisted what it felt to be the guild-like development to the point of seceding and establishing its own completely distinct Psychonomic Society. The American Association for Public Opinion Research followed the lead of the APA, committing itself to a "Code of Professional Ethics," while the University of Washington's Public Opinion Laboratory has broken the role barrier to the point of declaring that it will reject a contractual arrangement for a political poll if its phraseology is unacceptable to one of the major parties and will turn down an industrial poll if either management or labor withholds its consent. Harvard adopted an elaborate set of "Rules Governing the Participation of Healthy Human Beings as Subjects in Research" more recently, following the celebrated case in which a behavioral scientist had reportedly risked the health of University students in an experiment with hallucinogenic drugs. The statement's guiding principle is that "no one, whether students or other persons, should be exposed to unreasonable risk to health or well-being" while a subject of research. Furthermore, "the purpose of the research, the procedures to be followed, and the possible risks involved must be carefully and fully explained to the subject; the investigator must be satisfied that the explanation has been understood by the subject; and the consent of the subject must be obtained in writing without duress or deception."[8]

The dominant forces in sociology, however, have been most reluctant to admit the existence of a problem. Only 13 per cent of the sociologists sampled disapproved of the use of concealed microphones in a widely publicized study of jury deliberations (Burchard, 1958:688). Edward Shils (1961:1440), in appraising the general level of "responsibility" demonstrated by those engaged in social research, emphasized that a "considerable part" of the discipline's research is done without recourse to deception. What he was admitting by implication is that much *fails* to meet that standard.

Toward a Sociological Ethic

Alfred McClung Lee (1951, 1952:3), a founder of the Society for the Study of Social Problems, was one of the very few sociologists speaking directly to the issue of responsibility in research during the first half of the 1950's. Edward Gross (1956) followed a little later, although in a manner that tried to generalize the problem to the social sciences as a whole. But interestingly enough it was Talcott Parsons who was to play the central role in forcing the issue upon the official power structure of the discipline. His initiative took the form of a widely read paper, originally delivered before the annual assemblage of sociologists in the fall of 1958, titled "Some Problems Confronting Sociology as a Profession." Although he chose to remain securely within an orthodox frame by falling back on the conceptual device of role multiplicity, he added a set of new stanzas to the old refrain by arguing that the sociologist *as* sociologist played more than one role. In addition to the focal research role, Parsons depicted sociologists as sharing an applied function and a teaching role—the latter, in fact, claiming much the larger proportion of the total discipline's time. All these roles were quite appropriately conditioned and delimited by the ends of society. He hinted, too, of the need to spell out the normative nature of those limitations when he suggested that "the creation of codes for professionally proper ways of organizing such participation (referring in this case to the applied role) will . . . constitute one major task of our professional associations" (1959:559).

Thus it came as no surprise when the American Sociological Association's Committee on the Profession, with Parsons in the chair, reported in August, 1960, that it had appointed a sub-committee on "Ethics of the Profession" and had commissioned it with the task of "collecting and considering critical incidents which either directly or indirectly raise ethical questions involving the behavior of sociologists." "It is hoped," Parsons reported (1960:945), "that eventually a code of ethics with a solid empirical basis in case experience can be built up." The governing council of the ASA approved the direction taken but went on to establish a separate "Committee on Professional Ethics" with Robert Angell as chairman. The nub of the dilemma faced by the committee, and by the profession as a whole, was unintentionally evident in the phrasing of the original declaration of the Committee on the Profession—that "a code of ethics with a solid *empirical* basis in case experience can be built up"—and in that portion of the subsequent letter sent to the entire ASA membership soliciting its assistance wherein Angell stated that his committee shared the conviction that "standards should be *derived* from a consideration of the day-to-day experience of sociologists." Having assumed that as a discipline it was essentially "value-free," sociology now found itself in the embarrassing position of being pledged to create an ethic out of whole empirical cloth, a task which it had long affirmed as quite impossible. The committee members could not, of course, have been taken in by the language they chose; they certainly were aware that a set of standards lay in the background. The point to be emphasized is simply that the "value-free" ethos seemed somehow to demand that only "empirical," "day-to-day experience" be acknowledged as source. The discipline had come so to inhibit its moral impulse that it felt compelled to disguise a gnawing sense of responsibility even while speaking privately to itself. When this could occur in a field whose zeal in ferreting out contradictions and institutionalized deceptions in communal and professional life at large is unsurpassed, it seemed to suggest that the moment for self-disclosure could not be too distant. Catharsis or a radically new all-encompassing empiricism, one of the two appeared to be in order.

Still the judgment day was somehow postponed. Harry Alpert, involved as he had been as a representative of the behavioral sciences within the federal government, could innocently contend during a session of the 1962 annual meetings of the ASA devoted to the projected ethic that "I'm not sure I understand what ethical problems are." Substantive papers were invited which dealt with ethical problems of sociologists in government, as consultants, and in collaborative research; ethical problems that adhered to the research task *per se*—defining criterion of sociological activity—were ignored altogether. William Goode (1960) had not long before delivered a stinging rebuke to the professionalization of sociology that a formal ethic appeared to presage in his presidential address before the Eastern Sociological Society. When the request for actual cases suggesting ethical irresponsibility on the part of sociologists went out to the entire membership, only some sixty-five bothered to reply. The only letters printed concerning the issue in the society's official journal expressed opposition to a formal code. The first draft of the proposed Code was hardly a clarion call to subsume one's sociological activities within a larger commitment. The section on ethical standards in research included as a "principle" the admonition that the sociologist "is permitted to fail in his civic responsibilities when he is fulfilling his professional research role."[9] Even a modest codification of the going norms seemed headed for trouble. At the very time that the American Sociological Association had launched a program to engage a full-time executive officer at approximately $20,000 a year, move its headquarters from a university environment to the more convenient lobbying site of Washington, D.C., and increase its own financial dependence upon foundations grants and government contracts which it "serviced" to over 80 per cent of its annual budget, the ASA Council "voted to receive the revised version of the Draft Code of Ethics with thanks for the effort of the Committee whose report has made all

Association members more sensitive to their ethical responsibilities as professional sociologists."[10] The Code thus was buried with one hand while with the other the profession warmly clasped hands with the federal establishment. Talcott Parsons' sensitivities could be sublimated by appointing him to the editorial chair of the Association's new organ for specifically professional concerns, *The American Sociologist*. The occasional enthusiasms of the larger membership for things ethical might be directed instead to the behavior of other groups and provided periodic outlet through righteous resolutions at annual business meetings, although even this expression of the "responsibility" syndrome confronted an uncertain fate.[11] Given a modicum of rapport free from public embarrassment, the assortment of tranquilizers might take effect.

Camelot

Unfortunately, this is exactly what did not happen. Sociology—operating in terms of its code-free conventional norms—found itself in the summer of 1965 the central actor in an international drama that was overshadowed in Latin America only by the crisis engendered by the concurrent U.S. military intervention in Santo Domingo. It resulted in the halting or disruption of behavioral research throughout Chile and the rest of Latin America—whether of Latin or United States origin[12]—and led to a White House policy decision that now grants the State Department power to veto any government-funded social science research abroad. It revealed American sociologists as willing handservants of the United States Army's effort to throttle center-to-left political movements in a variety of sovereign states around the world,[13] triggered a hearing before a Foreign Affairs Committee of Congress, and promised to provide the richest mine ever for those who daily prospect for evidence to denigrate the promise that sociological research holds for the future. The research effort, designated "Project Camelot" by the Special Operations Research Office (nominally of American University) which developed it at the request of a group of high-echelon Army officers, sought to assess the causes of leftist insurrections in underdeveloped areas and to ascertain ways of blunting them. It held out as tempting bait the largest funding ever made available to a single research project in American sociology: from four to six million dollars to start with. The beginning of the end occurred when a well-known Norwegian sociologist, teaching at UNESCO's Latin American Faculty of Social Sciences, turned down an invitation to participate. U.S. Army sponsorship of an open-ended study of insurgency, he felt, was an anomaly; if it were truly free of Army control it would include the study of those domestic conditions in the United States that might profit from intervention by Latin American governments. Furthermore, European scholars would find their research impossible if they were forced to compete for the services of trained Latin American social scientists against a wave of American sociologists with relatively unlimited resources. When his knowledge of the project's sponsorship was balanced against the protestation by an assistant professor from the University of Pittsburg (whose trip to Chile had been largely underwritten by Camelot to assist in the recruitment of Latin American scholars) that the American military were not behind the project, the havoc to delicate political relationships and to social research was touched off. It is important to point out that none of the participants felt that the research would compromise their professional roles as sociologists. Many in fact felt the freedom they were granted appeared broader than that available in most research financed directly by universities. Rex Hopper, the director, was able to recruit personnel for Camelot who could be characterized as even more liberal than would be found among a cross-section of American sociologists, yet the appropriateness of a successful revolution was never an item for consideration. Two parallel but distinct vocabularies were maintained—one military with military justifications, the other sociological with social-scientific justifications—illustrating perhaps the sleight-of-hand manner in which role theory is able to transform military intelligence work into value-free social research without the slightest change in the activity itself.

The dominant figures of the profession maintained a discreet silence throughout the public outcry that was striking in its unanimity. Horowitz (1965:44) points out that "many 'giants of the field' are involved in government contract work in one capacity or another. And few souls are in a position to tamper with the gods." Furthermore, "many social scientists doubtless see nothing wrong or immoral in the Project Camelot designs."[14] It is difficult to accept either of these possibilities. One would rather assume that the silence was a product of infinite embarrassment and the determination to protect what remained of the profession's rapport with the intellectual world at large by closing ranks and reconstructing the foundations of the discipline's position regarding ethical neutrality. Only if the latter were not forthcoming would one be forced to take Horowitz' reading seriously. In October, 1965, the National Academy of Sciences and the National Research Council did establish a joint committee in response to the Camelot crisis to examine the implications that federal support in general had for the social sciences. By early 1967, however, it appeared that academically based sociologists were again being solicited for counter-insurgency studies, this time in reference to Africa (Van den Berghe: 1967). The only ethically relevant steps taken by the official structure of the discipline were the unilateral conclusion reached by Talcott Parsons in an editorial in the *American Sociologist* that the American Sociological Association was "a professional association" (although even this was immediately taken exception to)[15] and a decision by the ASA Council to once again appoint a committee to draft a code of ethics.

That the agents of the larger body politic were considerably less reluctant to view the research activity of social scientists as laden with value implications had been suggested by a 1966 memorandum from the Surgeon General to all those seeking Public Health Service grants (Stewart: 1967). It pointed out that such grants were contingent upon the voluntary involvement of subjects, assurance that they would not be risking permanent harm, the confidential treatment of the data, a guarantee that the findings would not be misused, and the assumption that all the activities engaged in and behaviors elicited were in accord with the law.

The filling and hauling of sociology's official and unofficial leadership may appear less schizoid if one examines the shift in self-image that had occurred on the part of the rank and file, for the abandonment of consensus about the system frame had been accompanied in the sixties by perhaps an even stronger disavowal of the neutral pose of the "priest." The ambivalence of the discipline's leaders may then have represented less their own confusion and more nearly the divided state of the membership. This interpretation would seem to be substantiated by the survey of sociological opinion undertaken by Alvin Gouldner in 1964. Although 45 per cent of the approximately 3500 who replied felt that the discipline's value-free ideal "helps sociology to remain independent of outside pressures and influences," nearly three-quarters acknowledged that "most sociologists merely pay lip service to the ideal." That the lapse could not simply be written off as human failure on the part of the majority to attain what was in principle an appropriate standard is seen by the agreement of some 70 per cent that "one part of the sociologist's role is to be a critic of contemporary society." A majority went on to deny that sociologists "contribute to the welfare of society mainly by providing an *understanding* of social processes"; contributing "ideas" for "changing" society was felt to be more important. Indeed, the weight of the membership's opinion appeared to favor rather than oppose the promulgation and enforcement of a code of ethics, even to the point of licensing those involved in applied functions. Sociologists were to be guaranteed freedom to express their political values even *within* their professional role, while more than three-quarters acknowledged that "sociologists must take some responsibility for how their findings are used by others." But perhaps the most intriguing clue to the potential direction of the reassessment taking place within the profession may be seen in the response elicited by the deceptively simple statement that "philosophers have interpreted the world; the point, however, is to change it." It would have been difficult to have selected a more characteristic phrase from the stock of prophetic Marxist literature. Yet less than half of the responding sociologists indicated that they disagreed: 26.6 per cent agreed and another 28.4 per cent selected a neutral response.

Sociology and the humanities

One of the developments within the discipline that helped reopen the door to prophecy was the renewed suggestion that sociology was one of the humanities rather than simply a science. C. Wright Mills had felt so inhibited by the latter word that he had been tempted to replace it with "study," hesitating to do so only because the phrase "social studies" rang reminiscently of high school civics. Thus his choice of "imagination" instead. The most direct call for a broadened image came the same year—1959—in Robert Bierstedt's presidential address before the Eastern Sociological Society. Pointing out that such giants in the history of the discipline as Veblen, Sumner, and de Tocqueville would almost certainly be deemed unacceptable as doctoral candidates in the 1950's, he argued that the reason they were able to make the contributions they had was that they were humanists first. Sociology should indeed be a science; but, Bierstedt claimed, it should not be *only* a science. Rather it must be seen as a bridging discipline between the sciences and humanities, possessed of an honorable place in the realm of humane letters as well as within the sciences. Nor was he unaware of the implications of his thesis. Although a second edition of his introductory text continued in 1963 to declare ethical neutrality a central characteristic of the sociological approach, Bierstedt (1960:8) had contended four years earlier before his peers that "not even the scientific sociologist can ultimately escape the ethical and political consequences of his own approach to the problems of society . . . objectivity may not be as desirable a criterion as it is commonly thought to be. . . . The greatest thinkers . . . have not been the neutral and objective ones, but those who have turned their biases to good account."

And Bierstedt was not alone. The same year saw Kurt Wolff (1959:592) call for "the injection of more self-conscious humaneness and historicity . . . into contemporary sociology." In 1962 Robert Nisbet, in an article whose title described sociology "as an Art Form," noted that none of the most distinctive ideas contributed by sociologists to the larger vocabulary of intellectual discourse—mass society, alienation, anomie, rationalization, community, disorganization—was a derivative of what we have come to call the "scientific method"; that the distinctiveness of sociology lay with its "revolt against the rationalist view of man and society"; and that its key ideas "have their closest affinity with an art movement, Romanticism."[16] By 1963, Peter Berger's *Invitation to Sociology*, subtitled *A Humanistic Perspective*, had appeared, while Paul Meadows (1964:20) declaimed the following year upon the partnership of the arts and the sciences as they fused in sociology through the latter's immersion in language, imagination, and values—concluding that "the human being, both as subject and as object, has always been closer to the world of meaning of the arts than of the sciences." The breadth of interest in such a general rapprochement between sociology and the humanities is suggested by the appearance about the same time of such new periodicals as *History and Theory* and *Comparative Studies in Society and History* and the joint publication by the Free Press of the two collections of essays, *Sociology and History* (Cahnman and Boskoff, 1964) and *American History and the Social Sciences* (Saveth, 1964). The genre had meanwhile broken through the inhibitions of the official power structure of the discipline when Robert Merton chaired a session of the 1960 annual meetings identified as "Sociology in Its Relation with History." And, the 1962 meetings included a special plenary address by Arthur Schlesinger, Jr., on the humanist's image of empirical social research. The concern reappeared as a session on "Sociology and History" in 1964, slipped back into "Historical Methodology in Sociology" in 1965, but then was reclaimed again as "Sociology and History" in '66 and '67. Indeed, the 1966 meetings included a session titled, quite unambiguously, "Sociology as a Field of the Humanities."

An additional manifestation of the movement away from the self-consciously natural scientific position was the shift in the substantive nature of the presidential addresses before the annual meetings from the 'fifties to the 'sixties. During the former decade the topics were almost exclusively technical in content ("Measurement in Sociology," "Sociological Analysis and the 'Variable'," "Priorities in Scientific Discovery," etc.). Only one, Robert Angell's "Sociology and the World Crisis," could be clearly accounted "prophecy." The reverse was the case in the sixties—at least to the moment of this writing in 1968: only one clearly reflected the "priestly" stance (Robert E. L. Faris' "The Ability Dimension in Human Society"). The rest were informed by, or appealed to, the "prophetic" urge: Howard Becker's "Normative Reactions to Normlessness," Lazersfeld's "The Sociology of Empirical Social Relations," Everett Hughes' "Race Relations and the Sociological Imagination," Homan's "Bringing Men Back In," Sorokin's "Sociology of Yesterday, Today, and Tomorrow," Wilbert Moore's "The Utility of Utopia's," and Charles Loomis' "In Praise of Conflict and Its Resolution."

Those who knew Howard Becker well were aware that he was—as Weber had been before him—disturbed by the unidirectional trend toward secularity. But, unlike Weber, he wished to make clear the *probability* of counteractive responses in the direction of the normative. Paul Lazarsfeld was even more revealing. He called quite explicitly for a return to an ethos of "muckraking"—tempered though it was by the phrase "in reverse." On one hand he would reintroduce the effort to stem undesirable social drift, on the other, the analysis of unrecognized social needs. Everett Hughes, disturbed by the discipline's gross failure to foresee the racial explosion in this country, admonished it for focusing so tightly upon the empirical and the repetitive and enveloping itself within a context that equated objectivity with indifference. He urged rather that its "detachment" be one of deep commitment, that we confront the vivid problems of "real life," participate in them intimately, and apply to them a "utopian imagination" that would project a variety of alternatives to its present structures. Homans, although remaining rigorously within the behavioral circle, called for the recognition that *man* was prior to "system" and that such an awareness was relevant to the sociological task. Sorokin, at the end of a long career as theorist and interpretive historian of sociological thought, saw American sociology moving into a period in which the classical concern with gross societal movement would again dominate our scholarly concern. And Wilbert Moore, picking up the key of "purposiveness" which Parsons seemed in his mature works to have replaced with "system," pleaded for a return to activism through the exercise of a utopian imagination akin to that urged earlier by Moore and seconded by Wendell Bell's plenary address the same year on "The Future as the Cause of the Present." Finally, Charles Loomis' address in 1967 moved a step beyond Moore by suggesting specific sites for "utopian" communities and offering his services as consultant.[17]

These *ex cathedra* declarations from the profession's elder statesmen were supplemented, indeed in many cases preceded, by the willingness of a wide array of younger sociologists to risk the censure of their peers by refurbishing the prophet's mantle and acting the part in their own research. Among the growing number one would have to include the names of Peter Berger, Lewis Coser, Amitai Etzioni, Nathan Glazer, Alvin Gouldner, Louis Horowitz, Leo Lowenthal, C. Wright Mills, Philip Rieff, David Riesman, Bernard Rosenberg, Maurice Stein, Arthur Vidich, and Dennis Wrong. Etzioni's call in 1965 for a *social analysis* that would deal with the "generic methodological, intellectual, and professional problems which the substantive sociologies raise . . ." (1964:614) is a distinctive case in point. Alfred McClung Lee's *Multivalent Man* (1966) was the first of what one might expect to be a wave of introductory texts in the recaptured mode.

Second Thoughts on a Value-Free Sociology

If the recent shift to a more "prophetic" style were limited to the discipline's increasing identification with the humanities and to expressions of uneasiness over her posture *vis-à-vis* the body politic, one might discount it as but a temporary manifestation of the larger activism that characterized the decade. But in fact, a considerably more basic reassessment of the foundations of sociology *as a science* was also underway.

Assumptions examined

We have already noted in Chapter 2 the sudden appearance, in 1963, of four major volumes on the philosophical and logical grounding of the social and behavioral sciences after a period of some twenty years during which *not one* had been made generally available. The first formal sign that such a fundamental re-examination might be underway was the inclusion by Howard Becker of two separate sessions on the basic assumptions underlying the discipline at the 1960 annual meetings. Although a rump gathering of sociologists of religion directed their attention to the issue at the end of the 1962 meetings, the first sessions under the rubric of the "Philosophy of Social Science" appeared in 1963. It reappeared as "Sociology and Philosophy" in 1965 and then settled firmly into the structure of the 1966 and 1967 meetings as the "Philosophy of the Social Sciences." Indeed, a semi-independent section of the membership of the parent Association was organized at the 1966 meetings under the title "Theoretical Sociology" to concern itself with "the critical examination of the epistemological foundations of scientific sociology" as well as to engage in the routines of substantive theory-building. And as we have seen, one final hint that the organizational center of the discipline was aware of the new introspective mood was the introduction for the first time of a special session of the annual meetings on the "Sociology of Sociology" in 1967.

Reassessment of Weber

The concern with the logic, philosophy, and sociology of the social and behavioral sciences was the result of one overriding fact. Social research practitioners were beginning to question the value-free stamp placed upon the discipline by Max Weber some forty years before. It was no longer a question of separating one's research role from those relevant to the institutional obligations one confronted in other areas of one's life. Teacher, government consultant, image merchant—these were not at issue. It was the sociologist at the heart of his scientific activity—the man engaged in "pure" empirical research—who sat beneath the sociologist's skeptical eye. And what he began to see carried him beyond the relativistic epistemology by which Weber's *wertbeziehung* ("value relevance") stance had sought to condition the rigor of the value-free claim.[18] Gunnar Myrdal, together with Arnold Rose and Richard Sterner, had as early as 1944 claimed in the theoretical section of their classic compendium on the Negro, *An American Dilemma*, not only that the sociologist engaged in research *did* have value biases, but that he *must* have them. At what point in the research process do the valuations enter? Myrdal suggested that there were a number:

> The processes of selecting a problem and basic hypothesis, of limiting the scope of study, and of defining and classifying data relevant to such a setting of the problem, involve a choice on the part of the investigator. The choice is made from an indefinite number of possibilities. The same is true when inferences are drawn from organized data. Everything in the world is connected with everything else; when shall one stop, and in what direction shall one proceed when establishing causal relations? Scientific conventions usually give guidance. But, first, convention itself is a valuation, hidden in tacit preconceptions which are not discussed or even known.[19]

Though Reinhard Bendix, Bernard Barber, and Arnold Rose sought briefly to reiterate the thesis in the early 1950's, it was not until the end of the decade, by which time Myrdal had republished the theoretical portion of the study in the collection of essays entitled *Value in Social Theory*, that the case began to command more than passing interest from the profession at large.[20]

Buttressed, then, by the ethos of re-engagement which had begun to pervade the larger culture, Myrdal's insight became the point of reference for a variety of new departures from the value-free model. Barrington Moore may have led off with his discussion of strategy in social science in *Political Power and Social Theory* in 1958. Werkmeister followed in 1959 with his analysis of the problem of "objectivity." Helmut Schoeck and J. W. Wiggins weakened an otherwise compelling case by encompassing two collections of essays—*Scientism and Values* (1960) and *Relativism and the Study of Man* (1961)—within a conservative polemic. A historical dimension was added in 1961 by Leon Bramson's *The Political Context of Sociology*, while Kaspar Naegele's and Edward Shils' essays introducing and concluding the Parsonian collection of the roots of the sociological tradition, the two-volume *Theories of Society*, suggested that second thoughts were being raised at the very heart of the alliance between the priestly mode and system analysis.[21] The reassessment of Weber's dictum was finally dramatized for the membership at large by Alvin Gouldner's influential essay

"Anti-Minotaur: The Myth of a Value-Free Sociology." The setting which drew forth Weber's persuasive proclamation of the value-free nature of science, both social and natural, had been one completely at odds with the present American academic scene. For it was one in which the lofty professorship at the German university of that day was being used indiscriminately as a position from which one could launch almost any ideologically-laden statement with complete unassailability. Yet Weber's motive was obviously moral:

> the myth of a value-free sociology was Weber's way of trying to adjudicate the tensions between two vital Western traditions: between reason and faith, between knowledge and feeling, between classicism and romanticism, between the head and the heart. Like Freud, Weber never really believed in an enduring peace or in a final resolution of this conflict. What he did was to seek a truce through the segregation of the contenders, by allowing each to dominate different spheres of life.[22]

That truce, Gouldner makes abundantly clear, is quite impossible. In at least three spheres—in the selection of problems, the preference for certain hypotheses, and in the choice of certain conceptual schemes—the intrusion of one's personal values is unavoidable. The Minotaur—the cleft creature, the half-man–half-beast—stood as symbol of a discipline in manifest need of demythologization.

Action, inexhaustibility, and freedom

Others who have joined in the effort to strip sociology of its value-free habit have included Llewellyn Gross and Gideon Sjoberg.[23] But the most radical effort was a slight essay by John Seeley that grew out of a departmental colloquium at Brandeis and appeared in the Stein and Vidich ensemble of essays published in 1963 in honor of C. Wright Mills. Seeley's stated aim was to locate himself, as a sociologist, "in social, moral, scientific space." This, in a scant twelve and a half pages, he was unable to achieve; but the route he selected was studded with provocative possibilities. He begins by pointing out that social scientists are the only ones granted a mandate to study the society that was the source of that mandate.

In other words, he is fully conscious of the paradoxical position of the sociologist and is willing to start out on his expedition from its slippery base. But he is able to do so only by acknowledging that we must discover somehow a "trans-social" vantage point outside the paradox or simply accept the fact that one's own personal values must be the guide. It is the latter position he adopts when he concludes that "the social scientist does and must criticize the society from a viewpoint that he cannot justify by an appeal to the society as it is" (Seeley, 1963: 56). He then sets forth three interrelated theorems that appear to follow from the initial paradox: the *social science is action* theorem, the *inexhaustibility* theorem, and the *freedom* theorem. The first means that whatever a social scientist does in his research, he inevitably intervenes in the very process he is attempting to study. The second, assuming the validity of the first, implies that one can never exhaust the content of one's social subject matter by one's description of it because the very act of description adds to it. The third follows in turn from the second. It is rooted in the awareness that "every theory regarding human behavior enters into human behavior . . . as a 'new factor' . . . an assertion, even if initially fully justified by inference from all previous cases . . . may and frequently does enter in a very short interval into the behavior of all the parties, in such a way as to make necessary its own qualification" (*ibid.*). It moves beyond Merton's self-fulfilling and self-denying prophecies, for it involves an inevitable dialectical principle operative to some extent in every piece of social research, and so denies the validity for social science of the axiom of recurrence that undergirds the logic of natural science. Seeley then goes on to suggest that this active, incremental, and liberating factor results in an implicit commitment to social *change* at a number of points in the research process, although he adds that at least at one point—when one chooses the background factors one will hold constant—the social scientist is making a countering contribution to stability. For his paradigm of the activity of social research as a whole he turns to psychoanalysis, "for the formal status of the knowledge gained in analysis is . . . that it cannot be embraced (or tested) until certain kinds of experiences have been had which alter, probably irrevocably, the intelligence that proposes to assess them."[24] He suggests that it may be analogous to the paradoxical posture of the man of faith for whom an initial commitment brings into his vision perceptions that justify a further venture in faith which in turn begins the cycle once again. Seeley acknowledges "participant observation" to be the accepted image of the process of which he speaks, but suggests that a more proper model of unreserved participation would in fact be the mystical experience. Indeed

> . . . the central social facts—love, hate, friendship, enmity—are constituted by faith, and entered upon, for any purpose except the most trivial comprehension, only in ways that set up the process of building knowledge on faith and faith on knowledge in a succession of steps that simultaneously opens one to some observations while blinding one to others. The most obvious statement might be that we can understand nothing until our modes of perception have been ineradicably set in many ways by some culture; but once this process is well begun, we can understand some things and not others. The knowledge has thus essentially in its very structure the nature of an historical or ontological process, in which successive steps in the activity produce irreversible changes in the actor so that the convention that approximates reality in the natural sciences—the contrary of Heraclitus' assertion that you cannot step into the same river twice—has no counterpart in the social sciences, or finds only a minor echo there (1963:64).

Implications for sociology

Seeley's thesis is an extraordinary one. If it—together with those other manifestations of the return to prophecy we have been confronting—meant that the value-free thesis as currently expounded almost universally in our introductory texts could no longer withstand close examination, then the revolutionary ferment we noted in Chapter 2 as it applied to sociology's grasp of its essential subject matter (the revolt of the conflict paradigm against the system paradigm) would indeed by accompanied by a concomitant revolutionary upheaval at the level of the sociologist's self-image (the reclamation of the prophetic paradigm in the face of what we have termed the priestly paradigm). It is possible, furthermore, that the relationship might be more than merely associational. Paradigms governing the sociologist's self-image may in fact be "primary," whereas those framing the image he has of his subject matter may be truly "secondary." Although the two may interact and feed upon each other, the fundamental agent may be the self-image, the fundamental function, the image of society.

Any informed response to the latter possibility would seem to hang in part upon the seriousness with which the discipline is apt to take what we have here simply described as the current "return to prophecy." If it is but a momentary aberration in what is in fact a linear movement in the direction of the priestly mode, then its role as an agent underlying the rather massive shift toward the conflict paradigm would have to be discounted. If, on the other hand, the case for abandoning the value-free motif that provides the underlying rationale for the priestly posture is a sturdy one, then the functional link I have hypothesized between a primary and a secondary paradigmatic level might appear somewhat strengthened.

There is very good reason, then, to examine the sociologist in some depth at that point at which he is engaged in the task that he would claim to distinguish him as scientist: in the activity of social research. To what extent must he be prepared—is he being prepared—to acknowledge that there, at the very heart of his activity as sociologist, he is unable to avoid recourse to standards of valuation or implicit commitment which lie beyond empirical adjudication—standards which are the final court of appeal for the current sociological reclamation of the prophetic paradigm?

Science: Dilemmas of Choice

7

Some sociologists have banished from their program all questions of value and have sought to restrict themselves to the theory of social happenings. . . . But the questions of human value are inescapable, and those who banish them at the front door admit them unavowedly and therefore uncritically at the back door.

Morris Cohen

Faith Versus Works

THE liturgy of the priestly mode in contemporary sociology holds, as we have seen, that scientists as scientists make no value-judgments and that, because sociology is a natural science, sociologists likewise are exempted. It is a position that is almost always hedged by the phrase "*qua* sociologist," even though the segmentation of man's activity into roles is itself a product of a sociological perspective and thus begs the question.

Yet even when sociologists are handed this trump card, it carries little or no indication of just exactly what the "qua" includes. If the value-free label signified only that the product of social research is indicative rather than imperative, an "is" rather than an "ought," then we must accept it as the self-evident truth that it has been for generations. If it stipulated that sociologists somehow have been spared the biases of other men, we would have to reject it out of hand, for we are well aware of our common human condition. If it claimed that sociologists in all their professional activities—including their roles as teachers and as consultants—could approximate value-neutrality, the thesis would be equally indefensible. What the dominant voices of the profession had come to argue in the post-war period was, rather, that when

Notes to this chapter will be found on pages 340–347.

sociologists engage in social research, they commit themselves to the limitations and power of a process that will minimize bias, for it is supported by a logic that is *in principle* free of the burdens of valuation. Bias that enters into our product is then simply the result of our failure to adhere to that logic precisely.

It is past time that the claim be examined in depth. We have pointed out already how it stands as keystone in the arch that straddles the poles of *priest* and *prophet*. We also have seen how our choice of such first-level paradigms may in fact govern our selection of second-level paradigms, such as system or conflict, which characterize our fundamental image of our subject matter. What we have not brought out is that the value-free thesis plagues the effort in process to create a truly international fraternity of sociologists as much as does the predilection to view social research as but the growing right arm of a paradigm of social reality already outlined in general form by Karl Marx. In this and the following chapter we will demonstrate the manner in which the value-free notion, although pointing to the empirical commitment that we all share, has muddied the waters of discourse, both domestic and international, much more than it has purified them; that sociologists in the West are beginning to discover that they have no more basis for drawing back, for security, into its womb than a maturing social scientific community in the East need bow before the semantic heritage of an intellectually unsophisticated nineteenth century.

The effort will be launched not from the mind-set of the logician of science, for I claim no unusual training in its mysteries. Rather it would continue in the lineage suggested in the volume's title: the sociology of sociology. It will necessitate occasional forays into the theory and nature of knowledge and associated realms, but will return each time to an empirical examination of just what must be included, *in principle*, if one is to engage in social research. If indeed the discipline in America over the past generation has been involved in a self-deception, then the central role sociologists play in examining our social universe could well radiate their own confusion and project it upon the folkways and mores of others. But even if no damage has been done, it would be well to cleanse the semantic inheritance of American sociology so as to set the stage for its reunion with an equally demythologized Marxist sociology.

The unfortunate thing about the value-free posture is that it is informed by an image of natural science that is at least a generation out of date.[1] The stance taken by most spokesmen for natural science in the West today views creative work in science as riddled by personal, idiosyncratic factors. This newer thread has probably seen its fullest expression in the writings of Michael Polanyi, a leading British physical chemist-turned epistemologist. His central work, titled appropriately enough *Personal Knowledge*, developed out of a series of lectures delivered nearly two decades ago. Polanyi is quite ready to acknowledge that the value-free posture is probably harmless in the exact sciences, because it is in fact disregarded there. The danger, he tells us, lies in the manner in which social scientists, seeking to shore up their claim to be scientific, have been taken in by the slogan. The fact of the matter is, rather, that "into every act of knowing there enters a passionate contribution of the person knowing what is being known, and this coefficient is no mere imperfection but a vital component of knowledge. . . ."[2]

One might have assumed that sociologists, because of their involvement in the sociology of knowledge and of science, would have been among the first to shake the film from their eyes. But somehow the sociological Adam was viewed as being spared the bias that accompanies tasting the fruit of good and evil by a dispensation but slightly different from that offered the intelligentsia by Mannheim a generation before: The "scientific community" or, in the singular, the "scientist *qua* scientist," simply replaced the intellectual as uniquely free from the original sin of subjective valuation.[3]

Not that sociology can claim any special foresight regarding the values that *should* frame man's social world. The logic of science offers no explicit guidance in delineating the "good" and the "bad" in social existence, and sociology can and should be looked upon as a *science*. Where one is forced to part company with the priestly mode in sociology is in its assumption that the sociologist *as* scientist can and/or should maintain a neutral posture *vis-à-vis* the values of the larger cultural context of which it is a part. The sociologist *qua* sociologist has never, even at the height of his doctrinaire rejection of the valuational process, actually ignored those values in the decisions he made *qua* sociologist. Arthur Schlesinger, Jr.'s observation (1962:769) that, "inside every sociologist, there is an humanist struggling to get out . . . ," would seem to have applied to *homo sociologus americanus* during the 'forties and 'fifties. The sociologist as "priest" may be wed by *faith* to a dogma that would place him close to the Zen ideal of simple perception uncontaminated by the maze that is valuation. But when we examine his *works* we find that he has not escaped and cannot escape the visions of heaven and the temptations of hell that condition every man's existence. Not teaching, not his applied role, but those actions that identify him as scientist—his research activities—are the "works" which this exercise in the sociology of sociology will now confront. For it is here at the very heart of his "role" as behavioral scientist that he is unable to avoid, *even in principle*, postures and decisions that undermine his claim to value-neutrality.[4]

Focus of Concern: The Autobiographical Character of Problem Selection

If we were to examine decision-making as it occurs in the process of social research—and examine it quite *instrumentally*—perhaps the first and most evident point at which value-judgments must of necessity enter is in the selection of the problem itself. Can neutrality be an appropriate pose when we are faced with the *choice* of the issue to be explored? The answer must be a completely unambiguous "no." "Only a tiny fraction of all knowable facts are of interest to scientists," notes Polanyi (1958: 3, 134):

> . . . if we decided to examine the universe objectively in the sense of paying equal attention to portions of equal mass, this would result in a lifelong preoccupation with interstellar dust, relieved only at brief intervals by a survey of incandescent masses of hydrogen—not in a thousand million lifetimes would the turn come to give man even a second's notice. . . . Our vision of reality . . . must suggest to us the kind of questions that it should be reasonable and interesting to explore.

But then even Weber (1949:72, 76), the father of the value-free image in sociology, had been willing to admit as much two generations before:

> All the analysis of infinite reality which the finite human mind can conduct rests on the tacit assumption that only a finite portion of this reality constitutes the object of scientific investigation, and that only it is "important" in the sense of being "worthy of being known."
>
> Only a small portion of existing concrete reality is colored by our value-conditioned interest and it alone is significant to us. It is significant because it reveals relationships which are important to us due to their connection with our values.... We cannot discover . . . what is meaningful to us by means of a "presuppositionless" investigation of empirical data. Rather perception of its meaningfulness to us is the presupposition of its becoming an *object* of investigation.

The central issue is in fact no longer contested, even by those who would continue to speak for the broader relevance of the value-free thesis. In a recent essay on problem-finding in sociology, Merton (1959) refers approvingly to Polanyi and specifies some of the idiosyncratic forces that lead us to focus upon one substantive area rather than another. Earlier, Parsons (1951b:167) acknowledged that "science is not simply a reflection of reality, but is a *selective* system of cognitive orientation to reality . . . 'facts' are not 'realities' but statements about realities. They may be true and yet highly selective in relation to any conception of the 'total reality'." Robert Lynd's classic *Knowledge for What?*, however, protested about the manner in which the recognition, once granted, was then ignored by the majority of sociologists.[5] The typical text passes over the issue.[6] Since the overall assumption already had been made that the scientist *qua* scientist is, or must try to be, neutral, sociologists following in the priestly mode find it relatively easy to absolve themselves of any sense of positive responsibility for the choice. The end result is neither "objectivity" nor "neutrality." It is a decision by omission —one that, although implicit, nevertheless has obvious value consequences. It is simply the decision to allow the choice to be made by someone else. The consequences for the larger society are equally self-evident.

Moral scientist, immoral grant?

By minimizing self-conscious responsibility for choice of a problem area, one is apt to be led by those who are willing and able to pay for his energies. Sociologists are not unaware of all this; they have written and have read of the "academic marketplace" and the "affluent professors." One of the younger generation who reached professional maturity during the period that the research bureau had multiplied across the universities of the land and come to dominate the research-training process describes some of the forces operative in latter-day sociological research as follows:

> On occasion (the research bureau's) members are painfully surprised at the unanticipated reception of their endeavors. However, from such experience they learn much—what is absolutely safe, what is questionable, what is risky, what is dangerous, what is fatal.
>
> . . . the selection of additional or replacement personnel comes to be predicted not solely on talent or demonstrated skill, but on the individual's capacity to subordinate scientific concerns to institutional needs. . . . Only those outsiders willing to take the vows of conformity, or whose regularity is so transparent as to require no proof, are admitted to the order. The "enthusiast" . . . is subordinated to the bureaucrat. . . . Moreover *the organizational researcher tends to lose his capacity for moral indignation*, which I suggest, is a crucial source of insight [my italics].[7]

As sociologists permit themselves to become tools in the struggle for power and legitimacy in the world at large, they find that they increasingly become the servant of the dominant economic and military interests of the day, for it is they who can afford the luxury of subtle persuasion and manipulation rather than the more brutal and direct weapons of social control such as the strike or boycott, sit-in or police action, which so quickly stir the public conscience. A sociologist who accepts the passive role and ignores the value dimensions that adhere to the issue of problem selection is making his small contribution to the dawn of that day in which power may be taken or held with the manipulated consent of a mass public.[8]

Social research may simply play the role of "anxiety-reducing" ritual for the powers that be. That is, problem areas may be so selected that the research conducted is almost certain to render legitimate the activity in question. In those instances where it does not, the results are easily filed away from one's superiors' eyes, from those of the public at large, or even from the rest of the scientific fraternity, for publication rights are often hedged with obligations to the sponsoring party. But C. Wright Mills's characterization of the milieu and mentality of the postwar products of our graduate programs is difficult to gainsay:

> Their positions change—from the academic to the bureaucratic; their publics change—from movements of reformers to circles of decision makers; and their problems change—from those of their own choice to those of their new clients. The scholars themselves tend to become less intellectually insurgent and more administratively practical. Generally accepting the *status quo*, they tend to formulate problems out of the troubles and issues that administrators believe they face. They study . . . workers who are restless and without morale, and managers who "do not understand" the art of managing human relations. They also diligently serve the commercial and corporate ends of the communications and advertising industries.[9]

Many have been tempted to absolve sociologists of any sense of guilt through analogy with the classic Niebuhrian phrase, "moral man, immoral society." The appropriate image then becomes "moral scientist, immoral grant." This is far too simple. The burden cannot simply be shifted to those who underwrite research.[10] Sociologists are free to accept or reject the conditions others would set for their employ. Furthermore, the mere admission of responsibility should not set them apart from natural scientists who are no less human than they. As Einstein (1932) observed, ". . . if an angel of God were to descend and drive from the Temple of Science all those . . . motivated by display and profit, I fear the temple would be nearly emptied."

If we are to be guided by the lessons that the history of the subordination of science to the interests of the nation-state has provided, then the readiness of the establishment to pay the piper if one but plays the tunes directed may indeed call for a more forthright acknowledgment of the risks involved and the internalization of an ethic that might help minimize those risks. If not, then "... as the physicists are busy engineering the world's annihilation," suggests Peter Berger (1963:152), "the social scientists can be entrusted with the smaller mission of engineering the world's assent."

But even if one were to deny the substantive threat posed by the commercial and governmental forces that underwrite most of today's social research, one fact should by now be abundantly clear. The choices made when one assumes the scientific role in preference to another, when one chooses to focus upon social phenomena rather than non-social, when one selects one particular problem for investigation over against all others—at these moments sociologists are forced *in principle* into value-laden stances for which there is no purely empirical authorization.

Conceptualization: The Crystallization of Bias

It is a bit startling that a discipline which looks to language as man's most distinctive attribute and which, along with anthropology and linguistics, sees language as structuring the very nature of social reality—that such a discipline is not fully conscious of the value-laden decisions that are implicit in the unavoidable task of selecting a sociological vocabulary. The decisions that underlie the development of a particular set of concepts—and the grammatical framework within which they are articulated—are, in point of fact, commitments that are made prior to those that are involved in focusing upon a particular area of concern, for they are necessary to the very formulation and expression of the problem in question.

Meta-linguistics

The raw data of empirical experience, as Heraclitus observed thousands of years ago, are always discrete and unique. The genius of the logic of science lies largely in its capacity to fabricate continuity from this stream of the unique. This it does by the use of categories, by inventing symbols by which we are able to pin the fluttering and ever-changing empirical datum to the typological mounting board. Its strong right arm is language, the system of concepts and syntax that is the core of any culture's inheritance. Social scientists—scientists in general—must select, improvise, or invent linguistic categories and their accompanying networks of grammar or logic. Yet they must do this with an awareness that the very linguistic tools they select act as a screen through which filter only those aspects of experience that are consistent with the conceptual scheme used.[11] The sociology and anthropology of language—particularly the branch that has come to be known as meta-linguistics—are in process of demonstrating this linguistic preconditioning through which any approach to the conceptualization of experience must pass. Through it we have become aware that the very linguistic tools and grammatical systems selected predispose us to observe and analyze selected areas of experience, that the very symbols and models that structure our systematic thinking will necessarily bias that which we perceive.

The logical empiricists struggled mightily to shape symbolic forms so that they would be devoid of valuation, and failed. They found, of course, that is was impossible not to use them in establishing the legitimacy of their own system over others. That natural scientists are becoming aware of the critical part played in their work by language may perhaps be suggested by the way in which Conant (1951:25) chose to define science as "an interconnected series of *concepts* and *conceptual schemes* that have developed as a result of experimentation and observation and are fruitful of further experimentation and observation." To Percy Bridgman this means that the day when we could look upon science as simply the systematic analysis of naked sensations is well past. *We* are inextricably bound up with our data: "wherever we go we find ourselves."[12] Perhaps Ernst Cassirer has made a greater effort to communicate this awareness to the present generation than any other philosopher of our period. The linguistic instruments we use not only act as a screen through which we sift the categories in which we are interested, but they set limits to the very questions we can ask.

Sociologists have not, of course, been oblivious of this characteristic of language. Many have followed closely the investigations of cultural anthropologists and linguists in this area, and some have contributed significant studies in their own right. The Sapir-Whorf hypothesis, which insists that the grammatical structure of a language perforce structures the very reality it seeks to communicate, has found its way into most of our introductory texts. Durkheim was able to face and acknowledge at least a part of its implication for science—i.e., that society was even the source of the basic categories of logic and science. He wrestled free of the relativistic dilemma in a fashion analogous to the tempting route taken by Marx before him, however, simply by assuming that he happened to live at a moment when the societally conditioned intellect of man became fully self-conscious.

Verstehende Soziologie

Max Weber was so thoroughly aware of the cultural and sub-cultural relativity of concepts that he elaborated the notion of *verstehen* to solve the dilemma. The fact that many of the concepts central to his own research appear to have transcended the restraints and bounds of immediate cultural empathy which the *verstehen* method laid down suggests that in fact he was forced to appropriate instead those categories that seemed to be more consistent with the implicit values and declared purpose of science itself, categories such as rationality and secularization. Parsons is among the many who find Weber's actions more helpful than his intent, for he is aware of the inextricable manner in which cognition is wrapped round with "cathexis" and, indeed, with valuation. The criticism that must be directed at most sociologists of the 'forties and 'fifties is precisely the same. Although aware of the role language plays in structuring reality, they simply failed to apply the fact to their own research enterprise. Wrapped safely in the dogma of ethical neutrality, they ignored the implicit and explicit value-choices that they inevitably made when they selected one category or conceptual scheme rather than another.[13] One can begin, then, to understand the frustration and anger with which C. Wright Mills viewed the sociological scene, for he simply saw it unself-consciously wed to a set of categories and conceptual networks that emphasized structure and stability at the price of dynamics and change. Mills's primary target was, of course, the structural-functional school of sociological theory and its leading spokesman,

Talcott Parsons.[14] It would profit us to review our earlier discussion of its paradigmatic base, for much that has struck the ideological nerve-endings of many a dissident sociologist would seem to be rooted in the implicit commitment that accompanied the choice by Parsons of a single key term.

Conceptual roots of Parsonian conservatism

Parsons is one of the most sophisticated minds that American sociology has produced—one that is, I believe, more fully aware of the necessary implications of the language he has chosen to use than are most of his critics. Putting aside the somewhat petty complaints about Parsons' capacity to operate with considerable ease at a very high level of abstraction, the most widespread criticism of the total impact of his theory is that it is biased, as we pointed out earlier, in the direction of stability. His closest collaborator over the years—Edward Shils (1961:1443)—remarks that "it is recurrently charged against the sociological theory of action, with its emphasis on systemic equilibrium, that it has no place for change. What is presumably meant is that it does not theoretically encompass enduring shifts of a whole society from one state to another state. There is truth in this charge." A lengthy string of his fellow sociologists—and some looking in from neighboring disciplines—have responded with the same indictment, although more often in harsher terms. They find but a secondary place granted the disruptive, the deviant, the tension-producing, conflict-generating, and change-inducing forces that appear to abound in our social experience. In its place we are offered "equilibrium" (dynamic though it may be), tension-reduction, and system-maintenance.

What is the key that unlocks this predilection for stability? We gave the answer earlier: He stacked his entire deck—and all the games he would later play with it—the very moment he settled upon the focal term "system" as the characteristic concern of sociology. And, it is important to note, he did so in full awareness of its implications.

The most general and fundamental property of a system is the interdependence of parts or variables. Interdependence consists in . . . *order* in the relationship among the components which enter into a system. This order must have a tendency to self-maintenance, which is very generally expressed in the concept of equilibrium . . . if [he adds in a footnote] the system is to be permanent enough to be worthy of study . . . (Parsons, 1951b: 107).

Not only does he focus the study of sociology upon "social systems," he also tells us by the selection of the term "worthy" in his addendum that he is well aware that the choices he must make as a theorist are not "value-free."

He could hardly be more explicit when by definition he attributes a "state of tension" to a *system* of action and then says that, ". . . other things being equal, it can change *only* in the direction of 'reduction of tension' " (1953: 83). He chose the title *The Social System* for the most elaborate exposition of his theory, well aware of the inevitable ideological stance that it implied, although perhaps unaware of the lack of linguistic and intellectual sophistication of his confreres. There was no room in Parsons' theoretical structure for conflicts *between* social systems; for any "between" implies, on the basis of his initial conceptual commitment, the presence of an overarching system of which the two units in question are but sub-systems. Such a perspective short-changes social change, for system is treated as the underlying conceptual reference. The social change that *is* involved in sociological analysis that his theory is equipped to handle must, by the conceptual priorities he assumes, simply represent a shift within a larger equilibrium. It focuses on tension reduction and functionalism rather than tension production and disorder because a system is *defined* as functional. It may well be that one of the belated effects was his decision to eliminate "self vs. collectivity" from among his original list of pattern variables, for if sociology does indeed deal ultimately in terms of systems, then there is no place in the longer run for an "either-or" image of "self-collectivity." Rather, the two are, by conceptual commitment, but varying perspectives in a large functional unity.

There are, however, two levels at which the legitimacy of the Parsonian approach may be questioned. One is when he and his followers seem occasionally to forget, in their enthusiasm for the rather towering consistency of the theoretical structure developed, that its integrity and beauty follow from its assumptions and do not represent empirical inductions. He has stated (1951:204) that his theory construction "is not an attempt to formulate a theory of any concrete phenomenon, but it is the attempt to present a logically articulated conceptual scheme." The integrity of his work, however, may have suffered occasionally from the complexity of his total output, for he seems to be oblivious of the contradiction that lies, for instance, in the manner in which he has offered the "Principle of System Integration" as a "law" of equilibrium on a level analogous to the inductively derived laws of biology and classical mechanics.

The second level of criticism is more central. It lies simply in whether or not we are willing to subordinate sociologists' concern with social man to a prior commitment to the paradigm of system and the particular ideological baggage it entails. Bendix and Berger (1959:112) spoke for the paradigmatic inclinations of many when they said that "attention must be focused on the boundary-extending as well as upon the boundary-maintaining activities of individuals, on the permissive aspects of culture and society which enable individuals to experiment with *what is possible* as well as upon the social controls which limit the range of tolerated behavior without defining that range clearly." As Turgot spoke vividly to his fellow prophets of Paris, "Like a mausoleum, a monument to the arrogance of the great and wretchedness of man, which seems to make us more aware of the emptiness of human affairs and of the death which it tries to hide, a system only serves to cover the shame of our ignorance."[15]

Mills's accusation that the structural-functional theory represented a fundamental distortion of social reality must be viewed as a criticism of a particular conceptual choice rather than as an attack upon Parsons' ideological intentions. Mills must simply be interpreted as claiming that an entirely new set of primitive categories would underlie the discipline of sociology—and not that Parsons is in fact politically conservative. Marx himself, as Charles Loomis (1967:876) recently reminded us, found system an extremely useful concept.

Fortunately, many sociological concepts are blatantly obvious in their value content. Sorokin's choice of the term "sensate" in contrast to the categories "ideal" and "ideational"; the waxing and waning attractions of such terms as "disorganization" as over against "deviant organization"; the "relativistic" and "absolutistic" categories of Putney and Middleton; Von Merig's "simplistic" versus "comprehensive" categories as developed in *A Grammar of Human Values*; and Peck and Havighurst's "irrational-conscientious" and "rational-altruistic" categories in *The Psychology of Character Development* may stand as unfortunate examples. Would that all conceptual categories were so open in their implications! The oft-repeated quip regarding the changing conceptual currents in psychology may be a bit more indicative of the subtlety usually confronted: "... psychology first lost its soul, then its mind, and finally has lost consciousness altogether."

But the best statement to date of the position in which sociologists find themselves *vis-à-vis* the commitments that the fabrication of concepts force upon them has come from Shils (1961:1448):

Sociological analysis, however much we succeed in systemizing, codifying, routinizing it—however close we bring it to the natural sciences in rigor of procedures, in the reliability of observation, and in refinement of demonstration—will always retain an important element of the personal. By this, we mean that the most elementary categories, the most fundamental variables, will have to be apprehended through an experience, through a kind of secular revelation. The operational definition of terms will be useful in the design of research; but what is defined will never be learned from handbooks, nor will it be learned ordinarily from the study of concrete investigations. The best of sociological theory will encompass these variables; but the theory itself will need the guidance of the "experience," or of the vision, of authority, and the refusal of order, of scarcity, of loving attachment, and of hatred. Even the possible mathematization of sociological theory will not evade this necessity of recurrent refreshment of the experience of the fundamental variables of sociological theory. The fundamental terms of sociological theory are primitive terms. Their meanings are apprehended in personal experience and through the secondary experience of contact with the vision, which expresses the deepest experiences of the greatest minds of the race.

We have seen how the value-free stance is violated in the very formulation of a research problem, both in terms of the selectivity of focus and through the particular way the problem is conceptualized. To the extent to which sociologists did admit an awareness of value-judgments in their research, they were likely to confess commitment on these two scores—but to conclude that, in fact, these are decisions that are in truth pre-scientific. From this point on, they would argue, the decision made need not in principle involve issues in which one must take a position that either explicitly or implicitly contradicts the stance of value-neutrality.

Certitude through mathematics

And, indeed, the elaboration of systematic conceptual models, the application of the cold tools of mathematics, and the harnessing of research design to the impersonal skill of the digital computer would have seemed compelling evidence in the view's favor. Bertrand Russell and Alfred North Whitehead's *Principia Mathematica* (1910–13) argued that it was in fact possible to formulate within one system of logic all the fundamental ideas of mathematics. Wittgenstein took up where Russell and Whitehead had left off in his *Tractatus Logico-Philosophicus* (1922), an analysis of the structure of language, which inspired in turn the dedicated efforts of the "Vienna Circle" in the late 'twenties and 'thirties. The latter group sought to redefine philosophy in what they felt had come to be the self-evidently value-free categories of symbolic logic in combination with a Machian empiricism. It led in turn to the linguistic analysis that dominates academic philosophy in Britian and America today. Cybernetic theory and the revolutionary advances made by the electronics industry during World War II had in the meantime presented man with a capacity to process, compute, and store information which, in terms of speed and volume, seemed clearly to free data-analysis from the subjectivity and the limitations of man's own nervous system and open the way to the bias-free handling of the multi-variate dimensions of the social scene that had till that time simply been beyond any but rough qualitative assessment. One was tempted to assume that the relatively simple framework of logic that Russell saw at the base of all mathematical thinking could be built into the structure and programs of such increasingly sophisticated electronic computers and that the combination of the two might provide scientists with a key to unravel systematically the natural world. The digital computer began, in fact, to suggest the grammar and thus the mathematical models that might appropriately frame sociological data, while programing technology became the operational *lingua franca*, the hybrid language, by which sociologists could identify fully with the natural sciences in general.

Disillusionment

But alas, there were rumblings in the background that disturbed the most sensitive. C. F. Gauss and G. F. B. Riemann had followed the non-Euclidean leads offered by Bolyai and Lobachevsky far enough to discover that there were infinitely many geometries available to man. The undefined primitive terms and axioms of Hilbertian geometry that had to be taken on faith began to replace the self-evident axioms and empirically rooted constructs of Euclidean geometry. The granite of mathematical logic that science saw as its firm foundation began to look a little more like simple sandstone after all.

Although it has taken decades for the non-mathematical world to be apprised of their significance, two radical discoveries were made in the late 'twenties and early 'thirties that caused even the sandstone to dissolve. Russell had contended in *Principia Mathematica* that it was possible to formulate within one system all the basic ideas of mathematics extant. By 1929 Skolem was able to conclude that not even the elementary number-system could be categorically formalized.[16] Two years later Kurt Gödel proved the famous incompleteness theorem, one of whose implications is that "no single logistic system . . . can tenably claim to embrace only logical truth *and* the whole of logical truth."[17] Efforts such as Russell's to construct proofs for *all* sentences that are true under the intended interpretation of the symbols were thus found to be hopeless. Not only did Gödel show that a sentence could be constructed about natural numbers which would easily be recognized as true under the intended interpretation but which couldn't be proven from the axioms by the rules of inference provided, but he also proved that *any* formal deductive system must have the same defect. Finally, Tarski capped the critique by demonstrating in 1944 that "any formal system in which we could assert a sentence and also reflect on the truth of its assertion must be self-contradictory."[18]

Existential roots of logic

What did all this mean to the scientist? It meant, among other things, that there is no ultimately self-validating mathematics or other logic that could take from man the necessity of *choosing* his axioms, *selecting* his logical models, and *accepting responsibility* for the particular grammar he chooses to apply to the problem confronting him. Even mathematical logic—the ultimate image of rationality—is wed to the same uncertainty that demands commitment in each of the other avenues of man's creativity. It can never become simply the province of the ultimate computing machine, for it is not—at rock bottom—capable of complete systematization. Always there will be an incompleteness that may be closed but momentarily for human purposes through human choice.

Mathematics, then, has taught us recently that logic is not one thing but a potentially infinite variety of axiomatic systems derived from man's fertile imagination. Even when one has *chosen* a particular logic, he operates within a system that remains dependent ultimately for its consistency on aspects of man's comprehension that lie outside the tautologies of symbolic logic and are more clearly expressive of man's existential nature. Percy Bridgman (1958:90–91) has put the impact of Gödel's theorem thus:

> It is a consequence of this theorem that mathematics can never prove that mathematics is free from internal self-contradictions. . . . Out of this experience mathematicians and logicians have acquired a new insight . . . that the human mind can never have certainty. . . . Gödel's theorem, as it were, cuts the Gordian knot with the insight that "certainty" is an illegitimate concept. . . . The reason mathematics cannot prove that mathematics is free from contradiction is that there are some things a system cannot do with itself. When we try to get away from ourselves by correcting what our senses or our perceptions or our reason presents to us, it is *we* who are attempting to escape. . . . But what we would like to do

can neither be done nor even talked about. Perhaps we have here a worthy candidate for the first law of mental dynamics, namely the law that we cannot get away from ourselves.

"Logic," then, is far from the self-validating and dehumanized grammar into which sociologists may securely slip after they have survived the necessity of selecting a problem area and a conceptual network. Rather, they shoulder the responsibility of settling upon one of a myriad of possible logical systems, none of which is able to validate itself in terms of itself. And by that selection sociologists, as with the choice of a conceptual framework, must accept responsibility for prefabricating their conclusions. If a sociologist follows an essentially Aristotelian logic, he will paint social experience in colors quite different from those that would come through given an initial commitment to a dialectical logic—pigments that impinge upon issues of ideology. When he chooses to drop his data into parametric rather than distribution-free statistical models (or vice-versa), he has made a *pre*-judgment about the nature of human nature that will inevitably carry with it a measure of metaphysical baggage.[19]

Game theory

A few final words would seem to be in order regarding one of the latest creatures of the fashion-minded behavioral scientist. When the most contemporary of sociologists turns to "game" theory, as he has done of late, he *begins* with social intercourse as a calculus of differential risks; one would hardly be surprised then if his ultimate projections appear archly and unconvincingly rational. Anatol Rapoport (1959:369) offers needed words of caution:

> . . . the theory of games . . . does not purport to describe how people behave in real-life situations or even in games, but only to discover the inherent *logic* of certain situations common both to games and to real life. It does say how people would behave (1) if they were guided entirely by unambiguous interests (that is, they could always decide in each situation involving both alternative outcomes and risks which outcome they would prefer at which risk); and (2) if they were able to utilize all the information available to them

and calculate the actual outcomes in determinate situations and expected outcomes in situations involving risks; and (3) if the rules governing the sequence and the range of permissible acts were explicit and fixed.

In other words, game theory operates on the assumption that its players are *not* human beings but unambiguously programed computers. Rapoport then goes on to add a set of remarks which seem to apply very distinctly to the human condition:

> The social scientist, therefore . . . must also be patient and tolerant of the mathematician, who, preoccupied almost exclusively with the tools of his deductive method, tends always to simplify situations beyond recognition. The mathematician must simplify, because only then can he begin working. The social scientist should not demand realism from the mathematician's models but only pertinence. . . . The social scientist must therefore muster his intuitive powers to distinguish the salient features of the social process from the trivial.

Hypothesis Construction: An Existential Leap of Faith

"Scientists—that is, creative scientists," Michael Polanyi (1958:143) reminds us, "spend their lives in trying to guess right." Many discussions have appeared recently that seek to characterize this peculiarly creative kernel that is at the heart of productive research.[20] Common to all these discussions is the view that of prime significance in almost all creative thinking is the operation of non-consciously rational factors. It is imperative that the investigator be steeped in the empirical data that cluster about his problem and be well trained, but it is equally clear that this is not enough. There seems, in fact, to be *no* relation between the degree of intelligence and a person's creativity—beyond an I.Q. threshold of about 120.[21] Instead such a-rational terms as *geistesblitz* (sudden illumination), insight, inspiration, intuition, faith, "effective surprise," paradox, passion, and a "vision of reality" clutter the literature. Some limited headway may be perceived in the correlation of certain general social, cultural, and psychological factors with creativity's appearance in particular intellectual sub-cultures in the contemporary Western, largely American scene. And the assumption that the logic of John Stuart Mill's "method of agreement" may influence learning on a non-conscious level seems increasingly profitable. Still, Peter Berger's observation (1963:13) that "in science as in love a concentration on technique is quite likely to lead to impotence . . ." would not seem an inappropriate moral to be drawn from the evidence to date.

Although there is an element of creativity in each step along the rather tortuous path of social research, few would disagree that the most creative leap is the formulation of an hypothesis. Most of what goes into research is literally "re-search": a searching *after* the fact—the fact that the hypothesis has already been made. All that follows can be thought of as simply an effort to disprove that hypothesis.[22] If alternative or subsidiary hypotheses are drawn forth during the research process, they are likely to be a derivative or analogy of the original hypothesis or a product of the peculiar constellation of observations to which one was drawn in testing the original hypothesis.

The logic that sustains scientific activity is the logic of the experiment—even in the social sciences, where control is usually approximated by manipulating symbols rather than people. And that logic is capable only of rejecting or failing to reject—at accepted standards of significance—the hypotheses explicitly (or implicitly) put forward. Testing the hypothesis may demand great skill, but skill is not enough for the ends of the scientific community. Francis Bacon, as we now know, was quite ill-advised in his glorification of inductive empiricism, for the mere collection of "data," however extensive, proves nothing.

Proof or disproof is meaningful only in a context that involves an hypothesis. If the "truth" of the matter has not been apprehended *before* the search for facts that might allow it to be sustained is undertaken, no "proof" is in the offing. The order of an actual piece of research as apprehended by a scientist's conscious mind—or, even in fact, the order perceived externally by a second person—may appear quite often to run at odds with the sequence described. The entire issue is clouded by the learning capacity of sub-conscious levels of the nervous system and cannot at present be resolved in terms either of self-consciousness or the perception of an observer. All we presently have to fall back on are the criteria and understanding of the process and logic of proof that have come to be held almost universally within the community of science. And it is abundantly clear that "proof" as scientists know it is apprehended formally as involving first of all an act of faith, a commitment of what is in fact a part of oneself, a risk taken, the fruitfulness of which is to be tested by the careful application of experimental logic but whose legitimacy prior to the empirical test has been quite existential. "It is often said that experiments must be made without a preconceived idea," noted Henri Poincaré (1907:129). "That is impossible. Not only would it make all experiments barren, but that would be attempted which could not be done."

If any of this sounds radically irrational, the fault cannot be laid to the lack of logical sophistication on the part of such a key figure in the history of the discipline's self-understanding as Max Weber. For the foregoing is little more than a paraphrase of a statement the latter made in his well-known essay on "Science as a Vocation" (Gerth and Mills, 1958:135):

> Nowadays . . . there is a widespread notion that science has become a problem in calculation, fabricated in laboratories or statistical filing systems just as "in a factory," a calculation involving only the cool intellect and not one's "heart and soul" . . . such comments lack all clarity about what goes on in . . . a laboratory. . . .
>
> Some idea has to occur to someone's mind, and it has to be a correct idea . . . such intuition cannot be forced. It has nothing to do with any cold calculation.
>
> Ideas occur to us when they please, not when it pleases us . . . ideas come when we do not expect them, and not when we are brooding and searching at our desks . . . inspiration plays no less a role in science than it does in the realm of art . . . the psychological processes do not differ. Both are frenzy in the sense of Plato's "mania" and "inspiration."

J. Bronowski (1958:62–63), writing recently out of the disciplines of mathematics and the philosophy of science, puts it most crisply: "The man who proposes a theory makes a choice—an imaginative choice which outstrips the facts. . . . To the man who makes the theory, it may seem as inevitable as the ending of *Othello* must have seemed to Shakespeare. But the theory is inevitable only to him; it is his choice, as a mind and as a person, among the alternatives which are open to everyone . . . it engages the whole personality. . . ."

Polanyi has in fact drawn up an impressive list of cases from the history of physics to illustrate this fact of scientific life: that a *passionate* conviction that one particular hypothesis is valid—although it flies completely in the face of all empirical evidence available up to that time—is highly fruitful scientifically. One of his examples was Einstein's simple conviction of the "reality" of atoms as actual particles, running as it did at direct odds with the facts to that date and against the grain of the then dominant operationalism of Ernst Mach—which led to the resolution of the riddle of Brownian motion in 1905. Our vision of reality "should," insists Polanyi (1958:134), "recommend the kind of conceptions and empirical relations that are intrinsically plausible and which should therefore be upheld, even when some evidence seems to contradict them." He then goes on to argue that "without such a scale of interest and plausibility based on a vision of reality, nothing can be discovered that is of value to science."

This "vision of reality" along with the "choice which outstrips the facts" mentioned by Bronowski and Weber's "frenzy" all suggest that the selection of fruitful hypotheses *of necessity* involves considerably more than a routinized application of a depersonalized logic. Hypotheses are the result of choices that must go beyond the assurance immediately available from the empirical evidence on hand. They represent commitments that involve risk and are conditioned by a wide variety of personal factors.

If more than a handful of American sociologists were fully aware of this during the hey-day of the priestly stance, they did little to reveal the fact. They wrote and spoke as if it were somehow possible in principle to be spared the burden of the implicit valuation that lies within such a leap of faith. The data of the empirical world will of course validate one profile of social man and reject another. But the image must be *hypothesized* before it has the opportunity of being validated. A sociologist who hesitates to draw hypotheses from the depth of his own social being and instead falls back simply upon images of man common to the larger sociological tradition denies his fellow sociologists the *opportunity* of assaying the validity of the image that moves him. The empathetic sensitivity to the meanings projected by one's subjects that Weber termed the method of *verstehen* is not, thus, the same thing as validation. It simply guarantees the *opportunity* of validation—of extending the range of social scientific research to images of social man that would otherwise never be presented for empirical testing.

This, I think, is essentially why a Robert Lynd could call, as he did in *Knowledge for What?*, for the creation of new and "outrageous" hypotheses. For every insightful hypothesis is an "outrage" to the evidence that has gone before, because it is in some measure at odds with the sufficiency of the data that has come to frame our image of the social world to that point.

Validation Through Risk

Many might argue that although value-judgments affect the steps leading to the testing of a hypothesis, the essence of a scientific logic lies at the point of verification and proof. Because the process of validation is value-free, the ethical neutrality of the sociologist *qua* sociologist is in fact guaranteed. The scope of the sociologist's role could thus be narrowed by semantic fiat, even though it is not so viewed by the larger discipline itself. But even if its dimensions encompassed only the verification stage, it would still be unable to eliminate, even in principle, judgments that were clearly valuational and ethically relevant in ultimate impact.

Although one might assume that the so-called "neutrality" of the scientific role is most clearly evident at that point at which a scientist squares his empirical evidence with his hypothesis, even here—at the most "objective" moment in the scientist's role—he is, of necessity, involved in either a personal or collective value-judgment. For scientific hypotheses are never "proven" beyond a doubt. Strictly speaking, "proof" exists nowhere outside of mathematics and formal logic, and we have seen that even these disciplines are not self-validating but depend upon the prior acceptance of axioms that are quite external to the logical system involved. Certainty, as Gödel warned us, is an illegitimate concept. The empirical world, on the other hand, is a probabilistic world. And when there is uncertainty, a demand arises for a judgment based upon non-empirical considerations. "It is clear," notes Polanyi (1958:24), "that a probability statement cannot be strictly contradicted by any event, however improbable this event may appear in its light. The contradiction must be established by a personal act of appraisal which rejects certain possibilities as being too improbable to be entertained as true." Bronowski (1959:56) is even more suggestive:

> In the nature of things, the description can match the facts only with a certain coarseness. . . . A scientist therefore has to decide what coarseness he accepts, if he is ever to come to conclusions. This decision is itself an act of judgment, and I suspect that it has subtle things to teach us about how we judge and how we value. Certainly it should teach us . . . that science involves the scientist as a person; a discovery has to be made by a man, not by a machine, because every discovery hinges on a critical judgment.

Significance levels

Most contemporary social research involves self-conscious and systematic sampling. This in turn subjects the findings to statistical analysis to determine whether or not the relationships uncovered could have occurred due to the chance selection of an oddly distributed although randomly selected, sample. Sociologists tend to label a finding "significant" if the possibility of the relationship occurring from a "chance" appearance of the distribution has been reduced to one in twenty or less. Thus they accept the fact that their conclusion that a relationship does in fact exist is going to be incorrect approximately 5 per cent of the time. Moreover, they must also accept responsibility for rejecting the significance of many distributions where the sample involved does not assure them that a mistaken judgment will be made but one time in twenty. Psychologists for some reason tend to demand more assurance regarding sampling than do sociologists. Their publications are more apt to limit statistical significance to distributions that exhibit relationships which could have occurred by chance but one time or less in a hundred. On the other hand, they must accept greater responsibility than a typical sociologist for rejecting the significance of considerably more distributions that do in fact accurately reflect the larger empirical scene.[23] In illustrating the case that "The Scientist *Qua* Scientist Makes Value Judgments," Richard Rudner puts the issue bluntly:

> . . . no analysis of what constitutes the method of science would be satisfactory unless it comprised some assertion to the effect that the scientist as scientist accepts or rejects hypotheses. But if this is so then clearly the scientist as scientist does make value judgments. For, since no scientific hypothesis is ever completely verified, in accepting an hypothesis the scientist must make the decision that the evidence is *sufficiently* strong or that the probability is *sufficiently* high to warrant the acceptance of the hypothesis. . . . How sure we will need to be before we accept a hypothesis will depend on how serious a mistake would be.[24]

The adjective "serious" throws the door wide open to the realm of subjective valuation. Rudner goes on to speculate regarding the level of sampling error that those involved in the Manhattan Project had accepted *vis-à-vis* the likelihood that the atomic chain reaction initiated within the University of Chicago squash court might have simply moved on to include other elements and thus have transformed the earth into a miniature sun or whether this issue had even been seriously confronted. Sampling error may be seldom introduced as a conscious factor in the activities and decisions of physical scientists, for they are inclined to presume that the materials they have access to have been physically equated with the larger "universe" from which they are drawn or that a sample of any useful size represents such a huge accumulation of the elementary particles involved that it operates for all intents and purposes as a "universe" itself.

It can and has been argued that the application of the logic of science does not seek to "validate" hypotheses but simply to establish probability statements. At least one philosopher of science has argued that the actual step of accepting or rejecting a hypothesis *is* a nonscientific one. The point is a valid one insofar as it is an admission that an existential choice is indeed involved in verification. But the thesis that it is not an integral part of the research role could not be taken seriously without ignoring the fact that scientists go ahead to base other decisions—whether or not to replicate the study, whether prior theories should now be abandoned, whether or not research should take new directions in the light of the findings—upon the "weight" they actually do grant the new evidence. In other words, even though a few may profess verbally to interpret the data as not involving any determination on their part whether or not the hypothesis had been rejected, their actual behavior thereafter is exceedingly clear evidence that they *do* decide to accept or reject the *significance* of the findings, operational evidence that would seem more convincing than any verbal statement to the contrary. Rudner (1953:4) goes on to argue, in fact, that even the acceptance of probability statements involves a probability of error:

> . . . the determination that the degree of confirmation is, say, *p*, or that the strength of evidence is such and such, . . . is clearly nothing more than *the acceptance by the scientist of the hypothesis that the degree of confidence is p or that the strength of evidence is such and such*; and, as these men have conceded, acceptance of hypotheses does require value decisions.

Most sociologists are unaware of the moral nature of the act of verification, for they simply appropriate the levels of acceptable error that appear as the common definition of the term "significant" in the sociological literature with which they are acquainted. Because they themselves do not feel that they are introducing personal standards of verification they are not likely to conceive of the step as in any way at odds with the image they have of their value-free role, although by the very act of choosing to fall back on the group's traditional standards they ignore what might have been their own personal criteria of "significance."

C. Wright Mills's habit of being little impressed with public rationales and self-images put him in a position to perceive at least some of the implications of all of this for sociology (1959:71–72).

> For what level of verification ought workers in social science be willing to settle? We could of course become so exacting in our demands that we should necessarily have nothing but very detailed exposition; we could become so inexac-

ting that we should have only very grand conceptions indeed.

Those in the grip of the methodological inhibition often refuse to say anything about modern society unless it has been through the fine little mill of The Statistical Ritual. It is usual to say that what they produce is true even if unimportant.

Precision is not the sole criterion for choice of method; certainly precision ought not to be confused, as it so often is, with "empirical" or "true." We should be as accurate as we are able to be in our work upon the problems that concern us. But no method, as such, should be used to delimit the problems we take up, if for no other reason than that the most interesting and difficult issues of method usually begin where established techniques do not apply.

Only recently have the official media of the profession deemed the problem worth airing. But in so doing (in an article in the *American Sociologist* headed, appropriately enough "The Sacredness of .05") the discipline has taken an impressive step toward acknowledging the claims that the prophetic mode would make of her. The paper in reference—written by J. K. Skipper, A. L. Guenther, and G. Nass—states quite baldly that not only should the substantive nature of the problem dictate which type of error—the risk of accepting a hypothesis when it is false as against the risk of rejecting it when it is true—is to be minimized, but also that, rather than establishing a specific level of error as the criterion of significance ahead of time, one should report the actual level of significance in conjunction with each finding. Indeed, the authors argue that it is the *ethical* responsibility of sociologists to recognize the statistical lack of sophistication of the layman and thus to present his materials in a fashion that is substantively intelligible to him.[25]

But most of all we need to be honest with ourselves. Verification is an act that involves risk and demands faith, just as any other distinctively human action must. Here at the very heart of the "objective" procedure of science we are forced to make choices either actively or by default that witness to our larger system of values.

Purity in Science: Ego Versus Alter?

Sociologists are almost universally adamant in insisting that a value-free sociology need not concern itself with the application of its findings. As one has put it, "The general position which science takes is that it is indifferent to its use. It need not be used at all, except to further research. 'Who' uses knowledge is relevant only if we first assume that knowledge will be used. The assumption that knowledge will be used is based upon an action premise, and not one of inquiry."[26] Yet we have seen that at each of the other stages involved in social research we have come to examine we could not in truth claim that a value-free posture was possible even in principle. Could it be that the capstone to the traditional catechism —that the scientist's neutrality *vis-à-vis* the issue of application—is no more freed of implicit valuation than research in its earlier phases? Here the value-judgments that are in fact involved are even more discreetly hidden behind labels that gained currency within the natural sciences a number of generations ago. I refer to the commonplace distinction between the "pure" and the "applied" sciences. Sociology has laid claim to the former, relegating the latter as far as it has been able to distinctly separate disciplines. This move has, of course, helped clarify functions and improved efficiency in academic organization. But it also associates sociologists with the not-so-subtly attractive image of "purity" as well, an image that itself rings a judgmental bell. "Pure" science is characterized as being an end in and of itself, and thus freed somehow from contamination by the marketplace of utility.

But when we view the issue *motivationally*, the distinction between pure research and applied research pales. Applied research does indeed satisfy needs—or seeks to do so. But so does pure research: It seeks to satisfy man's curiosity—a very deeply felt need for many men. The usual contrast between the ends of science in and of themselves on the one hand and the pragmatic demands of the marketplace on the other may just as easily be seen instead as a contrast between the self-centered satisfaction of a scientist's own felt need—the itch of unsatiated curiosity—on the one hand, as over against the felt needs of non-scientists on the other. The pleasant connotations that accompany "purity" begin, then, to fade. In their place emerges an image of self-interest. The adjective "pure" is an understandable product of the peculiar self-interest of the scientist *vis-à-vis* others who fail to feel the same need, or if they do, who fail to feel it as deeply as the scientist. The decision on the part of sociologists to abdicate responsibility for the applied function may no longer be seen as a consistent manifestation of a value-free stance. It is rather an embarrassingly real value-judgment—the preference for satisfying one's own needs rather than the needs of others. All of this is modified by the fact that the scientist is very much a member of a community—the community of science. And so the achievement of his own ends do indeed contribute to the fulfillment of the ends of the many others who identify themselves as part of that community. But the analysis in terms of self-interest is simply shifted to a group level. He chooses to meet the needs of his group and to devalue the felt needs of other groups who make up much the larger part of the total social fabric of which he is a dependent part.

Examined on the motivational level, then, the indifferent pose that sociologists currently affect may no more be tolerated as in truth indicative of a value-free stance than would a declaration of indifference on the part of one's spouse be accepted as a value-free statement in the context of the marriage relationship. In both cases one declares for *self* and in doing so inevitably denigrates the interests of the other.[27]

The point of this discussion is not that research which has been called euphemistically by the term "pure" is in fact "bad." It can indeed be a very great good. All I am saying here is that the old scientist's tale that indifference to application is to be justified by the value-free nature of science is sheer rubbish—but rubbish packaged so attractively and distributed so widely from so many admirable retail outlets that the scientist himself has become a "true believer." He is even less aware of its role as a disguise cloaking his self-interest than is the general public.

There have been, fortunately, a handful within the community of science with the perception and courage to voice their misgivings and to do so from widely disparate world views. Bronislaw Malinowski, Alfred North Whitehead, and Bertrand Russell stand out among them.[28] Even sociologists have not been completely immune to a sense of corporate accountability, for Talcott Parsons (1951a:43) has been willing to speak of "the scientist's obligation of responsible integrity in his role as trustee for society of the knowledge he possesses and hence in certain respects of responsibility for its uses." But it is Sidney Willhelm (1964:181–82) who is most suggestive, for he finds the priestly stance akin to the axiom that has been traditional to any aristocracy. "The elevated aristocrat aspires to sustain his power, while simultaneously he perceives no necessity to validate his behavior through an ideology that commits him to others or to generalized moral principle. . . . The aristocratic contention is simply, 'We do because we are.' " And is it only coincidental that mankind's first aristocracy took the form of a "priesthood"?

Knowledge *of* man is not neutral in its import; it grants power *over* man as well. And if power is to be dissociated from responsibility, we must at least acknowledge that the decision is embedded in valuation. As Peter Berger (1963:152) has observed, "there is an ethically sinister possibility in knowing the machinery of the rules . . . every sociologist is a potential saboteur or swindler, as well as a putative helpmate of oppression." We *do* live in a world of conflicting values. One may justifiably hold that it is preferable to jettison the issue of application, but this is not to act in a neutral fashion. Value-neutrality is a concept devised by man to assist him in achieving certain ends. It should never be taken simply at face value. Rather, one must assess the larger context that includes motivation and the use of scarce resources—the society's investment in the nurture of the child-become-scientist—as well.[29] In point of fact the cold winds of neutrality that have swept through sociology over the last two or three decades have been accompanied by an uninhibited scramble for research sponsorship wherever the financial support was forthcoming. Somehow the value-free quality of sociology was protected if hard cold cash called the tune rather than the sociologist himself. The dollar was simply exempted from the analysis of biasing factors.[30]

Pure research is not even in principle value-free. It is, rather, an astutely chosen term that reflects the priority granted by the scientist to the satisfaction of one of his own pressing felt needs and the depreciation of the felt needs of non-scientists. Pure? Perhaps, although it might be more appropriate to substitute the phrase "purely to the self-interest of the scientific community." And this, surely, cannot be equated with the implication that the scientist is somehow outside of the undulating stream of value-commitment that courses through the public domain. Indifference to all but one's own interests is not neutrality.[31]

We have looked at six phases of the research process that necessarily call forth value-judgments from those involved—judgments that demand criteria that lie beyond the immediate "givens" of the rhetoric of science. They centered about the selection of a problem, choice of concepts, preference among logics, investment in a particular hypothesis, the level of error one is willing to risk, and whether one will opt for the interests of non-scientists or only for one's own or those of his sub-community when faced with responsibility for applying his findings. Although the evidence offered would seem sufficient to defrock the sociological "priest" of his value-free cloak, it is by no means complete. For we shall now examine those additional aspects of social research that not only deny the neutrality of sociologists but may demand an implicit commitment beyond that normally assumed by the community of science as well. In other words, the sociologist *qua* sociologist may not only be forced in principle to abandon his neutralist pose, but his activity may introject a consistent and identifiable ideologically relevant bias within his larger social context as well.

The Commitments of Social Research

No one enters here who is not a dialectician.
Georges Gurvitch

Science as a Normative Enterprise

IN Chapter 7 we attempted to determine the degree to which sociologists must be prepared to acknowledge that even when involved in social research they are unable to avoid making value-judgments that lie beyond empirical adjudication. We suggested that if such trans-empirical judgment were impossible to deny, then the current reclamation of the prophetic mode in sociology could be expected to be more than merely a temporary manifestation of the larger activism that engulfed America and her younger sociologists in the 1960's. It might even imply, we pointed out, that the struggle between the system and conflict paradigms may in fact be but a function of a more fundamental shift from the priestly posture back toward the prophetic stance.

Logic and sociology of science

But before moving on to examine further evidence bearing upon the issue, a few comments concerning the very real differences that exist between the "sociology" and the "logic" of science would seem in order. Logicians recently have come to appreciate the gap that has always existed between the neat path that proof wends through an empirical exercise and the actual process of scientific

---

Notes to this chapter will be found on pages 347–351.

research. This development has been long awaited and speaks well of the influence that sociologists and psychologists of science are beginning to register upon the philosophic and larger scientific communities.

On the other hand some scientists may be tempted to dissolve the distinction between the two perspectives altogether. Indeed, the present volume may seem at times to be suffering from the same temptation. That is not, however, its intent, for the tasks of the two perspectives are quite distinct. A *sociology* of science, if it is to be considered within the circle of science itself, registers its findings, as we have already pointed out, in the indicative mood. Thus it is satisfied to describe, when examining the activities of scientists themselves, the behavior they exhibit, projecting it over time in the form of predictive generalizations. The *logic* of science is, however, a normative discipline; its findings are cast in the imperative. Once the end of science is defined as increased efficiency in the ordering of empirical phenomena over time—as is indeed the case today—then its *logic* may not settle for the mere description and projection of the behavior of scientists involved in research. Rather it becomes the servant of the community's corporate commitment, reflecting that commitment in the imperative voice with which she speaks.

The preceding two paragraphs have been set down to clarify the use, in portions of the present chapter, of what some might be tempted to disparage as but a "reconstructed logic" of science. Although Abraham Kaplan has recently (1964) offered an exceptionally persuasive case for what he has termed a "logic-in-use," it is clear that he is not unappreciative of the necessary distinction between a sociology (or psychology) of science and a logic of science, nor that he is unaware of the normative aspects of the latter.[1] Still, the immediate pages ahead must be characterized as "an idealization of scientific practice." Such an "idealization" accentuates a "context of justification" rather than a "context of discovery" and does so intentionally without belittling the sociological significance of the latter. It is simply that the "ideal-typical" approach we associate with Weber more nearly meets the clearly delimited purpose the immediately following discussion has in mind.

All empirical proof is ultimately tied to the logic of the experiment, while the logic of the experiment focuses on the issue of control.[2] The logic that has come to be the common vehicle of proof (of "justification" in ideal-typical terms) throughout the sciences—even when it is not consciously or systematically applied—is what John Stuart Mill called the "Method of Difference." Although Mill set forth five "Methods" underlying what Kaplan would characterize as the scientific "logic-in-use" of his day—"Difference," "Agreement," "Difference and Agreement," "Concomitant Variation," and "Residue"—the last two were merely approximations of the first three. He perceived that hypothetical links between two empirical configurations could be tested either by approximating a situation in which all the factors in the two configurations were *different* except one (the "Method of Agreement") or by approximating a situation in which two configurations demonstrated every factor *in common* but one (the "Method of Difference"). Both methods established criteria that could only be approximated empirically, but at the same time it was clear that the former method—that of "Agreement"—would be much more difficult to approach physically. Thus it was the latter route that came to be identified with the quite pragmatically derived logic of research that natural scientists label the "experimental method." The Method of Agreement serves as a restatement—after the fact—of the rational elements entering into semiconscious or subconscious comprehension of productive hypotheses, and thus a kind of implicit "logic-in-use."

Method of difference

With the Method of Difference, one began (again, in ideal-typical and skeletal form) with two configurations identical in every way. One—designated the control group—was to be held constant, while a new factor was to be introduced into the other—the experimental group. The consequent difference between the control and experimental groups could then be attributed to the factor introduced.

There are two particularly crucial steps in the process. One lies at the very beginning in equating the experimental and control groups. Although relatively easy to approximate in the physical sciences, it is elaborately demanding in the biological sciences where species must be bred over many generations to eliminate major variations in hereditary make-up. In the social and behavioral sciences even the proximate equating of experimental and control groups by physical means is impossible; yet there is no logic of proof apart from experimental logic. Thus the Method of Difference must be approximated by *selection* (by rough matching or by canceling out major differences through random sampling), which is in turn performed either physically in the present or symbolically through an *ex post facto* selection of relevant data.

After resolving the issue of the degree to which control and experimental groups can be equated by physical selection as against the liability of an *ex post facto* matching or randomization of what are but symbolic representations of a human sample, sociologists face the second critical step. They must try to introduce control at another level, in actually differentiating an experimental group from a control group. Here physical control is possible, although exceedingly difficult. Man is reluctant enough to be designated merely a statistical means to another's ends, whatever category he is assigned. When his actions are to be "controlled"—either negatively by consciously depriving him of something you grant to others of similar background (as would be the case if he remained part of the control group) or positively by treating him in a manner in which you do *not* treat the others (as would be the case if he remained within the experimental group)—he can be expected to be resentful and at least potentially uncooperative.[3] But again, the more thoroughly such control can be introduced, the closer one can approximate the canon of the logic of proof common to the community that is science. Contemporary sociologists more often than not decide that they are unable or unwilling to overide this resentment and settle instead for *ex post facto* symbolic manipulation.

Sociologists, then, are faced with decisions involving how much pressure to exert to bring individuals into their samples and the degree to which they should accept responsibility for changing or denying change to them.[4] They must make their choice knowing that, other things being equal, increased control will enhance the validity of their conclusions. In other words, not only does the logic of empirical proof involve an implicit commitment favoring *change per se*, but the sociologist's end is furthered in direct proportion to the degree to which the behavior of all those involved (*except sociologists*) are subject to the *controls* that are integral to experimental logic. Howard Becker (1950: 296) went so far as to characterize the commitment of scientists as a "faith in the possibility and supreme desirability of control . . . ," going on to observe that "the secular society in which he [the scientist] has grown up and which sanctions his preference system is endowed with sacred values by his enterprise; the quest for control [thus] becomes the quest for the Holy Grail."

Ethical restraints on physical controls

Now this may not be the kind of statement that would immediately endear one to those who have felt peculiarly burdened by the public's image of sociology, but it can be disputed on only one possible ground, and that is to point out, as I have already admitted, that most social research to date has limited itself to correlational analogies to experimental logic or to the *ex post facto* manipulation of symbols—to data *about* man rather than seeking to manipulate man himself. This is quite true, as is the fact that techniques of multiple and partial correlation, along with rather deft sampling methods, have carried us even further in the direction of approximating the essential logic of experimental proof while freeing us from the onus of actually experimenting upon fellow human beings. But these advances do not alter the immediate and direct relationship between the application of controls and the degree of confidence one can place in one's proof. All it tells us is that sociologists *qua* sociologists have been quite sensitive to what have been deemed "extra-scientific" considerations regarding the degree to which they would insist upon approximating the logic of the experiment, that they have all along introduced judgments of value that have no ultimate empirical legitimation into the very heart of social research. They have been moved by the values of their larger cultural tradition to compromise radically the ends they have as scientists, recognizing with that tradition that man cannot be characterized as fair game for whatever controls can be physically applied just so long as they increase our empirical knowledge of social behavior. It simply illustrates once again the very real way in which value-judgments must of necessity enter into the activity of the sociologist *qua* sociologist.

Implications of conceptual controls

But it also hides something of considerable long-range importance. Manipulating symbols of man rather than man himself may indeed be a greater actual threat to the traditional image of the humanity of man than any steps that have been taken to date to "control" him physically. Parsons (1951b:335–45) is among those few willing to acknowledge quite publicly that scientists find themselves forced to infringe upon the lives of others, although the illustrations he offers—the use of cadavers, the sensitivities of the Society for the Prevention of Cruelty to Animals, and the nuisance of being called upon to answer interviewers' questions—are startlingly at odds with his usual perceptiveness. But even those considerably more serious inroads made in the name of the behavioral sciences upon what Western man has come to look upon as his institutional and personal liberties—such as the use of hallucinogenic drugs and the tapping of jury deliberations—have been immediately halted when brought to the attention of the wider community, even though they have (at the time of this writing) as yet to result in the acceptance on the part of the discipline of any formal code of ethics. What sociologists appear completely unaware of is the long-run impact of coming to *conceive* of one's fellows as manipulable. Language—and the choice among symbols that it entails—pervades all meaningful social action, either overtly or covertly, consciously or unconsciously. The symbolic manipulation of man cannot be wholly isolated from the rest of a person's symbolically mediated relationships with others. As man's intellectual life more and more demands such symbolic manipulation, he runs the increasing risk of conceiving man in other areas of his life in terms that invite or are peculiarly amenable to a means-end relationship rather than those that support an attitude toward others as ends in and of themselves. Now this is clearly not in the order of a "clear and present danger" to the moral life of contemporary man, for social research does not yet play a major role in the total intellectual life of American society. If, however, such research should eventually guide the decisions that are made in all areas of our social life—as most of us would hope—the magnitude of the risk involved would become well worth considering. Even today one cannot help but be struck occasionally by evidence of routine, perhaps only semiconscious, manipulative behavior on the part of an occasional behavioral scientist who appears to have allowed a symbol system entirely appropriate to social research to invade the larger network of his symbolic interaction with others.

Social scientists, then, are caught up in a task whose logic demands that they enter the circle as agents of *change*. Furthermore, the substantive nature of that change —at least in this instance—is readily apparent. They must either conceive of their fellow human beings as manipulable or, preferably, take active steps to *control* their behavior, for the second option—lying as it does at the heart of the logic of the experiment—stands as the ultimate criterion for verification in science. It is no accident that *experiment* and *peril* are derived from the identical root. The common derivation should stand as an important reminder of the very real risk involved. Each person engaged in social research confronts the unavoidable task of judging the degree to which he is willing to compromise the certitude of his findings by modifying his involvement as an agent of change and control. It is a decision quite at odds with his priestly inclination to view himself simply as someone who communicates the "givens" of social "reality" and thus is one more indication that he is unable to remain, even in principle, value-free in his research activity.[5]

Observation and the Uncertainty Principle

Even if we were to ignore the rather complex manner in which control is inherent to the logic of experimental proof, we could not escape the fact that social research thrusts sociologists into a relationship with their subjects that involves an implicit or explicit value stance. Its root, indeed, is essentially the same as the paradoxical nature of one aspect of research in the physical and biological sciences, the unavoidable fact that observation has, as Planck puts it, "a more or less causal influence on the very process that is under observation."[6] Heisenberg, whose explorations in small-particle physics led to the enshrining of the phenomenon as a "principle" of physics, was more blunt. He saw such research as quite literally "transforming" its object.[7]

Although a considerable gap exists between the intellectual sub-cultures represented by the physical and the social sciences, sociologists and others speaking of or to the social sciences have begun to register their awareness of its implications.[8] Perhaps the classic Hawthorne study more than any other single incident has brought the potential effect of observation *per se* home to sociologists, documenting as it did the striking impact that the mere presence of a team of observers had upon industrial productivity. Talcott Parsons was quick to see that the scientist-subject relationship was itself a mutually interactive social system: "The point of origin for an observer's analysis of a system of action . . . must be such as to *include himself in the system being analyzed.*"[9] Parsons contends, however, that he is able to extract himself from the apparent paradox through *role* analysis, unaware, it would seem, that he has slipped back into a second net of unexamined conditioning factors by simply calling upon symbols that have themselves already been conditioned by the unique assumptions of science. Indeed, Parsons has gone so far in his search for an authority figure upon whom to rest his case as to read such role-duality into the methodological scriptures of Max Weber.[10] There is no evidence whatsoever that Weber made use of such a latter-day concept. If Weber had had access to the notion of role-playing, it might have ameliorated the disastrous manner in which his mind and spirit periodically succumbed to the strain of living out the contradictory commitments in his life. I use the term "ameliorated" rather than "resolved" consciously, for the role device, of which I have already spoken at length in Chapter 6, has proven no more durable an access to objectivity than has Mannheim's early faith in a free-floating intelligentsia or Marx's idealization of the proletariat. That an abandonment of the role-playing device in this regard is risky is abundantly evident in the autobiographical revelations by John Seeley in his *The Americanization of the Unconscious*, which reveals the interactive impact of the observations made by the *Crestwood Heights* research team of which he was a part. But this is exactly the point that is slowly dawning upon sociologists. Their observations *do* have an impact upon their subjects. If they all are as sensitive as John Seeley, they will find it impossible to prevent those reactions from feeding back into their non-sociological behavior.

Observation, thus, carries with it the same implicit commitment toward change *per se* as occurs in applying the controls that are part and parcel of experimental logic, change that is quite independent of the self-conscious interests of the subjects involved. Some may, of course, enjoy the attention they receive as subjects of research. More often, however, the opposite would appear to be true. The long-run impact on the subjects depicted in one recent community study led, if the town's newspaper is to be believed, to the inclusion in the annual Fourth of July parade of "a manure-spreader filled with very rich barnyard fertilizer, over which was bending an effigy of 'The Author'."

A widely utilized technique for minimizing the actual change—and thus the distortion—that occurs in the behavior of those being observed is to enter into the setting in a manner in which one's research role has been disguised. Those responsible for one such recent effort admitted, however, that "in deliberately cultivating a second self the research observer was engaged in something superficially like intelligence work or espionage."[11] One cannot help but wonder if the sociologists involved were able actually to convince themselves that they remained "ethically neutral." Julius Roth (1959:398) has listed a number of such "undercover" participant observation studies that had come quite casually to his attention, concluding that it took little or no specialized ability and admonishing his readers to "give it a try yourself." What could one lose—since sociologists are, after all, value-free? Lewis Coser, however, was willing to characterize the practice—which, in the particular case in question, involved the gathering of data of concern to the military—as a clear breach of professional ethics as well as a dangerous precedent.[12]

I would not wish to argue that disguised participant observation *per se* was or should be considered inappropriate ethically, for the sociological insight that might be derived might well be worth the price of the deception. It could be less objectionable than the disruption that would occur—say, in a therapeutic situation—by open and self-declared observation. But the issue is inescapably a moral one. One must decide the degree to which one is willing to accept the responsibility for interfering with an ongoing social process, for it is inevitable that one will do so to some degree in the shorter or longer run, whether the observational process is revealed or not. And one must judge the relative evils of deception on the one hand over against maximizing the disruptive influence on the other.

Although the phrase has been highlighted recently as the subtitle of an important recent volume titled *Unobtrusive Measures*, there is no such thing as completely "nonreactive research in the social sciences."[13] When a sociologist attempts to order empirical social phenomena over time, he acts within an epistemological framework that assumes that all social action is ultimately *inter*-active. If not immediately "reactive," an *ex post facto* response remains, inadvertently if not consciously influencing to some degree comparable behavior by those who are made aware by the study that such data are to be utilized in social research. In many cases the feedback will appear imperceptible; however, it is always a potentially disruptive factor. Indeed, the publication of the volume helps illustrate the value-laden nature of social research, for it suggests that sociologists have become sensitized to the impact they have on their subject matter and would wish somehow to minimize it. An alternative route has been suggested recently by Severyn Bruyn's *The Human Perspective in Sociology* (1966). He would project an image of sociologists as "participant observers," thus intensifying immediate reactions to avail the discipline of those intimate insights that flow from direct involvement. To the extent that the observer is successful in melding into the scene as a participant, the reactive factor may be muted and, in the longer run, minimized.

We are forced to conclude, however, that observation is one more stage in social research which poses an array of dilemmas that cannot be resolved without reference to value standards whose roots lie in extra-scientific considerations and, whatever the resolution, impinge upon the lives of others in a manner inconsistent with the view that sociologists are simply neutral agents in what is in principle merely a cognitive activity. But this is not all. To the extent that the procedures used affect the subjects under observation, they, like the actions involved in the logic of verification, represent an implicit commitment to *change*.

The Paradox of Prediction

Although embarrassed by many of their founding father's visions, sociologists are fond of quoting Auguste Comte's "*voir pour prévoir*" (to see in order to foresee) as an appropriate characterization of the activity of both science in general and sociology in particular. They tend, however, to ignore the fact that the phrase was followed immediately by a second: "*prévoir pour prévenir*" (to foresee in order to anticipate). The distinction between the two may at first seem inconsequential. But when it is read in the light of the transforming role Comte pictured for the science of sociology, it is very suggestive indeed. For the verb "anticipate" includes within its range of meaning a more active element than does "foresee." To anticipate something may suggest not simply that the actor foresees the likely course of events, but that he acts in some way in response to that foresight. He "anticipates" that which he "foresees" in some active manner.

Impact of knowledge

One of the very few discussions of the logic of social science specifically directed to the introductory student of sociology (Doby, 1954:5) states that one of the assumptions underlying the sociological enterprise is that "the real world is not changed by our knowledge of it." The author is not being entirely misleading, for this would appear to be the view that lies at the base of almost all contemporary sociological theory and research. The trouble is that the epistemology at the heart of most sociology today is quite dated. Alan Gewirth (1954:229–

41) posed the issue rather bluntly more than a decade ago by hazarding the question, "Can Man Change Laws of Social Science?" It would seem not only that he can but that he cannot avoid so doing. Edward Shils (1961:1413) appeared to sense the roots of the problem when he observed that:

> In purely cognitive respects, sociology could be a science like any other science, and it might well become such. Sociology is not, however, a purely cognitive undertaking. It is also a moral relationship between human beings studied and the student of the human beings. . . . Problems are raised by this relationship that sociologists have not yet resolved but which they cannot lightly disregard.
>
> I am quite confident that the rhetoric of the natural sciences, which are not in communication with the data of their inquiries, will have to be considerably revised for the purposes of sociology. This applies equally to reports on the most concrete research and to abstract theoretical treatises, and no less to theories of the middle range.

"To see in order to foresee"

Natural scientists seek to order the empirical world by discovering uniformities over time in the sequence of events that enter into the range of their interest. Although they examine what may appear to be unique phenomena or constellations of phenomena, they do so to extract from them or to see in them processes that are stable over time and thus are capable of generalization. We "see in order to foresee"—in order to predict future events or constellations of events. We also seek "understanding." But when understanding is spelled out operationally, it means "*voir pour prévoir.*" Evidence that such order *can* be extracted from the infinite complexities of the animate and inanimate world lies all about us. The dramatic successes of the physical and biological sciences and the insights that have stemmed from the social and behavioral sciences cannot help but convince even the most thoroughgoing existentialist that nature is permeated by stable processes and interactions.

"To foresee in order to anticipate"

But recall Comte's second phrase: "*prévoir pour prévenir*"—to foresee in order to anticipate. One of the curious abilities of man—and of a small but increasing number of electronic devices built by him—is that he not only is able to "foresee" but can "anticipate" as well. He can, in other words, *learn*. The capacity to readjust his behavior in response to regularities in his past experience appears to be a quality that entered into the phylogenetic history of protoplasmic organization at a very early stage.

Social and natural science

The logic of science is nothing more than a self-conscious statement of the means by which man tries to maximize the communal reliability and efficiency of his attempt to dislodge evidence of order—of sequences stable over time—from the "givens" of his empirical experience. It has been the gradual self-conscious *awareness* of this capacity, along with its systematic application, which we have come to call "science." Man has given a number of centuries to the task of comprehending this process as it applied to the physical and biological worlds but has failed to come to complete agreement over how it should be conceptualized. He has addressed himself to the same task in the social and psychological arena for a much shorter time, so it is not surprising that an even wider range of ambiguity hampers our efforts to come to grips with the degree to which this effort should be equated with or differentiated from the concepts that have proven fruitful in delineating the essential processes of learning in the physical and biological sciences. Sociologists have, as we have already seen, come down quite heavily on the side of a unitary logic. The paradigm for systematic learning in the social and behavioral realm has been equated with the essential rhetoric followed in the physical and biological realms.

There is no doubt that the identification has paid off in private and public support for the social sciences and in the power and prestige that this in turn has meant. And this has had its salutary effect. Sociologists have been freed from the somewhat manic drive to create a social utopia that had dominated their adolescence and have instead been encouraged to draw from the larger scientific community a sense of humility toward and dedication to the process of discovery itself. Unfortunately it has also provided him with a whole array of vested reasons to ignore factors that might differentiate the logic of his discipline from that of his elder brothers. And the prime casualty has been the loss in awareness of the significance of Comte's latter phrase, "*prévoir pour prévenir*."

Both "to see in order to foresee" and "to foresee in order to anticipate" are, as I have pointed out, most integral to the entire spectrum of the sciences. But the implication of the latter phrase is radically different in the social and behavioral sciences from what it is in the physical and biological. It may mean in both that knowledge of stable empirical sequences *may* be used in an anticipating way to alter the arrangement of those elements we have discovered within our physical, biological, or social environments. But of critical importance to the social and behavioral sciences alone is the fact that *the very discovery* of a stable social sequence must inevitably, by the very grammar that adheres to social or behavioral research, act to some degree as a new and unique element in the stream of empirical events that make up social and behavioral interaction. No matter what uniformities we uncover in the activity of sub-atomic particles or the chemical processes involved in the cell, that knowledge *alone* would appear to have no effect upon the order perceived.[14] The interactions will go their merry way regardless of our new knowledge of them. With that knowledge we may consciously alter the arrangement and prevalence of the particular atomic or organic processes of which we have become aware. But that knowledge by itself has no effect upon the recurrence of the sequences discovered.

This is not the case at the behavioral level. The simple *awareness of uniformities* that accompanies validation in the behavioral sciences is a cognitive factor which interacts with other cognitive factors that contribute to the matrix out of which the uniformities were originally precipitated. The result is a magnificent paradox. The social scientist's perception of uniformities represents *a new and unique event* that by its very appearance must to some degree in the shorter or longer run operate to deny the full validity of the perceived sequence when he seeks to reconfirm at a later time the order apprehended earlier. The logic of the social and behavioral sciences is, thus, unavoidably *paradoxical*.

Its significance is rather staggering. It means that the search for "laws" of human nature and for *fundamental* social processes that are *in principle* stable is ultimately destined to be futile. It also means that the contrast between pure and action research in the social sciences is a false contrast. *All* social research is in principle action research, with variations that can be legitimately characterized only in terms of degree, even though the degrees involved may be great. It means that if social determinism is evidenced operationally by the repetition of associated interactive factors and freedom by the appearance of the uniquely new, then the logic of social science is in principle a liberating logic, its grammar a transcending grammar.

Self-fulfilling and suicidal prophecies

Many sociologists will be tempted to respond immediately that the central thesis that I have put forth here is hardly new, that in fact it was given wide currency among sociologists long ago by Robert Merton (1949: 184–93) in his well-known essay, "The Self Fulfilling Prophecy." Merton did indeed reveal an awareness that man's cognitive expectations alter his behavior; but neither that awareness nor the particular form in which he put it (that bias *vis-à-vis* out-groups is accompanied by behavior which in turn leads to the fulfillment of such stereotypes) appear particularly revealing. A reference to "suicidal" prophecy was relegated to a brief footnote. The revised edition of *Social Theory and Social Structure* is, however, considerably more instructive. There Merton acknowledges, for instance, that such prediction "peculiar to human affairs . . . not found among predictions about the world of nature, . . . will enter into the situation as a *new and dynamic* factor, changing the very conditions under which the prediction initially held true." Indeed, he describes the situation as paradoxical, and mentions that "because it is familiar, it is conscientiously neglected, not systematically followed up in its implications" (1957: 129–30). Unfortunately, he himself fails to see its "systematic" implications. He is unaware that the phenomenon adheres to the logic of research in the social sciences *per se*. Unconsciously wed to the assumption that has proven so fruitful in the physical sciences—that "the real world is not changed by our knowledge of it"—Merton ignores, as have almost all Western sociologists, the full significance of what he confronts. Having discovered the dialectical logic of Marx and Engels to be of little or no value in ordering the inanimate world, the community of science in the West inverts the mistake made by Marxist science by failing to take dialectical logic seriously in social research.

Ernest Nagel, however, did seem to be disturbed enough by the potential inroads it might make upon a unitary philosophy for Western science to have proffered an elaborate counter-argument. He begins his rebuttal with embarrassingly reductive and outrageously unlikely examples involving the conceivable interference of the electronic communication elements linking a radar mechanism with the firing mechanism of an anti-aircraft weapon (and vice versa) in order to argue that such an interactive logic is not peculiar to the social sciences.[15] He goes on, however, to suggest that the apparent paradox dissolves when we recognize that all scientific laws are *conditional*. But to continue fabricating them without reference to their empirical probability also would seem to be in turn conditional, the latter condition being that one didn't mind building an edifice of fairy tales. He goes on to argue that "it is in fact sometimes possible to foresee, if only in a general way, what are the likely consequences for established social habits of the acquisition of new knowledge or new skills" (1961:471). The reservation is completely acceptable *if* we do not overlook the leeway Nagel provided for himself by using terms such as "sometimes," "in a general way," "likely," and "established social habits." He follows with a warning that "it is . . . easy to exaggerate the controlling role of deliberate choice in the determination of human events" (1951:472). From this point he infers that the rational "foresight" gained from social research, which might shake men loose from established patterns of ordered response, would in fact be typically overwhelmed by the restraints imposed by the culture in question. One can only point out that the paradoxical nature of social research does not in any way depend upon a deliberate, rational, or even conscious utilization of generalized information, although it is easy to sympathize with Nagel's generally pessimistic image of man's capacity to be moved by the merely rational. Strangely enough, however, he ends with a footnote reference to contemporary "game theory," suggesting that it could provide a framework within which the paradox could be handled. It is strange because, as we have already seen, game theory *assumes* complete rationality on the part of the participants—given the weighting of risks—and Nagel had just finished arguing that men were capable of little rational action at odds with institutionalized pressures.

Contrast with programed feed-back

A more casual way of denying significance to the paradoxical nature of prediction in the social and behavioral sciences is simply to label it a "feed-back" phenomenon and to infer, thereby, that it is something one might encompass rather neatly through the programing of digital computers. And although provision for feed-back is indeed built into their circuitry, such feed-back demands programing in advance. The fundamental paradox that confronts one in social research is incapable *in principle* of being provided for through advance programing, no matter how much information is available regarding man's behavior in analogous situations. Not only does knowledge of the degree and nature of past order introduce a new item into the matrix of elements involved; but even when a factor to compensate for one's previous experience with feed-back is added, its adequacy is in turn subject to the very same paradoxical fracture.[16]

But this does not mean that social scientists will never succeed in predicting the nuances of micro-social behavior or even, indeed, in projecting the gross outlines of certain dimensions of history. I am in hearty agreement with the efforts extended in these directions and seek myself to contribute to them. All it means is that in principle social scientists unavoidably destroy—imperceptibly much of the time, grossly at others—the validity of their own projections. To ignore this fact, as sociologists and other social and behavioral scientists presently appear to do, is to attempt to stride along the path of social science on but one leg.

The dialectical nature of social science

I have used the term "paradoxical" in characterizing the phenomenon before us; I was tempted to use the term "dialectical" instead. For Hegel's formulation of the thesis-antithesis-synthesis trinity does appear to be the peculiar logic in question, and Marx would appear to have applied it fruitfully at many points in his extensive historical forays. Marx's eleventh thesis on Feuerbach—that philosophers have only interpreted the world, the point is to change it; Engel's (1962:157) paraphrase of Hegel in which he claims that "freedom does not consist in the dream of independence from natural laws, but in the knowledge of these laws"; and the claim that scientific laws themselves are alterable—all these appear to be congenial to the dialectical frame.

Unfortunately, neither Marx, Engels, nor Lenin subscribed to the logic I have put forth, for none were in the final analysis wholeheartedly dialectical. Their primary commitment was to the noun "materialism" rather than to the adjective conditioning it. When the implications of a thorough-going dialectical analysis threatened the crusade against what they deemed "idealism," they would abandon man for nature. Lenin could say that the concept "matter"—to which their system was finally anchored—". . . epistemologically implies *nothing but* objective reality existing independently of the human mind and reflected by it." The mind, thus, was in no position to alter natural laws, for it acted only to mirror nature. "To be a materialist is to acknowledge objective truth . . . truth not dependent upon man and mankind . . . absolute truth."[17] In addition, Engels (1962:157) found that it was at least as easy to conceive of freedom as a product of necessity as vice versa; ". . . the *freer* man's judgment is," he wrote, "the greater is the *necessity* with which the content of this judgment will be determined."

A dialectical mode more congenial to the paradoxical nature of prediction in the social and behavioral sciences has been detailed in Georges Gurvitch's *Dialectique et Sociologie*. He makes clear that, unlike the Marxist tradition, the dialectical mode is *not* particularly fruitful in scientific analysis at the physical or biological level—only at the social. Although it is not excluded from the analysis of the *processes* of science in general—because science is a human and communal activity—it has a special relevance to the revelations that spring out of social research. He acknowledges that social scientists must act upon the assumption that there are deterministic networks to be unraveled, that there is no alternative to a causal analysis in ordering social data. Yet the ultimate product of such an assumption in fact mitigates against the stability of the order revealed. Thus through the very activity of social research itself, social reality continually steps outside of the ordered network in which sociologists perceive it and turns every closed system of theory into a self-defeating fiction.

Gurvitch has not been entirely alone in appreciating the implications of the classic observation that those who could not remember the past were condemned to repeat it. Had Karl Mannheim's life not been cut short, he might have more fully resolved the dilemma he had earlier posed in taking the sociology of knowledge even more seriously than had Marx himself. From a position that would naïvely exempt the intellectual from the social conditioning that he saw dominating the ideologies and utopias offered by the bourgeoisie and the proletariat, he had begun toward the end of his life to articulate a faith in the emancipating process of social science itself. Neither class nor the elimination of class could emancipate man from the compulsions of his culture or subculture; but self-conscious involvement in the dialectic of social-scientific enlightenment and societal reconstruction might.

George Herbert Mead's training in philosophy apparently provided him with the breadth and conceptual framework necessary to catch a glimpse of something of the same process. For Mead went beyond the natural scientific assumption that effects could at least in principle be reduced to their causes by arguing that there was in the effect an "emergent" that in turn would condition the context such that the so-called "effect" was incapable of being deduced from the so-called "cause."[18] American sociologists, although acknowledging Mead as perhaps their most creative theorist, appeared to extract from his larger pragmatic humanism only those portions that would fit into the mold of an epistemology borrowed from natural science.

But the sensitive eye and mind do exist. Not perhaps in the sociological texts, although even here the last paragraph of Simpson and Yinger's *Racial and Cultural Minorities* speaks almost directly to the point: "it may well be . . . that an understanding of the nature of events is a new variable that changes the results. . . ." But they too fall back on the comfortable reservation that "the laws are still true—*if*." If, we might add, social scientists give up the effort to *predict* and limit themselves to unraveling order in the past.

Werkmeister shows a very real appreciation of the phenomenon under discussion, seeing it, however, as a factor that limits a sociologist's role rather than endowing it with special importance.[19] Barber views it similarly, suggesting that it provides a rationale for limiting oneself to short-range predictions only, although he does not go on to make the additional observation that Gurvitch would make, that one should therefore limit one's theory construction to the short-range as well.[20] Barrington Moore appears to grasp its implications more fully. He points out that the very logic of the social and behavioral sciences may not be entirely congruent with the "hard" sciences, that the Hegelian dialectic might provide a more adequate support. The difference lies not simply in the degree to which we may have confidence in our generalizations; it is a matter of "principle" as well. "Increases in knowledge about human society have contradictory results. . . . As we learn more about a political and economic situation in the attempt to forecast its outcome, the additions to our knowledge thereby change the situation and increase the number of possible ways in which it can turn out."[21]

The theorems offered by John Seeley that we discussed earlier focus upon essentially the same phenomenon, but project "freedom" as the paradoxical product. As social scientists inevitably intervene in the social process in the course of their research (the "social science is action" theorem), and because that intervention in principle alters and/or increases their potential subject matter (the "inexhaustibility" theorem), the theoretical posture they bring to their research acts as a *new factor* to break the chain of the recurrent that natural scientists assume as they seek to generalize from their observations of empirical phenomena over time (the "freedom" theorem). In other words, the deterministic chain is broken by social scientists as they react to the awareness they have of the regularities they believe they have discovered in their research. The argument is weak only at one point. Seeley states that *every theory* we may have regarding human behavior has this characteristic. Although no one involved in social research ever is completely certain that the evidence he has gathered of order in the social world does in fact reflect the universe of such equivalent phenomena, the peculiar paradox of which I speak is not operative unless or to the degree to which the order perceived was indeed an accurate reading of the empirical situation. Whenever a social scientist does isolate a specific manifestation of order in the social world, his awareness of that order represents an entirely new factor in that world and will feed back, through his own actions and the actions of those to whom he communicates that awareness, to deny to some degree the full validity *of that order* in the future. A researcher's theory or hypothesis will not exhibit this paradoxical tendency if it is not a reflection of actual empirical order, even though it might have an equivalent effect on a social scientist's behavior, for the *actual* factors responsible for the order he is examining may function as they had before because they remain untouched by the false assessment.

Paul Streeten's introduction to Myrdal's collected essays (1959:XXVIII) suggests, rather delightfully, that the typical sociologist may be playing a role today somewhat analogous to that played by that unhappy prophet, Jonah. Like Jonah, the sociologist makes relatively accurate predictions based upon what he has been persuaded is a correct reading of man's past. And although in both Jonah's case and the sociologist's the readings usually are accurate, both are upset and indignant over the fact that God's (nature's) hand somehow stays their execution. Jonah prophesied the destruction of Nineveh for its multiple transgressions, but the Ninevites heeded the prophecy and sought God's forgiveness through a radical return to His ways. And because the glory of God lay not in His justice but in His grace, they were indeed saved. In the process, Jonah's prophecy of their destruction was of course falsified. Hence a demoralized and indignant Jonah, for his claim to omniscience had clearly been denied. The parallel with the sociologist is clear. Actual or potential subjects are to some extent influenced to break out of routinized behavior as they gradually become aware of the behavior that is expected of them. And when they do, the sociologist is once again proven wrong and once again must return to the foot of the scientific—and academic—table, that is, unless he is aware of the paradoxical logic that adheres to his enterprise. If he is so aware, he may begin to identify with that which liberates as well as with that which orders. He might in fact go so far as to render unto the physical sciences that systematic order that is theirs and unto social man the dimension of spontaneity that is his.

Streeten goes on to point out that the projections of Marx and Toynbee illustrate the effect of prediction upon patterns of social regularity. The very truth of much of Marx's analysis of the nineteenth-century European and American bourgeoisie appears to have acted in part as a self-defeating prophecy as that bourgeoisie acceded to modifications in its power *vis-à-vis* the proletariat. Toynbee's role differed from Marx's in that he was aware of the paradoxical impact of historical generalization and so projected what he conceived to be the ordered rise and fall of civilizations to assist Western man in denying the continued validity of those projections. When one realizes the scale of the latter endeavor one is tempted to conclude that the effort represents one of the great self-mortifications of the human mind.

Other examples of the therapeutic impact of knowledge abound. Psychoanalytic therapy rests upon the profound reaction that may occur when a person becomes consciously aware of the links that tie his present compulsions to his personal history.[22] At least one analyst of Max Weber's view of history as a process of secularization, depersonalization, and bureaucratization has suggested that it was used by Weber semiconsciously as an intentionally self-defeating prophecy.[23] Certainly sociologists since Weber's time have responded to it in such a manner.

David Riesman's "other-directed" characterization, along with the work of dozens of other social observers, helped to short-circuit what might otherwise have been a rather prolonged period of unreflective conformity in American society. Certainly his addition of the category "autonomous man" to the otherwise self-contained fabric of the *Lonely Crowd* thesis has been quite revealing. Because "autonomy" was offered as an "ought," it confused the self-consciously value-free social scientists among his readers. Yet the phrase "autonomous man" stands as a most appropriate characterization of the social scientist himself, when he becomes aware of the manner in which his knowledge of social regularities acts to free him from their re-enactment.

The point of taking this elaborate excursion into the paradoxical logic that frames the social-scientific role should by now be quite apparent. Although the sociologist may try to project an image of himself as dedicated simply to the task Comte characterized by the phrase "*voir pour prévoir*," he is tied, like it or not, to the additional responsibility characterized by Comte in the terms "*prévoir pour prévenir*." The dialectic within which the discipline is caught invokes an implicit commitment to break free to some degree, however minor this may seem in any particular case, from the uniformities that his method has enabled him to perceive in the cross-currents of past social interaction. Rather than standing outside of the stream well insulated by value-proof garments, he commits himself in the most "pure" research to *altering* that stream, to frustrating the continuity of the rhythms that course through social existence, to freeing the future from the past. All this will occur in some measure even though he accepts no responsibility for communicating his findings to his subjects—or even to his fellow social scientists—for the initial and unavoidable change is the one that occurs in his own expectations and behavior as they respond to the new and unique recognition of past patterns. What he has been viewing as a neutral delineation of things as they are appears instead to involve a *commitment to change per se*. And for a sociologist of sociology it is almost equally important to realize that a wide sampling among those speaking to and for the larger discipline today are gradually displaying awareness of the essentially dialectical nature of their enterprise.

Communication as Change

Sociologists of science are quick to point out that science is a communal enterprise. Robert Merton, in fact, describes it as essentially "communistic" in character.

When they do so they do not intend simply to describe the proliferation of research "teams" and "institutes" that characterize the actual administration of much contemporary research. They mean rather that communication—the sharing of data and results—is integral to the nature of the beast. It is an essentially cumulative activity that has meaning only in terms of how it speaks to man's prior knowledge and how it may contribute to its further accumulation.

But the social nature of science is even more radically grounded. It is rooted in the definition of the term "empirical" itself. For the raw data of science, empirical evidence, is distinguished—and limited—by the fact that it must be amenable to observation, and thus verification, by more than one person. This is the heart of the criterion of "objectivity" that is the mark of science. Scientific research *must* be communicated to others in order to legitimate itself.

Although the preceding discourse about the paradoxical nature of social research was and can be isolated from the more or less formal communication by the scientist of the results of his research, almost all discussion of sociological "feed-back" or the "self-fulfilling" and "self-defeating" prophecies assumes that the interaction involved will be between the scientist and his subjects or audience. The impact of such processes, then, really belongs to the present phase of the argument rather than to the section just completed. Although the structure of the dialectical process is the same, in the former discussion the interaction involves the cognitive and evaluative processes of the scientist himself, whereas in the present case the interaction is an essentially cognitive one between the scientist and his larger audience.

American sociologists have shown surprisingly little concern with the issue of communication, although two recent developments may have stimulated interest in it. One was the selection of the question of *how* sociological work should be communicated to policy makers and the general public as the first theme of the meetings of the International Sociological Association in Washington in 1962. The second is the interest generated by the effort of the Council of the American Sociological Association to develop a code of ethics for its membership.

Gatekeepers to communication

When a social scientist sets out to communicate his findings, he finds himself engulfed in a series of decisions that only the extraordinarily naïve would seek to settle on the basis of the empirical data confronting him alone. A whole series of "gatekeepers" stand between him and effective communication with a wider public, not the least of which is the inner censor that Mead termed the "generalized other." A sociologist may or may not be astute enough to realize that, other things being equal, he will be responsible for changing the pattern of the very social interaction he confirms in direct proportion to the breadth and success of its communication. Nonetheless, the impact of his actions on others are no less real even if he is unaware of it.

The communication burden is shared by a whole covey of "gatekeepers" even as he seeks to communicate with his confreres in his own discipline: major professors, team directors, section chairmen, editors, editorial consultants, "referees" are all high on the list. Anyone who has shepherded a major piece of research through to publication will confirm that that which is finally communicated carries with it the stamp of a number of value systems in addition, or in contrast, to his own—masked as they may be in changes of vocabulary, shifts in emphases, or differences in evaluation. The young Thomas Huxley (Kantor, 1953:58) wrote feelingly of his efforts to break through the "gatekeepers" of his day, and in his presumably less ideologically laden field, in the following manner: "I have just finished a Memoir for the Royal Society which has taken me a world of time, thought, and reading, and is, perhaps the best thing I have done yet. It will not be read till May, and I do not know whether they will print it or not afterwards; that will require care and a little maneuvering on my part. You have no notion of the intrigues that go on in this blessed world of science. Science is, I fear, no purer than any other region of human activity, though it should be. Merit alone is very little good; it must be backed by tact and knowledge of the world to do very much."

A contemporary sociologist's situation is not entirely different. Diana Crane's recent study, "The Gatekeepers of Science: Some Factors Affecting the Selection of Articles for Scientific Journals," is a correlational analysis of the institutional ties that link editors of the two major official publications of the American Sociological Association and one of the comparable publications in economics with the authors of the papers that survive the screening process. She finds that "the evaluation . . . *is* affected to some degree by non-scientific factors." The data suggest that the primary factor is similarity in training, i.e., exposure as graduate students to the same methodological, theoretical, and stylistic traditions at the same cluster of institutions, while a secondary role is played by personal ties themselves (1967:200).

The official media of an entire professional association may be swept up by value-ridden images of what is "appropriate" or "inappropriate" to the time. Sociologists concerned with the general area of "social problems," as we mentioned in Chapter 4, felt compelled, under threat of becoming inaudible during the heyday of the vogue of value-neutrality, to found their own society and their own journal.[24]

The not always polite curtain of implicit and explicit valuation bends and twists the immediate products of social research and acts through feed-back to alter the very substance and structure of such activity. Kurt Wolff (1946:547) points out that "extra-scientific, extra-objective factors enter into his [a researcher's] own work not only when he thinks about publishing a certain book or paper—and where, in what form, with what emphases, for what public—but also when contemplating writing itself with reference to the possibility of its publication. In other words, the *selection* of fields, frame of reference, in brief, the *constitution* of his work are co-determined by consideration of publication."

Ethical implications

Concern with the ethical implications of the communication process, however, is relatively new to sociologists. The traditional attitude is illustrated by the resolutely satisfied manner in which Arthur Vidich admits that the question of what impact *Small Town in Mass Society* would have upon members of the community who were readily identifiable in the book had been quite consciously ignored.[25] A contrasting position is suggested by the image of the teaching (*communicating*) role of the sociologist held by Talcott Parsons. The responsibility, he tells us, is similar to that borne by a physician with a disturbing diagnosis to report.[26] If one differentiates sharply between the "teaching" role and communication, then the issue has not been joined. But it would be difficult if not impossible to separate them, particularly in cases where the research is published in a form intended to appeal to non-sociologists as well as sociologists, as was the case in marketing Vidich's own volume.

Another example of the sensitivity of some behavioral scientists to the responsibilities inherent in the communication process may be found in the sharp protest against the therapeutic use of delinquency-prediction scores registered by the Council of the Society for the Psychological Study of Social Issues when it discovered that test results would be explicitly or implicitly shared with high-scoring subjects. Their concern was rooted in the fear that the "feed-back" would act as a self-fulfilling prophecy. It is worth mentioning, however, that those lodging the complaint were not sociologists but psychologists, members of a profession that has for some time operated within the context of a formal code of ethics.

When may those who would publish their research in intimate detail justly claim immunity from the charge of irresponsibility when in fact some of those in the subject population may be injured by the publicity? I have already suggested that such publication might be justified by the long-range gain to be derived. By withholding the information gathered, much of the liberating impact of that new knowledge might be lost. Joseph Fichter and William Kolb (1953: 544–50) offer a tempting alternative. They see sociologists freed of the responsibility of protecting the anonymity of their subjects to the extent to which the subjects' behavior has placed them outside the larger moral community that encompasses both the citizen and the social scientist. Who is to determine when the line of no return has been crossed? The "duly appointed authorities" of that body politic. In all fairness it should be added that Fichter and Kolb also would have sociologists consider their image of the nature of science, the likelihood of injury, and the degree to which society has need of the data. Still, their willingness to abandon their own moral standards because political authorities declare that the subjects have abandoned theirs is a startling suggestion coming from a Jesuit priest and from a sociologist who has since admonished his discipline to build its theoretical base upon an Hebraic-Christian image of man.

There is no ready answer to offer sociologists caught in the dilemma of communication. Indeed, it might be out of keeping for a sociologist of sociology to offer one. It is sufficient, at least for the moment, to point out that the dilemma itself cannot be denied. Communication, a feature integral to the intersubjective and cumulative character of science, demands judgments that are trans-empirical in their root. But this is not all. Communication, when seen in conjunction with the paradoxical nature of prediction *per se*, magnifies the implicit *commitment to change* manifested by the latter.

Social science's commitment to change

In the present chapter we have gone beyond the simple affirmation that value-judgments are in principle demanded throughout the research process. We have pointed out the manner in which the application of the logic of the experiment, together with observation, the paradox that adheres to prediction, and the communication of one's findings all represent, inferentially, not simply the demand for value-laden choice, but a particular substantive commitment as well. Each, we have discovered, involves an implicit affirmation of *change* as well. And if sociologists will but recall that Howard Becker has made a convincing case for identifying change as the central commitment of the "secular" pole of a continuum whose opposite pole he has identified as the "sacred," they will begin to realize the full implications of the value-laden garments they don as they enter upon the task of social research.

The sociologist of sociology cannot help but take such evidence into consideration as he seeks to discern the contemporary state and potential direction of his larger discipline. And when he discovers in addition that the perspective outlined in these last two chapters is playing a part in the larger shift from the "priestly" toward the "prophetic" pole among his contemporaries, he is encouraged to take the latter paradigms ever more seriously as crucial keys to the paradigmatic struggle between those who would view the fundamental nature of their subject matter in system terms and those who would perceive its core to rest in conflict.

The Presumptive Faith of Science

That which one would insinuate, thereof one must speak.

Richard Luecke

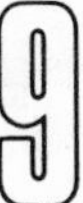

Possibilities

THE evidence presented in the preceding two chapters has detailed the numerous points in the research process at which investigators are forced to make choices and personally intervene, thus calling forth decisions and actions that reflect or imply valuations that transcend the empirical data they confront. It would appear, then, that sociologists cannot even in principle claim the value-free label, that they must move beyond the priestly posture of neutrality and accept responsibility for value-laden action that is essentially prophetic in nature.

And yet even as valuation is admitted to the heart of the sociological task, it may be possible to argue that there may after all be a means by which the decisions that confront sociologists might perhaps be made simply on the basis of a kind of overall commitment to the scientific task that is consistent with the priestly mode. It is conceivable that once one has taken the initial step of faith that is involved in ordination in the church of science, the interpretation that follows may provide an implicit metaphysic and derivative ethic upon which the decisions demanded in the research process might then be based without the necessity of stepping outside a scientific frame of reference. This would not "free" sociologists of

---

Notes to this chapter will be found on pages 351–357.

value commitment. Rather, that commitment would focus about a choice in favor of the metaphysic implicit in the epistemology to which one commits oneself in the use of the logic of science rather than the decision to call into play a metaphysic (and derivative ethic) from some other source. Another way of putting it is that one might *reify* the ontological and "anthropological" assumptions lying within the epistemology peculiar to science rather than bring to bear a concept of existence and an image of man rooted in considerations that lie clearly beyond the framework of that sub-culture.

The fact of the matter is that at least one major social theorist—Howard Becker—would seem to have felt that the trick was possible, for his phrasing of the value issue was both broad enough and precise enough to open the door to its realization. I refer to his contention that "no value-judgments which derive from sources other than the supreme value-judgment that control is ultimately desirable are ethically permissible by the scientist in his specifically scientific capacity" (1950:297). The critical phrase is "which derive from sources other than," for it permits scientists to utilize standards that are *derivative*, that lie as logical correlates of, or presuppositions to, the central commitment of science.

Now this may seem at first glance to be a highly tendentious undertaking. But it is worth pointing out that this, in fact, is exactly what F. S. C. Northrop has been urging (Chapter 5). He acknowledges that it is quite impossible to derive an ethic *directly* from the end-product of the social or physical sciences. But, he argues, a normative ethic can and should be derived from an analysis of those primitive concepts that are at the heart of man's most reliable route to knowledge. In other words, a universally normative system of values should and must reflect the *assumptions* implicit in the logic of science. To mention Northrop approvingly at this point does not alter our earlier negative appraisal of his overall thesis. His is not necessarily the *proper* route to fundamental standards of value for *all people*. However, it is a *possible* source of values for those scientists who are determined to resolve issues that arise in their research without stepping outside a scientific frame of reference. Indeed, it is the path that those who stand uncompromisingly under the value-free banner that dominates contemporary sociology *should* take if they would consistently follow the logic of their stance.

The Ground of Science

Unfortunately, the task of formulating such a derivative ethic stumbles at the very start over terminological difficulties, the lack of interest on the part of most American sociologists, and a continuing confusion over the terms "objectivity" and "value-neutrality." One might wish, for instance, to distinguish "presupposition" from "assumption" by suggesting that the former, when brought to the light of consciousness, is transformed into the latter. But because the philosophers of science have not yet agreed upon such usage, we may perhaps be pardoned if we use the two terms interchangeably.[1]

Some of the most sophisticated neo-positivists might defend their philosophical aloofness by quoting Wittgenstein to the effect that "whereof one cannot speak, thereof one must be silent." If so, they are simply helping to illuminate the very nub of the issue before us. For, as Richard Luecke (1960:1152) would invert Wittgenstein, "that which one would insinuate, thereof one must speak." A presupposition, we have suggested, is like a postulate in mathematics. "Postulate" derives from the Latin *postulare*, which means "to demand." Thus, the metaphysical "demands" that science makes of us will be brought into the open and, as a further step, will be examined in terms of the normative guideposts they furnish.[2]

The presence of a layer of presumptive faith beneath the surface routines of science has not gone completely unnoticed by sociologists. Weber himself was very much aware of its presence, and this awareness was largely responsible for the fundamental and self-conscious relativism of all his work.[3]

Karl Mannheim not only was conscious of the metaphysical baggage that accompanied any pursuit of empirical knowledge, but advocated its explicit avowal.[4] Talcott Parsons, whose baptism in sociological theory came largely through Weber's works, preached the same doctrine in one of his first published essays, an exposition that later grew into *The Structure of Social Action*.[5] Although most sociologists broke quite self-consciously with their philosophical past during the 'forties and 'fifties, a handful continued to probe at the discipline's roots.[6] Not only do some realize that their social-scientific activity is grounded in implicit philosophic assumptions, but a few are aware that these assumptions may have *theological* implications as well.[7] A bit shocking, perhaps, but at least Talcott Parsons would not disagree. For he speaks of science as being bound by a cultural framework "which is in part philosophical—which level is in turn interdependent with the theological. It can function effectively only within this framework of discipline."[8]

The Historical and Prehistorical Context

To argue that science is an activity sharply structured by a unique theory of knowledge and its attendant metaphysic is not to suggest that it is somehow radically alienated from the human enterprise in general. Although most contemporary examinations trace the origins of science to the recording and calculation of astronomical events and geometric relationships in early Babylon and Egypt, a case may be made for going back at least as far as the appearance of language during primate evolution. For with language the progenitors of *homo sapiens* were for the first time endowed with a capacity for conceptual generalization that might be shared with others and built upon from generation to generation. Actually, we could retreat further, close to the very base of the tree of organic evolution. The Latin term *scientia* derives from *scire*, "to learn or to know." And we are aware that very simple forms of life are capable of learning, of associating elements in their environment in such a manner as to alter their behavior systematically in response to them. Such "adjustive" behavior involves generalizing from one raw stimulus to another and generalizing from empirical experience is the essential activity of science. As George Herbert Mead (Strauss, 1956:21) put it, "the scientific method, as such, is after all, only the evolutionary process grown self-conscious."

Anything we could reasonably term "conceptualization" enters the evolutionary record much later, although studies of non-primate mammal forms would seem to indicate that abstract thinking is not an exclusive attribute of the higher primates. Nevertheless, somewhere along the line of man's efforts to civilize himself he became self-conscious of his ability—both actual and potential—to conceptualize in *symbolic* form. This self-consciousness came ultimately, in the Western tradition, to rest upon a thin line of Greeks who, having emancipated themselves from the inhibitions of the sacred institutions that framed their larger culture, were somehow caught up—for perhaps the very first time in man's precarious venture on this planet—with an insatiable drive to understand the curious makeup of their world *simply as an end in and of itself*. Bringing to the task both the deductive inclinations of a Plato and the inductive proclivities of an Aristotle, they possessed themselves of all the essential elements of an approach to knowledge that, two thousand years later, would transform both man's world and man's nature.

The Roman transposition of the Stoic doctrine of "right reason" into the notion of "natural law," a concept acceptable to the Christian Fathers, tied the roots of Western science for over a millennium to a stern and inhibiting master—"reality." Still, it contributed as well a theological rationale that encouraged dedicated Christians to respond to the rediscovery of the classical world and the technical advances of a reawakening Europe by seeking to glorify God's creation by unraveling His handiwork. Even so, an epistemological uneasiness was apparent as early as Galileo's confrontation with the problem of the real versus the nominal. At approximately the same time Descartes began his private excursions into the problem of knowing, a journey that led him to conclude that the least doubtful datum of existence was an inner awareness of the doubt itself. It is unfortunate that both he and the guardians and interpreters of the larger intellectual tradition misunderstood the real significance of the exercise, Descartes by seeing in it the basis for a dualism of mind and matter and the others by viewing it as having supported the prior reality of the conceptual over "self" consciousness. The latter stand could not help but diminish the significance of the existential, which has plagued philosophers of science ever since.

The elaboration and coordination of the empirical and mathematically deductive strains that came to the fore toward the end of the Renaissance were brought to fruition in the first great physical synthesis achieved by

Newton. Although he appeared to view his work as simply a revelation of the glory of God the Creator, this very identification of his findings with the ultimately real —a product of the natural law heritage—contributed rather to an image of a universe whose reality might be quite adequately detailed in terms of a mechanistic materialism, with God at first assigned simply the role of the great Clock-Maker and later, when science came to realize that "first causes" were quite superfluous to its focal concern, simply discarded as irrelevant. Together with the legacy of Locke and the French rationalists, this attitude shaped the anti-metaphysical climate within which the great strides in physical and biological science were to be taken in the nineteenth century.

But a second stream of thought had appeared in the seventeenth and early eighteenth centuries that provided the philosophical framework for the revolutionary scientific image that was reflected in the new physics at the turn of the present century. This was the strain of skepticism that was born in a portion of Locke's incompletely systematic perspective and was nurtured toward adulthood by Bishop Berkeley and David Hume and modified only slightly in the *Critiques* of Immanuel Kant. Whereas Newton and Locke established separate households for nature and God; Berkeley, Hume and Kant sought the complete divorce of nature from reality. Science now had before it a conceptual context that made it an end in itself with a vengeance, for it was no longer to be justified as a revelation of anything but its own purpose.

This view became the frame upon which the amaterial images of the new electromagnetic physics of the late nineteenth century were stretched, for the symbols of Newtonian physics were no longer sufficient. Einstein's general and special theories of relativity were simply later formulas expressive of the same essential instrumental approach, even though Einstein himself could never accept the nominalism, the lack of concern over the "reality" of the concepts used, that his theories came to symbolize for the new age.

The Principle of Economy

The classic statement of the new position appeared during the generation immediately preceding Einstein in the writing of Ernst Mach, particularly in his extremely influential *Die Mechanik in ihrer Entwicklung*, published first in 1883. Mach's contention that *economy* should dictate scientists' choices among alternative models for conceptualizing empirical phenomena was a long-awaited breakthrough toward characterizing science in entirely instrumental terms. Scientists, argued Mach, must cast off their earlier assumption that scientific precepts should be mirror images of the "real" and accept instead the operating criterion by which one model has displaced another throughout the history of science—economy.

Predictive efficiency

Not only is this, historically speaking, the manner in which the scientific community has come to select the "more fit" schema or equation, but it represents the position which by far the larger proportion of practicing scientists take today. Mach's views were taken up by Henri Poincaré in France and Karl Pearson in England and influenced the latter's *The Grammar of Science* (1892), a volume that, together with Mach's *Die Mechanik*, has been largely responsible for setting the tone for interpreting science both within and without the discipline since that time, at least in Western Europe and America. They did so directly through the broad reception that the Pearson volume found in an England that had been steeped in the utilitarianism of Bentham and Mill and in an America hearkening to the philosophy of pragmatism, and later—indirectly—through the influence Mach's views had upon the Vienna Circle in the late 'twenties and early 'thirties. Einstein himself acknowledged his debt to Mach for freeing him from the inhibitions that would have tied his imagination to a picturebook version of science, encouraging him instead to seek a conceptual framework that was directly at odds with the way in which the empirical world pressed itself upon man's direct sensory experience. And in this response to Mach, Einstein also saw efficient prediction as the scientist's end: "it is the goal of science to discover rules which permit the association and foretelling of facts . . . it also seeks to reduce the connections discovered to the smallest possible number of mutually independent conceptual elements."[9]

Kepler's principle—*natura simplicatatem amat* ("nature loves simplicity") had become, three centuries later, "*scientists* love simplicity." We select, as scientists, those concepts, symbols, and logical frames that precipitate "order" within the empirical world most efficiently. And when the ordering of phenomena is spoken of in the context of man's immersion in time, it becomes thus "anticipating the future course of phenomena."[10]

Use of the term "*pre*diction" may obscure the fact that the essential logic involved might equally encourage *post*diction.[11] Once science became emancipated from the notion of causes as forces, its logic could be applied backward or forward in time, depending upon whether its focus of concern was the last of a series of events or the first—and depending upon the practical exigencies involved in applying the controls inherent to the experimental logic. It is this second consideration that forces almost all scientific research to follow quite literally a *pre*dictive pattern rather than a *post*-dictive one.

Even the notion of proof has been revised radically when viewed operationally. In the syllogistic sense of the verb, we can "prove" nothing about the continuity of patterns discovered in empirical data; we can merely *predict* the discovery of a sequence of events in terms of its appearance in other comparable contexts. Statistical logic attempts to overcome this limitation by enabling us to *dis*prove *null* hypotheses. But the proof is essentially a semantic device, based simply on the fact that only one contrary case is necessary to upset a negative hypothesis, whereas an infinite series of cases would be necessary to guarantee a positive hypothesis. Proof and disproof remain essentially *a posteriori* rather than *a priori* concepts, and because the future is always a *tabula rasa*, a blank, prediction alone remains.

Problems of usage

This whole discussion could become very puzzling unless we keep in mind that it occurs within the context of the Anglo-American use of the term "science." A great deal of conceptual and intellectual confusion has arisen simply because this is a term with a considerably narrower meaning than the German word *Wissenschaft*, with which it is too often equated. The English term "science" has been largely limited by common practice to the disciplines that fall, in English-speaking areas, within the academic fields encompassed by the physical, biological, and social or behavioral sciences. *Wissenschaft*, on the other hand, includes all forms of knowledge that may be treated systematically, including such areas as theology. Furthermore, there is nothing inappropriate in describing science—or sociology—as does Peter Berger in his recent *Invitation to Sociology* (1963:4), as "an attempt to understand" as long as one recognizes the peculiar kind of *understanding* that is involved. Science is an instrument for efficiently ordering empirical phenomena over time, regardless of the subjective intentions of the scientists involved or the gratifications they seek. This does not necessarily mean that scientists aren't moved by criteria of beauty in structuring their models. A model wins long-run acceptance by a discipline, however, only on the basis of economy in prediction.

There appear to be traces of an awareness of the role played by the principle of economy in science from sociology's very beginnings.[12] And although Max Weber regarded *verstehen* as essential to the nature of the sociological task, he regarded such empathic understanding as prefatory to the traditional image of a causal explanation. Sociology, thus, was seen as a "science which attempts the interpretive understanding of social action *in order thereby to arrive at a causal explanation of its course* and effects."[13] Causality, in turn, he defined in essentially the same instrumental terms: "a statement of probability that things we have described as orthodox today will recur in a specified manner."[14]

Of the classic figures in sociology, George Herbert Mead may have grasped the instrumental nature of science most fully. Science to Mead could not be satisfactorily characterized as seeking simply to "know" the world. Rather, its unique contribution lay in its ability to inform us of what is likely to happen when we *act* in a particular manner. The past, thus, is significant to scientists only as it enables them—and those to whom the evidence of past order is communicated—to *act in the future* with greater assurance concerning the consequences of that act.[15] Benjamin Ginzburg in his strategically placed article on "Science" in the *Encyclopaedia of the Social*

Sciences took essentially the same position, as have numerous sociologists since.[16]

It is sheer conceptual economy that welds a community of interest from the disparate personal motives and biographies that enter into science. With it we are able to free science from the animistic taint that began with "right reason" and led, through natural law and "reality," to the *anima* that even today continues to haunt the term "cause." What we are in fact left with as the criterion by which one empirically justified formulation is accepted and another is denied within the corporate enterprise of science is simple *predictive efficiency*.

Inter-subjectivity: The Roots of the Empirical

Instrumentalists, however, are not free from the temptation to overstate their case. Percy Bridgman, father of operationalism—fundamentalist cousin of the instrumentalist view—did a particular disservice for his fellow scientists when he tempted many to exaggerate the character of their activity as "nothing more than doing one's damndest with one's mind, no holds barred." For the criterion for maximum efficiency in prediction upon which scientists operate establishes an implicit set of rules within which "one's damndest" is rather severely restrained.

It has been traditional to describe scientists in terms of their preference for *objectivity* over *subjectivity*, the kind of preference that led the French Encyclopedists to give more space to the article on "Furnaces" in their magnificent summation of the spirit of their times than they provided for "Faith." That such preferential treatment itself was evidence of a faith of which the authors of the *Encyclopédie* were not fully aware may simply be a commentary on the distance our self-comprehension has come since that day.

The Positivists followed hard on the heels of the Encyclopedists in France in responding to the magnetic appeal of "objectivity." They wished to be "positive"—to be completely assured—in cataloguing human knowledge, so they turned quite self-consciously against the "subjectivity" that they saw engulfing all but the activities of the small band of mathematicians and natural scientists of their day. They were ready, with Hume, to destroy everything in Western man's intellectual heritage not contributing to that "objectivity": "Does it contain any abstract reasoning concerning quantity or number? No. Does it contain any experimental reasoning concerning matter of fact and existence? No. Commit it then to flames: for it can contain nothing but sophistry and illusion."[17] Just as Baudelaire would put on gloves whenever he made love, so—as one perceptive interpreter has phrased it—"the hands of the scientist are gloved to keep the subject from contaminating the object."[18]

Objectivity identified with value-neutrality

The only unfortunate thing about all this is that scientists have not been content to accept objectivity as simply the semantic opposite of subjectivity. Instead, they have used the former term as if it were an exclusive vehicle for the approach to "truth," while assuming that "passion" is its opposite. Scientists, rather than seeing science for what it is uniquely and superbly equipped to be—a logic by which the raw phenomena of experience may be transformed into *objects* which may then be addressed communally—have been tempted to view themselves as uniquely free from the distortions that are generally the mark of man's apprehension of his existence. The fact of the matter is that *all* activity, including the objectivity of the scientist, must of necessity presuppose *motivation.* And scientists cannot isolate themselves from what Parsons would term "cathexis," the layman, simple "passion."[19] It would seem wise, therefore, to join the many contemporary logicians of science by dispensing with a term so burdened by the distortions that have accompanied two or three centuries of overly broad usage.

Public nature of scientific data

The adjective that is coming to be preferred today in both scientific and philosophical discourse is "empirical" —from the Greek *en* (in) + *peira* (a trial, experiment). The empirical would then quite appropriately characterize that data which is amenable to the logic of the experiment, a logic that we have already suggested is the basis of approximate proof in science, of reliable prediction. It is amenable to the logic of the experiment because it meets one crucial condition: *that it may be observed by more than one person.* Now this may seem a rather mild demand—and hardly one upon which an edifice as exclusive as science might be built. And yet this is all that we really need say. In its insistence on being as "positive" as humanly possible about what it concludes, science has defined itself in *plural* terms; it could not, even in theory, operate in the singular. In order to guarantee reliability, scientists have, over the generations, eliminated from the realm of fact—from the raw material that is to be processed into varying degrees of predictive generality—all those elements in experience that are not potentially available to more than one witness at a time. This development did not occur by faith or all at once. It came slowly and pragmatically with the discovery that any other approach simply would not meet appropriate standards for reliable prediction. The issue did not hinge in a quasi-moralistic way on the "unreality" of the subjective. Investigator after investigator simply found that too many errors were made when one accepted any and every sensation, image, or impression reported by one's fellow investigators directly into the procedural machinery of science. Gradually concepts were dropped which had been accepted into the language as generally indicative of interior states but which could not meet the minimum standard of reliability implicit in the demand for a plurality of witnesses. "Spirit" was dropped from the realm of inanimate phenomena, "soul" from the animate, and "mind," by many, from the psychological. If and when any have been readmitted, they have been accepted only, as have "mind" and "self," on terms that define them as conceptual shorthand that stands for intervening variables that are rooted in publicly verifiable actions.

The present awareness regarding the communal nature of scientific evidence is a recent development, coinciding approximately with the widespread use of the term "empirical." Karl Pearson (1957:6), following the lead of Ernst Mach, spoke of "judgments independent of the idiosyncracies of the individual mind." Herbert Feigl (1949:11) may have originated one of the popular versions when he spoke of the criterion of "inter-subjective testability":

Knowledge claims which by their very nature cannot independently be checked by anyone else . . . are not of the kind that we seek in the sciences. Religious ecstasy, the elations of love, the inspiration of the artist, yes, even the flash of insight on the part of a scientific genius are not in themselves scientific activities . . . they do not validate knowledge claims.

A second version, that of the "public" nature of scientific evidence, has come increasingly into play of late. There is some likelihood that it may prevail in the longer run both because it avoids raising the phenomenological and semantic problems that inhere in the stem of the term "intersubjective" and because it has an overtone of the "civic" about it which could be attractive to an enterprise whose support must depend increasingly upon the good will of those who control the public purse.

Sociologists, fortunately, were appraised early of the corporate nature of science and of the criteria that were set for its raw data. Durkheim's successful argument in favor of the existence of "social" facts demanded an image of sociology that rested upon this public quality of verification,[20] while Weber made quite clear that even the insight granted by the method of *verstehen* had to stand or fall before similarly concrete standards of verification.[21] George Herbert Mead's social behaviorism carried the intersubjective standard over into the graduate education of a whole generation of sociologists trained at the University of Chicago, many of whom have played leading roles in the development of the discipline over the past three decades.[22] Thus it was possible for Robert Bierstedt to say in full confidence not long ago in a presidential address before a major regional sociological society that "all of us would agree that in order to qualify as knowledge a proposition needs to be public in character, the product of shared experience."[23] More than any other social system developed by man, science has an automatic policing system. Indeed, all of its active participants are policemen. Science is at heart a communal enterprise because its raw data must meet criteria that are supra-personal truth claims, as Merton has pointed out, which must be subjected to pre-established *impersonal* criteria.[24]

The reliability that attends empiricism has carried us beyond many of the "dreams of reason" that possessed the rationalists and seedling empiricists of the eighteenth and early nineteenth centuries. Still, the enactment of such a "by-law" by a community dedicated to efficient prediction, although opening one door, has closed another.

Paradox of Descartes' exercise in doubt

The double doors to understanding were laid bare by Descartes in his famous exercise in skepticism. His own resolution of his doubt—into a metaphysical dualism—I would not defend. But that he confronted and recorded a dilemma that faces those who take the grammar of science seriously cannot be denied: "examining attentively that which I was, I saw that I could conceive that I had no body, and that there was no world or place where I might be; but yet that I could not for all that conceive that I was not. On the contrary, I saw from the very fact that I thought of doubting the truth of other things, it very evidently and certainly followed that I was." And a little later: "What causes many, however, to persuade themselves that there is difficulty in knowing this truth . . . is the fact that they never raise their minds above the things of sense. . . ." If we were to grant priority to the "I" rather than the "think" of his famous "I think, therefore I am"—as indeed it would appear that Descartes himself had in fact actually done ("but . . . whilst I thus wished to think all things false, it was absolutely essential that the 'I' who thought this should be . . .")—we would have to conclude that it was Descartes who first uncovered the dilemma that engulfs the practitioner of science (1952:24, 28): that, in establishing the criterion of intersubjectivity in order to guarantee reliability, the logic of science filters out the very element in human experience—the *intra*subjective sense of personal existence—upon which the value of such a venture is predicated. The quest may have been entered into before, perhaps by Augustine when, struggling to clarify the concept of time, he agonized, "For so it is, O Lord my God, I measure it, but what it is I measure I do not know." And essentially the same answer may have been given many times since. Certainly it is evident in the existentialist's insistence that "existence" precedes "essence," that subjectivity is one's ultimate point of reference. It is revealed as well in the closely related perspective of

Edmund Husserl, who locates the source of all knowledge in a "pure stream of experience" (*Erlebnisstrom*) that is apprehended by the subject in its immediate giveness, with the objective-scientific method as merely a secondary typification of selective elements drawn from it.

The identification of knowledge with but a derivative level of awareness may have had its origins in Locke's conclusion that nothing was to be discovered in the intellect which had not been perceived before through the senses. If so, the greater the pity, for Locke had at another point made quite clear that knowledge of the existence of *oneself* was not so dependent.[25] However, the evident successes of science simply overwhelmed those who continued to lean toward the implications of Descartes' exercise in doubt. They had to await the twentieth century's rediscovery of Kierkegaard's existential rebellion to recover its significance.

Even the identification of sense-experience as the raw data of science is an overstatement of the case if the inter-subjective criterion is not added or the particular sensory channels appropriate to it are not identified. For a person "senses" *intra*subjectively as well as *inter*-subjectively. The monopoly that scientists have staked out for the term "sensory" is unwarranted; it smacks, in fact, of a kind of reification that is hardly appropriate to the instrumental view science has come to take of itself. It lies at the heart of the difficulty posed by Mach's attempt to reduce knowledge to sensory elements and to build thereon an exclusively scientific system of knowledge. The same oversight was fatal to the integrity of the logical empiricists who, drawing their essential inspiration from Mach, simply added a more sophisticated appreciation of the role of language. Both they and the radical wing among linguistic analysts foundered, in addition, upon an unwillingness to appreciate the manner in which even language alienates the subject from himself.

But none of these comments is meant in any way to deny the appropriateness of the criterion of intersubjectivity through which evidence must pass if it is to be accepted as potential raw material for science. Although the need for such a criterion developed only gradually, hand in hand with the historical emergence of a self-conscious scientific community, it is today a universal standard, common to all disciplines that limit their concern to the empirical. Art may be "I," but, as Claude Bernard so rightly insisted, "science is *We*."

Recurrence: The Manifestation of Order over Time

Scientists' obsession about being positive—to be as *certain* as possible about that which they speak—is, as I have indicated, inextricably intertwined with what they perceive as their legitimate goal—the economical ordering of experience over time. This has entailed, wisely and in fact necessarily, limiting the raw data entering directly into its peculiar logic to those phenomena that can be checked by other observers. Now these two factors—the predictive aim and the intersubjective route—are in turn intimately related to a second presupposition. It is that science is focally concerned with—and its end products are stated in terms of—the empirically *recurrent*. Prediction is after all but the projection of past order into the future. And the intersubjective criterion is often stated, or met, by the capacity of one scientist to *repeat* the observations reported by another.

Though the significance of the recurrent undoubtedly made its way into the mind of historical—and probably even prehistorical—man simply as a pragmatically fruitful stance in his effort to understand his world, historians of science tend to grant Hume the honor of having first made systematic note of it. For Hume, realizing that postulating a hidden force linking causes to effects would not enhance the reliability of knowledge and that such a "force" was logically unprovable, simply concluded that reasonable inductions were those that conformed to *past* regularities. The animistic spell that had gripped the pursuit of publicly reliable knowledge was thereby broken and scientists were permitted to go directly about the business of delineating the recurrent aspects of the world in which they were immersed.

Laplace's demon

Unfortunately, there were those who either would not or could not accept the simple instrumentalism that lay at the heart of Hume's stance. The mechanistic imagery of nineteenth-century technology stepped in as the earlier animistic imagery was sloughed off, tempting Laplace to create a cosmology in which a hypothetical intelligence might be capable of knowing at one moment of time "all the forces by which nature is animated and the respective positions of the entities which compose it . . . nothing would be uncertain for it [the intelligence] and the future, like the past, would be present to its eyes" (Polanyi, 1958:141). It was the same demon that was to grip Henry Adams as late as 1906 when in his autobiography he set forth the premise that he might determine the course of history by projecting the differentials found at but two of its points, the thirteenth century and his own lifetime. Laplace's "counter reformation," influencing as it did the materialistic ideologies of the last century, had to await the precocious brilliance of a John Stuart Mill for its demythologizing. For Mill recaptured Hume's anti-metaphysical spirit simply by *defining* the concern of science in terms of uniformity. "Any facts," Mill declared, "are fitted, in themselves, to be a subject of science, which follow one another according to constant laws."[26] Mill went astray only when he made the method of empiricism synonymous with that of all knowledge, a confusion that still infects a small portion of the present generation as a result of the selective semantics of the logical empiricists.

Idiographic versus nomothetic

The seeds of a dual epistemology were planted before the turn of the century, however, through the neo-Kantian efforts of a Heidelberg School of philosophy dominated by Wilhelm Windelband. Windelband projected two formats for studying history, a generalizing and an individualizing one, with *natural* history identified with the former and *general* history with the latter. Wilhelm Dilthey, using Windelband as his springboard, distinguished between *idiographic* (particularizing) and *nomothetic* (generalizing) modes of knowledge, holding that this division entailed differentiating subject-matter rather than merely method. Heinrich Rickert, another of Windelband's disciples (and, later, teacher of Heidegger), elaborated the distinction further, stating that simplification and absolute validity—to be contrasted with the individualizing and immediately "realistic" manner of the "historical" or "cultural" studies—were the goals of natural science. The distinction was not one of subject matter, but of approach, with the *values* of an individual providing the ultimate clue as to when and where one approach was to be preferred to the other. It is Rickert's image of science as a generalizing discipline concerned with the projection of uniformities over time that has set the standard for most Western scientific investigation, social as well as physical and biological, ever since. History inherited the particularizing mode.[27]

Regularity, the conviction that nature does not change basically over time, is thus a second by-law of the corporate activity of scientists, though a by-law passed by science rather than philosophy or nature. Nature, as Heraclitus taught us long ago, confronts us primarily with flux, an ever-changing spectrum of sensory experience, both public and private. It is we who have fashioned the sophisticated weapon of science to pin it down, to order it, to predict its many manifestations. "With what right do the sciences of nature seek to predict nature?" asks J. F. A. Taylor.

> The answer is, it must be admitted, by no right whatever. . . . Experience of nature will enable us to predict nature only on the assumption that nature behaves uniformly on all occasions, so that the part of its career which has been observed may serve as evidence for the part of its career which has not. Yet for this belief in the uniformity of nature . . . there neither is nor can be proof in any ordinary sense. Reason cannot prove it. . . . Nor can experience supply to it any confirmation which will not itself have presupposed the uniformity of nature and therefore have begged the question. That was Hermes' momentous bequest to philosophy, the annihilating percepture that the fundamental principle of empirical knowledge is amenable to no proof . . . (1958:486).

"*Laws of impotence*"

There are those who have argued that certain so-called "laws of impotence," such as the Second Law of Thermodynamics and the Heisenberg Principle, suggest exceptions to the view that science focuses upon the recurrent rather than the unique. The Second Law, for instance, describes the ultimate heat-death of the universe based upon the phenomenon of entropy—the movement of heat from warmer to colder objects—which in turn is viewed as a movement from ordered to disordered structures. Because such a heat-death clearly would be a *unique* occurrence *vis-à-vis* that universe, it is argued that science thus focuses upon the unique as well as the general.

But such a rendering of the nomothetic-idiographic distinction assumes more for it than it claims, particularly if one follows Rickert's lead and sees the two as different epistemologies rather than implying different subject matter. For science is not satisfied with moving simply from the particular to the general; its focal orientation toward *prediction* suggests that patterns discovered within the flux of raw experience are indeed projected back upon that experience to delineate *particular* constellations of phenomena that may be expected to arise at *particular* times. The Second Law does not apply to one moment in time. It simply generalizes a phenomenon of heat transfer that is characteristic of *all* closed systems. If we assume that the universe *is* a closed system, we are simply applying a general rule to a specific case. Science centers around the establishment of the general rule. It is the same kind of an argument that might be made regarding the dynamics of evolution. Men trained both in science and natural history obviously have sought to trace the particular route it has taken upon the earth. But in their scientific role—as contrasted with the equally important role of the natural historian—their concern, and Darwin's, has been with the general principles that could be discovered running uniformly throughout the process.

Somewhat the same confusion has appeared in some of the interpretations of the "uncertainty principle" in physics. Here, we are told, science once again focuses upon the unique, some going so far as to say that quantum physics has introduced history into nature. History has in fact *never* been separate from nature *in terms of the ultimate character of what we seek to understand.* It is only the epistemologies we use in trying to come to grips with it that have been distinct. The generalizing nature of science has not been affected by quantum mechanics. All that the discoveries of Heisenberg and Bohr have suggested is that there may be a point beyond which our perceptual abilities are unable in principle to go in comprehending the microcosmic world, and therefore that we may have to be satisfied in treating such levels of phenomena in terms of probability statistics. It may be beside the point to point out that others—Einstein, de Broglie, and Schroedinger among them—felt that the barrier is only temporary and that the ordering of the infinitely small will be taken up again as man's ingenuity is addressed to the task. Much more to the point is that the Heisenberg Principle is *itself* a phenomenon rooted in the recurrent. *It* is the stuff of science, not a specific empirical incident. The fact of the matter is that anyone seeking in an empirical way to deny the fundamental nature of the recurrent assumption in science would first have to presuppose it in support of his own effort.[28] Thus, even the so-called "laws of impotence" witness to the recurrent, even if only to the recurrent limits to our perception of the recurrent!

"*Chance*"

Nor does the pragmatic value that scientists have discovered in the concept "chance" free it from the embrace of the nomothetic. Chance merely signifies our conclusion that the empirical factors involved in a situation are too complex or subtle to bother with, given the particular ends in mind, or, in the context of the "uncertainty principle," that the interaction between observation and the observed rules out any but a macroscopic, statistical approach. The latter—the statistical method—then goes on to presuppose the regularity implicit in probability theory.[29]

Limiting character of verstehende Soziologie

This nomothetic or generalizing image entered sociology most directly through the studies undertaken by Max Weber to clarify the framework by which the logic of the natural sciences might be applied to sociological data. Although acknowledging that historian Eduard Meyer was quite correct in viewing each event in human history as unique and joining Dilthey in his claim that the method of *verstehen*—of empathetic understanding—was imperative to the meaningful analysis of human action, Weber developed a method of abstracting the general from the particular of social history by means of conceptual configurations—"ideal types." These constructs, although tied intimately to the particular cultural or sub-cultural framework under examination, would enable social scientists to apply the very same experimental logic to *Geisteswissenschaften* (which included history and the social sciences) that had already proved to be the *sine qua non* of *Naturwissenschaften* (natural science). Although at times Weber succumbed to the lure of the idiographic, plying the trade of historian, jurist, and statesman, this should not distract us from his awareness of the contrasting methodological postures involved. And, contrary to the views of many, his formal dedication to the *verstehen* approach (a method which he himself appeared to ignore in a considerable portion of his sociological writing) did not *contradict* any essential element in the logic of the natural sciences, including the criterion of intersubjectivity and the concern with the discovery of uniformities running through the maze of the unique. It simply tended to limit the range of concepts he considered focal in the ordering of social phenomena to those that reflected the subjectively meaningful actions of individuals and the mind-sets of the cultures or sub-cultures he examined. This was an unfortunate limitation, true, for it failed to appreciate the fact that the corporate goal of science—efficient prediction—would not coincide with the value-orientation and related conceptual structures of any culture or sub-culture *except* the scientific. And so sociology has moved on since Weber's time, honoring the essential mode by which he would extract the general from the particular of history (the logic surrounding the use of the ideal type) and ignoring the constraint imposed by his inordinate emphasis upon subjective intentionality.

Weber was not the only one writing toward the turn of the century who had come to accept sociology as nomothetic. Ernest Troeltsch was affected deeply by the Windelband-Rickert-Dilthey position as well, although only now are some of his more pertinent comments on the generalizing logic of social science becoming available in English. Durkheim played essentially the same role within French sociology, declaring that "uniformity of effect" established the "reality" of the *conscience collective* just as it demonstrated the relevance for science of physical phenomena.[30]

A nomothetic approach to sociology as a science is well-nigh universal among recent and contemporary sociologists. The specific manners in which it is spelled out vary in form but not in substance, Merton (1962:41) offering "order," Parsons (1951b:5) preferring "determinate relations of interdependence." Other versions include "typical and recurrent situations and patterns," "regularity," "causal closure," "invariant relations," even simply "that which is common and general."[31] Where the idiographic is introduced it is for an essentially nomothetic purpose, unique cases being used to negate particular general propositions. Such uniqueness represents neither the goal nor the presumption of the rhetoric of science. Its aim is to extract order from the flux that man confronts through his immersion in time. Thus the scientist both presumes and seeks the recurrent.

The Relational: The Web of System

When Copernicus suggested that no single element within the universe could be altered without altering the whole picture—that if you tinker in one place, its impact would of necessity reverberate across the vastness of the cosmos and down through the corridors of time—he was merely giving voice to a third "by-law" characteristic of science. For science entails, in addition to intersubjectivity and recurrence, the assumption that the foci of its concern exhibit the nature of *system*, that none of its elements be isolated in any final sense from one another but rather be linked, ultimately, through a network of essentially determinate *relationships*. This is the basis on which science is characterized as *systematic*. It is but a simple derivative of science's corporate intention—predictive power of maximum efficiency. Prediction is the movement from one empirical constellation to another over time, and if we are not to discount our intent from the very beginning we must simply *assume* the relatedness of all such phenomena. Thus, when the most eminent of recent historians of science, Sir William Dampier (1949: 467), defines science as ". . . ordered knowledge of natural phenomena and the rational study of the *relations* between the concepts in which these phenomena are expressed," he has chosen to emphasize the relational aspect for very good reason. He is aware that science has no need to concern itself with the "inner" nature of any of its terms, for the utility, even the "truth," of the relationships sought is quite independent of the *relata* themselves.[32] The individual elements composing the raw data may indeed be the most "real" of realities. The point is, however, that science simply is not concerned with their status *per se*. Its focal commitment to predictive efficiency enables it to be merely "relational."

The admonition that "hypotheses are not articles of faith" but merely "foundations for calculation," which Osiander added in his "Address to the Reader" at the beginning of Copernicus' treatise on the solar system, may well have been simply a practical device to protect Copernicus from censure by a Church that had committed itself to an Aristotelian cosmos. But the seed planted in caution was to grow into the mighty oak from which one of the fundamental tenets of contemporary science was hewn. The general public was largely unaware of its growth and transformation until Einstein shattered the common-sense identification of science's product with everyday images of the real. For Einstein tore from natural man his last stable point of reference—the grey ghost "ether"—shocking him into an awareness that, to the eyes of the scientist, "there is no hitching post in the universe." The Ptolemaic and Copernican solar systems became one and the same thing and could be distinguished now only in terms of the point of reference selected for calculation. Choice between the alternatives could be made only in terms of the criterion of economy in prediction. With space denied any absolute referent, the instrumental character of science had been finally and completely laid bare. There would be no Rosetta Stone, no Linear B, to use in translating the terms of science into the language of the "absolute" or the "ultimately real." These would have to be supplied from beyond its logic or perceived within it through an act of faith. The growth of natural science is, then, analogous to the utility of a monolingual dictionary in a completely alien tongue. Both provide means by which we may identify one element in the system in terms of other elements. Neither carry us beyond that system to grasp the "meaning" of an item *per se*.[33] Thus the so-called "Laws of Nature" are simply predictive *relationships*.

The fact that sociological theory as it has matured over the past generation has come to focus upon concepts designating social *relationships* rather than individuals or groups of individuals may, in the light of the foregoing, appear more understandable—inevitable, perhaps. Just where the shift began it would be hard to say. But certainly the strain that dominates contemporary sociology and its investment in social psychology would seem to have flowered at the philosophically sophisticated hands of George Herbert Mead when he bequeathed to American sociology its focus upon the relational concept of role. Another strand, entering sociological theory by way of continental sociology and British social anthropology, is the paradigmatic image of society as "system." Karl Mannheim, reflecting both the English and continental traditions, argued quite explicitly that sociology focuses on relationships and configurations of the parts rather than on the parts themselves,[34] while Parsons' preoccupation with system-analysis, drawn from the common "systematic" predispositions of Weber, Pareto, and Durkheim, has argued that the *only* way of describing behavior within the frame of "action theory" was in relational terms.[35]

What Kenneth Boulding has termed the "relational image,"[36] then, is an inherent part of the equipment of science, physical and social. Its eyes are focused upon relationships rather than upon the interpretation of the quality of an element in the relationship in and of itself.[37]

Significance for a Sociology of Sociology

If we would understand the full significance of the paradigmatic revolutions confronting the discipline today, we must understand the epistemological framework within which it operates—particularly if sociology would remain within the extended family of science. Indeed, the word "understanding" implies that one is *standing under* a contextual frame of some sort. Even though such a frame has developed quite un-selfconsciously over the generations and centuries and one can do excellent scientific work without consciously being aware of it, this can grant the sociologist of sociology little solace. For his task demands more than a facility for empirical research. If sociology may be conceived of as a "science"

—and we discover near unanimity on this point within the discipline today, even though some would see it as more than a science as well—then the "sociologist" of such a science must inform himself of the implicit as well as explicit cognitive postures demanded. For cognitive elements in man's communal and sub-communal life, we know, are interactive with his cathectic and evaluational life as well. Indeed the *raison d'être* for the present chapter lay precisely in this fact.

It was suggested that the priestly mode in sociology might be able to withstand the present challenge from a re-emergence of the discipline's earlier prophetic stance if it could reinterpret its claim to "value freedom" by calling for freedom from all value postures *except those that were derivative of a commitment to the scientific task itself*—and do so in a convincing and attractive manner. If it were able to do so then one might have to grant the substantive paradigm of system more staying power as well, for it seemed to have emerged as a functional expression of the more fundamental movement on the part of sociologists toward a priestly self-image. If not, then one would expect the reclaimed prophetic image to carry the conflict paradigm into a dominant position in its wake.

We have in the present chapter only set the stage for such an assessment, for we have merely delineated the *cognitive* commitments that underlie natural science. The "end" of such a community—viewed instrumentally (and thus empirically and historically)—we discovered to be "efficient prediction." This is the focal "commitment" of the scientific task. Supporting it, we discovered, were three assumptions or presuppositions. These pragmatically validated and communally sanctioned "by-laws" were those I have labeled the *intersubjective* (or "empirical"), the *recurrent* (or "nomothetic"), and the *relational* (or "systematic"). Our next step will be to examine the *derivative* image of man and his society which such a screen necessarily filters from the larger flux that is experience when it is applied to the social scene. If that image is both convincing and attractive, then it could be offered as an ontological and "anthropological" (in its philosophical sense) base from which one might then draw a derivative ethic for the resolution of those immediately trans-empirical decisions—and perhaps a justification for the implicit commitment to "change"—which we discovered, in Chapters 7 and 8, unavoidable in principle as well as fact during the process of social research. The sociologist as priest would then be able to claim a cathectic and evaluational posture consistent in its derivation with the cognitive commitments underlying sociology as a science.

Sociological Man as Natural Man

Mind mastering clay,
gross clay invades it.

George Meredith

10

Introduction

In discussing the "presumptive" faith of science, I suggested that there might be a way in which a criterion could be established that would avoid the necessity of moving beyond the bounds of science to resolve those value-laden issues that are an unavoidable part of the research role. One could follow the lead of F. S. C. Northrop and build those norms upon the postulational base of science itself. That procedure, as we pointed out, would seem to be quite consistent with Howard Becker's admonition that only those value positions that reflect a scientist's central commitment to economy and reliability in the ordering of experience over time *or its derivatives* were appropriate within the scientific role itself.

Because the assumptions made by scientists *derive* from this central dedication to conceptual efficiency, normative behavior based on these assumptions also would fit the "derivative" criterion set by Becker and Northrop. The discussion that follows will seek to transform that pragmatically and historically derived epistemological screen through which the experienced world must be filtered so that it is accessible to the methods of science into a philosophic frame of reference (a "metaphysic," if you

---

Notes to this chapter will be found on pages 357–364.

will) from which a philosophical anthropology ("man's fundamental nature and essence") and an associated ethic might be drawn that would provide the normative base found to be necessary to sociological research. What we will be about, then, is a "reification" of the epistemological stance of science as it is characterized by its larger community today. This reification, though it be an "anti-metaphysical metaphysic," would then grant at least one possible basis by which a sociologist might fashion such norms, yet without having to turn for them to any source beyond the scientific community itself. If value-neutrality is indeed the larger banner under which the sociologist as priest is to move into and through the research role, then this would appear the most consistent response available. If such a derivative ethic seemed both plausible and attractive we would then be in a position to argue that the priestly image together with the system paradigm might successfully withstand the renascent force of the prophetic mode and the conflict paradigm in the "revolutionary" struggle for paradigmatic supremacy within contemporary sociology.

Efficiency as End

The grammar of science has focused above all on efficiency in prediction. Although the discussion that we have begun will focus upon the epistemological by-laws that support that end, a few words concerning the reification of the goal itself are in order. Some have regarded *efficiency* itself the clue to a derivative ethic. Wilhelm Ostwald (1905), for instance, would have had us replace Kant's categorical imperative with an "energetical imperative" whose central tenet would be, simply, "Do not waste energy." Although this particular approach has had little direct influence upon the search for norms within science in the last generation or two, the Second Law of Thermodynamics furnishes what might appear to be substantive support.[1] McQuilkin DeGrange (1953: 494) would seem to be the only recent overt American advocate of this position, deriving his inspiration from Comte rather than from Oswald or the Second Law. F. S. C. Northrop (1953:331) himself appears to have been captured in part by the promise of economy when he argued that cultures should be judged "better" or "worse" in terms of the *amount* of sensory raw data their conceptual systems could "take care of." One is also tempted to view pragmatism with its sifting of "truth" in terms of its relative contribution to problem-solving as a reflection of the same essential spirit, growing as it did out of a milieu in which the efficiency ethos of the age of science had come to dominate the American intellectual scene. The efficiency theme may then have moved back into the mainstream of sociology through Durkheim's (1955) serious interest in pragmatism and could well have been an important factor in preparing the way for the functionalism that was to dominate his sociological analyses and to influence so much of sociological and anthropological theory since. And more than one sociologist has seen in Parsons' structural-functional theory much the same: an analysis that orders social data essentially in terms of their contribution to the *functional efficiency* of the system involved.[2]

Man as Object

If a calculus of efficiency may be offered as a surrogate ethic for a science that would draw normative guidelines from within its own frame of reference, then the depersonalization that accompanies objectification would structure its doctrine of man. For a reification of the *inter*-subjective criterion—the first of the three presumptive conditions we saw flowing from the commitment to predictive efficiency—would by definition grant only a secondary, reflective significance to that which man experiences *intra*subjectively. And thus the existential in man—that which speaks to the nature and destiny of his most private self—would be denied. The central mystery of *being*—collective and individual—would have been adroitly eliminated. From but a "public" perspective questions of ontology, as logical empiricists have claimed, are quite literally "non-sense." We would then come to live in a depersonalized and disenchanted world in which the primary reality of our experience—the awareness of one's *intra*subjective self-hood that remained the residue in Descartes's attempt to carry doubt as far as he could—is abandoned. Indeed, the first selection in a popular collection of readings for the introductory student in sociology is entitled "Undermining the Student's Faith in the Validity of Personal Experience" (O'Brien, Schrag, Martin, 1964:15).

Reports that may earlier have been greeted with at least mild surprise fall, when viewed in terms of the priority of the intersubjective, neatly into place. An assembly of scientists greets the playback of a recording of the noise of a cat's nervous system with "wild applause." A noted biophysicist states before a meeting of his colleagues that "our common meeting ground is the faith to which we all subscribe . . . that the phenomena of behavior and of mind are *ultimately* describable in the concepts of the physical and mathematical sciences." A famous philosopher-mathematician asserts that "the average practicing scientist is a materialist."[3] No advantage appears to accrue from hypothecating a subjective dimension of existence when one is operating simply upon a physical or organic level of investigation. The full implications become visible only as one moves on into the behavioral sciences to hear such not completely lighthearted observations as the one in which man is described as "a ten-cycle computer in a one-tenth ton chassis with one-tenth horse power motor," followed by the only appropriate conclusion: "Get rid of him."[4] In point of fact one may not have to get rid of him. Characterized in such terms, he has already disappeared.

The path of science *is* a path of renunciation. We must forgo the temptation to confront experience in its personal immediacy.[5] Eddington's pointer readings point only to themselves; ignored, of necessity, are the existential factors that commit us to science in the first place. Were objectivization—the exclusion of or dispensing with the cognizing subject—to stand alone, we might have an elegant network of maps that detailed the public byways, but we would be unable to appraise the personal significance of any intersection.

Impoverishment of the "self"

The denial of a non-empirical base to cognitive understanding is but one item in a vast body of evidence supporting the view that mid-twentieth-century man seeks to flee from the self. Indeed, the reduction of the concept "self" in social and social-psychological theory to the status of an intervening variable is almost a perfect case in point. The social behaviorism that sociologists have abstracted from the full body of George Herbert Mead's work would identify truth with the logic of science, whereas the latter in turn is justified by a pragmatic philosophy that links the two through their mutual attachment to efficiency. The "self," which until Mead's time referred to elements falling within the bounds of man's *intra*subjective comprehension, was captured and transfigured through a brilliantly consistent application of an *inter*subjective frame of reference that left it merely the result of an interaction between a socially derived "me" and a biologically based "I." "The proudest assertion of independent self-hood," Mead could then be quoted as affirming (1929:395), "is but the affirmation of a unique capacity to fill some social role." Here was no simple assertion that behavioral scientists had to reject the world of the subject in the astringent manner of a J. B. Watson. The self was to be fully claimed for the object world, the implication being that there was no residue, intellectual or otherwise, that might have any further claim to the concept. Sincerity itself, as David Riesman has suggested, is debased, for a self composed simply of roles in flux possesses no stable point of reference. There appears to be even too much of the "personal" in "personality" for the latter to remain a viable concept for sociologists *per se.* Talcott Parsons heads a long list of contemporary theorists who assume that roles rather than personalities are the units of social structure with which social psychologists should be primarily concerned.[6] "Mind" likewise has been reclaimed as an exclusive vehicle for the rhetoric of empiricism. Erving Goffman (1959:252–53) is able to paraphrase this aspect of Mead—and, in doing so, to be blessed officially by sociologists in general—by acknowledging that "in analyzing the self we are drawn from its possessor, from the person who will profit or lose most by it, for he and his body merely provide the peg on which something of a collaborative manufacture is hung. . . ." He has no identity other than those attributes that are "psychological in nature . . . and (which) seem to arise out of intimate interaction with the contingencies of staging performances." "The self, then, as a performed character, is not an organic thing that has a specific location, whose fundamental fate is to be born, to mature, and to die; it is a dramatic effect. . . ." What better way to obliterate the existential dimension in man than to deny it its language?

If one is tempted to deal with man in depth, one need only add the psycho-biological imagery of Freud. "Sincerity" becomes, as we have seen, but an attribute of the self that is taken in by its own propaganda. With the expropriation of "self" in the name of that which is publicly verifiable, problems of ethics are transformed into problems of socialization, and conscience is reduced to the social relativism of Mead's "generalized other." The image of man as but a role-playing animal is in turn re-enforced in the larger discipline by the perspective of the sociology of knowledge, and the two are linked through reference group theory.

Many scholars have pointed to the elusiveness of Mead's characterization of the biologically given "I" and even more have been disturbed by the manner in which behavioral scientists have tended to depreciate even those elements of the "I" that Mead identified as the agents that initiate social interaction. But critiques have typically gone no further than the kind of uneasiness expressed by Dennis Wrong's paper on "The Oversocialized Conception of Man in Modern Sociology," an uneasiness that does not spring from a fundamental confrontation with Mead's approach to understanding *per se*, for Mead not only thought that he had freed himself from metaphysics but also from what he casually described as the "philosophic riff-raff known as epistemology" (Strauss, 1956:22). This results, as Paul Pfuetze has noted (1961:267), in a system that is *entirely* pragmatic. "His simple formula was: Man can if he will; and he will if he knows; but he can only know through the technique of science." But the pragmatic use of the logic of science—*and none other*—to delineate self-hood is itself cluttered with metaphysical presuppositions. T. V. Smith, one of Mead's students and colleagues, was aware of this over thirty years ago when he wrote of Mead that "a metaphysics was emerging from his speculations to help his sociology cope with the recalcitrant ways of his psychology."[7] Mead, unfortunately, was unaware that he was simply projecting the instrumentalism of science back into the world of the subject, the very world that scientists must rule out of court in order to proceed at the level of reliability that they demand of themselves. To suppose that such an approach could be sanctioned on *a priori* grounds alone—or, as Mead thought, by a metaphysically untainted pragmatism—reflects a naïveté perhaps understandable in the flush of excitement over America's first major contribution to philosophic dialogue. But pragmatism, we have come since to realize, is no more free of epistemological, and thus metaphysical, presuppositions than any other philosophical tradition.

The societal context in which pragmatism came to flower in America may have protected it from the harsh implications of its suppositions, for the ethos that ran through Mead's image of social man was in fact humane and democratic. But that ethos is viewed increasingly as excess baggage in a new secularized era that seeks its bearings solely in the empirical. H. Richard Niebuhr (1960: 139–40), although one of the most sophisticated champions of the scientific community among recent theologians, put the dilemma posed by sociology's image of self-hood in the following terms:

> Our western morality is built on the recognition that nothing is more important, more to be served and honored, apart from God himself, than human I's and Thou's—the selves we are and the selves among whom we live. But the morality of personal worth maintains itself in our subconscious minds like an alien in a strange country where no one understands and few acknowledge his presence. These selves among selves are required to direct their attention to things, to impersonal powers, forces, relations, and concepts. They are the knowers, but only the known is acknowledged and honored; they devote themselves to the cause of knowledge, but only the publicly, generally present is accorded the recognition of being real and valuable. These selves are true and false to themselves and to one another, but only the truth and falsity of their statements about things assumed to be objective is considered important. They live in the intense subjectivity of decision, of anxiety about meaning, of commitment to their causes. They live in faithfulness and in treason. They must deal in their isolation with the questions of life and death, of being or not being. They must enact the dramas of devotion to great and little causes, suffer the spiritual pains

of betrayal and being betrayed, of reconciliation to life and of revolt.

But as selves they are epiphenomena in the dominant world view of our society. Poetry and religion may portray them, but poetry and faith are officially regarded as dealing with the mythical. What alone is acknowledged, accepted and actual, is the object. So far as selves can be made objects—set before the mind as projected, eternal realities—they have their place. But then they are no longer selves; they are not I's and Thou's but It's.

So we live in a depersonalized and disenchanted world in which we are taught to doubt the primary realities that we experience—the self and its companion selves and in which we are taught to flee from the knowledge which lies near the beginning of wisdom—the knowledge of ourselves . . . the world in which all selves become objects for objective knowledge on the one hand, for objective manipulation in the market and the political arena on the other, is not a world in which the morality of personal value can flourish. . . .

In his two series of Gifford lectures published as *Self as Agent* and *Persons in Relation*, John Macmurray follows Mead insofar as they both build upon an interactionist base. Macmurray, however, avoids the reductionist trail. Instead he is fully cognizant of the postulational commitments that are incurred when one accepts the scientific frame as one's ultimate referent. Focusing upon the personal rather than fleeing from it ("I exist as an individual only in a personal relation to other individuals"), he points out that

. . . any objective or impersonal knowledge of the human, any science of man, whether psychological or sociological, involves a negation of the personal relation of the "I" and the "You," and so of the relation which constitutes them as persons. Formally, such knowledge is knowledge of the "You," that is, of the other person; but not of the other person in personal relation to the knower, but as object in the world. I can know another person *as a person* only by entering into personal relation with him. Without this I can know him only by observation and inference; only objectively. The knowledge which I can obtain in this way is valid knowledge; my conclusions from observations can be true or false, they can be verified or falsified by further observation or by experiment. But it is abstract knowledge, since it constructs its object by limitation of attention to what can be known about other persons without entering into personal relations with them (1960:28).

It is a mistake to view such an impersonal stance as unjustifiable. It can be justified—but only, Macmurray contends (1960:29), "by relation to a personal intention which includes it." It is simply that the logic of science, standing on its own legs—or the closely related legs of Mead's pragmatism—fails to provide even a language, to say nothing of guarantee, for such a context of personal intention.

Reductionist tendencies in Parsons

Although Talcott Parsons stands head and shoulders above most of his critics in the perceptiveness with which he deals with the value-laden societal context within which sociological theory itself must operate, portions of his work since *The Structure of Social Action* suggest that he has been unable to resist completely the lure of a reductive objectivity. He even stumbles at one point into accepting the hoary three-stage version of the history of cognitive structures (theological-to-metaphysical-to-positive) that is so basic to Comte's vision of history.[8] The posture obscures the fact that social scientists have not and cannot even in principle free themselves from philosophical presuppositions, even though Parsons in his better moments has gone a considerable distance toward acknowledging that fact.

Parsons (1961:32) does indeed declare that action theory is incompatible with reductionism, that "neither the theory of mechanics in the older sense nor that of the nineteenth century physiology would be adequate if simply 'applied' to the behavioral field." Unfortunately, his theory has over the past two decades seemed to move in precisely that direction (Scott, 1963:716–35). Although claiming that much of his inspiration has come from the humane Weber—both in terms of the method of *verstehen* and the related interpretation of "meaningful" action as indicating goal-directedness—Parsons blunts its significance by claiming that Weber had gone too far in distinguishing between the approaches of the natural as over against the social sciences. Granting but lip service to *verstehen*, Parsons seems to have settled upon the "goal-directedness" of complex organisms as the single differentiating factor. He is not satisfied with accepting as his point of ultimate reference Weber's acknowledgment of what may be termed the existential involvement of scientists even within the scientific role. Rather, Parsons seems to frame the role of the scientist in terms of action theory itself, providing no clear base for viewing science from any perspective that would stand outside its own presumptive circle. "Parsons," as John McKinney has noted (1954:569), "demonstrates a tendency to state what the nature of things is." He slips by implication over into the tempting role of implicit metaphysician rather than making completely clear that sociological theory must be judged *simply* in terms of its ultimate contribution to the economical ordering of empirical experience.

Societies as equilibrating mechanisms

George Lundberg, characterized widely as reflecting the positivistic metaphysic of a Comte, came in fact to claim the latter-day Parsons as a brother-in-arms. In his paper describing "Some Convergences in Sociological Theory," Lundberg (1956:21–27) saw Parsons and Bales in a portion of their *Working Papers in the Theory of Action* (1953), as neo-positivists who proposed "to force sociology into the framework of physics," the very same language that Parsons had used against Lundberg and Stuart Dodd in the earlier *Structure of Social Action.* For Lundberg points out that the central terms by which Parsons had arrived at his theory (along with categories drawn from Bales with which Parsons explicated it) were immediately analogous to those of Dodd. Indeed, the first three of the four generalized conditions Parsons and Bales offered as "laws of equilibrium" were acknowledged by Parsons to be in fact analogous to the three Newtonian laws of mechanics, all neatly reduced to the language of physics. As Parsons and Bales (1953:85, 102) admit,

> what we have here . . . are the dimensions of a four-dimensional space in the mathematical sense of that term. . . . We will further assume that the space thus defined is "Euclidean," in the sense that . . . it is "rectilinear," that there is continuous linear variation along each of the dimensions, and that time enters into the analysis of classical mechanics.

> . . . the first three of our generalizations are clearly analogous to the three Newtonian laws . . . it would seem likely that there is a very important analogy between the scheme we have developed in this paper and the classical mechanics.[9]

They then added, with more insight than they suspected at the time, "If this supposition stands up . . . it is evident that it should turn out to have far reaching implications. . . ." They see such implications in the potential provided for quantitative analysis; the more striking implication, however, lies in the manner in which the analysis documents the degree to which Parsons succumbed to the very reductionist trend in the social sciences that had elicited his initial foray into sociological theory a quarter of a century before.

A latter-day behaviorism

In developing the four "laws of equilibrium," Parsons clearly abandoned Weber's method of *verstehen* and the latter's claim that sociology is to be characterized by a conceptual scheme drawn out of the value motifs of the *human* sub-culture involved when he stated that the conceptual framework developed was appropriate to the analysis of *sub-human* activity as well.[10] Parsons (1953:64) admitted to having found, in fact, that the theory of action could be fruitfully spelled out in "modified behavioristic terms." The distance he had come from his early antipathy to the behavioristic mode is illustrated by his inclusion within *Toward a General Theory of Action* of a monograph by Edward Tolman illustrative of his new mood. In it Tolman uses "behavior" and "action" interchangeably, differentiating both from mere movement or response in terms "only of the *organism-environment rearrangement* which it produces." Movements or responses are identified "in purely intra-organismic terms." Parsons' elaborate emphasis upon "meaningful" in the term *meaningful action* then is reduced, by Tolman's illuminating essay, to an analysis of "the ways in which (the action) tends to manipulate or rearrange physical, social, or cultural objects relative to the given actor." Tolman (1953:279, 281) in turn refers for support to a volume in which E. P. Guthrie and G. P. Horton had suggested the use of the two terms *act* and *action* "for the response defined in terms of the environmental-actor rearrangement which it tends to produce." The reductionism in which Parsons had been caught may perhaps be made evident by the title of the particular Guthrie-Horton volume involved: *Cats in a Puzzle Box*. Tolman's learning theory may be labeled "purposive behaviorism." But as E. R. Hilgard (1956:187) remarked about it, because all the raw data are rooted in the world of physics and physiology "the system remains a behaviorism."[11]

Evaporation of conflict of interests

Another intriguing aspect of Parsons' general shift has been his elimination of the "self vs. collectivity" polarity from those dimensions of the social act that he has termed "pattern variables." Concerned with consistency in social theory as he has been, he must have gradually come to realize that an approach which begins by presupposing "system" and continues by analogy to a number of theorems basic to biophysics simply contained no viable place for the apposition of "self" to "collectivity."[12] Would that one could so easily eliminate or demote the central dilemma of social existence!

Fortunately, Parsons (1960:478) is not so consistently "systematic" as he would have us sometimes believe. For he has not entirely ignored the obligation to relate action theory to other levels of knowledge. "At each end," he tells us, "is a set of limiting conceptions of nonaction 'reality.' At the lower end is 'purely physical' reality. . . . At the upper end is 'nonempirical,' perhaps 'cosmic,' reality. . . ." But although he speaks of the latter as "an 'existential ground' of operative cultural systems," he sees "no significant interpenetration" on the part of either. The crucial failure in his writings in recent years, then, lies at just this point: that, although he tends to identify action theory with "reality," he sees "no significant interpenetration" of that reality by the reality of an existential mode of understanding. A clue to his difficulty might possibly be found in his rather unfortunate inclination to identify the non-empirical with the "cosmic"—a strategy no more likely to enhance the significance or plausibility of the non-empirical than the immediately analogous but discarded efforts of theologians to locate a God somewhere "out there" in cosmic space.

What seems to have happened is that Parsons' appropriately increased involvement with those who are caught up in empirical research has led him gradually to restructure his theory in terms that meet the presumptive conditions of effective and reliable scientific work. Yet in the process he has been unwilling to forsake the identification of the "real" *per se* with social theory that animated his early revolt against the positivistic and behavioristic forces he saw threatening the social and psychological sciences in the 1920's and 30's. Although he has typically been more aware of the value issue in sociological theory than his critics, his resolution of the dilemma has taken the form of a changing mixture of philosophical sociology and sociological philosophy, which has confused more of his readers than his prose and which awaits clarification in the context of a careful and unambiguous statement of the epistemological base upon which the various stages of his sociological theory have been grounded. In the meantime, his inadvertent movement toward a startlingly mechanistic (and, most recently, organismic) image of social man may illustrate what is in store for those who would base their image of man—and a system of norms consistent with it—solely upon the postulational base of empiricism. To reify the assumptions of science at the expense of the private and personal, to transform for any but heuristic purposes what Martin Buber has termed the "I-Thou" relationship into an objectivized interaction of an "I" and an "It" is to risk much more than F. S. C. Northrop, Howard Becker, or any of those fully and consistently dedicated to a value-free sociology have suspected. *It can be done*, as I believe I have begun to demonstrate. But in the process man is reduced to an *object*. And *objects*, by definition, are denuded of any but *external* significance. Nothing need restrict one's relationship to them but the exigencies of the communal nature of sociology itself. "Selves" are no longer inviolable because they too have become "objects." The moral restraints implicit in the "self-collectivity" contrast dissolves as the "self" is seen simply as the product of the collectivity. Selves become merely "objects of interest," objects that may be used by the collectivity that is science to satisfy *its* self interest. With the latter-day Parsons, they may be seen to possess no centers of integrity that lie beyond categories derived from the biological and physical sciences. The ethic one is able to derive from such an "anthropology" is thus simply a pragmatic one, restrained only by the ultimate criterion for membership in the scientific community: that one contribute to its effort to predict the world of experience with increasing efficiency.

The Escape from Freedom

We discovered earlier that the second "by-law" of science was the assumption of *recurrence*, a stance that must be presumed if empirical phenomena are to be ordered over time. When reified, it is hardened into a *determinism*. Scientific research neither discovers nor demands such a posture. Determinism is its product only when its logic is regarded, with Northrop, as the clearest clue to a universal "reality." Those, like Ernst Mach, who reject the relevance of the concept of "reality" itself, may seem to becloud this distinction, although a completely instrumentalist stance would have a behavioral import identical to that projected by those who accept the search for reality as relevant.[13] Einstein (1941) exemplified the many who have been tempted to go beyond the assumption of recurrence and to characterize it as a dimension of reality when he noted that "the more a man is imbued with the ordered regularity of all events the firmer becomes his conviction that there is no room left by the side of this ordered regularity for causes of a different nature."

Sociology is far from free of the same temptation. George Homans (1963:100) evidenced it recently when he stated that "the sociologist and the historian are . . . both determinists. Indeed I think any effort at explanation implies a deterministic assumption." Bernard Barber (1962) stands among those who would prefer the term "determinate," although Reinhard Bendix (1951:187) declares simply that "modern social science teaches us to regard man as a creature of his drives, habits, and social roles, in whose behavior reason and choice play no decisive part." Or, as one popular introductory text (O'Brien, Schrag, Martin 1957:1) has put it, "the basic assumption of sociology . . . [is] . . . that human behavior is *elicited by stimuli* which can be identified and reliably observed." No taint of early Parsonian "voluntarism" here!

Freedom as a feeling-state

Intimately involved, of course, is the traditional commitment of the Western world to "freedom." Indeed, as Waddington acknowledges in *The Scientific Attitude* (1941:110), "freedom is a very troublesome concept for the scientist to discuss, because he is not convinced that, in the last analysis, there is such a thing." Sociologists, rather than denying the term outright, have tended to redefine it, perhaps because they realize that the word has taken on too sacred a cast to be rooted out of the common vocabulary. In their search for redefinition they take their cue from Max Weber's inclination to view it as but a "feeling" correlated with the rational linking of means and ends (1949:124–25):

> we associate the highest measure of an empirical "feeling of freedom" with those actions which we are conscious of performing rationally—i.e., *in the absence of physical and psychic "coercion," emotional "affects" and "accidental" disturbances of the clarity of judgment*, in which we pursue a clearly perceived end by "means" which are the most adequate in accordance with the extent of our knowledge, i.e., in accordance with empirical rules.

Freedom as functionality

Lundberg seemed to have picked up this thread in Weber and, through it, concluded that freedom was the feeling one has when an induced situation was flowing freely. A. K. Davis (1953:443) merely adds the vocabulary of functionalism when he identifies it as "a subjective feeling of personal well-being which results from the objective fact of living in a functioning society." If man then only *feels* that he is free he must, concomitantly, only *feel* that he is a *responsible* creature. Or as Robert Merton (1952:15) has put it, "sociologists generally assume that . . . to understand is to excuse, that the conception of individual responsibility is alien to social determinism." Neither freedom nor responsibility is to be dropped out of the vocabulary; but those of us involved in or acquainted with the behavioral sciences are to be emancipated from the inclination to identify a feeling state with a cognitively valid statement.

Responsibility as revenge

"Indeterminists are wrong," we are told by Gwynn Nettler (1959b:693) in defense of his study identifying cruelty with free will and dignity with determinism, "in that they run counter . . . to the assumptions required, to date, by scientific endeavor."[14] His conclusion is that "neither the evaluation nor the control of human behavior requires that we concern ourselves with 'moral agents,' " that "the concept [responsibility] is a harmful honorific, good only for revenge" (1959a:382, 384).

Laws about laws

Parsons has made a genuine attempt to emphasize the reality of choice by the manner in which he characterizes his pattern variables. Building upon Weber's conviction that moral values could be irreconcilably and mutually exclusive, he pictures the patterned pairs as dichotomous, rather than as mere polarities on a continuous dimension. Choices, then, must be made between the two alternative orientations—or, at the very minimum, a choice is made between mutually exclusive constellations of the patterned pairs. Unfortunately, it doesn't quite come off. Those who have applied his categories in empirical research appear to use them as polarities capable of merging one with the other toward the center of a scalar continuum. As behavioral scientists, they see no heuristic value in Parsons' attempt to retain a measure of his earlier voluntarism. Weber himself saw the exclusive nature of values as a characteristic of the world of phenomena *prior* to its conceptualization in scientific terms, not as something to be built into the fabric of the scientific mode of understanding itself. That Parsons may not have even convinced himself is suggested by McKinney (1954:569), who observes that:

. . . science evokes the postulate of uniformity. The uniformity of nature is a major premise of science, and it of course is implicit in the systems of all three men [Parsons, Mead, and Lundberg]. Owing to the fact that all the endeavors of science are predicated on this premise, there is a frequently observed tendency to treat uniformity as more than a postulate. Such a tendency is manifest in the work of Parsons. Uniformities seem to "inhere" in nature very frequently for Parsons. Probabilities are sometimes spoken of as being demonstrative of uniformities of nature . . . the uniformity was assumed in the first place. . . . The uniformity of nature cannot be "demonstrated" by assuming it in advance; consequently, "uniformity" remains merely a necessary postulate.

The relentlessly determinate nature of science is perhaps made most evident in Parsonian social theory by the way in which the whole is couched in terms of system analysis. I have already observed that those who criticize Parsons' emphasis upon equilibrium theory as the result of a conservative political stance are snapping in the wrong direction. They may be barking at the right tree, but its epistemological roots are the culprit, not its ideological fruit. For Parsons is simply taking more seriously than perhaps any other major theorist the fact that the logic of science assumes closure in principle. It operates upon the presumption that phenomena available to it are all related in and over time—that they possess the nature of a closed system. Parsons may reflect this postulate more clearly than others simply because he is striving to provide a conceptual framework at the very highest level of abstraction. Kenneth Boulding (1963) has put the implications of such a stance brilliantly:

> Any point of view depends upon certain value presuppositions. . . . Not even general systems . . . can escape this iron law. . . . The first of these presuppositions is a prejudice in favor of system, order, regularity and non-randonmess and a prejudice against chaos and randomness. Along with the poets, the general systems type has a "rage for order" as Austin Warren has called it. . . .
>
> The next prejudice is . . . that the whole empirical world is more interesting ("good") when it is orderly. It is to the orderly segments of the world therefore that the general systems man is attracted. Like the blessed man of the Psalmist, his delight is in the law, though not necessarily of the Lord, and in that Law doth he meditate day and night. . . .
>
> If he delights to find a law, he is ecstatic when he finds a law about laws. If laws in his eyes are good, laws about laws are simply delicious and are most praiseworthy objects of search.[15]

Kierkegaard may have contended that there is no system conceivable to man that could contain human existence, but his is the tradition that sociology has denied. Weber's leap of faith—that "there are no mysterious incalculable forces that come into play, but rather one can, in principle, master all things by calculation"—was rooted, as was Marx's, in the Hegelian vision that knowledge is real *only* as a system.[16]

Freedom and causality as incommensurable

As Peter Berger (1963:122) has pointed out, an affirmation of freedom by man poses "*a priori* difficulties within the framework of a sociological argument." For "freedom is not empirically available . . . it is not open to demonstration by any scientific methods. . . . An object, or an event, that *is* its own cause lies outside the scientific universe of discourse. Yet freedom has precisely that character." He goes on to maintain that freedom and causality are not contradictory; they simply are incommensurable. His argument is rooted in the distinction between the cognitive and the existential, between the mode of nature and the mode of history—contrasting epistemological categories that have come increasingly into play over the last intellectual generation in both philosophy and theology. A person need not have lost his freedom to decide merely because someone else may frequently *predict* the direction his decision will take. But neither is it sufficient to suggest, as both Berger and William Kolb appear satisfied in doing (1961:13), that freedom is not to be identified with unpredictability. Freedom is not *simply* unpredictability, for this would subject the notion to the very reductionism that they and I would seek to avoid. On the other hand it would be foolish to deny that as we increase our ability to predict the behavior of others we increase our potential capacity to control that behavior as well. What we must avoid is the temptation not only to identify unpredictability and freedom in any one-to-one fashion, but also to suggest that there is no relationship whatsoever. If we succumb to the latter we must settle either for the psychologistic view that dominates the functionalist approach—that one is free to the extent that one "feels" free (or its sociologistic twin which argues that one is free to the extent that the system of which one is a part is "flowing smoothly")—or abandon the evidence that is the empirical world and stand instead upon a simple rhetorical statement of faith. By recognizing that nature and history, the cognitive and the existential, although not identical, address themselves to aspects of the *same* reality, we are in a position to avoid both simplistic alternatives.

Causality speaks *only* of those elements in the "real" that are recurrent. Freedom, although possessed of an existential dimension that transcends the categories of nature, has an empirical character as well. The latter is suggested by the abundant evidence that links predictability with control. Behavioral science, if it improves infinitely upon its capacity to predict human social behavior over the long run, will extend in like measure its capacity to control man, reducing in inverse ratio the empirical content of any image of man as a creative or responsible agent in the traditional sense of those terms. Freedom has a *content* that cannot be *identified* with the idiographic, with unpredictability. But if there is no reason to believe that such uniqueness may not in principle be eliminated, then the term itself will be emptied of significant content except for the poet and the antiquarian.

Freedom and causality as nested

In other words, the ultimate problem that adheres to the issue is not solved, as Berger suggests it might be, simply by keeping a Kosher kitchen—by separating the meat of causality from the milk of freedom. For one must turn to one form of discourse or another for one's clue about when and where to shift one's menu. And the direction one takes then inevitably affects the nature of the diet that results. The key lies in the discovery that the menus are not alternative. They are nested within each other.

The nomothetic is engulfed by a sea that includes the idiographic, the categories of nature set in a frame that involves history as well, the cognitive extracted from a base that is also existential. Though it has served man's purpose to precipitate order from the larger solution that includes the unique, the latter remains within the larger solvent that is immediately salient in human experience. Empirically speaking, this merely suggests that the Heraclitean flux remains a crucial part of the ground from which one may isolate Democritean atoms.[17]

Again we conclude that one may indeed build an

image of—and an associated ethic for—social man from a fundamental assumption of the behavioral and natural sciences. But such reification—this time of the postulate of recurrence—leaves us with man as a product of impersonally determined forces. Freedom and the responsibility that derives from it are reduced, in sociology, to feeling states that derive from a social system functioning smoothly and are bracketed in quotation marks in the analysis of power. Man is transformed into a dependent variable whose nature it is to respond rather than to initiate. In conceiving his every action as but a reaction, he becomes merely an expression of forces beyond himself and, with no inhibition other than the restraints of his fellow scientists, sociologists are tempted to orient themselves toward social man as independent variable to dependent variable. Scientist and "man" are no longer reciprocal. The relationship is transformed into that of an "I" and an "It." If in fact sociologists take a step toward consistency by including themselves within the determined circle, then they absolve both ego and alter of risk as well as responsibility. The contemporary version of the escape from freedom is complete.

The Retreat to Relativism

A third postulate that must enter into our discussion is the one I have labeled the "relational." Along with the screens of inter-subjectivity and the recurrent through which the data of science must be sifted is the filter that reduces our experience to a network of predictive relationships, thus eliminating concern for the character of an experience *per se*. This position cannot be equated abruptly with an ethically relativistic stance, for the relational postulate may simply be applied when appropriate to the particular ends a person has in mind when he takes on the scientific role. However, *if* sociologists are to look no further than their own presumptive tradition for the norms they must apply in social research, *if* they are to be consistent in their declaration that no value-judgments are proper in that role beyond the commitment to reliable prediction and to attitudes that derive from that commitment, *then* they reify the relational stance and it does take on the format and character of *relativism*. And there is considerable evidence to suggest that this is exactly what has occurred throughout a broad spectrum of the behavioral sciences.

Cultural relativism

It is most visible, perhaps, in anthropology. There, in the form of the doctrine of cultural relativism, it has been regarded by many as "one of the major achievements of contemporary ethnology" (Bidney, 1953a:693). That it is not regarded simply as an instrumentally derived rule of thumb is suggested by the way in which its opposite—ethnocentrism—has been the anthropologist's *bête noire*. Ethnocentrism is not looked upon merely as inaccurate; ethnocentrism is morally wrong.[18] And this has meant that cultural relativism is not just a method but a philosophy—even a guide for practical conduct as well. Herskovits (1951:24) was commendably honest in making this quite clear:

> As method, relativism . . . seeks to understand the sanctions of behavior in terms of the established relationships within the culture itself, and refrains from making interpretations that arise from a preconceived frame of reference. Relativism as philosophy concerns the nature of cultural values, and, beyond this, the implications of an epistemology that derives from a recognition of the force of enculturative conditioning in shaping thought and behavior. Its practical aspects involve the application—the practice—of the philosophical principles derived from this method, to the wider, cross-cultural scene. . . .
>
> In these terms, the three aspects of cultural relativism can be regarded as representing a logical sequence which, in a broad sense, the historical development of the idea has also followed. That is, the methodological aspect, whereby the data from which the epistemological propositions flow are gathered, ordered and assessed, came first. . . . Out of these data came the philosophical position, and with the philosophical position came speculation as to its implications for conduct.

What does all this mean for one's approach to values? Herskovits (1955:364, 366) tells us that it asserts "the validity of every set of norms for the people who have them, and the values these represent." It provides us with the "leverage to lift us out of the ethnocentric morass in which our thinking about ultimate values has for so long bogged down." Unfortunately, it leaves us deeply imbedded in a second morass. As praiseworthy as an open sensitivity to the perspectives of others may be, we are left with no reason that would justify our being tolerant of them, for after all—as Herskovits has made quite clear—our values, ethnocentrism among them, are by their very existence valid for us. Or, as Bidney notes (1953b:424), "Herskovits does not explain how it is theoretically possible to have cultural relativism without ethnocentrism, in view of the fact that cultural conditioning necessarily leads the members of any given society to prefer their own value system above all others." Bidney suggests that cultural relativism is in fact a kind of ethnocentrism: a *serial* ethnocentrism in which each normative pattern is judged *only* in terms of itself. Not only, with Protagoras, is man the measure of all things; now *each* man may claim such omniscience.[19] That a methodological and philosophical reaction to the stance has begun to set in suggests the beginning of an appreciation of the fact that science itself is the product of a specific value-orientation and an awareness that thorough-going cultural relativism is in fact destructive of its own claims.

Relativizing role of sociology

Sociologists have not succumbed to the temptation to reduce the relationism of its method to a relativistic ethic as openly as anthropologists, although to the extent to which it is presented in the texts as built upon a cultural sub-structure it acts to transmit the relativistic ethos streaming from its grounding discipline. It can, however, claim to have spawned its share of methodological perspectives—Weber's *verstehen*, Mannheim's explorations into the sociology of knowledge, W. I. Thomas' "definition of the situation," and, most recently, reference group theory. Even Florian Znaniecki (1940:7) was able to define "truth" as "any element of any system of knowledge taken . . . from the standpoint of the men who believe that they understand this system, who are actively interested in it and regard it as containing objectively valid knowledge about the object matter to which it refers." Peter Berger (1963:52), writing out of an immediately contemporary context, can see a "relativizing motif" as one of "the fundamental driving forces of the sociological enterprise." Berger moves beyond such relativism in his own stance, but only by couching his sociology in what he terms a "humanistic" context. Most sociologists have been unwilling to subject the image of man that their image projects to any such larger framework.

Relativity of the system stance

We have returned again and again to the system image that reigned as sociology's dominant paradigm in the 'forties and 'fifties and to Talcott Parsons, the paradigm's major apologist. Taken literally as an approximate statement of social "reality," the image Parsons (1951b:61) projects is one of a *relativized* man. "There is," he admits quite openly, "an inherent relativity in this frame of reference." For any element in action is seen as relative to the system within which it is viewed, while the system itself is relative to the system or systems within which it acts as element. Science itself, Parsons has made clear (1961: 337), assumes a "systematic" stance: "the concept of system is so fundamental to science that, at levels of high theoretical generality, there can be no science without it." This in turn has elicited the related concept of equilibrium, which has drawn such a steady stream of criticism from fellow theorists. For Parsons (1961:337) is able to contend that equilibrium, then, is also "an inherently essential part of the logic of science. . . ." This stance has drawn him in recent years toward cybernetics, whose input-output vocabulary is amenable to the mechanistic imagery we associate with the reductionism of the electronic computer. Parsons is not himself guilty of any one-to-one identification of such a conceptual structure with "reality" *per se*, but neither is he clear about how he would distinguish the two. We have seen that he states quite explicitly that scientific and philosophical categories tend to merge in his total frame of discourse. This blurring of epistemological boundaries in turn can only contribute to the more unsophisticated reductionism that is evident in the work of less talented theorists, research personnel, and some of the popular merchants of sociologese.

Functionalism

This temptation has nowhere been more evident than in the behavioral sciences' prolonged and rather intimate "affair" with functionalism, of which Parsons' structural-functional theory is but one contemporary expression. Functionalism may have had its roots as far back as Comte's *consensus universalis* or perhaps in Spencer's suggestion that integrative forces continually offset societal pressures for differentiation. Certainly Pareto's concept of society as a moving equilibrium influenced the Parsonian version. But the main line of development seems to have come largely via anthropology through William Robertson Smith and Franz Boas to Durkheim, and then on to be made quite explicit in the works of Malinowski and Radcliffe-Brown. Although few concepts have carried as wide a range of freight as has functionalism, common to all characterizations has been the notion that the phenomena under consideration are to be viewed in terms of their contribution to the interaction involved in some larger system. This being the case, it is startling that the discipline had to wait until the late 'fifties for Kingsley Davis' suggestion (1959:760) that the posture which it demands is simply that of the logic of science itself:

> Functionalism is most commonly said to *do* two things: to relate the parts of society to the whole, and to relate one part to another. . . . It strikes me that . . . [these] simply describe what *any* science does. Every science describes and explains phenomena from the standpoint of a *system* of reasoning which presumably bears a relation to a corresponding *system* in nature. . . . if there is a functional method, it is simply the method of sociological analysis.

Unfortunately, neither pre- nor post-Davis sociology has seen the point. What we find, rather, is unambiguous evidence to the effect that both anthropology and sociology as they are presently constituted seem ever so ready to transform a methodological postulate into a substantive reality.

Radcliffe-Brown explicitly acknowledged his indebtedness for the functionalist approach to Durkheim. But the manner in which Durkheim viewed the person as but the imprint of an "impersonal" *conscience collective* upon a body distinct in space and time set the stage for a sociology that granted but secondary significance to the individual. Upon such a base Durkheim (1953:56) then built an ethical relativism in which he could observe that ". . . all moral systems practiced by peoples are a *function* of the social organization of these peoples, are bound to their social structures and vary with them. . . . Each society has in the main a morality *suited* to it. . . ." Here then was planted the seed of a largely automatic utility: that which *is* is *good*—at least for those intimately involved. Health is defined in terms of "normality," while generality, largely statistically derived, is the criterion of the latter. Crime, for instance, becomes a "factor in public health, an integral part of all healthy societies . . ." because it is "normal" statistically (1938: 67).

Functionalism as a "school" made its formal appearance in 1922 with the publication of Radcliffe-Brown's *The Andaman Islanders* and Malinowski's *Argonauts of the Western Pacific*. Both saw culture as a *gestalt*: Any particular element within a culture or society was to be viewed from the perspective of its contribution to the whole. The way may well have been paved in Malinowski's mind by the Ph.D. he received in mathematics, in whose language the elements of any single system are defined as functions of one another, while his tendency toward reductionism could only have been re-enforced when he worked, after his degree in mathematics, in the fields of chemistry and physics. His anthropology—born out of a period of convalescence from tuberculosis—denied the significance of the historical and distributional studies dominating the scene until his time and pointed instead to the manner in which each element in a cultural configuration contributed to the overall "functioning" of the institutions involved. This functionality was ultimately spelled out in terms of the "needs" it fulfilled, needs defined primarily in biological terms although not exclusive of levels that he characterized as "derived" and "integrative." The reductionism within which he was caught, however, prevented him from becoming aware of the very real ambiguity residing in the term "need." For even where it freed itself from the primary biological base, it could be identified instrumentally only in terms of that which man *had* sought. Thus the alternative to reductionism was a redundancy. Radcliffe-Brown too had to fend with a similar two-edged sword. When he wasn't speaking in organismic terms, he was caught in a Durkheimian net which saw the mere survival of a cultural characteristic as *prima facie* evidence of its positive value to the maintenance of the societal system involved. The influence of these two—Malinowski at London and Radcliffe-Brown in Australia, at the University of Chicago during the middle 'thirties, and then for ten years at Oxford—was enormous, extending well into the mainstream of American anthropology and sociology and enabling at least one informed anthropologist (Firth, 1955:247–51) to report that *all* of British anthropology in the 1950's was functionalist. Although American anthropology has by and large exhibited greater restraint, Walter Goldschmidt (1962:666) is one among many who grasp the element of survival value from the functionalist heritage and claim it as the value-free foundation upon which they may build a "scientific" critique of cultural forms.

Although Kingsley Davis has denied the significance of functionalism as a particular mode of sociological interpretation, his influential *Human Society* published in 1949 would appear to have been a classic expression of the functionalist position. However, it is at the level of community study—perhaps most closely analogous to the field of vision of the cultural or social anthropologist—that the functionalist viewpoint has been most evident in American sociology. And it is perhaps no accident that here too we find some of the most ideologically laden efforts appearing under the guise of empirical research. The Lynd's *Middletown* and *Middletown in Transition* set a tone that was tempered in the works of W. L. Warner and his students only by the restraints of a considerably more sophisticated methodology. The analogy between Durkheim's functional assessment of religion and latter-day analyses of American ceremonialism by Warner (1953) is striking indeed.

Functionalist approach to religious phenomena

In applying the functionalist frame to the sacred, Durkheim (1953:52) could conclude that association was the generating source, or efficient cause, of the religious experience, and that God is only society transfigured and conceived symbolically:

In the world of experience I know of only one being that possesses a richer and more complex moral reality than our own, and that is the collective being. I am mistaken; there is another being which could play the same part, and that is Divinity. Between God and Society lies the choice. I shall not examine here the reasons that may be advanced in favor of either solution, both of which are coherent. I can only add that I myself am quite indifferent to this choice since I see in the Divinity only society transfigured and symbolically expressed.

The fact of the matter is that society became the ultimate through the simple process of reification. Durkheim was not registering a profound insight but merely following a logic consistently to its end.

Although neither Malinowski nor Radcliffe-Brown went so far as to identify the social and the divine, they passed on a legacy that views religion as essentially but "functionally" prerequisite to the continuity of a cultural network, a social group, and the individual himself. Religions persist because they are "part of the mechanism by which an orderly society maintains itself in existence. . . ." In "counteracting fear, dismay, and demoralization, [religion] assures the victory of tradition and culture over the mere negative response to thwarted instinct" (Malinowski, 1955:53). Thus a leading anthropologist at our most distinguished university (Howells, 1956:22) feels free to *define* religion in one of his texts as but "the normal, psychological adjustment by which human societies build a barrier of fantasy against fear." Fantasy though it be, Howells sees it as *necessary*, thus offering one more wearying example of the age-old temptation on the part of members of an elite to *encourage* belief by part of the general population in what they themselves are able to do without. Merton (1957:44) has observed that "the functionalists, with their emphasis on religion as a *social mechanism* . . . may not differ materially in their *analytical framework* from the Marxists, who, if their metaphor of 'opium of the masses' is converted into a neutral statement of social fact, also assert that religion operates as a social mechanism. . . ." The only difference in the present case is that Marxists would appear to be more honorable. They would destroy the fantasy rather than encourage it and profit by it. On the other hand the Howells approach might be more effective than a direct assault upon religion, given the context of the American scene. For while appearing on the surface to support the functional value of the belief, such an appraisal destroys—at least for those dedicated to or moved by the criterion of truth—its operative agency.

This strain, with a strong assist from anthropology, runs through sociology from Comte to Durkheim and on to the less ambitious but similarly functional appraisals of religion by theorists such as Karl Mannheim (1950), Kingsley Davis, and W. E. Moore (1945). Unfortunately, the strain speaks less appropriately to and of the Judeo-Christian faith, the scaffold from which Western culture was built, than to faiths that have lain outside the prophetic tradition. Much Christian theology has come in fact to view beliefs rooted in the social and personal utility of the faith as in fact *demonic*. Sociology, borrowing its approach to the sacred from anthropologists steeped in field data relevant to non-prophetic faiths, has found itself trying to apply the functionality discovered therein to faiths that are correlated with theological structures which, while acknowledging the recurrent invasion of the functional into their forms, *reject by definition* those modes that reflect it. Even the term "religion" has been rejected by those faiths for the very functional nature that it has come to signify.

But even more critical for our present concern is the redundant nature of the functionalist rhetoric. For under its assumption that extant cultural norms must somehow contribute to societal cohesion or survival, it becomes possible—as Clyde Kluckhohn and Dorothy Leighton (1946:176) have illustrated—to view the hanging of innocent people as witches as a functional means by which an outlet for communal distrust has been provided and the fabric of the culture maintained intact. Or one can, with Childe (1960:15), see headhunting as a method of facilitating the maintenance of an economic system. As Polanyi has suggested (1957:482), "No matter how cruel, treacherous, or abysmally stupid a custom may be, it will be presumed to fulfill a social function. . . ." The most disparate figures—the Hitlers and the prophets of Israel—are, adds Hannah Arendt (1953:482), indistinguishable in their functionalism. Perhaps it is time we realized, with Evans-Pritchard (1956:313), that it was not the savage who transformed society into divinity, but Durkheim.

Robert Merton (1957:26–32) did sociology a major service when he pointed out that functional analysts have typically adopted three interconnected postulates: the functional *unity* of society ("a condition in which all parts of the social system work together with a sufficient degree of harmony or internal consistency"), *universality* ("in every type of civilization, every custom, material object, idea and belief fulfills some vital function"), and *indispensability* ("every custom . . . represents an indispensable part within a working whole"). Noting that these assumptions are commonly reified in research inspired by the functionalist viewpoint, his plea was that they be translated into hypotheses which might be tested empirically.

Functionalism identified with the sociological method

Kingsley David argued instead that functionalism itself be dropped as a special mode of interpretation, but that the postulates be retained as *postulates*—although without reification—for they were in his mind simply fruitful assumptions built into the fundamental perspective of sociology as a science. If Davis is correct, then the dangers of which Merton has spoken loom large indeed. Davis (1959:764) himself mentioned that "functionalism adopts a kind of language that is peculiarly close to the purposive and moralistic reasoning of ordinary discourse, yet tries to use it in the opposite way. . . ." That the danger is a pernicious and ever-present one might be suggested by the fact that Merton (1957:51) is willing to settle for a definition of "function" that hinges on the teleologically ridden terms "adaptation" and "adjustment."

That the problem is not resolved simply by including the notion of dysfunctionality as well is clearly evident. Harold Fallding (1963:7, 9, 10) has been willing to acknowledge quite openly, even in the context of a paper supporting the use of functional analysis in sociology, that analysis in functional-dysfunctional terms does indeed involve evaluation. "To ask the function of any social arrangement is to call for its justification—or alternatively for its condemnation. The positive and negative polarity inherent in the terms (eu-)functional and dysfunctional should betray at once that evaluation is afoot. A great deal of unnecessary hedging in sociological work would be obviated if this could be frankly admitted. . . . Evaluating social arrangements as functional or dysfunctional is equivalent to classifying them as normal or pathological." The criterion typically offered for "normality," however, remains embarrassingly ambiguous: "stability and adaptive change in the combination demanded by the time and place." And when he feels pressed to suggest a criterion upon which conflicting functionalities might be integrated, what does he provide? The criterion of *economy*. The involutions of the reification process completed, we find that we have merely returned to our point of departure. Functionalist theory simply projects into the nature of society that which had been accepted initially as the central intent of science: economy in the ordering of experience over time. There was, in fact, no other place to go, for the alternative to the reification of the postulates of science is, as Ernest Nagel has pointed out (1961:520–35), the recognition that the criteria about which the functionalist approach centers—"internal consistency of a system," "functional unity," "indispensability"—simply are not amenable to empirical control because they cannot be given independent and verifiable reference.

Functionalism, as Ernest Gellner points out (1962:177), "blinds us to what is best and what is worst in the life of societies. It blinds us to the possibility that social change may occur through the replacement of an inconsistent doctrine or ethic by a better one, or through a more consistent application of either. It equally blinds us to the possibility of . . . social control through the employment of absurd, ambiguous, inconsistent or unintelligible doctrines." And if Kingsley Davis is right in his contention that the postulates of functionalism are simply those that inhere within the sociological perspective in general, then we see the magnitude of the blinders it has chosen to wear. If the blinders are then exchanged for lenses that reify those postulates for fear of compromising the empirical task by stepping beyond its own epistemological posture in justifying the value-laden choices faced in the research task, then we are in a desperate way indeed. The relational stance that necessarily adheres to a scientific rhetoric will have been transformed into the moral relativism of a *1984*.

Thus our picture is complete. The sociologist need not step beyond the bounds of the scientist's central commitment—to economy in prediction and its epistemic derivatives—for an image of man and a network of norms by which to resolve the choices that are demanded of him in the process of empirical social research. But in inhibiting himself in this manner—as the priestly posture would appear to encourage him to do—he should, if he is to be consistent, be willing to see man as but an impersonal object with no center of inviolable integrity, determined and thus manipulatable, guided only by a relativistic attachment to the moralities of the social nexus in which he finds himself at the moment. Though the call to a full-fledged value-neutrality may appear uncomfortably inhibiting in the immediate restraint it demands, the psychic compensation is clear: nothing need restrain the enjoined sociologist in his relationship to his human subjects but the practical exigencies of the power structure he confronts.

The Communal Ethic of Science

We have seen where the derivation of an ethic from the "primitive postulates" of Northrop's natural science and/or from Becker's conception of the central value stance of the scientist must necessarily lead. There is, however, one further route to a system of norms from within the circle of science itself that must be explored. That channel is by means of the Weberian method of *verstehen*: through empathic identification with those norms that we find expressed within the particular culture or sub-culture involved. In other words, one might emulate the values that appear characteristic of science as a *community*—to be contrasted with those that I have just shown may be logically derived through a reification of its epistemological assumptions. Though the two are related, the approach by means of the ethic that adheres to the communal nature of science would not only appear the more humanely attractive, but it is a path that has been deemed highly appropriate by an increasing number both within and without the behavioral sciences. Furthermore, the strength of its appeal may be expected to be enhanced as that community continues to increase in size and comes to play an influential role at those critical points of power wherein decisions of major ideological significance are made.

Perhaps the most cogent spokesman for this perspective within the behavioral studies is David Bidney (1953:415–47), trained in both anthropology and philosophy. Bidney, a sharp critic of the relativizing motifs that have dominated anthropology since the turn of the century, is equally unhappy with the reductive normativism of F. S. C. Northrop. He realizes that empirical "facts" are not simply sterile products of a value-free approach: "So-called facts are really *truth values*, human evaluations as to the truth of one's ideas concerning the order of nature and cultural experiences. . . ." But of the three categories of value—truth values, moral values, and aesthetic values—"truth values are *primary* . . . they underlie all other judgments of value." And, since it is the scientific community which is uniquely dedicated to the pursuit of truth, "it is the spirit of science, at once rational, progressive, and self-corrective, which may serve as an absolute norm for culture as a whole. . . ." This has a very practical meaning in terms of man's search for an absolute set of cross-cultural norms. "Instead of the slogan 'Workers of the world unite,' or the implied, but not articulated, 'Politicians of the world unite,' we might substitute the call, 'Scientists of the world unite.'" The traditional democratic freedoms of the West will in the process be guaranteed, Bidney argues, because "the scientist requires a social and cultural environment . . . which permits him complete freedom of thought and experiment in the pursuit of scientific truth and cultural knowledge."

The position is echoed on many sides. Richard Rudner (1958) responds in the affirmative in a paper titled "Can Science Provide an Ethical Code?"[20] Science not only assists inductively by clarifying means-ends linkages, but offers an ethical code *emulatively*, because the ideals traditionally associated with it may be drawn upon, and *deductively*, by noting that no other norms are necessary. Robert Hannaford (1962:30) is most explicit. He lists consistency, responsiveness, responsibility, self-evaluation, co-operation, honesty, and dedication as attributes demanded of scientists. "Indeed," he argues "these attitudes are hardly separable from the operation of a democracy." Polanyi (1962:54) would go considerably further. He not only finds the "free cooperation of independent scientists . . . a highly simplified model of a free society . . . ," but he sees a direct analogy between the "invisible hand" offered by Adam Smith as the guiding directive of a *laissez-faire* economy and the interactive mechanism that directs the communal marketplace of productive scientific theses. Among the many who have taken similar postures are Nevitt Sanford, C. E. Ayres, Jacob Bronowski, René Dubos, and Russell Bayliff.[21] The latter suggests in fact that the scientific community may be seen as the "fullest" manifestation of Christianity the Western world has yet seen. What we seem to approach, indeed, is a Durkheimian image of society in microcosm, a sub-community that has begun to sacralize itself.

But a slightly different version of essentially the same identification is offered by sociologists of science in the West when they see the scientific community dependent for its fullest fruition upon a democratic political context.[22] One is then able to argue, as Thomas Hoult (1968) recently has done, that sociologists' vested interest in "democracy" justifies the projection of such democratic values in their research role.

Subjects as means and objects of control

Unfortunately, although many of these characterizations are appropriate descriptions of the ethic of scientists in their interaction with one another, all ignore the fact that they do not represent the *entire* range of their behavior as scientists. For a scientist not only relates himself to other scientists, but if he is a social or behavioral scientist he also relates himself to others who are not of his in-group—those human beings who are his *subjects*. Although physical scientists may be excused for having overlooked the fact, those involved in the human sciences operate with a dual ethic—one appropriate to their fellow scientists and the other demanded by their interaction with the "out-group" that is the focus of their research.[23]

And these, if one is to operate at maximum efficiency, are radically at odds.

What is the nature of that subject-oriented ethic? It is simply one that roots itself in the image of the subject as means to the scientist's ends. "Science," John Macmurray reminds us (1961:184), "is knowledge of the other as means." His end we have delineated at wearisome length. Existentially it may perhaps be termed the satisfaction of curiosity—the scientist's curiosity, not the subject's; instrumentally it is seen as increased efficiency in empirical prediction. These ends may be guaranteed, other resources being equal, to the degree to which he is able to apply the logic of the experiment to that outgroup. And, as I have suggested earlier, this demands the application of *control*, for control is central to the logic of experimental verification. The subject, then, not only may but *should*—given simply the ends of the community of science—be treated as a means rather than as an end, as an object for manipulation and control, with no restraint whatsoever except as it is tactically imperative in a given context.

Perhaps the image appears overdrawn, a fictional characterization of the kind of intellectual arrogance which sees man as but a fit subject for experimentation. Yet, as one president of the American Sociological Society claimed in his presidential address, "There are no such things as inalienable rights. The only rights we know about are those which a community from time to time chooses to grant and respect" (Lundberg, 1944:3). And the only community that could claim to be in a position to grant and respect norms of an objective and cross-cultural nature would be, from the perspective under discussion, the community of science. It needn't feel overly sensitive about the issue of "freedom" for, as we have seen, sociologists may have concluded as Lundberg did (1944:4) that "men are free when they feel free. They feel free when they are thoroughly habituated to their way of life. It follows that within the limits of human conditioning, the feeling of freedom is compatible with an almost unlimited variety of social conditions." Once committed to satisfying his curiosity, a social scientist may not of course "feel" free until he has unambiguous power to apply the controls that maximize verification, whereas the means to his ends—the subjects involved—may be so indoctrinated in the value of such research that they may be led to "feel" free as they submit. Dostoevsky's Grand Inquisitor (1960:127–8) would, in that case, have spoken for those in the sciences gratuitously labeled "human" when he observed coldly that "people are more persuaded than ever that they are completely free, yet they have brought their freedom to us and laid it humbly at our feet . . . (for) man seeks to worship what is established beyond dispute. . . ."[24]

Martin Buber has provided our generation with a vocabulary that, although in the poetic mode, speaks poignantly to the stance we describe. If a social scientist regards his subjects as simply means to the achievement of what Bidney termed "truth-values," he transforms a potentially I-Thou relationship (in which ego relates to alter as an equally inviolable end) into an I-It relationship (which sees alter as an "object"—an object simply of ego's interest). The image is hardly new. Aristotle spoke of the treatment of others "as a living tool" and Kant "as a means merely." The second form of the latter's categorical imperative ("So act as to treat humanity, whether in your own person or that of another, in every case as an end in itself, never as a means") is of course but a statement in propositional terms of something that Buber sought to communicate in a more existential fashion.

The sociological tradition itself has approached the polarization of the I-Thou and I-It through Tönnies' *Gemeinschaft-Gesellschaft* typology and the many derivations, including Parson's pattern variables, which stem from it. Sociologists usually locate the ethos of science at the *Gesellschaft* end of the continuum, a pole which Parsons (1935:310–11) has characterized as involving a "kind of calculation of advantages which . . . when it is thought of *only* as a means to [specific ends] we think of as . . . a perversion."[25] It might be illustrated by the contrast between the manner in which a Freud could picture Charcot as praiseworthy when the latter maintained a servant in his home beyond her serviceable years so that, upon her death, he could demonstrate his diagnosis of her illness in an autopsy, and the instructions written by the anthropologist Kroeber to an associate, at the death of Ishi—a lone Indian survivor of a stone-age culture—that "as to the disposal of the body . . . yield nothing at all under any circumstances. If there is any talk about the interests of science, say for me that science can go to hell. We propose to stand by our friends."[26]

The sociologist as priest, then, is not only unable to claim "value-neutrality" in his research activity, but must eventually face the fact that if he would seek his normative guidelines for social research from *within* his scientific commitment—either by deriving them from its epistemology or by emulating its communal ethic—he must settle for a posture that cuts dramatically against the grain of the humane image of man that has been the West's heritage from its Hebraic and Greek forebears. There may of course be some who would accept the new pledge, one in which predictive efficiency becomes the very mark of high morality. It seems safe to assume, however, that as the implications of a fully consistent priestly paradigm begin to permeate the consciousness of the discipline, it will serve instead to re-inforce the current return to prophecy.

The Marxist Analogue

> It is not the consciousness of men that determines their existence, but on the contrary their social existence determines their consciousness.
>
> Karl Marx

The Marxist Paradigm

In my earlier discussions of the re-emergence of the prophetic mode and the manner in which the conflict image had come to challenge the system paradigm in sociology, I made occasional reference to the renewed awareness within the larger intellectual community of methodological and theoretical contributions of Karl Marx and the strain of thought that has borne his name.

Sociologists, to their credit, were among the first to decipher the fresh handwriting on the wall. Some very few—Hans Gerth at Wisconsin high among them—had nurtured the flickering flame all through the 'fifties. (It was no accident that Madison was the birth-site of *Studies on the Left* and later became the organizational center of the student protest movement.) Nor was it happenstance that C. Wright Mills, whose biting prose made it impossible for sociologists to ignore entirely the harsh realities of class, power, and conflict through this same period, was Gerth's student before he became his collaborator. Mills was aware that beneath the surface novelty of much of sociology's grasp of social man lay a set of assumptions voiced first with intellectual rigor by Marx and that much of the remainder would not have found its way into the discipline's bloodstream if Marx

---

Notes to this chapter will be found on pages 364–372.

had not insistently thrust the strong light of empirical scholarship into areas earlier set aside for the humanities.[1] Indeed, none less than Mills's focal antagonist on the battleground of social theory—Talcott Parsons—felt it necessary to admit in the early 'sixties that Marx was one of the symbolic grandfathers of his larger theoretical frame.[2]

Marx as sociologist

Marx was now being seen essentially as a sociologist rather than as an economist.[3] Peter Berger (1963:168) pointed out that Marxism's general appeal is quite similar to "a theoretical system of sociologism—that is, a system that interprets all of human reality consistently and exclusively in sociological terms, recognizing no other causal factors within its preserve and allowing for no loopholes whatever in its causal construction." The question posed by T. B. Bottomore's paper before a plenary session of the American Sociological Association in the fall of 1965—"Kark Marx: Sociologist or Marxist?" —meanwhile was answered by the unprecedented numbers who responded with their presence.

The relevance of Marx and the tradition he left to sociology had not, of course, been completely obscured during the 'forties and 'fifties in America. The sociology of knowledge, in particular, found it impossible to ignore its indebtedness, through Mannheim, to Marx's awareness that ideological and intellectual frames of reference might be viewed as but reflections of more underlying social positions, summed up in the classic observation that "it is not the consciousness of men that determines their existence, but on the contrary their social existence determines their consciousness." Paul Lazarsfeld (1962: 760) found himself acknowledging in a presidential address before the A.S.A. that his analysis of the sociology of empirical social research was blood-brother to the manner in which the Marxist appropriates the stance of the sociology of knowledge when he contends that modes of intellectual analysis are a function of the introduction of new methods of production. Philipp Frank (1961:198) in fact had been inclined to argue that dialectical materialism's contention that the propositions of science were to be understood in terms of their link with other social processes and not just in terms of the logical matrix of which they were a part is identical to the posture of the sociology of science—a posture echoed from within the sociology of science *per se* by Bernard Barber (1962: 56).

The kinship between the Marxist and sociological frames of reference was seen extending to the very heart of the latter's system paradigm when, in delineating the structure of functional analysis, Merton stated that Marxism's analysis of religion was matched point by point by a functional analysis if the former's judgmental tone is transmuted into a simple statement of fact.[4] Kingsley Davis (1959:769) then drove the point home when, as we have already noted, he concluded that such a functionalist approach was identical with the underlying methodological assumptions of sociology.[5]

Perhaps even more compelling evidence of common lineage may be found in the understanding the two postures share concerning the manner in which man is himself to be conceived. The dominant image within contemporary sociology has been provided by George Herbert Mead: Man is, beyond the biological slate upon which his selfhood is to be written, simply an ensemble of those human relationships within which he has been socialized. "The essence of man is not an abstraction inherent in each individual. In its reality it is the totality of social relations." "Man is, in the most literal sense of the word, a *zoon politikon*, not only a social animal, but an animal which can develop into an individual only in society." "Man is a member of society. Consequently his consciousness is formed and developed under the determining influence of the social conditions of the life and activities of man. Consciousness is indissolubly tied with language and from its inception has a social character." Society, in turn, "is not merely an aggregate of individuals; it is the sum of the relationships in which these individuals stand to one another." It is unlikely that any informed student of sociology would deny that these statements indeed characterize the main current within the discipline—or, indeed, that they ring specifically of Mead. In point of fact the first two and the last are direct translations from the writings of Karl Marx. The other item came from a contemporary Soviet philosopher's effort to paraphrase the Marxist understanding of man's fundamental nature.[6] Contrary to the impression of most American sociologists, Marx's stance may not justifiably be characterized as simply the paradigmatic parent of contemporary conflict theory. It is at a number of crucial points startlingly congruent with system theory as we have come to know it in Western sociology.[7] Charles Loomis contributed a delightful exercise to the re-education of candidates for advanced degrees at a number of our better graduate schools recently when he confronted them with selections from Marx which not only assumed the system stance and spoke in terms of function, but dwelt heavily upon what Marx termed a "constant tendency to equilibrium."[8] Almost all, given a choice among a list of names including those of Marx and Parsons, identified the latter rather than the former as their author. The fact of the matter is that Marx's overall position took, in his later years, a markedly "systemic" tone. One prominent theorist has gone so far as to label Marx rather than Weber the primary architect of the self-conscious use of ideal types in constructing systematic social theory (Hughes, 1958:87–88).

There is no doubt that much that Marx wrote stands unabashedly in the prophetic and conflict traditions. Still, if Marx is in process of reclamation by sociologists who regard the ideological tradition that has grown out of his and Engels' writings as an unqualified ally in the battle against the priestly and system modes, it would be well to examine the historical credentials for such a claim. If an equally convincing—perhaps even a more compelling—argument can be made that dialectical materialism as projected by Marx, Engels, and Lenin is at base highly analogous to the priestly and system paradigms, then the renewal of sociologists' interest in Marx might have a distinctly different effect on the future of the discipline than most sociologists currently assume.

Historical Antecedents

It is common practice to trace the lineage of empiricism from Newton to Bentham and then on to modern social science. It is equally possible to argue—as indeed it has been contended by informed Western scholars[9]—that one must extend the line forward from Bentham not only to sociology but directly on to Marx and Lenin as well. For Marx and Bentham shared a common materialist base and saw the method of science as the key that would unlock its implications for society. Talcott Parsons picks up the same thread and sees it woven into the origins of modern sociology.[10] Marx (1926: 188) himself recognized Hobbes as one of his intellectual progenitors, while Engels (1918: 17) added Francis Bacon and John Locke. All three, plus Marx, were in turn viewed by the Vienna Circle as among those to whom a philosophy that took its cue from the logic of science had to acknowledge its indebtedness (Ayer, 1959: 4).

Lenin did of course go out of his way to reject the Vienna Circle's immediate forerunner, Ernst Mach, just as other Marxist spokesmen since have opposed a full-blown logical empiricism. But Philipp Frank (1961: 196–200) had been among those of the latter school who believed that logical empiricism and Marxism shared the same epistemological foundation. He argued that Lenin's opposition to logical empiricism was tactical rather than fundamental. For the two postures rested on at least three common doctrines: that science was "materialistic"; that the criterion for the truth of a proposition was rooted in an essentially instrumental logic; and that the propositions of science must themselves be interpreted in scientific terms—more precisely in what we now term the sociology of science. Marxism and logical empiricism therefore confronted the same pair of opponents: idealistic philosophy on the one hand and a literal projection of Newtonian mechanics as the basis for all science on the other. Frank felt, then, that when dialectical materialism is applied in a fully instrumentalist fashion, the epistemological bases of Marxism and logical empiricism will coincide. That Frank's view was not unrepresentative of those positivists who sought to reduce all knowledge to the metaphors of science is suggested by the Marxist tone that ran through the Vienna Circle's original manifesto, the heavy hand of Marx that inspired so much of Circle-member Otto Neurath's *Empirische Soziologie*

(1931), and observations similar to Frank's offered by logical empiricism's most influential apologist to the general intellectual public, A. J. Ayer (1959:9).

The Open-Ended Nature of Marxism-Leninism

The non-Marxist social scientist in the West, however, finds it extremely difficult to accept the suggestion that Marxism-Leninism might in fact share a common presumptive base with natural science because of the dogmatic tone he finds running through so much of Marxist scripture. What he may forget is that its progenitors were both political activists *and* scholars, that the polemic demanded by the former task was not to be identified in any one-to-one manner with the social-scientific spirit that conditioned their scholarship. There is absolutely no doubt that one can document the rigid and dogmatic nature of their political style. But what the larger scientific community in the West has failed to realize—enveloped as it has been by the selective distortions of a conflicting ideology—is that an equally compelling case may be made that the basic stance taken by the founding fathers of dialectical materialism is in the best tradition of social science. That is, they were openly and self-consciously aware that, whatever their hypotheses might be, it was harsh empirical experience that acted as the final court of appeal. They recognized themselves as fallible, acknowledged prior error, and expected their projections to be but approximations of the economic, social, and political events that lay ahead. Their commitment as social scientists was not to any particular vision of the future, but to the epistemology that characterized natural science in general. As political activists they were of course dogmatic; but as scholars they both professed and demonstrated an open-endedness that was to be closed only by empirical facts.

Marx states, for instance (Feuer, 1959:225), that "I am not at all in favor of raising our own dogmatic banner . . . saying: Here is the truth, bow down before it!" Rather he saw his outlook as but the "self knowledge" of an age about itself, freed from preconceptions and subject only to the evidence of nature and history. Although his political self tempted him to proclaim the inevitability of revolution in the transition from a bourgeois to a socialist society, his social-scientific second self led him to acknowledge that the transition could occur in certain settings—such as England and the United States—without revolution.[11] Indeed he even went so far as to declare that communism itself might not be the final resting point of social history (Pappenheim, 1959:116).

Engels' major contribution to the Marxist corpus was his effort to set forth the full significance of the posture's natural-scientific assumptions, emphasizing as it did the tentative nature of any cognitive formulation. We must, he admonishes us, remain

> . . . extremely distrustful of our present knowledge, inasmuch as in all probability we are just about at the beginning of human history, and the generations which will put *us* right are likely to be far more numerous that those whose knowledge we . . . have the opportunity to correct. . . .
>
> In other words, the sovereignty of thought is realized in a series of extremely unsovereignly-thinking human beings; the knowledge which has an unconditional claim to truth is realized in a series of relative errors. . . .
>
> . . . an adequate exhaustive scientific statement of this interconnection, the formulation on thought of an exact picture of the world system in which we live, is impossible for us, and will always remain impossible. If at any time in the evolution of mankind such a final, conclusive system of the interconnections within the world—physical as well as mental and historical—were brought to completion, this would mean that human knowledge had reached its limit, and, from the moment when society had been brought into accord with that system, further historical evolution would be cut short—which would be an absurd idea, pure nonsense.[12]

Engels goes on to tell us that the same approach must be applied to the concept of "materialism" itself, for "with each epoch-making discovery even in the sphere of natural science (not to speak of the history of mankind) materialism has to change its form."[13] This relative "openness" filters right down to the issue of the assessment of the primacy of economic factors in the diagnosis of political and social dynamics. Engels (Marx and Engels, 1942:427) openly acknowledged that he and Marx had over-emphasized the former and had not granted other elements in the interaction sufficient weight.

Although his writing reflects the tone of one more

immediately caught up in direct revolutionary activity, Lenin too showed an appreciation of the approximate nature of the knowledge that he sought to convey: "the limits of approximation of our knowledge to objective, absolute truth are historically conditional . . . every ideology is historically conditional. . . ." ". . . dialectical materialism insists on the temporary, relative, approximate character of all . . . milestones in the knowledge of nature gained by the progressing science of man."[14] He was so disturbed by "crude" or "rigid" interpretations of materialism that he declared that an "intelligent idealism" would be preferable.[15] Lenin would have philosophy dissolved among the various branches of science and everything but science declared historically relative. The absolute was that toward which science points. Its "absoluteness" reflects back upon the *method*, granting it a share in the certainty that does indeed lie beyond the limits of a merely heuristic logic. Nor should we overlook the fact that close to the heart of the vision of science that Marx, Engels, and Lenin shared was a dialectical logic which, whatever its limitations may be as a support for nature, guarantees a remarkable degree of openness to the *process* of scientific growth. As Engels paraphrased Hegel (Feuer, 1959:199), "truth lay now in the process of cognition itself, in the long historical development of science, which mounts from lower to ever higher levels of knowledge without ever reaching, by discovering so-called absolute truth, a point at which it can proceed no further."[16]

A case, then, can be made for the open-ended nature of Marxism, for its contention that it draws from the ethos of the natural sciences a willingness to be judged and reframed by the evidence of nature and of an empirical grasp of history. Marxism is rooted ultimately in the affirmation of a selective approach to "reality." But since all approaches to knowledge are based finally on a point of reference taken on faith, this cannot be seen as a liability peculiar to dialectical materialism. It may be a strength, because the foundation is openly declared, not hidden.

Demythologizing Marxism

Western social and behavioral scientists are likely to reject evidence such as this less because of first- or second-hand acquaintance with the Marxist scriptures or with the actual ethos of scientific communities in Marxist lands than because it simply runs against the grain of their image of the presumptive limits within which Marxist social science must operate. The trouble with this kind of reaction is that it is no more sophisticated than the typical Marxist conception of the handicap that Judaic-Christian assumptions must be for Western scientists. Neither is likely to take into consideration the demythologizing process that has been occurring in the other over the past generations. In each case the opposing community tries to engage a complex of images that have long been rejected by the intellectual elites most directly involved. Although the original symbol systems are brought into play upon ceremonial occasions, they no longer claim their original referents. "Materialism" is no longer wed to the imagery of a pre-Einsteinian universe, the "dialectic" no longer caught simply in the web of an inverted Hegel.

A recent explication of the Marxist conceptual base offered by one who considers himself within the circle of "orthodox" Marxism (Friestadt, 1960:63) views historical materialism as but the equivalent of the sociology of knowledge. The dialectic is simply the recognition that the categories required in science are not immutable building blocks of nature but temporarily useful terms to be superseded as other concepts give evidence of more adequately reflecting the empirical evidence. "Necessity" is, in turn, only the presumption of causality; to assume anything else would simply undermine the fundamental notion of the universe as a closed system and would limit, on an *a priori* basis, the infinite enterprise of science. Nothing, it is acknowledged, forces one to accept a scientific path rather than a more subjective one; a deliberate choice must be made. But once chosen, it governs the character of everything that is thereafter claimed. "Matter," that ontological anchor to the entire Marxist edifice, becomes merely "the totality of invariants (and covariants) belonging to the realm of science"—identical, we are advised, with the scientific community's use of the term "nature."

The conclusion to which one is pushed, then, is that, contrary to the ideological proclivities of many in the scientific and broader intellectual communities of the West, a *demythologized* Marxism—indeed, the Marxism that is coming to dominate the technical elites of Eastern Europe and Russia—is far from an uncongenial context for nurturing the natural-scientific viewpoint. Although the Stalinist period did much to delay the development, even *orthodox* Marxists (in the sense of claiming fidelity to political bodies identifying themselves as Marxist and occupying positions of national power in the East) are able to claim, quite justifiably, an identification with what even non-Marxist scientists will have to admit is an orthodox natural-scientific stance. If a Judaic-Christian ethos provided the initial constellation of factors conducive to the rational empiricism that took systematic root in the fifteenth, sixteenth, and seventeenth centuries in Western Europe,[17] then perceptive sociologists, historians, and logicians of science would do well to confront the obvious possibility that a nineteenth-century Judaic-Christian heresy—a demythologized Marxism—might well be even more conducive to science's growth in the future.[18]

Science as a communistic community

Bernard Barber (1962:107, 130, 293) has suggested that active rationality, utilitarianism, universalism, individualism, progress, meliorism, and an open-class system represent the matrix that has provided the nutrient for the growth of modern science. All but individualism he finds characteristic of a Marxist context, although even here he would acknowledge that science can never hope to be completely freed from a measure of political control. Indeed, he goes on to acknowledge that a factor he terms "communality"—called more bluntly "communism" by Merton—is an additional imperative within the mix, a situation in which all scientific output is conceived of as communal property, available to all trained scientists for their common benefit. He adds, tellingly, that "in science, if anywhere, the utopian communist slogan becomes social reality: 'From each according to his abilities, to each according to his needs.' " His earlier bow in the direction of 'individualism" would appear, then, to have been little more than a gesture, particularly in light of his concluding observation that "it cannot be assumed that there would be no restrictions on science even in a socialist society, although it is possible that there might be fewer than in capitalist society." Here, from one of our foremost sociologists of science—and one who is well aware of the aberrations that colored the development of science in the Russia of Stalin—is an acknowledgement of the congruence of the Marxist and scientific frames that is as courageous as it is provocative.

But as important as all of this has been for our effort to assess the prospects of sociology's re-engagement with Marxist theory, something of even greater significance to our immediate concern with the paradigmatic prospects for the discipline has been implied. We have already mentioned that those sociologists who are in process of reclaiming Marx have sought him out in large measure because of the support he would seem to give to the prophetic and conflict approaches. What they have not realized is that the dominant images projected both by classical Marxist theory and a demythologized yet orthodox reading of that theory would be more likely to approximate—and thus re-enforce—that image of man and associated ethic we have already found to reside in the most consistent application of the priestly and system paradigms.

Object and Matter

The labels "dialectical materialism" and "scientific socialism" are not simply phrases to deceive the innocent. Although Marx and Engels did see in the language and substance of natural science a vehicle that would grant their political theories a status and stamp that no other ideologies would be in a position to challenge, they quite honestly framed their anti-metaphysical metaphysic in its terms. They did not need to distort the natural science of their age, for nature *was*, in the middle of the last century, simply *matter in motion*. They did not have to reify the assumptions of science for it had already been done for them. They entered a world whose intellectual elite had already come to accept matter and necessity as the regulative features of the natural world. All they saw themselves involved in was the extrapolation of the world of nature to include social and historical man as well. It is far from fortuitous, then, that the fundamental dimensions of the reality they regarded as "real" turned out to be essentially identical with the reified form of what we have since come to realize are the *presuppositions* of the logic of science. But again let us turn to the evidence.

As Weber observed on one occasion, a materialist conception of history is not a cab one can get off and on at will—one has to stay on for the ride. The "cab" is entered by way of criteria that govern scientific verification: the demand that any item introduced as the raw data of science be directly available to comprehension by more than one person. A position that grants precedence to science must inevitably screen out the uniquely inward experience. Philipp Frank (1961:198–99) draws the analogy with dialectical materialism in the following terms:

> If we look up the definition of the word "materialism" in the official textbooks of diamat, we find roughly the following: "By *materialism* is meant the conception that science speaks of a world that is completely independent of any arbitrariness, a world that is neither the creation of a world spirit . . . nor the creation of individual consciousness. . . ." If . . . we observe how this definition is applied in practice, we find that all scientific propositions are to contain only terms that occur in statements about observable facts. . . . Everything in the world that is describable through intersubjective expressions is called "matter" by diamat.
>
> This is not to say that matter actually has the properties which Newtonian mechanics or even the newer physics attributes to matter. Such an opinion would be "mechanical materialism." According to diamat, every investigation of the world that makes use of intersubjective expressions is an investigation of matter.

Frank then goes on to indicate that the conception "comes very close to the viewpoint that science is based on an intersubjective language, which Neurath and Carnap have designated more precisely as the physicalist language" and with which, as we noted earlier, Frank is in general agreement.

The case is quite easy to document from the writings of the dialectical materialists themselves. For following hard upon Marx's initial inversion of Hegel ("the ideal is nothing other than the material when it has been transposed and translated inside the human head . . ."), Engels (Marx and Engels, 1935:219) contended that "the material, sensuously perceptive world to which we ourselves belong is the only reality. . . . Its premises are men . . . in their actual *empirically* observable process of development. . . ." To this Lenin was later to add:

> There is nothing in the world but matter in motion. . . . Blei is absolutely right when he says . . . that "personality" is a *quantité négligeable*, a cypher, that man is an "incidental factor," subject to certain "immanent laws of economics" . . . for the concept matter . . . epistemologically implies *nothing but* objective reality existing independently of the human mind and reflected by it. . . . And it is this sole categorical, this sole unconditional recognition of nature's existence *outside* the mind and perception of man that distinguishes dialectical materialism from relativistic agnosticism and idealism.[19]

The fact that the most orthodox of priestly inclined, system-oriented sociologists project their theory and research from the assumption that "it is not the consciousness of men that determines their being, but on the contrary, their social being that determines their consciousness" should by now not appear to be the creative product of a uniquely sociological imagination. What before was congruence now becomes ideational diffusion: that which lay implicit within a reified nineteenth-century natural science was made explicit in Marxism, while indirectly it infected the "orthodox" image of man in American sociology over the past generation through the discipline's capitulation to the priestly paradigm of a value-free social science.

Determinism and Necessity

The second by-law of science noted in Chapter 9 was the repetitive regularity—the "recurrent"—which the scientist seeks to extract from his confrontation with the empirical. Reified by the science of the last century and projected into its social sphere by Marxism, the prism dissolves and all—the prism and the scientist together—become manifestations of an "iron necessity" that is seen to characterize both nature and society. Spontaneity, creativity, existential risk—none could be deemed relevant. Rather "it is a question of the laws themselves, of these tendencies working with iron necessity toward inevitable results" (Marx, 1932:13). "In the social production of their existence, men enter into relations which are determined, necessary, independent of their will" (Marx and Engels, 1955:362).[20] Necessity became the mother of existence itself: "the freer a man's judgment is in relation to a definite question," Engels (1962:157) tells us, "the greater is the necessity with which the content of this judgment will be determined." Engels, all to his credit, is consistent enough to have insisted that even the appearance of Marx's materialistic conception of history was determined (Marx 1935:393).

The view, as I have suggested, was not the invention of either Hegel or Marx. It came out of a posture which, seeking to extract the recurrent from man's experience with his world, had come slowly through the very real advances of an adolescent science to dominate the nineteenth century's vision of reality. This search for regularity eliminated by very definition the ultimate relevance of the unique. The latter could act as a continual goad and corrective to that enterprise, but scientists had to focus upon the recurrent if they were to justify their attempt to generalize over time. Even Marx's admonition that "the philosophers have only interpreted the world, the point is to change it . . ." was not—either in his mind or the interpretations of orthodox Marxists since—viewed as in any way contradictory to the larger determinist frame. As Lenin insisted (1930:114), "all that happens in history is subject to the law of necessity."

He could say nothing else, given the context of his Marxist commitment or the scientific font from which it drew. According to both, the individual *is* an abstraction, for he would otherwise be by definition unique. And uniqueness stands simply as a residual category to challenge the ingenuity of a generalizing logic. It was to *order*, paradoxically as it may seem, that the revolutionary Lenin was dedicated: "The recognition of the fact of natural order and the proximate reflection of that order in the mind of man is materialism."[21] Marxism has appeared to re-enforce the prophetic and conflict paradigms because we stand *outside* a Marxist context. *Within*, the priestly and system modes dominate.

The immediate relevance of all this to recent and contemporary sociology is suggested by our earlier discussions of functionalism as it has been appraised by Merton and Kingsley Davis. Quoting Merton to the effect that the Marxist theory of religion is essentially the same as functional theory in method of analysis, Davis went on to suggest that "if Marxist sociology does not differ methodologically from functional analysis, it seems doubtful that any kind of sociology does." And indeed it does not—if we speak of a demythologized orthodoxy in reference to Marxism and to a sociology that would base those choices forced upon it in research upon a consistently value-free stance.

Relativism and the Dialectic

The final epistemological derivative of the corporate intent of science that we discussed in Chapters 9 and 10 was a "relational" posture which, when reified, approaches a Machiavellian relativism devoid of any central referent beyond predictive efficiency. Deprived of any existential base, the scientist—social or otherwise—is limited simply to unknotting the scrambled skein that is the empirical and fabricating a network of predictive schemes, each of which is validated only in terms of its links with others. The inherent value or ultimate character of that which one orders over time cannot be known, except insofar as one creates a metaphysical base through the reification process itself. One is caught as one would be in a monolingual dictionary; the thread of explanation travels down intricate byways only to turn back upon itself. "Economy" and its handmaiden "control" are the only clues for guidance. The Second Law of Thermodynamics is as compelling as *The Origin of Species*; death is as appropriate as life. Love is to be described but not emulated; justice is a slogan but efficiency is the end. When a social scientist is completely consistent in his value-neutrality, human action is reduced to behavior and behavior in turn to the meaningless flux that is process.

Fortunately, even a demythologized Marxism cannot be simply reduced, in ethical terms, to the bland leading the bland. For its step-father was the concern for justice that rings through Biblical prophecy and its vision was second cousin to the Second Coming. The utopia it projects is in fact immeasurably more consistent with the larger Hellenistic and Hebraic tradition than is the Book of Revelations, and its identification with the disinherited is considerably more relevant to its ends than the moralisms of the "Protestant Ethic."

Still, having granted this, the dedication of the orthodox Marxist to equalitarianism is burdened by an image of man that is nourished at the relativistic well of a reified science. As Engels (1962:125) himself points out, "knowledge is here essentially relative, inasmuch as it is limited to the investigation of interconnections and consequences of certain social and state forms which exist only in a particular epoch and among particular peoples and are by their very nature transitory. . . . We therefore reject every attempt to impose on us any moral dogma whatsoever as an eternal, ultimate and forever immitigable ethical law on the pretext that the moral world, too, has its permanent principles which stand above history and the differences between nations." The only absolute, so the orthodox Marxist argues, is relativity itself, and the "good" is no exception.[22] Thus, his revolutionary energies need be inhibited by no final line of restraint beyond the pragmatic, and the universality of his vision may be reduced in fact to an equalitarian denial of individual integrity.[23] This is possible because of Marx's inability to ascribe reality to a "human essence . . . inherent in each single individual." Rather, that "human essence" is but an "ensemble of the social relations" (Selsam and Martel, 1963:228). Indeed, Blau and Moore (1959:167) suggest that this is precisely why Marx's approach is compatible with the sociological perspective[24]—and, again, is the consideration that led Merton to demonstrate that the rhetoric of functionalism was identical to Marxism and Kingsley Davis to suggest that all sociological research shared the same presumptive base.

Perhaps, then, Charles Loomis' selective sampling of Marx—one which highlighted the latter's references to "system," "function," and a "constant tendency to equilibrium"—cannot be pushed aside as simply idiosyncratic. Even Alvin Gouldner (1959:269)—spokesman though he has been for the return to prophecy—sees

Engels and perhaps Marx as "deeply concerned about system analysis." Bukharin, he points out, saw system as the key to formal sociological analysis long before it acquired paradigmatic status among American sociologists.[25] Indeed, once initial Stalinist suspicions were overcome, cybernetics, the handmaiden of system analysis, took the Soviet intellectual scene by storm.

Existenz

The implications of all this are startling. Both classical and an orthodox demythologized Marxism-Leninism project an image of social man that is strikingly similar to the one that emerges when sociologists in the West pursue social research in as consistently a value-free manner as possible. The paradox is brought about because sociologists, in rejecting any extra-scientific value frame, are forced either consciously or unconsciously to reify the assumptions that underlie the logic or the communal ethic of natural science. We saw in Chapters 7 and 8 that it was impossible for a sociologist to move through his research without calling upon some value base beyond that which is empirically given to resolve the choices thrust upon him or to justify the nature, the degree, and the implications of his intrusion upon human subject matter. The specific nature of the presuppositions underlying the norms of science were etched in Chapter 9, while their reifications were noted in Chapter 10, along with the problems that attended any serious attempt to anchor one's values in an extrapolation of the communal ethic of social science. The present chapter has shown the manner in which the Marxist "anti-metaphysical" metaphysic was itself grounded in such reification, simply because the mature Marx, with a major assist from Engels (and, a generation later, from Lenin), in enclosing socialism within the relatively unsophisticated language of nineteenth-century natural science, inherited the latter's reified imagery. Along the way we have seen instance after instance of how sociologists—particularly the converts to the priestly and system paradigms—have reflected the same temptation and the same inheritance.

At the same time I have tried to make clear that the congruence uncovered is *not* between social or natural science as it has been or is currently practiced within

Soviet Russia or some of its East-European satellites on the one hand and the general practice or intention of sociologists in America on the other. There is all too much evidence available illustrating how classical Marxism has been radically distorted by the heavy hand of Russian history to suggest the former, while in the latter case it is clear that no major American theorists have self-consciously modeled their social imagery after either the classical Marxist model or what I have called its contemporary demythologized but orthodox version. I have merely said that if one were to take the value-free stance seriously and to conduct his research simply in its terms, the end-result would be an image of social man startlingly like the orthodox Marxist image. Notice that I have *not* said *the same image*. The classical Marxist position was motivated by a trans-empirical sense of ultimate social justice that it inherited from its Hebraic and Hellenic roots and which cannot be accommodated, finally, by its scientific aura; it is therefore more humane than a reified science. Nor have I sought to suggest that American sociologists are in any danger of succumbing to either horn of the dilemma. They most assuredly deny the Marxist metaphysic and tend to honor the value-free posture in the breach. As Gouldner (1965) found in his survey, the great majority of sociologists are well aware that mere lip service has been granted it—that its actual value has lain in its public relations potential.[26]

Yet it is too tempting not to point out that the general correlation drawn between the "orthodox" Marxist metaphysic and the priestly mode and the system paradigm in recent American sociology is far from a private vision on my part. Essentially the same conclusion comes from a full-fledged participant in the development of Marxist thought itself—Jean-Paul Sartre. I refer not to the Sartre of that monumental defense of human freedom and of the precedent reality of the intrasubjective that appeared as *L'Être et le Néant*, but to the author of the audacious attempt to cleanse the Augean stables of Marxism with the broom of *Existenz*: the 755-page *Critique de la Raison Dialectique* published in 1960. So far only the one-hundred-page introduction, "Question de Méthode," has been made available in English translation as *Search for a Method*. Indeed even the mammoth *Critique* itself was offered as but the first of a two-volume effort to free what Sartre terms "modern" (sometimes "Stalinist," sometimes simply "lazy") Marxism from the rigidities of its nineteenth-century context.

Although the major thrust of the volume is directed against what is passing as orthodox Marxism, its relevance to sociology *per se* is suggested by *Search for a Method*'s subtitle: *The Sartrean Approach to the Sociology and Philosophy of History*. What Sartre sets out to accomplish is the explicit annulment of orthodox Marxism's marriage to the assumptions that have guided the development of natural science. Early in the introductory essay Sartre (1963: 32, 33n) states that when Marx declares that the materialist conception of the world simply signifies nature as it *is*, "he walks into a world of object-men"; and when Lenin speaks of consciousness as simply a reflection of the material base, "he removes from himself the right to write what he is writing. . . . Both these conceptions," Sartre argues, "amount to breaking man's real relation with history, since in the first, knowing is pure theory, a non-situated observing, and in the second, it is simple passivity. In the latter there is . . . only skeptical empiricism. . . . The only theory of knowledge which can be valid today is one which is founded on that truth of microphysics: the experimenter is a part of the experimental system."

The analytical, systematic rationality of orthodox modern Marxism—and of recent sociology—is, Sartre tells us, appropriate only for the natural scientific examination of inert materiality, in and of itself. As soon as such a materiality is examined in its interaction with man, then a dialectical rationality must be introduced. Although contemporary Marxists grant obeisance to the term "dialectical," Sartre sees them compounding the error of bourgeois theorists not only by joining them in casting a positivistic net over the works of man, but in searching for a dialectical logic in the materiality of nature *per se*. Sartre would have Marxism break cleanly with even the demythologized base of Marxist neo-orthodoxy and undergird its very real politico-economic insights with an essentially existential foundation.

The manner by which a society organizes its economic production and distribution does indeed dominate its social, political, and intellectual activity. The linear logic involved is the dialectic and the setting is one that sets human needs over against the realities of economic scarcity. Violence cannot be avoided in the movement toward justice and freedom, for if a laborer is to become conscious of the manner in which the economic system has minimized his share of the product of his work, he must internalize that scarcity. Such internalization is the premise to violence.

But instead of accepting orthodox Marxism's commitment to "materialism" (or sociology's analogous commitment to "empiricism") as its point of departure, Sartre affirms the precedence of man's life experience as it forms itself through the action and reaction of *pour-soi* (being-for-itself) upon *en-soi* (the material, external world), *praxis* (action) upon the *pratico-inerte* (all those factors that confront man as a finite being). Instead of modern Marxism's determined network of historical necessity (or sociology's assumption of recurrence), Sartre perceives a dialectic of freedom continually presenting man's *project* (his effort to "transcend himself toward") with ever new moments of *totalization* (unifying acts). Rather than accepting Marxism's inclination (and that of what I have termed a fully consistent priestly mode in sociology) to restrain its moral relativism by an implicit commitment to social control alone, Sartre insists that each man's freedom is limited by the freedom of every other man. Where *objectification* (the projection of oneself through one's work into nature) is demanded, the reductive categories of the material (the sociologist's "intersubjective"), the determined (our "recurrent"), and the relativistic (our "relationality") are to be enveloped by the claims of the existent life history, the unique, and the inviolate. Even the end of the scientific enterprise—efficient prediction—is to be subordinated to the ends of a humane future, with a dialectically modulated *comprehension* standing in its stead. The man who is foreseeable becomes in Sartre's mind an "object"—an object to be made a means for the ends of other men. Standing in the tradition of Weber's *verstehen*, "comprehension" is an act whereby one seeks to live the existence of the other—to reproduce the *project* of the other.

Sociology (indeed, "anthropology" in its generic

sense) is important to Sartre, for it would sensitize both the "philosophy" that is a "true" Marxism and the "ideology" that is existentialism to the *mediations* (in social scientific terms, the intervening variables) that stand between the uniquely existent individual and the pervasive economic factors. Such mediations—infant experience, sibling status, peer group pressure, the rupture between generations and so on—are very real elements in the life experience of any individual and the outcome of any particular situation. Yet Sartre sees contemporary sociology as sharing with orthodox Marxism the same debilitating objectivist frame by affirming the radical autonomy of its object.

What form has this taken in sociology over the past few decades? A three-fold "autonomy," each of which prostitutes the very real potential of the discipline to be both informing and humane. Its pretensions to an *ontological* autonomy result in the reification of collectivities—particularly, Sartre notes, when such groupings are defined in terms of their functions. Its assertion of *methodological* autonomy is a denial of the open-ended character of history, transforming processes and actions into presupposed unities. What Sartre tèrms its image of the *reciprocal* autonomy of the experimenter and the subjects of the experiment is a falsification of the necessary interaction of the two—an interaction that impinges upon the existential and empirical life and future of each. The "analytical" reason of a sociology that takes system as its point of departure is a fundamental distortion: "The *existing* man cannot be assimilated by a system of ideas." Indeed, "a system is an alienated man who wants to go beyond his alienation and who gets entangled in alienated words" (1963:19, 115). Neither words nor the past may freeze the future. Individual *praxis*, the *project* of man upon the *pratico-inerte*, guarantees freedom to the future. Positivistic reason has its place in the *totalization*, but only as an interval nested within a larger reason that is dialectical. Here, then—from a self-conscious "Marxist" we find almost the identical linkage between the paradigms that dominated sociology in the 'forties and 'fifties and those rooted in orthodox Marxism. However, the key to the present plight of sociology lies, according to Sartre, in its claim to reciprocal autonomy. The result is a cauterization of the breach between researcher and subject, symbolized by the oath taken to a fictitious value-freedom that has transformed both into objects of nature rather than creative and responsible agents of history.[27] And although it was an ontological commitment that led Marxism to its initial deconsecration of man, the same reciprocal perversions dominate her neo-orthodox epistemological assumptions today.[28] Both modern Marxism and a sociology dominated by a priestly image of its calling have reified the categories by which they have approached the study of social man, sociology inadvertently and Marxism-Leninism much more self-consciously. Man's selfhood in sociology *becomes* the internalization of those categories and concepts—of "role," "internalization," "generalized other"; "system," "functional perquisite," "equilibrium maintenance" replace his dialectical interaction with others.

Sartre would find the emphasis which the younger Talcott Parsons placed upon "voluntarism," upon man's actions as irredeemably purposeful, as a crucial contribution to American sociology, which both the later Parsons and the discipline itself have typically ignored. Man is defined ultimately in terms of *praxis*—purposeful activity—and not through the automatic functioning of *processus*. Nor can existence—social or otherwise—be signified by such a biomechanical term as "equilibrium"; rather it is characterized by "a perpetual disequilibrium, a wrenching away from itself with all its body" (1963:151). The human future is not, fundamentally, to be an extrapolation of the past; indeed, man is defined by Sartre as a flight *out of the present* into the future.[29] For the very activity that is knowing, we are reminded, changes that which would be known. This is, perhaps, the essential insight of existentialism: that man retains the capacity to "invent his own law."[30] The "totalization" of any one instance is capable of transcendence through the interaction of knower and known in the next. The fundamental logic of sociology becomes, in this light, the grammar of emancipation.

The Young Marx

Still, Sartre's critique of "modern" Marxism and the dominant thrust of recent sociology cannot claim to be the primary reference for the latter's renewed interest in Marx. Instead, it has quite clearly stemmed from the recovery of and response to the early manuscripts of the youthful Karl, manuscripts that began to appear in English only in the late 1950's, with the entire set available only as recently as 1961.[31] C. Wright Mills (1959:171), troubled as he had been by the reduction of the sociological imagination to the pursuit of "grand theory" and an "abstracted empiricism" within the context of a "bureaucratic ethos," was perhaps the first within American sociology to be moved by the manner in which the essays' focus upon *alienation* might contribute to an understanding of the plight of recent sociology. "I know of no idea, no theme, no problem," he wrote of alienation, "that is so deep in the classic tradition—and so much involved in the possible default of contemporary social science." Alienation, in other words, was not merely a powerful concept for dissecting the larger body politic, but was also an image that spoke to the condition of the typical American sociologist himself.

Alienated social research

Indeed, if one were to take Marx's four-fold characterization of alienation quite literally—the alienation from the product of one's work, from the process of work itself, from one's true nature as a worker, and from others—and apply it to the activity of the research sociologist, the result would be an indictment equivalent to the one we have already spelled out in our characterization of the sociologist who would carry the priestly posture of a value-free sociology to its logical extreme. Following the language by which Marx defined the term as closely as possible, the convert to the prophetic and conflict paradigms could argue that alienation would be evidenced by sociologists caught up by the priestly mode and the system image in:

(1) the relationship . . . [of the sociologist] to the product of . . . [his research] as an alien object which dominates him . . . (2) the relationship . . . [of sociology] to the act of . . . [social research and] . . . his personal life . . . as an activity which is directed against himself, independent of him and not belonging to him. This is self-alienation . . . (3) Thus alienated . . . [social research] turns the species life of man,

and also nature as his mental species-property, into an alien being and into a means for his individual existence. It alienates from man his own body, external nature, his mental life and his human life. (4) A direct consequence of the alienation of man from the product of . . . [his research], from his life activity and from his species life is that man is alienated from . . . [non-scientists, his subjects or potential subjects] and [from] the objects of their labor.[32]

For the 27-year-old Marx, science was not to be regarded as a pleasure subject simply to the itch of curiosity and the exigencies of one's social context. It was to remain the servant of mankind (1939:199). "Objectivization" was itself "the practice of alienation" (Marx, 1964:39). History was not to be objectified through the impersonal lens of science, for "history does nothing, it 'possesses *no* immense wealth,' it 'wages no battles.' It is *man*, real living man, that does all that, that possesses and fights; 'history' is not a person apart, using man as a means of its *own* particular aims; history is nothing but the activity of man pursuing his aims" (Marx, 1956:125). In brief, "This communism . . . equals humanism" (1959:102).

Marx as Messiah

To Erich Fromm, responsible in large measure for the publication of the early manuscripts in English and their widespread dissemination over the last few years in America, this means that recent social science has been alienated from its true calling insofar as it has modeled its assumptions and its logic upon the natural sciences. In doing so, both social scientists and their human subjects are transformed into "things." The young Marx —and Fromm would argue that the mature Marx remained loyal to his early humanistic vision—saw that a dissected man was a destroyed man, a manipulated social context led perforce to a dehumanized society, and the knowledge gained thereby would be a false knowledge.[33] It is this that fired the imagination of the pre-*Manifesto* Marx: an image of man as inviolate end. And it is this, Fromm holds, that has become the scandal of "orthodox" Marxism—a liberating New Testament to the rigid scriptures of scientific socialism. Indeed, Fromm is so taken by the existentialist and humane spirit of the early Marx that he sees it as direct heir to "prophetic-Christian

Messianism" and thirteenth-century Thomism, and close neighbor to Meister Eckhart and Zen Buddhism. It becomes, in his mind, a "synthesis of the prophetic-Christian idea of society as a plane of spiritual realization, and of the idea of individual freedom . . . a doctrine of salvation in nontheistic terms."[34]

The effort to "humanize" the scientistic thrust of orthodox Marxist-Leninism has been with us, of course, for some time. Revisionist strains have been legion, many with precisely this intent. American scholars as early as 1941 had begun to confront Marx as humanist through Herbert Marcuse's *Reason and Revolution.* But unlike Fromm and many who have recently been influenced by the availability in English of the early materials—particularly the *Economic and Philosophic Manuscripts*—there had been no systematic effort, with the exception of Raya Dunayevskaya's *Marxism and Freedom* published in 1958, to claim that the existential posture of the "young Marx" with its focus upon "alienation" was in fact the same "Marx" who lived and wrote until the age of 65. It is this latter contention that deserves careful scrutiny, both in the light of sociology's current reassessment of the significance of Marx and as it speaks to the appraisal of "orthodox" Marxism as I have characterized it to this point. For if the "real" Marx were indeed the Marx of the *Manuscripts*, then the analogy we have drawn between the priestly mode in sociology and the Marxist corpus might appear to some to be less tenable.

Young Marx versus old Marx?

There is no doubt whatsoever that Soviet Russian ideologists have held to, and continue to hold to, the view that the early manuscripts represent but a Hegelian—and thus "pre-Marxist"—stage in the youthful Karl's development.[35] Could it be, then, that it has been they, controlling as they have the "orthodox" image of Marxism-Leninism for half a century, who are responsible for relegating the *Economic and Philosophic Manuscripts* to a "pre-Marxist" stage and not Marx and/or Engels themselves? Unfortunately, it is difficult to refrain from placing the initial blame on Marx himself—on his apparent assumption that his early essays would threaten the natural-scientific stature he later claimed for his system as a whole, a posture that might elicit a warm ripple of empathy from the many contemporary sociologists who appear tempted by a similar charade. For Marx withheld the early manuscripts from publication in his lifetime, stating to his translator in 1886 that "the semi-Hegelian language of a good many passages of my old book is not only untranslatable but has lost the greater part of its meaning even in German" (Marx, 1953:151). Indeed, Marx had long before—a scant four years after the *Manuscripts* were originally written—turned his back upon the language of alienation when, in the *Communist Manifesto*, he and Engels ridiculed the German True Socialists for their focus upon an "alienation of humanity." Even upon Marx's death, Engels cast aside a request that they be made available to the public anew with the disdainful comment that "Marx had also written poetry in his student years, but it could hardly interest anybody."[36] Although there are those who would put the major blame on Engels' shoulders rather than on Marx's—when he re-read *The Holy Family* in 1867 Marx indicated that he found nothing in it which would shame him[37]—Engels claimed that Marx had read and approved the manuscript of the archly scientistic *Anti-Dühring*.[38] In any case it was not until after the October Revolution in Russia that the Social Democratic Party of Germany, inheritor of the Marx archives, granted the Soviet government permission to reproduce them. An additional ten years went by before even an incomplete Russian translation was made available in 1927.[39] And their potential impact upon the continental scene was deferred until 1932 when the *Manuscripts* appeared in volume three of *Historisch-Kritische Gesamtausgabe*.

Unfortunately perhaps for American sociology, the task of converting the larger corpus into the passionate humanism that Marx appeared to presage in his early essays is a difficult one at best. One is handicapped from the start by what even as sympathetic a reader as C. Wright Mills (1962:112) has termed the "cryptic" manner in which the focal term "alienation" is used.[40] It appears to stand at times as a causally prior necessity, at other points as a logically prior assumption. In the *Manuscripts* themselves it is the cause of private property, while in *The German Ideology* the relationship is reversed.

We have already pointed out how, in the *Communist Manifesto*, Marx and Engels had derided the German True Socialists for dwelling upon the notion of the "alienation of humanity." Marx (1939:68) had in fact already made the shift in *The German Ideology* when he noted sarcastically that "the philosophers" viewed history itself as a "process of the self-alienation of 'man.' " For Marx came to project that which he discovered in Hegel to be a general phenomenological characteristic of the "self" as it is inhibited by a wide variety of institutionalized restraints into the class structures of capitalist society, although emphasizing relationships involved in the act of labor. Self-alienation thereby became simply a socio-economic relationship; alienated labor simply wage labor; the personal power of capital, social power; and "man" but an ensemble of social relations.[41] Thus his early humanism gravitated in the direction of a scientific socialism. Although he remained a passionately political animal, Marx opted for the vocabulary and stance of the scientist in his intellectual work. He could thus claim with considerable justification that he was not a "Marxist": his concern as a social scientist was to set forth the natural order that laborious empirical work might extract from the history of capitalist society and its progenitors.

It is, as even T. B. Bottomore has come to acknowledge, impossible to reconcile Marx's early humanism with his later scientific stance. As committed as Bottomore has been to the significance of the early materials—having collaborated with Fromm in making them readily available in English—he has had to conclude that "the general inclination of Marx's work, when it is traced from his earlier to his later writings, is clearly away from the philosophy of history and toward a scientific theory of society, in the precise sense of a body of general laws and detailed empirical statements."[42] It is a judgment with which a host of other scholars have had to reluctantly concur.[43]

The case that Fromm builds for a mature Marx who continues to ground his intellectual endeavors in an image of man that accentuates spontaneity as over against necessity, freedom as over against order, the existential as over against the empirical, the individual as over against the social, and love over against hate, has served as an important stimulant to the intellectual communities of the communist and non-communist worlds. In the former it may serve as a strategic channel through which the humane sensitivities that remain the residue of our Hellenic and Judaic inheritance may confront the reified anti-metaphysic that is orthodox Marxism; in the latter it is serving to challenge the slogan of value-neutrality that identifies the priestly mode in sociology and related disciplines. Both movements would appear "functional" from the point of view set forth in this volume. Yet beyond the transient need felt by each intellectual generation to break the rigid paradigmatic mold of its predecessor is a larger commitment: a commitment to simple accuracy in mining the sediment that is history. And through this commitment alone the evidence in support of Fromm's claim that the early and the later Marx represent a single consistent whole is at best open to serious doubt.[44] Having ignored the young Marx through oversight or calculation does not in turn permit a simplistic reading of the Marx who lived and wrote till the age of 65.

But the fact of the matter is that the thesis I have set forth will not have to remain in abeyance until the historical issues that govern the quarrel over the integrity of the Marx corpus have been resolved. For what I have suggested is simply that the *orthodox* interpretation of the lineage that begins with Marx and moves through Engels to Lenin is startlingly similar to a sociology informed by the system paradigm and the priestly mode. Only when one envelops that tradition in a larger existential context (with Sartre) or reduces it to the humanistic sentiments of the youthful Karl (with Fromm) is one able to conclude that the Marxist posture would unambiguously re-enforce the prophetic and conflict models. Still, the very fact that even a demythologized neo-orthodox Marxism is being confronted from within her own ranks by *Existenz* and the humanism of the early Marx strengthens the analogy that we have drawn. Both the scientific and larger intellectual communities have pushed their boundaries, in the present generation, beyond the limits set by ideological assumption and national interest. One might expect, then, that paradigmatic battles would no longer be fought in isolation, that the contest between system and conflict and between the priestly and prophetic mode we witness today in American sociology would be faced, albeit with different vocabularies and semantic traditions, within the Marxist world as well. The culture of science—social as well as natural—is now an international culture, and the outcome of paradigmatic revolution therein promises to be international as well.

The Calling of Sociology

Much sociological writing seems suspended between two images. One of these conceives society as the arrangements of sleepwalkers and the other as a play involving both actors and audience, a stage and a realm behind the scene. Obviously, both images are appropriate, and both are incomplete.

Kaspar Naegele

12

Stock-Taking

I have called this book "a sociology of sociology." Many a reader—having followed the author along the paradigmatic trail blazed in the first six chapters, examined the dilemmas of choice and implicit commitment confronted in social research in the seventh and eighth, noted the presumptive faith of natural science and sociology's temptation to reify those assumptions in the ninth and tenth, and seen how the same issues have risen to plague those who stand within a Marxist frame in the past chapter—perhaps indeed all who have journeyed this far—would contend that the trek, although a provocative one, should not really be identified as a "sociological" exercise. For have we not couched the indicative within an imperative context and set a science within a frame that includes history and philosophy?

Even if this were true, need we admit duplicity, to masquerading as a "sociology of . . ." when the book is in fact an "argument for . . ."? There are two considerations that would make such a judgment premature. The first is rooted in the assumption that any and every science—sociology included—seeks to characterize the future through a study of order precipitated from the past. Because sociologists themselves are moved by con-

Notes to this chapter will be found on pages 372–374.

tending philosophical and ideological postures, we must assess the factors confronting them in these areas before we can project their probable impact upon the sociological generation to come.

The claim of predictive reliability, however, is only the lesser part of the case for the defense. The more important consideration must lie with the paradoxical nature of the task I have undertaken—which I drew to the reader's attention at the very beginning of the venture. Because I had set forth to characterize a discipline and its future by means of that very same discipline, whatever "openness" regarding the nature of the *subject matter* that I brought to the enterprise had to be shared with the *method* as well. Thus the reader is not in a position to make a fully informed assessment of the appropriateness of calling the book a "sociology of" sociology until the substantive nature of the discipline is finally set forth. On the other hand, if the reader were willing to assume the author's integrity, he might—by extrapolating the book's position to this point—project in at least rough outline the image of the nature of our discipline and the context within which it must act. Let us see.

I completed my examination of the revolutionary currents that had brought forth the conflict stance to challenge the system paradigm in recent American sociology by marking how a "dialectical" image had been introduced as a possible basis for a cease fire between the two warring schools. I then went on to point out that accompanying the rebirth of conflict theory had come a reassessment of the value-free stance that had accompanied the system image. This latter discovery suggested that the thesis developed by Thomas Kuhn in *The Structure of Scientific Revolutions*—the point of departure for the entire volume—would be insufficient to the task of analyzing revolutions in the social and behavioral sciences. For we found that the social and behavioral sciences precipitated *two* paradigmatic levels rather than the single level addressed by Kuhn, because such sciences are forced to encompass the scientist, his activity, and his self-image as part of their subject matter. Indeed, I suggested that the paradigms of which Kuhn spoke appeared to be functions of, or at least secondary to, a more primary level. The system paradigm appeared to be a product of a prior commitment to a paradigmatic image of the sociologist as *value-free*; the conflict paradigm an outcome of the paradigmatic vision of the sociologist as *engagé*.

It should be abundantly clear by now that those involved in social research are incapable, even in principle, of disengaging themselves in the manner in which value-freedom has typically been understood in sociology. If one is more sophisticated and perceives the latter phrase (with Howard Becker and F. S. C. Northrop) as merely limiting one to a set of values that are assumed by, or lie implicit within, the scientific stance—or, indeed, are necessitated by the communal life of an ongoing scientific sub-community (as with David Bidney)—then one may indeed remain free of *other* values, at least in principle. But Chapters 10 and 11 suggested the sacrifices that would have to be made: efficiency would become ego's transcendent end and control his indisputed means, with his relationship to alter inhibited by no vision beyond an image of man as an ordered object in a completely relative field. Some might stretch their valuation the additional half-step demanded by a demythologized yet essentially orthodox Marxism, but in doing so they would have to abandon the humanistic sensitivities of the early Marx that had led to his persuasive analysis of alienation.

Prognosis

But it takes no extraordinary sociological perception to conclude that this more subtle route through the valuational dilemma will not appeal to more than a handful of sociologists, East or West. Although many of them will continue to act *as if* it were acceptable merely by intellectual and ethical default as they cling to the traditional identification of value-neutrality with objectivity, the overwhelming majority would find any stark rejection of those images and associated ethics which the West derives from its Hellenic and Hebraic roots—or, indeed, of those analogous metaphors which undergird the mythic life of other world-wide religious-philosophical communities—to be quite untenable. And well they might, for the demanding lens of science has had to sacrifice the personal, existentia dimension in human experience with its accent upon man as inviolate end, freedom and responsibility as substantively real, and one's intra-subjective experience as transcendent so that its logic might fulfill with integrity *its* special calling: delineating order over time. That which is common to the sciences is not a product but a means, as the traditional phrase, "the scientific method," reminds us. And when a "method" or "logic" seeks guidance only from within itself, it projects the very same feature upon its subject matter. The sociology that seeks its bearings internally thus sees man as but *means*. Such a posture not only *must* be rejected, but *is*: Sociologists in America not only are well on their way to rejecting a simplistic identification of objectivity with value-freedom, but have become increasingly willing to acknowledge the appropriateness of alternative value references within which to frame their research.

Prophecy or priestcraft?

In the ideal-typical language of this volume, then, the discipline can be expected to continue to move toward a reclamation of its original *prophetic* understanding of itself and away from the exclusively *priestly* paradigm that dominated the post-war period to the end of the 1950's. The sociologist as priest, viewing his office as but a means by which any given social reality may be revealed to the layman, had overestimated his capacity to refrain from transfiguring the quality of that reality through the selectivity of his perception and the special interests that adhere to his office, as the custodians of orthodoxy traditionally have been inclined to do. On the other hand, the sociologist as prophet is consciously committed to an image of society that transcends any given social reality. He therefore uses his predictive powers to portray quite realistically a future state of empirical reality that quite normally may be expected to ensue given no change in that social matrix other than the potential impact of his own prediction. He differs from the sociologist as priest not in any temptation to distort the reality of a given situation—he is equally dedicated to honoring the empirical facts—but in his awareness of the value-laden choices and implicit commitments confronting those who would extrapolate evidence of past order into the future and in his decision to respond to them in a way in which his own comprehension and predictive agency will make it a significant factor for change through its impact upon his fellow sociologists and the "lay" public. The "priest's" perceptions and predictions cannot, of course, avoid having an impact that is rooted in the same feedback principle. But because he draws his image of man and thus an implicit ethic consciously or unconsciously from a frame of reference that honors ordered efficiency above all, the manner in which he resolves the value-decisions confronting him in the precipitation of that order will muffle the impact of his projections and/or turn them from self-defeating prophecies to self-fulfilling ones, from liberating change to increased stability. Although the criteria upon which one may draw thus lie outside the epistemological competence of science alone, a decision regarding the relative emphasis to be placed upon the one mode as over against the other cannot be avoided; if it is not resolved explicitly, it will be implicitly. My own predilection to re-emphasize the integrity of the discipline's original prophetic inclination should now be self-evident, and it is clear that more and more sociologists lately have turned in the same direction.

Having opted for a revival of the prophetic image, should I then urge that conflict be chosen in preference to system as sociology's substantive referent? I think not, at least if we seek a conceptual frame at the highest theoretical level. There is no need to assume that just because we have uncovered a correlational, functional, or even causal link between the prophetic and conflict paradigms on the one hand and the priestly and system images on the other that the relationship need be expected to project itself compulsively into the future. Indeed, if we are to be completely serious about the prophetic paradigm, its capacity to deny complete continuity through the impact of the awareness of past order would undermine such continuity. But there is a considerably more fundamental reason for my—and the discipline's—unwillingness to settle for "conflict" as sociology's ultimate substantive referent.

Legacy of Talcott Parsons

The scientific community has become increasingly aware over the last two or three generations that its singularity, its one common bond, lies in its dedication to the extraction of order from the flux of human experience. Social existence may well be fundamentally out of joint, conflicting, unsystematic. But even if it is, the presumptive cement that serves as bond between the varying sub-communities of science would be incapable of responding to that circumstance other than by viewing it as but one more challenge to its own ability to bring cognitive order out of apparent chaos. This I have tried to make clear in Chapter 9 by tracing the route taken by that community toward self-understanding and by revealing the "by-laws" that appear to govern its activity. One of these by-laws, you will recall, is the assumption that *all* empirical phenomena are in the final analysis interrelated. Its derivation, like the derivation of the by-laws of intersubjectivity and recurrence, had been solely pragmatic. Seeking to order experience over time, those who came to identify their activity with the adjective "scientific" eventually had to conclude that any other assumption would inhibit their search, prejudge the limits of order available to them. Presuming the "relational" character of empirical phenomena thus guaranteed the *open-mindedness* of the scientific task, not its bounds. And yet, paradoxically, its product has had to be portrayed ultimately in "system" language. For that which is completely interrelated is *by definition* a system. Talcott Parsons is right in recognizing that the term must be regarded as *a*—perhaps *the*—primary sociological referent if sociology is to be viewed as a science. It is what Kingsley Davis meant when he identified functionalism in its broadest sense with sociological theory in general. From such a perspective, "functions" are the *relata* that link the structural features of a society. This is not to say that conflict becomes an illegitimate concept. But even it must be approached in fundamentally "system" terms if one wishes to remain within the frame of reference that has undergirded the development of natural science. Conflict if not patterned is abandoned to the idiographic sensitivities of the historian; only by redefining sociology as history might it be reclaimed. Thus, conflict is *presumed*—must be presumed—to be "functional" in the most general sense of the term.

Where Parsons has gone astray has been in adding to

this presumption a misinterpretation of Newton's fundamental "laws" of motion. As Catton has deftly pointed out, the latter were in fact axioms which held that physicists need not bother to "explain" *continuity* of action. The axioms simply represent a way of registering the assumption of order that science must make. Parsons—and Dodd and Lundberg—read into Newton's "laws" a strain *toward* equilibrium, a notion that has no presumptive place in the fundamental grammar of science, behavioral or otherwise. Social phenomena may or may not illustrate homeostatic tendencies at any given time or place—the issue is clearly an important one and one that is open to empirical examination.

Conflict or system?

The fundamental error in Parsons' general theory is that it tends to build what is merely a possibility into the very rhetoric of its underlying vocabulary. It is a mistake that Freud did *not* make, even though he too was organismically informed; Freud set forth both a life *and* a death wish, suggesting that he took much more seriously than Parsons one of the central themes of our Hebraic heritage. Parsons' disclaimer of William Kolb's effort to do just that—to build a theoretical structure upon an essentially Hebraic base—is at least consistent, for Parsons' equilibrating predilection would appear to have considerably more in common with the central predisposition of Eastern religious-philosophical thought. "System"? Yes, by the very assumptions necessary to maintain an open frontier to the pursuit of further evidence of order. "Equilibrium"? Maybe yes, maybe no; but in either case it must remain at the level of hypothesis, to be assessed in terms of the empirical evidence applicable to the particular case. Certainly it would not appear self-evidently fruitful to grant it paradigmatic status given the present level of our knowledge of social man. "Conflict"? Unfortunately, no. It is incapable of serving as the *fundamental* paradigmatic referent simply because its ultimate implication undermines sociology's assumption of, and search for, order. Conflict can serve as the conceptual keystone only if sociology is to be regarded primarily as one of the idiographic humanities. And although I have taken pains to document (in Chapters 4 and 5) that the undercurrent running through the discipline in the 1960's flowed strongly in that direction, the economic and prestige factors that accompany membership in the community of science in the present generation are certain to continue to block its course in the forseeable future. Furthermore, many of those who have argued the case for conflict appear in fact to have retained an implicit system approach—one that has a readily identifiable root in a patterned historicism.

A final reason for concluding that the present paradigmatic battle, if limited to a choice between system and conflict, is more likely to be won by the former lies with the impact of computer technology on sociology. Originally regarded simply as a means for circumventing what earlier had been viewed as insurmountable in social research—the manipulation of large numbers of variables, complex calculation of lengthy statistical formulas, and the storage and retrieval of mountains of data—the systematic quality of the digital computer is fast coming to be seen as a powerful model in its own right for the structure and functions of social systems, while well above the horizon is the prospect that Fortran—the Esperanto of the digital world—may in fact become the instrumental language of social analysis. Both developments cannot help but reinforce and deepen the system image at the level of theory. Again, the conflict image need not be ruled out. It may indeed gain a new lease on life, as the surge in the direction of game theory has suggested. But game theory—as well as any other models of conflict that can be programed—must, by the very nature of the logic that has been built into the computer and programs its use along with the rules that govern the relationship between "players," presuppose a system context. Even simulated war games are governed by the larger assumption of system.

The dialectical image

But what of the hint provided at the end of Chapter 2 that a "dialectical" image may play an increasingly attractive mediating role between the system and conflict paradigms? The decision on the part of Charles Loomis, who had identified himself with the former camp in both his *Social Systems* and *Modern Social Theories* volumes in the early 1960's, to title his presidential address before the American Sociological Association in 1967 "In Praise of Conflict and Its Negation" would appear to grant both official sanction and considerable encouragement to the possibility. Underwritten by the recent "recovery" of Marx as sociologist, the option might be strengthened by the suggestion that the dialectic foundered at Marx's and/or Engels' hands when they extrapolated it beyond the social sciences and used it as a stencil for the entire realm of nature. Thus, with the discovery that it was considerably more of a nuisance than an aid in the physical and biological sciences, social and behavioral scientists in the West abandoned the dialectic altogether. As the realization grows that the substantive focus of sociology includes social research and the resultant awareness that the very precipitation and comprehension of past and present order will inevitably to some degree be fed back through social interaction to deny that order, a dialectical paradigm becomes increasingly tenable. Neither "system" nor "conflict" need be denied; rather they become necessary elements within a larger dialectical *gestalt*. Formally, system would still take cognitive priority over conflict simply because the former must be presupposed. But conflict is always in principle a partial product, even though it in turn contributes, as in the classical formulation of the dialectic, to a new moment of stability.

Suddenly the compelling critiques offered in the name of a new "humanistic" sociology can be seen as more than simply cries of anguish over an intellectual adolescence that has been outgrown. All speak to the idiographic in human experience when it is in dynamic relationship to the nomothetic, the disjunctive linked with the functional, conflict harnessed with system. Although reaching beyond the traditional language of science, the metaphors they offer point toward a presumptive base for sociology that is itself interactive. If the dialectic does not seriously challenge conflict and system for paradigmatic status during the 1970's, it will not be because of inadequate formal credentials.

Epistemological pluralism

At the same time, a note of caution would seem in order. As powerful a searchlight as sociology indeed promises to be, its conceptual apparatus is not and cannot be the measure of all things. We and our world may well be in the singular, but the epistemologies by which the modern world has been structured and is known remain perforce in the plural. Sociologists might wish to claim an all-encompassing clarity and insight for their chosen field, but they should be aware of the danger of mixing both metaphors and logics. When we were children we spoke as children—as Comte, as Marx, even as Durkheim; but now that we are grown we must put away childish hopes and recognize that epistemological segmentation is the price that we must pay, at least in our time, for clarity. Sociology cannot contain the wealth and depth of all socially relevant experience within its own conceptual, theoretical, and logical reservoirs. If it would claim the cognitive reliability that is the peculiar presumptive power of a scientific rhetoric, it must set competing claims in another frame. *Praxis,* "ecstasy," "subjective realism," "authenticity" all refer to an image of man that would underline his existential integrity, his freedom to risk, and the moral nature of his responsibility, and would grant his history a fundamental direction and relevance. It is a portrait that I would honor. But it is not one that should drive us from methodological surefootedness, away from the patient and precise ordering of the given empirical world toward a well-intentioned but woolly-headed confusion of tongues. The dilemma that in fact gnaws at the base of sociology today lies precisely here: how to commit outselves to an enterprise that must screen out the existential and yet claim it as a fundamental referent.

Nested Frames

The key that would unlock the paradox is the recognition that the competing frames are not simply alternative but nested as well. The eyes we all have—scientists and nonscientists alike—register experiences that cluster about the complementary poles of the intrasubjective and the intersubjective, the unique and the recurrent, the existential and the relational. Given a preference for efficient prediction, some—eventually all at times—will use a polarized lens to filter out the first of each pair and focus simply upon the second, projecting order over time in the manner of science. Given the opposite aim—the delineation of the intrasubjective, unique, and existential in experience—a complementary lens may be substituted that blocks the opposite polarities, thus projecting those elements of experience that the present generation has claimed in the name of *Existenz*. But notice the analogy carefully. Neither polarized lens is of any value—indeed, nothing whatsoever will be registered—if the original eye is not present. Each of the alternative lenses rests upon (or is *nested within*) the prior experience and perceptive capacity of the given eye for both its utility and its meaning. At one level, then, we may speak appropriately of alternative lenses or frames of discourse. But in doing so we should never allow ourselves to ignore the fact that a nested hierarchy of lenses—one artificial and one given—is the more fundamental epistemological paradigm.

How is it that sociologists have missed this self-evident feature of man's experience? Why is it that they have continued so long to assume naïvely that man is *either* scientist *or* layman, social researcher *or* potential subject, sociologist *or* member of a larger, all-encompassing community? The reason lies, as we discovered in Chapter 6, in the manner in which sociologists have reified the concept of role. Although borrowed from the language of drama, the term took on the texture of "reality" in the social behaviorism extracted from the larger corpus of George Herbert Mead and became, with system, one of the fundamental points of reference for recent American sociology. Finding the concept a powerful tool within their discipline, sociologists lifted it bodily out of the realm of its special competence and applied it as a primary criterion for framing the nature of man's original, "given" eye. The two, then, were identified. All we were left with were alternating lenses, alternating roles. The nested relationship had dissolved.

The activities of sociologists as scientists, however, are always and in principle nested in a larger frame that includes the intrasubjective, the unique, and the existential. And it is because we are never able to extricate ourselves from that context, even when we take on the "role" of sociologist as scientist, that the image of man resident within the rhetoric of science may serve as a powerful tool in the service of a more fundamentally realistic and humane paradigm.

The Sartrean Alternative Reconsidered

We mentioned toward the end of Chapter 11 how social scientists operating within a Marxian context might find the humanistic elements in Marx or a Sartrean reinterpretation a strategic route by which to shake themselves free of the scientistic frame of orthodox Marxism. To do so, liberties would have to be taken with the historical record, for the evidence available to date suggests that neither the early Marx nor Sartre represented the epistemological or the substantive position taken by the "mature" Marx, to say nothing of Engels or Lenin. Still, given the relative success by which the Christian West has been able to reinterpret the essentially apocalyptic message of the New Testament to fit the existential needs of each passing intellectual generation, the task would not be impossible. What does seem quite unlikely is that either one in the foreseeable future could attract and contain the larger community of Western—and thus largely American—sociologists. For better or for worse, the "Marxist" label worn by both will eliminate them as potential victors in the paradigmatic struggle we witness today in American sociology. Research even in sociology is too closely tied to the vocabulary and needs of the body politic in the United States, and the latter is too self-consciously anti-communist, to allow either to become major contenders in the foreseeable future.

The case against the Sartrean posture is more complex. It cannot be challenged on the same basis as Fromm's portrait of an "original" Marx, for Sartre explicitly denies the fundamental validity of much of the Marx corpus. But two elements within the latter that he does accept diminish the likelihood that a Sartrean *Existenz* will ever serve as a context for sociology in the West. They are its emphasis upon *negation* and upon *violence*.

Negation

The dialectic that provides the structural framework for Sartre's posture is grounded, as with Marx, in Hegel: not the trinity that is thesis-antithesis-synthesis, but rather that of affirmation, negation, and the negation of the negation. The latter—the negation of the negation—is a key phrase in the *Critique*. Its significance lies in the allegation that only the future may harbor the positive; all that is present demands a negative response. Man's freedom here and now—and of course man is condemned always to live in a "here and now"—lies simply in his capacity to say "no," epitomized ultimately in his ability to say "no" to existence itself, to move from "Being" to "Nothingness" through suicide. Only that which man must negate is in fact conceivable; the nature of his ultimate freedom is not. When one moves beyond the words to the man, negation stands out with equal vividness. Sartre's political activity has always been action *against*, beginning with his work with the French underground against the Nazis and continuing with his opposition to orthodox Marxism, to the shifting power structure of France, to the Algerian war, and more recently, through participation in a mock war crimes trial, to American involvement in Vietnam. That pattern has, of course, been shared with many Frenchmen over the past generation. Its specifics, however, have not: the refusal to join the Communist party while advocating that the French proletariat and others should; the rejection of the Nobel prize for literature; a refusal to honor invitations he had accepted to speak before academic circles in the United States because of the Vietnam war; perhaps even his simple refusal to marry. The ideology, the philosophy, and the man appear as one in their predilection for negative action; they may also be one in their inability to grasp the ordered, the structured, the positive, as anything but a further negation of negation. This could be a heavy burden to a student of society who already is all too aware of the flux that is his subject matter, who seeks to find order in the eddies of change itself, who may search for theories of the short or middle range that promise relatively reliable prediction over limited periods of time. And although the concepts of negation and the negation of negation may appear to inform those moments of history heavy with violence and revolution, they are apt to appear curiously situation-bound when we address ourselves to cultural contexts and eras other than our own.

Violence

Such negation spills over into his image of man *per se*, granting ontological and ethical status to violence. "Man is violent . . . against the anti-man (that is, against any man) and against *his Brother*, as being such that he can at any time become an anti-man" (Sartre 1960:689). Such violence cannot be avoided, for if the laborer is to become conscious of the manner in which the economic system has minimized his share of the results of his work, he must internalize an awareness of scarcity. This internalization is then *defined* as the premise to violence. His treatment of "scarcity" in turn makes the Sartrean package even less acceptable. Shifting from the term "desire" in *Being and Nothingness* to "need" in the *Critique* in order to justify a Marxian treatment of "scarcity," he falls into the same trap that, as we saw in Chapter 5, has claimed many sociologists. That is, he seems to assume that man's "needs" may be determined simply by cataloguing those things man has striven for in the past. In doing so he reproduces the very error he had set out explicitly to challenge: that of projecting limits on future behavior on the basis of past behavior. He would, in other words, move back within the very circle of a deterministic logic that *Existenz* was formulated to avoid. Furthermore, "scarcity" is defined merely in economic terms. Provide an economy that creates and assures universal abundance and an era of freedom—with its absence of conflict (even an end to the negation of the negation)—is upon us. This would represent a shockingly naïve understanding of the human being as a social animal, for there is utterly no evidence to lead anyone sensitized to the subtleties of social existence to believe that once a human being's material needs have been met his strife with his fellows will cease—or, indeed, when an entire society's physical needs have been so satisfied. The evidence of man's ceaseless striving for ego advantage is simply all too abundant to demand detailing here. No, the Sartrean effort, although it may challenge the priestly and system modes as they are set forth in both Marxist and non-Marxist contexts, is not in a position to offer American sociologists a suitable framework even in the longer run.

An increasing number of sociologists would argue—as we noted in Chapters 2 and 6—that a "socialized" phenomenology might be sufficient to that task. Certainly the renewal of interest in Husserl by philosophers and the recent translation and publication of Alfred Schütz' *Collected Works* and his early *Phenomenology of the Social World*, together with the vivid and sociologically sophisticated efforts of such younger social theorists as Peter Berger, Thomas Luckmann, Edward Tiryakian, Harold Garfinkel, and Burkart Holzner, signal an important new turn for "general theory" and one that promises to raise the profession's level of contextual awareness considerably.[1]

Roots

Husserl, trained as he was in mathematics, physics, and philosophy, set out to construct nothing less than a completely reliable "science" of the subjective. Aware that natural science was burdened by a set of largely unrecognized assumptions, he claimed that through a technique of self-conscious "phenomenological reduction"—the apperception of the impact of phenomena upon one's consciousness devoid of reference to the actual presence or absence of external objects—he had framed an epistemology freed of all but self-evident assumptions. The phenomena abstracted were in turn seen to structure themselves within a format of universally present and relatively invariant *Ideen* and found to relate themselves, in the life histories of individuals in society, to an inverse "suspension of doubt" in the "reality" of "everyday life" on the latter's part. Needless to say, the self-evident nature of the position was questioned by many—with perhaps his most promising student, Martin Heidegger, breaking away to become philosophy's leading exponent of existentialism and succeeding to Husserl's chair at Freibourg. Rather than claim either the certainty or the freedom from presuppositions that Husserl was wont to do, Heidegger focused upon the element of risk that adheres to an existence that must confront, as its primary datum, the threat of "non-being." Instead of projecting a set of systematically interrelated and quasi-Platonic *Ideen*, the latter drew a portrait of the concrete individual forced to accept the responsibility of making choices in a setting of substantive freedom. Rather than painting experience in the neutral hues of an invariant structure of consciousness whose appeal would be to man's search for rational order, his canvas was colored by a call to the commitment necessary for "authentic existence." Instead of the cool bracketing out of all but the impact made by phenomena upon the consciousness, Heidegger reclaimed for philosophy dimensions of human experience that had been abandoned as idiosyncratic by both science and philosophy. In other words, instead of seeking to grasp by introspection the phenomena of both inter- and intrasubjective experience, within the web of an essentially "scientific" frame of reference, Heidegger renounced the value of the intersubjective "lens" of science for an understanding of the human condition that he felt was available to it through the depth of the intrasubjective alone.

Alfred Schütz

Still, a social theorist such as Alfred Schütz, who sought a firmer base than that provided by existentialism and yet would not abandon the subjective dimension of human experience, could find much that was attractive in the phenomenological stance. For one thing, he saw it sharing with existentialism the conviction that the knowledge that one must die and the fear of that death stood as primordial data of human existence, although it would have to be seen as presenting itself within the phenomena of consciousness rather than as the direct threat of "non-being" to "being," as would be the case with Heidegger. It is Schütz' interpretation of man's reaction to that threat, however, that provides the key to his larger posture. Following Husserl, man is seen as inverting the phenomenologist's doubt of all but the phenomena of consciousness: in order to cloak his anxiety, man *suspends doubt* in the paramount reality of "everyday life." "Everyday life," together with the "natural attitude" with which it is associated, then becomes the paradigmatic focus of analysis. It is in turn characterized as "action" oriented—that is, the meaning reflected by the "natural attitude" toward the world of "everyday life" originates in and is instituted by chosen, motivated "acts." The individual, although confronting a world that is largely a shared world of *typical* images and meanings (whose genesis is set forth in terms akin to those of Cooley and George Herbert Mead), discovers his "projects"—his purposes—confronted by unique constellations of events that demand choice. Whether his "act" (the outcome of his choice) is identical with his "action" (his preconceived project) he alone knows; others may only approach certainty by sharing in the common definitions of "everyday life." Even the failure to act is choice, for it is an explicit or implicit decision *not* to act. Still, the desire to change one's environment is regarded as such a central factor within the "natural attitude" that Schütz considered "work" the archetypal image of human reality.

Only when an individual is confronted by a problem for which no resolution is provided by the range of typical meanings available in "everyday life" is the "natural attitude" threatened. He is forced at that point—if he would seek a solution—toward a Kierkegaardian "leap of faith" from the "natural attitude" to an alternative "finite realm of meaning"—one which fails to share a common cognitive frame with the "natural attitude." One such realm is sociology. Man as sociologist is to accept the former world of "everyday life" as his subject matter—his *only* subject matter—but in doing so he is to superimpose an additional layer of typicalities that are justified by the aims of the new province. He does so by constructing ideal types through the method of *verstehen* in the manner of Max Weber, especially models of "rational" actions. To these he applies the logic and standards of verification common to natural science, except that Schütz (1962:65) would not limit the term "empirical observation" to sensory perceptions of the "outer" world, but would extend its meaning to include that experience "by which common-sense thinking in everyday life understands human actions and their outcomes in terms of their underlying motives or goals."

The aim of such a social science, Schütz tells us, is to reconstruct, in a simplified manner, the way in which "healthy, wideawake adults" interpret their world. Yet it does not purport to be identical, even in principle, with that world. It self-consciously distorts the "natural attitude" by abstracting from it those aspects that fit the fully systematic model appropriate to the ends of science. The result is an image of social man as but a puppet of the typicalities of sociation and in reference to which such terms as "motive," "action," or "project"—immediately appropriate to the realm of the "natural attitude of everyday life"—should always, when confronted within the province of science, be interpreted as if in quotation marks. It is a distortion that must be justified by the systematic understanding—and thus predictive utility—afforded by the latter realm of meaning.

Although much of this is compelling, it is startling to discover that Schütz could then go on to portray the sociologist *qua* sociologist as aloof, detached, and completely uninvolved in "action"—as impinging only upon the cognitive dimension of existence, as *merely* an observer and not an actor in the world about him. Indeed, he goes so far as to state that his theoretical activity may not even be considered "work"—a crucial clue to the respect he would grant sociology (and, apparently, all of the pure sciences)—when one recalls that "work," to Schütz, served as the ideal-typical mode of human action. Indeed, scientific activity is viewed as a point of refuge where, having made the "leap" into disinterestedness, the sociologist and his colleagues may somehow now find themselves freed even of that existential anxiety that was set forth as the source of the suspension of doubt in "everyday reality." It is clear that he has, with relative accuracy, described the "natural attitude" reflected in the everyday life of the *sociologist of his day*; still his naïve acceptance of that self-image places the utility of Schütz' entire effort in question.

The phenomenological task draws its fundamental attractiveness from its claim: the assertion that it is able to deal cognitively, systematically, and reliably with the *intra*subjective as well as the intersubjective. Added to this has been its appreciation of existentialism's fundamental point of reference (the threat of "non-being") and the genetic and dialectical relationship that the two philosophies have demonstrated over the years—the manner in which man, even "social" man, is viewed primarily as "actor" rather than as "respondent"; its corresponding emphasis upon change rather than stability; its provision for fundamentally discrete realms that cannot be contained within a common *cognitive* scheme; the awareness of the manner in which the product of a science is limited by its assumptions; and the sophisticated manner in which Weber's *verstehen* sociology and the interactionism of Cooley and Mead are interwoven. Yet the cost would appear too great for sociologists to bear, moving as they are into a period of epistemological self-awareness.

The root of the trouble lies with Husserl's explicit—and Schütz' implicit—point of departure: the conviction that there was a *presuppositionless*, or at the very least a persuasively self-evident, mode of confronting experience that would be amenable to systematic, cognitive, and thus *reliable* explanation; that there could indeed be a "science" built upon a base that included experience that was in principle private in its immediate giveness. In other words, the phenomenological reduction became the twentieth century's peculiar contribution to the perennial quest for a certainty that would escape the net of implicit commitment accompanying any presumptive context. Instead, it has simply joined that lengthy lineage recited in Chapter 5, each of which, presuming finally to free cognition from valuation, has had rather to accept the label of a philosophical predisposition. For it shifted its complexion from a radical psychologism through a "neutralism" to a transcendental idealism even in the hands of Husserl himself and, upon Husserl's death, was splintered into a wide variety of disputatious "schools" by his followers.

This pretension of freedom from substantive assumptions was carried over immediately to a comparable pretension regarding the suspension of doubt that is the *epoche* of the "natural attitude": the world that is "everyday life" is treated as self-evidently an "ultimate or "paramount" reality and becomes the center of Schütz' attention. Some would be tempted to identify the "original given lens"—the full range of man's inter- and intrasubjective experience of which I spoke earlier—with such a "natural attitude" toward the "everyday" world. Indeed this would appear to be akin to the tack taken by Gibson Winter in his recent and provocative *Elements for a Social Ethic: Scientific and Ethical Perspectives on Social Process*. Unfortunately, it is quite clear that this was *not*

Schütz' intention. He would restrict such a "natural attitude" to the *typicalities* that frame a "wide-awake" and doubt-free apprehension of "everyday life"; it is not designed to encompass all of experience, even all of social experience. Rather, it is self-consciously limited to a single "province of meaning" that is reputedly shared socially as the "natural" one in the adult workaday world. It is this "world" from which the individual turns only when confronted with a "problem" that is unresolvable within it, with a "shock" that breaks the limits of the "natural attitude" and forces one to leap into another "finite province of meaning."

One of the provinces is, as we mentioned earlier, the realm of social science. But even sociologists, according to Schütz, must limit themselves to second-order typologies of the first-order typifications that form the content of the "natural attitude." The appropriate empirical referent of one's sociological conceptualization, then, is doubly narrowed thereby, a renunciation that is not likely to be accepted by a discipline that has often exhibited an even more voracious appetite for the socially atypical than for the typical. And when one notes the substantive nature of those areas that must be ruled out because they fall outside the realm of the "natural attitude of everyday life"—those social phenomena which reflect unresolved conflict or are in response to atypical crisis situations on the one hand or which depart radically from the archetypal image of "work," as "play" would appear to do, on the other—one is forced to conclude that the limitation not only will not do but should not do.

The phenomenological tradition, as it is mediated by Alfred Schütz, then, is unsuited in its present form for either the immediate or contextual needs of sociology. It founders initially in its claim to be both presuppositionless *and* reliable; its attempt to escape a positivistic realism on the one side and a naïve idealism on the other results in a methodological reification of a mundane and doubly typified "everyday life" drained of the leaven of both fundamental anxiety and play; and it perceives the sociologist *qua* sociologist not only in the discredited and simplistic value-free terms that dominated the sociology of the 'forties and the 'fifties, yet goes further by denying him even the active quality denoted by "work." As impressive as its aim to safeguard the subjective, purposive dimension of experience may be, the price asked cannot help but be deemed unrealistic by a sociology approaching epistemological sophistication.

Peter Berger

This is not to say that fruitful revisions of the phenomenological lineage represented by Schütz may not be forthcoming. Indeed, one of the most intriguing would appear in process of development at the hands of Peter Berger. Though acknowledging a major debt to Schütz—as his works to date clearly testify—Berger adds an accent that is decidely his own. Rather than penning sociology within the narrow boundaries of a scheme of second-order typifications and perceiving its aim as but the reconstruction of the common-sense world of man living his everyday life among his fellow men, he would allow its subject matter to encompass both the broad range of "social facts" of a Durkheim and the empathetic sensitivity of a Weber. Berger's aim is to shake man free—even if but for a moment—of the fictions that he himself has constructed quite unselfconsciously into an "everyday reality" that in fact serves to imprison and manipulate him. Although Schütz, too, recognizes "common-sense reality" as a human product, he treats it with almost sacred regard, as all of us tend to treat that which we regard as of paramount reality. Berger, however, would *de*sacralize it as our larger tradition would desacralize all that is simply the product of man himself. The "natural attitude" toward "everyday life" becomes, in Berger's hand and those of his associates, not the be-all and the end-all of the entire sociological enterprise but rather an exceptionally fruitful focus for an enlarged exercise in the sociology of knowledge. Where Schütz would have sociology simply seek to "understand" that "common-sense world," Berger conceives sociology as a medium by which we are able to transcend the determinate forms and meanings we ourselves as men have given it. In other words, through a process analogous to the way in which a psychoanalyst assists his patient in uncovering and thus understanding the compulsive routines and meanings he himself had fashioned in response to his need for security, sociologists may, through an extension of the perspective of the sociology of knowledge, portray to the layman the manner in which society—or one of its sub-systems—routinizes its own structures and meanings in the name of "reality" or "the natural" and so subjects man to a socialized prison of his own making or, when those norms have been unselfconsciously internalized (as they are typically held to have been), to the unauthentic life of the puppet. When the genesis of a particular social compulsion, cognitive or behavioral, has been carefully and accurately described —and understood as such—the conditions necessary to transcend it are at hand. One then becomes capable of "standing outside" the internalized norm, the prescribed role, the cultural expectation, or the structural niche for a shorter or longer period. Indeed, the cognitive norms of the language of contemporary sociology—role, system, generalized other—are themselves seen as socially derived fictions equally capable, in principle, of being transcended.

The attractiveness, then, of a phenomenologically *informed* format for the sociology of the 1970's may be quite formidable. It will have to take the general direction of the Berger modification, however, if it would seek paradigmatic stature, for the posture of Alfred Schütz—following hard upon that of Husserl—is essentially a *priestly* one: satisfied with the approximate communication of that which is regarded as paramount reality rather than motivated by the claim of transcendence. And we have already acknowledged that sociology is now directed—and can be expected in the immediate future to move—toward the *prophetic* pole. That Berger has built up abundant momentum in the latter direction is self-evident.

But the strength of Berger's posture is also its weakness —at least *vis-à-vis* its acceptability as paradigm for the many within the discipline who continue to view sociology as integrally related to natural science. As influential as his *Invitation to Sociology* has been, it was greeted—when reviewed in the profession's major official journal by one of the discipline's less conservative minds (Selznick, 1964:285–86)—with undisguised hostility as an attempt to transform an even-tempered science into a "debunking" exercise. Perhaps the sub-title Berger gave the volume—*A Humanistic Perspective*—provides the crucial clue. Most sociologists in America, although they are becoming aware of the manner in which the social sciences may begin to serve as a bridge between the "two cultures," will not in the immediately foreseeable future be willing to renounce their image of sociology as a science nor return to the *Wissenschaft* definition traditional to the Continent, encompassing as it does *any* systematic cognitive endeavor. Yet the latter represents, by and large, the intellectual context out of which—and in terms of which—Berger speaks. This is not to say that it is wrongheaded. Such a return may well be our appropriate destiny in the longer run and Berger, again, one of its prophets. At the very least it represents a spring to which the more segmented, specialized inclinations of the New World have periodically returned for creative insight and for breaking parochial linguistic habits and which gives every appearance of maintaining the strength necessary to play a similarly liberating role in the future. But from the evidence that is the state of contemporary sociology it is quite clear that such a frame places too great a burden on the undeniably attractive vision that Berger has begun to share with the larger profession and makes his imagery incapable at the moment of winning a clear-cut victory in the battle for paradigmatic supremacy or even for serving as the basis for a collaborative ceasefire.

The test of the Berger version of the phenomenological posture, then, must await the passage of a decade or more, by which time he and his associates and students will have blocked out more fully the range of its implications and resolved those apparent inconsistencies that are the price of any major new theoretical departure. By that time, too, those generations of graduate students who returned during the 1960's to the prophetic stance abandoned by their predecessors will be an increasingly dominant factor in the discipline. Among those issues that one would expect by that time to have been resolved would be Berger's apparent reluctance, in the midst of an insistence that sociology be seen as a "debunking" dialect aimed at establishing conditions which would make transcendence of a given social reality possible, to in fact give up the traditional value-free characterization of the discipline, together with the related legacy of Husserl and Schütz which argues that the sociological enterprise appropriately strives to be but "an act of pure perception."[2] Imperative, too, will be a clarification of the essential difference, if any, between his expanded image of a sociology of knowledge and sociological theory, humanistically conceived, in general. The most fundamental problem facing Berger, however, is his apparent unwillingness to grant the processes involved in the structuring of a given "reality of everyday life" ontological status equivalent to those that contribute to its transcendence—in other words, his inability to date to grant those forces that would guarantee stability to the flux that is human social experience the same stature he would give the disjunctive.

The larger discipline, although increasingly sensitized to its contextual setting by those writing from a phenomenological and/or an existential, historical, or philosophical perspective, will almost certainly continue over the immediate years ahead to continue to perceive of itself as a science intimately linked to the natural sciences through its dedication to the delineation of order in the social world. Although there will be fierce rear-guard action on the part of those who would save the phrase "value-free" for its undoubted public-relations value, the concept is fated to wither appreciably. Or, if it is to survive, it must be transformed into the modest and accurate claim that the verbal product of social research is always to be stated in the indicative, never in the imperative. The major shift will be the increasingly open admission that neither sociology nor any other science has operated nor can operate simply from within its own functional integrity for its normative standards, if one would sustain the values that the West derives from its Hellenic and Hebraic roots and other cultural traditions. The conditions for such an awareness have always lain implicit within the nature of sociology, for science could easily be seen as but one among many human communal activities. It was not until relatively recently, however, that the sociology of knowledge spawned a fledgling sociology of science to document in engaging detail the humanity, the ineradicably value-laden color, of that sub-culture. Now it in turn has given birth to a "sociology of sociology," promising to advance the discipline's awareness of its own peculiar life-style—and the fictions that support it—enormously. That this book seeks to contribute to that end cannot be denied, but it should be clear that the outlines of the picture drawn herein are etched deeply enough into sociology's recent history to have made this particular effort expendable.

Primacy of the personal

What the sociology of the immediate future will seek is some intelligible manner of grasping the strengths and the limitations of its "scientific" perspective relative to the larger context it has finally acknowledged as being contained within, yet neither succumbing to the tempting but tautological trap of returning to the epistemology of the science it would envelop nor resigning itself to the web that is paradox. One such possibility has been offered by John Macmurray, a Scottish philosopher so moved by the interactionist implications of sociology to have titled the volumes that were to sum his life's work and point toward a new departure for philosophy *The Self as Agent* and *Persons in Relation.*

Acknowledging that the metaphorical sensitivities of existentialism have served to focus our attention on the crucial philosophical problem of our age—the crisis of the personal—Macmurray, although content to remain within the rhetoric traditional to his discipline, sets forth from a radically new point of departure. Rejecting as egocentric the assumption that the self may act as pure subject in registering the world as object, he offers "action" as the fundamental quality of existence, substituting *personal intention* ("I do" or "I intend") for the "I think" of idealism, the "It is" of realism, the "I perceive" of phenomenology, and the "I am" of existentialism. Even the "I" that "does" or "intends," however, is seen to transcend the traditional egocentric predicament by being viewed as constituted, at an ontological and not merely a scientific level, by the relationships between persons, by the implicit reading of "You and I" within the explicit "I." Not "Self" but "Person" —intentional, acting, and reflective of its interpersonal nature—stands as the key contextual referent and "Personal"—the relationship to the "Other" as end rather than as means—as the fundamental criterion for integrity.

Scientific research and theory-construction are then subordinated to the claim of the personal, justifiable not in and of themselves but only in terms of contextual motives that would seek through them the conditions necessary to expand the dimension of the personal. This is due to the fact that such scientific activity represents a temporary withdrawal from the personal relationship back to the egocentric stance that would see the effort as but a means to the resolution of the scientist's cognitive problem. When the research of theoretical activity focuses upon human behavior, the intentional, acting character of persons—together with the mutual treatment of the other as end that signifies the personal—must be sacrificed in some measure in exchange for the power of a grammar that would perceive man as determinate object and treat him as means. Approximation to such reflective objectification is unavoidable even in everyday informal experience; it is, however, always to be judged in terms of the intentional context that surrounds it. Where Macmurray tends to fail is in his inability to suggest—beyond the usual bow in the direction of technological application—the various ways in which the behavioral sciences, once a contextual frame is acknowledged, may be *peculiarly* suited to guaranteeing an extension of the personal. It is just such a calling for sociology that will be explored in the final pages before us.

Dialogical Possibilities

There will be those who will have read this volume with the hope and expectation that they have stumbled across another club with which to beat once again what they feel to be the pretentiousness of sociology's claims as a science. But if they do they will be taken in by an altogether private vendetta, for the full import of what has been said here lays the foundation for what may appear to be an outrageously extravagant appraisal of the contribution a *science* of society may be expected to make to buttressing and extending those humane images that represent our inheritance from the city states of Greece and the tribes of Israel. Though it has been my intention to draw a harsh caricature of a sociology that would seek its center of reference within itself—the value-free claim—the discipline's informal life-style, never succumbing to its own propaganda, has played and will continue to play a remarkably liberating and responsible role in the drama of human existence.

All the pieces of the puzzle lie before us and need now but to be fitted together. Those that had been missing have been recovered: first, the realization that the scientific rhetoric that distinguishes sociology demands a *context*; and second, the appropriation of the *personal*—or some metaphorically equivalent paradigm—as that context for sociology. An epistemology that would reduce social experience to simply a network of determinate objects is transformed thereby into *man's most reliable instrument for extending meaningful responsibility and substantive freedom*.

The extension of responsibility

The larger intellectual world, pressed to the wall during the first half of the present century by the formal assumptions and claims of the scientific community, turned to the sanctuary provided by the intrasubjective and countered with the inverse blinders of *Existenz*, for here at least the personal might remain inviolate. Unfortunately, in the process, existential man had to renounce all claim to *social* responsibility, because any extension from the experience of the immediately intrasubjective demands the reintroduction of "order" and the latter—if it were to approach reliability—remained the province of a rejected science. Indeed to turn for one's compass to *Existenz* exclusively could prove at least as tragic as the opposite recourse, the reification of the intersubjective assumptions of science, as may be illustrated by the early Heidegger's dramatic plea to the German people to follow their *Führer*, on the one hand, and the later Marx's identification with the materialism of science, on the other. It was the dilemma Sartre sought to bridge philosophically in his *Critique de la Raison Dialectique*.

The larger culture of which we are a part has traditionally assigned the cultivation of "responsibility" to the family, the church, and the school. The means assumed to be particularly appropriate to its extension have been exhortation and the cultivation of discipline. Serious consideration at the adult level is reserved for the discipline of ethics, an exericse that appears too often satisfied with the verbal manipulation of a variety of contending frames of reference, examined in terms of their logical integrity by the philosopher and in terms of their consistency *vis-à-vis* given traditional doctrines by the theologian. "Social" ethics has of recent decades begun to be distinguished from its parent as an effort to apply such norms—the roots of which lay historically in face-to-face personal encounter—to situations that reflect the more secondary, indirect interaction that typifies contemporary complex societies. But even in the latter case the accent has been upon the application of normatively *given* standards upon descriptively *given* situations. The contribution of the specialist is seen to lie in linking the two logically (and/or theologically), not in extending responsibility *per se*. The latter task is left by and large to exhortation, example, and differential acculturation. It is into this breach that sociologists and their colleagues in neighboring social sciences have marched.

Once again we must acknowledge a fundamental debt to Max Weber. For it was he who insisted that the ultimate aim of the sciences of social man was the enhancement of one's "sense of responsibility."[3] The term itself—the Latin *re+spondere*: "to promise"—reflects the notion of "accountability," "answerable for one's conduct." Thus when one extends the domain of man's accountability he enlarges his responsibility. And this is exactly what the epistemology of sociology as a social science is uniquely equipped to do. Notice the phrase "uniquely equipped." It is not used for affect value. I intend to suggest quite baldly that *no other human endeavor*—preaching, example, the formal or informal study of ethics—*may claim such an advantage*.

A child is not held responsible either in law or more informally for much (in law, any) of its behavior because it does not realize the potential impact of its acts. Even an adult may be held "irresponsible" under law if it can be determined that he was at the time incapable of comprehending the potential results of his behavior. If, in other words, he is unable to *predict* the "response" that his action will elicit, he is *ir-respons-able*. Yet it is precisely this gap that a social science is armed to narrow. Its logic enables it, when applied with a trained intelligence, imagination, and patience, to extract the recurrent from the maze that is social experience and project it into the future, thus informing us of the consequences of the alternative steps that lie immediately before us. By constructing a network of order over time we are provided with a map by which we may move with foreknowledge into the future and therefore be held in fact answerable for the impact of our conduct. Granted that direct existential awareness may assure us of the ineradicable nature of choice *per se*, still we are provided by it with no grounding in the social world that we share with others and are sustained only by myth and metaphor in our search for reliability. Exhortation serves merely to focus our attention; the reiteration of habit but to add to the burden of our compulsiveness. The sciences by their intersubjective restraint guarantee a measure of social reliability otherwise unavailable to us. And sociology, concerned as it is with the common denominators of social action in any and every substantively differentiated sphere, would thrust its torch into every niche and cranny of our social world, judging nothing to be too petty or commonplace for its attention, and thus extending the domain of the "responsible" far beyond the boundaries traditionally marked out by ethicists. It demonstrates, thus, a universality of concern seldom shown even by our avowedly universalistic religious tradition.[4]

Such universality of concern shades over into the compassion of which Peter Berger[5] has spoken and on toward the humility that Merton documented in his early study of Calvinist roots of seventeenth-century science. For the cognitive conditions for such qualities are laid down when one uncovers the determinate dimension in any human action. It undergirds as well the substantive realization so central to the sociological stance, that man is not man except in community: that he cannot simply chose in the privacy of his existential selfhood the path that will guarantee social maturity and ethical sensitivity, but that he is largely dependent upon responsible interaction with others for his integrity.[6] Sociology can in a very real sense, then, claim a prime position within the role that a mature Heidegger could grant science as a whole: that of "the shepherd of being" (Underwood, 1961:141).

The Weberian case is, then, a sturdy one. If one would

accept the definition of responsible behavior offered—a situation in which the actor is aware of the approximate impact his action will have on others—then sociology, concerned as it is with features that underlie all forms of social interaction, would appear to provide the paradigmatic mode for the most reliable extension of responsibility in the human social sphere. Though taken in and of itself it may project an image of man that would deny the traditional notion of responsibility altogether, its actual result—when viewed within a larger context in which choice has a measure of substantive reality—is to enlarge the domain of man's accountability. Rather than settling for the modest claim that sociology enables the trained professional to discover more efficient means-ends linkages (as valid an assertion as that is), we may begin to see it for what in fact it is: a tool far more powerful than logical and theological analyses traditional to the discipline of ethics and/or the powers of exhortation, imitation, and habit to expand the range of man's responsibility. There is indeed no other medium but the traditional recourse to "revelation" by which responsibility may be or has been reliably extended. Whenever and wherever such advances have taken place, they must have occurred in a fashion which, although pragmatic and unselfconscious, was immediately analogous to the logic that we have come over the last few generations to systematize as social science. And if one would take our reading of that logic with full seriousness, the gap between it and what theology would identify as "revelation" may have already largely disappeared.

There are, however, two marked boundaries that must encompass and condition what has been claimed. The first is simply this. A "shepherd" may have, indeed typically has, an aim that may not be in the ultimate interest of his flock. Machiavelli, authentically heralded today as the first self-conscious social scientist of the modern period, could serve a just prince or an evil prince with equal effectiveness. To enlarge the realm of responsible action says nothing whatsoever of its qualitative content. One may enhance the impersonal in as telling a manner as the personal, the manipulation of others for the satiation of one's own needs as adequately as for the fulfillment of the others' own aims. In either case one is "responsible." The choice cannot be dictated by a logic rooted in the intersubjective, for the latter (as we saw in Chapters 9 and 10) provides no fundamental point of departure but merely a network of predictive relationships. The choice, then, must be made in dialogue with the intrasubjective, for it is there that the texture of experience registers its deepest impact. It is there, as the philosophers and theologians of *Existenz* have served to remind the present generation, that issues of "being" and "non-being," the grounding of good and the grounding of evil, of alienation and authenticity, are to be confronted. And only if one perceives at that level that it is the integrity of the person that must serve as social compass will we be in a position to avoid the egocentric predicament that is the product of intentional or unintentional reification of the presumptions of science. Once again we find that the scientific frame is not merely alternative but nested as well: it resides, whether it would or not, in a larger world of experience that includes the intrasubjective.

The nurturing of freedom

The second boundary is established by the paradoxical nature of social science, which we pointed out in Chapter 8 and mentioned in our discussion of the dialectical paradigm. The paradox lies in the startling fact that the actual procedures necessarily and in principle adhering to social research are shot through with an implicit commitment toward *change*. Unavoidable in the application of the control necessary to approximate the experimental paradigm that governs verification, confronted in the interaction that is observation, magnified through the acts of communication that define science as a plural enterprise, it is seen most dramatically in the impact that the very perception of order within social experience has upon the future behavior of those who share that perception. We discovered that the inverse of Merton's "self-fulfilling prophecy" syndrome—"suicidal" or "self-denying prophecy"—must be extended to cover, in some measure over the shorter or longer run, all social research; that in the very process of precipitating and comprehending recurrent patterns of social behavior we were introducing factors that would act in principle to deny their full validity when projected into the future. We were therefore forced to conclude that all social research was in some measure "action" research; that, by the very fact that the sociologist himself was part of the interactive circle of action he sought to predict, social "laws" are not, cannot be, stable over the long run. Only by projecting an imaginary social universe in which there were no history and no social scientists (indeed, no laymen who could come informally and pragmatically to comparable perceptions) might sociology continue in its secure assumption that there are indeed fundamental social "laws" to be deciphered and proclaimed valid at least until man's biological structure has itself taken new form. And not only are we unable to provide adequately for such "feedback" through experience with it over time, but the very paradox itself is not amenable to statement as "law," for in either case such provision or such a "law" would be subject to the very same erosion—and again in principle.

Merton's hesitancy to advocate, for the present generation at least, any aim beyond the derivation of theories "of the middle range" may well have resulted in part from his sensitivity to the prophetic nature of social prediction. Certainly the advice would seem to have been in the right direction. But even this admonition will have to be reinterpreted or rephrased, to add a temporal dimension to its concern for level of generalization, if it is to provide fruitful guidance to the novitiate. The stance taken by Merton's younger associate in the sociology of science, Bernard Barber, would appear preferable. Barber recommends that, largely because of the paradox under discussion, we limit ourselves to continual short-range prediction.[7]

It is an immediately analogous transcendence of the given structures of everyday reality that informs the comic motif that dominates the invitation to sociology that Peter Berger would set before us. The tragic destiny of a *1984* is not at all suitable in its light; rather it is the clown-like figure of man, caught up in the compulsive routines of a drama he assumes has been authored by nature or by God, that occupies center stage.[8] The tragic mode must give way to the comic, first because of the image projected by an Adam who is congenitally indisposed to acknowledge to himself that it was in fact he who allotted the roles and wrote the script and, second, because sociology has the capacity to reveal the human comedy in its full dimensions. But most important, although the vision is precarious, through it Adam may be freed at least momentarily to reconstruct the order of his existence in terms of a more authentic script. It is no accident that humor is man's most potent weapon for self-disclosure nor that he stands alone among the animals in possessing it. For it is intimately tied to his unique capacity to create his own culture together with his ineradicable temptation to deny his responsibility at one moment and his freedom to create anew at the next.

The general character of the liberating process of which Berger speaks is not, of course, a fundamentally new insight. Only its specific application to the breaking of the bonds of fictitiousness that appear all to "functional" in the social sphere is new. Furthermore, dialectical philosophy and theology have long linked freedom with the perception of order. What is unique in the present formulation is that it moves beyond the level of mere assertion and/or faith to the description in empirically relevant terms of the epistemological basis for the claim. Through the sociologist's capacity to grasp the fact that social research actually stands *within* the dialectic that is social interaction, he stands in an enviable position to spell out the substantively verifiable manner in which the very perception of order will contribute to freeing one from compulsive repetition. And, as in the case of "responsibility," there is every reason to assert that his calling, because of its patient dedication to the harsh master that is empirical fact, holds a key far more reliable and sustaining than the traditional recourse to sheer rhetoric and admonition to guarantee the extension and preservation of man's liberating and creative faculties.

But once again the limits of a logic rooted in the intersubjective alone must be drawn, for "liberation" as well as "responsibility" is a two-sided sword. One may turn one's freedom from the shackles of the past toward aggrandizement as readily as to compassion. One may free oneself from restraint all the better to restrain. One may destroy the security that others find in an ordered past to feed one's own private security, shatter a functional relationship at large to nourish one at home. One may be freed to achieve community or to accomplish mastery. The final grounds for choice, as we have seen earlier, although informed by the empirical, lie rooted in the intrasubjective. Only if we assume that the presumptive framework to which sociology as a science makes claim is contained within a larger dialogue that includes the existential—and is drawn by the latter toward a fundamental respect for personal integrity—may the freedom we enhance be distinguished from nihilism or, through the conscious or unconscious reification of but the assumptions that grant sociology its power, lead us to transform man into mere object.

One may be tempted to characterize the overall posture now before us as a simple extension of a term that is traditional to the vocabulary of philosophy and that we have made considerable use of to this point: that is, the adjective "dialectical." There is no doubt that it does indeed apply to the manner in which sociology contributes interactively to the substantive extension of both man's responsibility and his freedom. It is not, however, equally appropriate for designating the larger stance for at least two reasons. The first, of lesser importance, is the fear that it would serve too handily the inclinations of those who are tempted to substitute categorization and conceptual stereotyping for the exercise of reason and the effort to comprehend. The message is not Hegelian, consciously or otherwise: experience is the residual epistemological category, not idea. It is equally apparent that it is not an extrapolation of Marx, early or late. It should be taken, not in a private shorthand, but for what it is: the product of a wide range of intellectual influences and sympathies.

The second, and by far the more important, is the fact that "dialectical" has traditionally been used to characterize the nature of a single logic, to be distinguished thereby from other singular logics such as the Aristotelian. A crucial characteristic of the present formulation, on the other hand, is that it seeks to engage two quite distinct epistemologies within the framework of *dialogue*. Sociology does not thereby abandon the logic traditional to natural science for one appropriate to history. It does not seek to replace Aristotle with Hegel, Mill with Mills,

Parsons with Sartre. Existential sensitivity is no substitute for empirical verifiability—or vice versa. What it says is that the two predispositions—the one suitable to the concern for reliability evidenced by natural science and the other appropriate to the risk demanded by a sensitivity to the ground that is personal existence—must inform each other if either is to bear fruit for man. Indeed, it says more than that. It declares that they *do*—that social man unavoidably orients himself in terms of two levels of experience, the intersubjective and the intrasubjective, the public and the private, the empirical and the existential—and that to continue to ignore that fact, as the sub-cultures grouped around either pole have been tempted to do, reflects in cognitive form but the egocentric predicament that has been the mark of man's creatureliness, individual and corporate.

It is for these reasons, then, that I would choose the term *dialogical* to characterize the epistemological situation in which we find ourselves. It does not reflect a metaphysical or ontological dualism of any sort: experience, its grounding referent, is one. It is the modern world's vocabulary and grammar and the structures that frame socialization in her separate intellectual sub-cultures that have created that dualism. There is no doubt that the two polar rhetorics in fact shade one into the other—indeed, have only gradually come to be differentiated from each other in recent centuries. When and if they will regain the unity they once claimed is for the future to reveal. The present generation may hope at most to begin to rebuild lines of communication. The sociologist, with ears professionally sensitized to evidence of dialogue—and its absence—is in a privileged position to amplify both the subliminal evidence for, and the conscious disclaimer of, such interaction, to assist in revealing the fact that even epistemology as currently structured must be viewed as an essentially "social" enterprise. But in the process he will be forced to reconstruct his own image of the calling of sociology.

Sociologist: Witness to Dialogue

Thomas Kuhn, whose *The Structure of Scientific Revolutions* served as port of embarkation for the voyage we have taken through the turbulent seas of sociology, has much to offer those who would aspire to chart the shoals and hidden reefs that comprise a sociology of sociology. An awareness that a science must, as it moves toward maturity, coalesce about a single substantive paradigm is balanced by his discovery that the ordering of empirical phenonena within a given field takes place within the bounds of the accepted *gestalt* only until the amplitude it has afforded man's predictive understanding has heightened the community's awareness of anomaly as well. For when the latter has persisted in the developmental history of a natural science it has led ultimately—after a period of trial, epistemological soul-searching, and conflict—to the revolutionary rejection of the former paradigm and the crowning of the new. It is a tale not simply of steady progress made as one level of order is precipitated upon the sediment of previous evidence of order, but one in which a period of sustained development alternates with very real and very harsh competition for paradigmatic supremacy.

The rewards that the stencil offers a sociology of sociology were revealed in the first portion of this volume. We found that sociology did tend to move out of an eclectic adolescence toward coalescence about an orthodoxy spelled out in terms of system and the derivative notion of function; that the late 'fifties and early 'sixties found the field wrestling with the issue of fundamental social "change"—a stubborn anomaly when addressed by a conceptual model which saw in stability its final point of reference; and that the 'sixties brought with them a major movement, particularly among younger sociologists, toward replacing system with conflict in the position of prime paradigmatic honor. At the edge of battle stood a small band of mediators proffering a "dialectical" flag as a means to an honorable peace without victory or defeat.

To take the latter group seriously, however, would be to reject Kuhn's central thesis and the epistemological assumptions upon which it drew its strength. Revolutions by definition imply the overthrow of the orthodox and the acquisition of supreme power by the victorious combatant, while the revolutionary model itself was projected as infinitely repetitive. Kuhn's error lies precisely where one might expect it to lie: with the fact that, trained in the physical sciences, he brought to his task the assumption of recurrence native to that province. But his exercise was in neither the history nor the philosophy of science, it was rather in sociology, the sociology of science. And in its pursuit he—as with the great majority of trained sociologists—was simply unaware of the fundamental paradox that differentiates the logic of the social sciences from that of the physical and biological. For in an exercise such as his own the very knowledge we gain of the periodic cresting of paradigmatic revolutions in the past may be fed back as a new and unique factor in science's communal life, enabling the latter to break with the compulsive routines that would lead once again to monopolization of orthodoxy by a single paradigm. As a result, "revolution" may, after a time, no longer be the appropriate image. With the growing realization that all specific conceptual and empirical activity within a science is dependent ultimately upon a larger "given" *gestalt*, scientific communities may themselves come to accept a fundamental pluralism as an appropriate style for the life of scientific mind just as much of the larger populace of the West has come to accept pluralism in civic and religious life as an appropriate response to an awareness of the repetitive nature of revolutions in the history of the civic sphere. There is, indeed, some slim evidence already available that this has in fact already begun to occur within the natural sciences themselves.

It is with the social sciences, however, that one should expect the pluralistic motif to come to the fore initially. Hard evidence in support of one paradigm to the exclusion of another is too difficult to come by to dull the social scientist's appreciation of the long-range value of "peaceful" paradigmatic co-existence. This need not mean any slackening of competition—indeed, competition can only be guaranteed when it is encompassed by an allegiance to a larger loyalty. But it does mean, for sociology, that the candidacy of the "dialectic" would be immeasurably strengthened. For it, like the paradigm of "democracy" in the truly pluralistic state, grants a place to competing paradigms, if but a secondary place. Loyalties to competing paradigms within either the "dialectical" or the "democratic" frames play active and fruitful roles.

Kuhn's analysis, then, is epistemologically short-sighted—a visual handicap which, although inherited from his epistemological lineage and not to be blamed on Kuhn himself, is none the less real. The dialectical paradigm may be expected to gain ground in the decade of the 'seventies at the expense of both the system and conflict motifs. There is little likelihood, however, that it will be reported or perhaps even seen as dominating the sociological scene for one very self-evident reason. And that is, of course, because its public image has been so terribly bruised by its association with the term "materialism." The professionally knowledgeable will strike it from their applications for public funds while editors will cast it from manuscripts for elementary texts. Sociology, having just won the battle to distinguish itself from "socialism," will be archly conscious of any future semantic booby-trap. Yet a paradigm need not be consciously voiced to play its part. A growing accommodation and mutual appreciation among those publically espoused to system and those wed to conflict may come to be its only badge. In the longer run, however, the association with the Marxist heritage may act in fact to strengthen the dialectic's claim. With the recognition that the phrase "dialectical materialism" is as little likely to be abandoned in Eastern Europe as "God" will in fact die in the vocabulary of the West—together with the conscious effort of both camps to build conceptual bridges and the specific steps taken in the 'sixties to transform national sociologies into a truly international discipline—there will be much sustained effort to reframe the dialectical in terms that transcend ideological frontiers. Although most of that effort may be expected to come from the conceptually more flexible West, the author himself was witness to the suggestion by a prominent Soviet colleague in the context of an informal discussion that system theory might well be appropriate for the analysis of social structure while dialectical theory was reserved for the analysis of social dynamics.

We pointed out at the end of Chapter 2 a second major addendum that we would have to make to the Kuhn thesis. In extrapolating his model to the social sciences we discovered that it was necessary to introduce an additional paradigmatic level, one that would focus upon the sociologist's self-image. This was due, again, to the fact that the socially relevant activity of the social scientist—including, therefore, the image that guided his research role—was itself a prime candidate for inclusion within the sociologist's range of concern, particularly when the specific area under consideration was the sociology of science. Thus the contrasting images of the sociologist as prophet and as priest were introduced and it was noted that the typically implicit choice for emphasis between them appeared to govern one's choice between such substantive paradigms as conflict and system. The paradigm addressed to the sociologist's self-image was deemed primary, that designating the substantive nature of sociology's subject matter secondary, for a prophetic posture appeared to beget the conflict model and a priestly stance, system. Earlier in the present chapter, however, we suggested that as the fundamentally dialectical nature of social research became more apparent, the former linkages would be apt to part; that the recent return to prophecy within the discipline might well avail itself of the tool of system analysis, while the conflict paradigm could in fact mask a dedication to some more fundamental posture which, if it were to be revealed, would represent the sociologist in priestly terms strikingly akin to those projected by Comte's positivist society of the future.

Although I have both revealed and admitted my support for the current reclamation of the prophetic mode, it does not mean that I would at the same time deny the priestly. Rather, informed by the dialogical nature of the relationship between intra- and intersubjective experience, I would both expect and encourage a pluralism at the level of self-image, just as I would expect and encourage it at the level of substantive paradigm. Although the prophetic and the priestly modes enlighten one's image of the fundamental nature of sociology's subject matter, the former is rooted in a sensitivity to the intrasubjective, the latter in a preferential response to the intersubjective. Although sociology as a science lays peculiar claim to the latter, we have discovered that it is impossible—not just inappropriate, but impossible—to resolve the value-laden choices forced upon one in social research without recourse to the existential level of awareness. Not even when the sociologist turns implicitly or explicitly to a reification of the epistemology or an extrapolation of the norms of science itself does he avoid such dialogue, for the choice cannot be dictated by the intersubjective alone. It not only provides no point of reference, but would deny the reality of the choice itself.

Thus it is that although the one will appear dominant at one moment in sociology's history and the second at another, the prophetic and the priestly modes will continue in dialogue—as they do in the larger religious-philosophical life of our kind. If one would seek a term that would envelop both the active and passive, the liberating and the ordering, nature of our calling as sociologists, perhaps *witness* may do. The sociologist would be *witness* to the profoundly social dialogue that is man.

Notes

2 "Normal" and "Revolutionary" Sociology

1 Only six articles published from the inception of the *American Sociological Review* through 1965 are listed under the subject heading "psychoanalysis" in its indices; indeed, only one of these appeared later than 1946.

2 See, for instance, John McKinney (1954: 565–74) and George Lundberg (1956: 21–27).

3 Alex Carey (1967: 403–16) concludes his re-evaluation of them with the pertinent suggestion that an exploration of the reasons for the unquestioned acceptance of the findings "would provide salutary insight into aspects of the sociology of social scientists" (416).

4 Still, the integrative assumptions of the orthodox paradigm remained sturdy enough through the first half of the decade of the sixties to enable James Petras and Michael Shute (1965) to draw an immediate parallel between them and the "conservative" responses of such sociologists as Seymour Lipset, Nathan Glazer, and Lewis Feuer to the Free Speech Movement at Berkeley in 1965, overriding whatever empathy that might have remained from their own early "radical" years.

5 Gunnar Myrdal (1955: 1056). Robert Merton had earlier demonstrated (1949: 37–46), however, that dialectical materialism's treatment of religion was, if deprived of negative judgment, essentially identical with a functionalist interpretation.

6 Norman Birnbaum's analyses touching the issue began to appear as early as 1953 with an article contrasting Marx and Weber in the *British Journal of Sociology*. They have included two essays in the *Transactions of the Third World*

Congress of Sociology (1957) as well as critiques in *Sociological Review* (1955) and *Commentary* (1956). The most helpful to an understanding of the paradigmatic climate of the post-war period and to a perception of the range of alternative paradigms lying beneath the discipline's glossy surface was a review article, "The Sociological Analysis of Ideologies" (1960), published as a separate number of *Current Sociology*. See also his critique of David Riesman in Lipset and Lowenthal's *Culture and Social Character* (1961). Pungent estimates of the immediately contemporary sociological scene are available in essays titled "The Crisis in Marxist Sociology" (1968) and "Conservative Sociology" (1968), while an analysis of the larger societal context is being published as *The Crisis of Industrial Society* (1969).

7 "*. . . a general theory of the processes of change of social systems is not possible in the present state of knowledge*. The reason is very simply that such a theory would imply complete knowledge of the laws of process of the system and this knowledge we do not possess. The theory of change in the structure of social systems must, therefore, be a theory of particular sub-processes of change within such systems, not of the overall processes of change of the systems as systems" (Parsons, 1951a:486).

8 See Parsons (1968:xii–xiii); for the "late analytic" phase distinction, see Demerath and Peterson (1967:97).

9 Parsons admitted his inclination to regard biology as sociology's "nearest neighbor in the community of sciences" as early as 1955 (Parsons, 1955:399). For his recent work in the social-evolutionary vein see his "Evolutionary Universals in Society" (1964:339–57) and *Societies: Evolutionary and Comparative Perspectives* (1966), together with a companion volume to the latter, promised at the time of this writing, to be titled *System of Modern Societies*. Note the manner in which the word "system" remains dominant in the latter. See also S. N. Eisenstadt's "Institutionalization and Change" (1964a:235–47) and "Social Change, Differentiation, and Evolution" (1964b:375–86).

10 See, for instance, Bernice Kaplan's paper, "Contrasts between Anthropologists and Sociologists at Annual Conventions," delivered before the 1967 meeting of the American Anthropological Association.

11 Irving Horowitz' (1967, 1968) "professionalist," "occupationalist," "anti-sociologist," and "un-sociologist" typology is unique only in that it saw the light of day in print.

12 See Talcott Parsons' "Comment" (1961:138–39). Also

see Paul Lazarsfeld's acknowledgment of a similar bifurcation in "International Sociology as a Social Problem" (1962:741).

13 Pierre van den Berghe's "Dialectic and Functionalism: Toward a Theoretical Synthesis" (1963:695–705).

14 See Charles P. Loomis "In Praise of Conflict and Its Resolution" (1967:875–90). It is intriguing to note that the word "Resolution" in the title, as published later in the *American Sociological Review*, had in fact been "Negation" in both the preliminary and final printed *Program* of the 1967 American Sociological Association meetings.

3 Sociology: The Prophetic Mode

1 It did, however, re-enter the main current of professional —as contrasted with lay—discourse in the late 'fifties, perhaps in part through association with the concept "alienation." See Leo Srole (1956:709–16); Robert Dubin (1959:147–64), Richard Cloward (1959:164–76), E. H. Mizruchi (1964); Albert K. Cohen (1965:5–14); Herbert McClosky and John H. Schaar (1965:14–40); E. L. Struening and A. H. Richardson (1965:768–76); and Marshall Clinard (1964).

2 The *Manuscripts* were first published—though only in part—in 1927, with the first complete German text in 1932. The 1959 English version was through the Foreign Language Press, Moscow. The 1956 and 1963 translations were T. B. Bottomore and M. Rubel (eds.), *Karl Marx: Selected Writings in Sociology and Social Philosophy* (1956, McGraw-Hill Paperback Edition, 1964); and T. B. Bottomore (ed.), *Karl Marx: Early Writings* (1964).

3 C. Wright Mills's *The Sociological Imagination* (1959) and his posthumous *The Marxists* (1962) carried the term into sociological theory proper, while Jean-Paul Sartre's *Critique de la raison dialectique, précédé de question de méthode* (1960)—the first portion of which was translated by Hazel E. Barnes as *Search for a Method* (1963)—may be expected to have a fundamental effect upon the nature of that theory in the decade ahead. Two book-length critiques assessing the relative success of Sartre's attempt to reclaim the early Marx for existentialism—and *vice versa*—had already appeared in English by early 1965: Wilfred Desan's *The Marxism of Jean-Paul Sartre* (1965) is much the more successful, if only because the main body of Walter Odajnyk's *Marxism and Existentialism* (1965) seems to have been written without access to either the *Critique de la raison dialectique* or Barnes's translation. Odajnyk's volume is a master's thesis drawing from essays by Sartre

that led up to the *Critique* and, for a supplementary chapter or two, upon the manuscript of Desan's own volume. Norman Birnbaum stands among those sociologists who, though they find the term significant, do not believe it can be translated without residue into the language of science.

4 Edward Shils (1961:1423). "The traditions from which the theory of action springs are not all equally oriented toward the more consensual position of contemporary theory. The powerful impulsion given by Hobbes and the utilitarianism that came from it contained an alienative tendency, which the moderate political views of its nineteenth-century proponents did not eradicate. Nor did Durkheim fully overcome such elements in his inheritance from Saint-Simon and Comte. For many years, sociology was viewed by its adherents as something outside the existing social order and necessarily at odds with it. Sociology conceived of itself as a necessarily dissensual factor in society; its observations emphasized the dissensual processes, toward which it took a tone of severe disapproval.

"It is still a proud boast of some sociologists that sociology is an 'oppositional' science. Some of those who take pride in the oppositional character of sociology are former or quasi-Marxists—who, without giving their allegiance to Marxism, wish nonetheless to retain its original disposition.

"It is, however, not only the Marxian influence in sociological analysis that has sustained this alienated standpoint. It came into sociology much earlier than the first contacts of sociology with Marxism. Marxism and late nineteenth-century German sociology both drank from the wells of inspiration provided by German Romanticism and by the radical Hegelian version of alienation" (*Ibid.*: 1421–22).

5 Berger's opposition to the sociological use of the term is due to his insistence that a prophet is a man through whom *God* speaks; that this in turn is "one of the most awesome fates that could befall a human being"; and that he is "determined to frustrate any hopes for prefabricated messianism." See *The Christian Century*, March 27, 1963, p. 415 and May 15, 1963, p. 649. Since this volume tries to be a *sociology* of sociology, it feels justified in turning to a broader tradition of usage that does not exclude the non-theological.

6 Isaiah 11:3–4, *The Holy Bible*, Revised Standard Version, Thomas Nelson, 1953.

7 See John B. Bury (1920), Morris Ginsberg (1953), Frederick J. Teggart (1949 and 1942), and Kenneth E. Bock (1956:1–132).

8 One could have turned as easily to the impressionistic summary of the period given by Shils (1961:1422): "The numerous investigations into industrial sociology, mass communications, criminality and delinquency, educational institutions, elites, urban communities, adolescents, and the aged, are conducted in a radically iconoclastic mood. This iconoclasm is not merely the realistic dissipation of erroneous views; it is almost always directed against authority. . . . The result is an outlook that radically distrusts the inherited order of society."

4 The Cloak of Neutrality

1 In their delineation of "The Setting of Sociology in the 1950s," Lipset and Smelser (1961:1,7,8) saw the new posture indicative of "the complete triumph . . . of the new 'scientific sociology.' " History itself was viewed as weighing the balance in the latter's favor, for the process was seen as but "an instance of the tendencies toward the secularization of knowledge which have characterized Western civilization for many centuries." Those who remained within the tradition that was dying were characterized as "people who incline toward political sensitivity and broad moral concerns, who see sociology becoming less problem-oriented, less vital, less concerned, less committed, less historical, less humanistic, more sterile, and more conservative politically. . . ." Even a president of the Society for the Study of Social Problems (Lindesmith, 1960:98), in addressing that little band of sociologists who had organized the society in 1951 as a supplement to the American Sociological Association because they were disturbed by the growing tendency to abandon the entire social problem area to "applied" sociology and social work, was ready to argue that "in his scientific role he [the sociologist] is concerned merely with what things are, not with what they ought to be." The commitment to no commitments had a number of intriguing ramifications. It led one of the profession's leading specialists in the sociology of science (Barber, 1962:298) to observe that "neither scientists taken as a whole group, nor any individual scientist alone can be considered responsible, in any sensibly direct fashion, for the social consequences of their activities." Granted that the statement was conditioned by the phrase "in any sensibly direct fashion" and had been set within the context of a volume which

sought to embrace science within a larger societal frame, still this was an extraordinary renunciation—one which had met with public censure in all other human pursuits.

Conclusions comparable to those of Lipset and Smelser were common during this period. See, for instance, Hinkle and Hinkle (1954) and Parsons (1959).

2 Talcott Parsons (1959:550) has observed that "Max Weber was probably the first major theorist to assert the fundamental importance of carefully distinguishing between problems of scientific generalization and those of evaluation and policy, and to work out a clear methodological basis for the distinction."

3 Florian Znaniecki (1940:5–6), who played a major role in transmitting Weber's views from the European scene to America, explained the method of *verstehen* as follows: "Just as a conjugal relation which he observes is to him really and objectively what it is to the conjugal partners themselves, or an association what it means to its members, a given system of knowledge must be to him also what it is to the people who participate in its construction, reproduction, application, and development. When he is studying their social lives, he must agree that, as to the knowledge which they recognize as valid, they are the only authority he need consider. He has no right as a sociologist to oppose his authority to theirs: he is bound by the methodological rule of unconditional modesty. He must resign his own criteria of theoretic validity when dealing with systems of knowledge which they accept and apply." Ernest Gellner (1962:153) notes, however, that "it is *not* true to say that to understand the concepts of a society [in the way its members do] is to reveal it . . . masking some of it may be a part of their function."

4 Matilda Riley (1960:914–26), drawing from the same essential data but simply contrasting 1959 with 1950, offers similar evidence. Race and ethnic relations fell from 4th place to 8th, while the sociology of organization rose from 16th to the vacated 4th position. Methodology changed places with marriage and the family, moving from 3rd to 2nd; and theory moved up to 5th. Summarizing her data, she quoted Talcott Parsons' impressionistic but appropriate observation that sociology was moving from a concern with "how to cope with clear-cut evils in the society" to an examination of "what kind of society it is" and "where it is going."

5 Shils (1961:1434), interestingly enough, indicted much of his own work when he noted that "the more genuinely

general and abstract the propositions of sociology become, the less they will contain of a genuinely critical response to the contemporary situation."

6 Rothbard (1960:173) observes that "instead of choosing his own ends and valuing accordingly the scientist supposedly maintains his neutrality by adopting the values of the bulk of society. In short, to set forth one's own values is now considered biased and 'non-objective,' while to adopt uncritically the slogans of other people is the height of 'objectivity'."

5 Sociology: The Priestly Mode

1 This, in fact, is exactly what Henry A. Murray and C. D. Morgan (1945:8) would appear to contend when they say that "since there is only one acceptable method of testing the value of anything and that is by experience, there will never be a sound basis for a philosophy of life until the experiences of a vast number of different types of men and women have been accurately reported, assembled and formulated in general terms." Lundberg (1958:722–23) would appear of like mind, observing that "the fact that there are differences of opinion in a large society as to what these values are itself represents an unnecessary social lag. For in such recent developments as scientific public opinion polling, the values of a population and the unanimity and relative intensity with which they are held can also be determined."

2 Erich Fromm (1955:20), for instance, is constrained to declare that "a sane society is that which corresponds to the needs of man—not necessarily to what he *feels* to be his needs . . . but to what his needs are *objectively*, as they can be ascertained by the study of man." Clark Hull, Bronislaw Malinowski, A. J. Ramsperger, and J. C. Flugel have taken essentially the same position. Isidore Chein, I feel sure, would himself be amused by a re-reading of an early essay (1947:235) in which he seems to identify morality with means-ends efficiency and nothing more: "The key to a science of morality may be found in a remark made by Sigmund Freud to the effect that, rather than ask about the purpose of life, we should ask about the purposes for which men live. The fact of the matter is that men do have purposes and that, from the viewpoint of these purposes, actions are not indifferent. Some actions result in the purposes which instigate them: these actions are *good*. Some actions have consequences which interfere with the attainment of action ends: these actions are *bad*."

3 See A. K. Saran (1962: 220–23) for an additional critique of Gouldner's thesis.

4 "Religious methods have been able to produce in the past unity and cohesiveness of a national level; in *our* time, a therapeutic world order based on sociometric principles should be able to attain the same result without resorting to militant war and violent revolution." See J. L. Moreno, "Psychiatric Encounter in Soviet Russia," an undated pamphlet reprinted with some alterations from *Progress in Psychotherapy* (1960), Vol. 5, pp. 1–24. The quotation is taken from page 27 of the pamphlet.

5 Rubin Gotesky, in a paper presented before the Society for the Scientific Study of Religion, October, 1960.

6 H. Richard Niebuhr (1960: 132–33).

7 John F. A. Taylor (1958: 489–90; 496). Also see his *The Masks of Society* (1966), especially Chapter VII.

8 Alfred North Whitehead (1938: 229): ". . . without judgment of value, there would be no science." Vannevar Bush (*New York Times*, 1955): Science is "built on premises which we accept without proof or the possibility of proof." Jacob Bronowski (1959: 62): "The Activity of science . . . is not neutral . . . [It is] directed to one overriding end . . . accepted as the supreme value." Philip Siekevitz (1958): "The highly rational world of experimentation rests upon nothing more nor less than an abiding faith in the rationale of experimental approach" William Zurdeeg (1958: 51): Science functions "within a larger framework which is convictional."

9 "The ultimately possible attitudes toward life are irreconcilable . . . their struggle can never be brought to a final conclusion. Thus it is necessary to make a decisive choice. . . . You serve this god and you offend the other god when you decide to adhere to this position (of science)" (Gerth and Mills, 1958: 151–52). Also: ". . . whoever lacks the capacity to put on blinders . . . may as well stay away from science. He will never have what one may call the 'personal experience' of science. Without this strange intoxication . . . without this passion . . . you have *no* calling for science" (*Ibid.*: 135). "And still less can it be proved that the existence of the world which these sciences describe is worthwhile, that it has any 'meaning,' or that it makes sense to live in such a world" (*Ibid.*: 144).

10 ". . . science is, like all socially organized activities, a moral enterprise . . . a set of activities devoted to definite moral values and subject to clear ethical standards. The proximate a-morality of the individual scientist is only possible . . . because of a more ultimate, relatively absolute

the sociologist's self-image. This was due, again, to the fact that the socially relevant activity of the social scientist —including, therefore, the image that guided his research role—was itself a prime candidate for inclusion within the sociologist's range of concern, particularly when the specific area under consideration was the sociology of science. Thus the contrasting images of the sociologist as prophet and as priest were introduced and it was noted that the typically implicit choice for emphasis between them appeared to govern one's choice between such substantive paradigms as conflict and system. The paradigm addressed to the sociologist's self-image was deemed primary, that designating the substantive nature of sociology's subject matter secondary, for a prophetic posture appeared to beget the conflict model and a priestly stance, system. Earlier in the present chapter, however, we suggested that as the fundamentally dialectical nature of social research became more apparent, the former linkages would be apt to part; that the recent return to prophecy within the discipline might well avail itself of the tool of system analysis, while the conflict paradigm could in fact mask a dedication to some more fundamental posture which, if it were to be revealed, would represent the sociologist in priestly terms strikingly akin to those projected by Comte's positivist society of the future.

Although I have both revealed and admitted my support for the current reclamation of the prophetic mode, it does not mean that I would at the same time deny the priestly. Rather, informed by the dialogical nature of the relationship between intra- and intersubjective experience, I would both expect and encourage a pluralism at the level of self-image, just as I would expect and encourage it at the level of substantive paradigm. Although the prophetic and the priestly modes enlighten one's image of the fundamental nature of sociology's subject matter, the former is rooted in a sensitivity to the intrasubjective, the latter in a preferential response to the intersubjective. Although sociology as a science lays peculiar claim to the latter, we have discovered that it is impossible—not just inappropriate, but impossible—to resolve the value-laden choices forced upon one in social research without recourse to the exis-

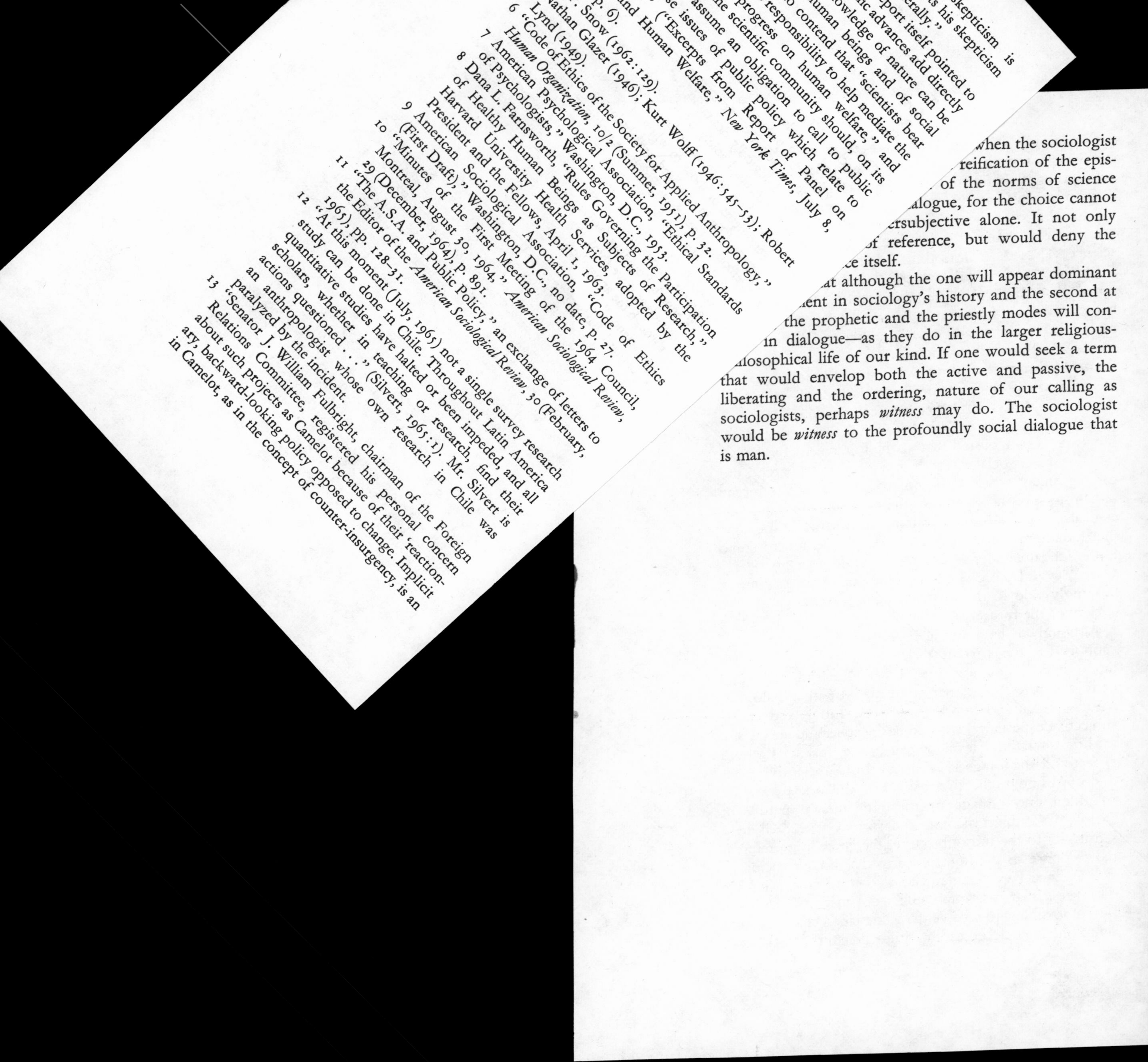

when the sociologist
reification of the epis-
of the norms of science
alogue, for the choice cannot
ersubjective alone. It not only
f reference, but would deny the
ce itself.

at although the one will appear dominant
ent in sociology's history and the second at
the prophetic and the priestly modes will con-
in dialogue—as they do in the larger religious-
ilosophical life of our kind. If one would seek a term that would envelop both the active and passive, the liberating and the ordering, nature of our calling as sociologists, perhaps *witness* may do. The sociologist would be *witness* to the profoundly social dialogue that is man.

. . . Nathan Glazer (1946); Kurt Wolff (1946:545–53); Robert Lynd (1949).

6 "Code of Ethics of the Society for Applied Anthropology," *Human Organization*, 10/2 (Summer, 1951), p. 32.

7 American Psychological Association, "Ethical Standards of Psychologists," Washington, D.C., 1953.

8 Dana L. Farnsworth, "Rules Governing the Participation of Healthy Human Beings as Subjects of Research," Harvard University Health Services, adopted by the President and the Fellows, April 1, 1963.

9 American Sociological Association, "Code of Ethics (First Draft)," Washington, D.C., no date, p. 27.

10 "Minutes of the First Meeting of the 1964 Council, Montreal, August 30, 1964," *American Sociological Review*, 29 (December, 1964), p. 891.

11 "The A.S.A. and Public Policy," an exchange of letters to the Editor of the *American Sociological Review*, 30 (February, 1965), pp. 128–31.

12 "At this moment (July, 1965) not a single survey research study can be done in Chile. Throughout Latin America quantitative studies have halted or been impeded, and all scholars, whether in teaching or research, find their actions questioned . . ." (Silvert, 1965:1). Mr. Silvert is an anthropologist whose own research in Chile was paralyzed by the incident.

13 "Senator J. William Fulbright, chairman of the Foreign Relations Committee, registered his personal concern about such projects as Camelot because of their 'reactionary, backward-looking policy opposed to change. Implicit in Camelot, as in the concept of counter-insurgency, is an

assumption that revolutionary movements are dangerous to the interests of the United States and that the United States must be prepared to assist, if not actually to participate in, measures to repress them' " (Horowitz, 1965:3). For an expanded version, see I. L. Horowitz, *The Rise and Fall of Project Camelot* (1967).

14 Horowitz (1965:44). For instance William Goode (1966:255), at the time Vice-President-Elect of the American Sociological Association, wrote that "Camelot was and is morally defensible."

15 Talcott Parsons (1966:124–26); Robert E. Barnes (1967: 22–24).

16 Robert Nisbet (1963:156). See also his *The Sociological Tradition* (1966) where the theme is developed at length.

17 Howard Becker (1960:803–10); Paul Lazarsfeld (1962: 757–67); Everett Hughes (1963:879–90); George Homans (1964:809–18); Pitirim Sorokin (1965:833–43); Wilbert E. Moore (1966:765–72); Charles P. Loomis (1967:875–90).

18 Talcott Parsons provides a helpful analysis of the complementary nature of Weber's *Wert-Frei* and *Wertbeziehung* postures in *The Structure of Social Action*, pp. 600–601. He concludes that "Weber's principle of value relevance, while it does introduce an element of relativity into scientific methodology . . . does not involve the skepticism that is the inevitable consequence of any radical relativity."

19 Gunnar Myrdal (1959:153–54). The original theoretical sections of *An American Dilemma* were republished, together with later essays on theory, in this volume.

20 As Reinhard Bendix (1951:192) put it, ". . . it is less our opinions on day-to-day problems and more our major underlying assumptions that call for explicit acknowledgment: our beliefs concerning the relation of knowledge and human power, the role of science in society, the position of the intellectual in the community—these are among the problems which we must clarify for ourselves." The following year Bernard Barber (1962:294) observed that "too many scientists . . . have been so much the victim of a certain positivistic bias . . . that they have even denied that science itself rests on values . . . society as a whole rests on a set of moral values and . . . science always functions within the context of those values. These social values pose certain non-empirical problems to which science, being concerned only for the empirical, cannot give answers—problems of meaning and evil and justice and salvation."

21 Barrington Moore (1958) went so far as to suggest that

the logical structure of social scientific knowledge might not be identical with that of the advanced natural sciences. W. H. Werkmeister (1959:153–54) noted that "the social scientist is himself an integral part of the culture in which he lives. The normative ideas characteristic of his culture pattern . . . may effect the selection and formulation of the problem, the approach, the collection of relevant data, the recording of observations, the interpretation of the 'facts,' and the manner in which the results are finally presented." Kasper Naegele (1961:9) acknowledges quite explicitly that "discovery and presupposition go hand in hand. One must create some sociology before one can know what it is; and one must know, at least, what it might be, before one can help create it." Edward Shils (1961:1448) concludes that "there is (in sociology) . . . a personal element that is decisive. . . . The fundamental terms of sociological theory are 'primitive' terms. Their meanings are apprehended in 'personal' experience and through the secondary experience of contact with the 'vision' which expresses the deepest experiences of the greatest minds of the race." See also Helmut Schoeck and James W. Wiggins (1960 and 1961) and Leon Bramson (1961).

22 Alvin Gouldner (1962:212–13). Gouldner's thesis regarding the moral base of Weber's *Wertfreiheit* had in fact been developed the previous year by Bruno Leoni (1961:158–74).

23 See Edward Gross (1960:441–48 and 1961:125–43); also see Gideon Sjoberg (1966) for an array of case studies, including one of his own, which reveal the implicit and explicit value judgments encountered in the process, or as a result, of a wide array of empirical studies undertaken by sociologists.

24 Seeley (1963:63). The analogy is elaborated at length in Seeley's collected essays, published as *The Americanization of the Unconscious*, International Science Press, 1967. The essay noted here is reprinted as pp. 149–65.

7. Science: Dilemmas of Choice

1 As early as 1927 Morris Cohen (1927:453) was able to observe that "some sociologists have banished from their program all questions of value and have sought to restrict themselves to the theory of social happenings. This effort to look upon human actions with the same neutrality with which we view geometric figures is admirable. But the questions of human value are inescapable, and those who banish them at the front door admit them unavowedly and

therefore uncritically at the back door." More recently James Conant (1952:62) has pointed out that the activities of science "are shot through with value-judgment . . .", while a paper published over a decade and a half ago and titled "The Scientist as Scientist Makes Value Judgments" (Rudner, 1953:6) states in part: "The traditional search for objectivity exemplifies science's pursuit of one of its most precious ideals. But for the scientist to close his eyes to the fact that scientific method *intrinsically* requires the making of value decisions, for him to push out of his consciousness the fact that he does make them, can in no way bring him closer to the ideal of objectivity. To refuse to pay attention to the value decisions which must be made, to make them intuitively, unconsciously, haphazardly, is to leave an essential aspect of the scientific method scientifically out of control . . . objectivity for science lies at least in becoming precise about what value judgments are being and might have been made in a given inquiry—and even, to put it in its most challenging form, what value decision ought to be made."

2 Michael Polanyi (1958:1). James D. Watson's *The Double Helix: A Personal Account of the Discovery of DNA* (1968) is a delightful case history in point. It is a stance that Bridgman, the empiricist and operationalist, approached toward the end of a distinguished career as physicist and philosopher. See his "Remarks on Niels Bohr's Talk" (1958:175).

3 When Paul Furfey (1959:517) sought to develop a bibliography of items dealing descriptively with the value-judgments of "the fair-minded and unprejudiced scientist," he was able to uncover but three—and not one of those was written by a sociologist or published in a sociological journal. One reference was to a paper written by the psychoanalyst, Laurence S. Kubie (1958:597–98), in which Kubie suggests a number of levels at which the research activity of the normal scientist is apt to reflect unconscious needs and valuations: ". . . there are significant relationships between masked neurotic components in the personality of an apparently normal scientist, and such things as (a) the field of work which he chooses; (b) the problem within that field which he chooses to investigate; (c) the clarity with which he habitually uses his native capacity for logical thinking; (d) the ways in which he attacks scientific problems; (e) the scientific causes which he espouses; (f) the controversies in which he becomes entangled and how he fights; and (g) the joy or sorrow which is derived from the work itself and also

from his ultimate success or failure." Rollo Handy (1956:325–32) finds that anxious people try to control or hide their anxiety by engaging in superformal and precise behavior.

4 "Questions of value should not be taken *uberhaupt*. Located as snarls in social inquiry, questions of value become specific and genuine. They need to be answered by sociological analysis of specific disciplines and problems arising in them. Not only the content of values in social inquiries should be detected, but how values creep in, and how, if at all, they condition the direction, completeness, and warrantability of the results of research." This statement by C. Wright Mills (1963:466–67) comes close to suggesting what I am about in Chapter 7.

5 The very same anguish is found in Mills's statement in *The Sociological Imagination* (1959:66–67) when he caustically observes that, "there is, in truth, *no* principle or theory that guides the selection of what is to be the subject. . . . 'Happiness,' . . . might be one; marketing behavior, another. It is merely assumed that if only the Method is used, such studies as result—scattered from Elmira to Zagreb to Shanghai—will add up finally to a 'full-fledged, organized' science of man and society. The practice, in the meantime, is to get on with the next study."

6 One of the more honest (Doby, 1954:12) acknowledges the substantive elements involved, but then rests content with a pious wish that somehow this should not be: "This aspect of research is often a question of motivation and interest; many 'accidental' things go into the selection of a problem area. The possibility of obtaining prestige, security, or even the solution of a personal problem may determine the area in which the scientist is interested. We cannot deny the importance of such highly private considerations, but science is public. These 'ought nots' become a part of science itself."

7 Wilson Record (1960:413). Robert Angell (1958:6) would carry the argument a step further. Going beyond a simple acknowledgment of the shift from the prophetic role to the commitment to science *per se*, he suggests that the value-free position has even led to an aversion toward the study of moral conduct: "For a generation social scientists have proudly kept judgments of fact separate from judgments of value. . . . Although this 'value-free' position does not imply that moral standards and moral conduct should not be studied, there has often been a disinclination to study them . . . they have seemed some-

how scientifically tainted."

8 Of nearly one-quarter of a billion dollars spent on social research of all kinds in a recent year, nearly two-thirds came directly from and was performed by industrial and commercial organizations. (Harry Alpert, 1959:74–75). The larger part of this takes the apparently innocent form of research relating to the relative effectiveness of advertising, although when one realizes that the immediate intent of the latter is in fact to *create* frustration, the blush of innocence is quickly lost.

9 Mills (1959:96). Loren Baritz (1960:209–10) is less restrained: "Many industrial social scientists have put themselves on auction. The power elites of America, especially the industrial elite, have bought their services—which, when applied to areas of relative power, have restricted the freedom of millions of workers. . . . They are now beginning to control conduct. Put this power—genuine, stark, irrevocable power—into the hands of America's managers, and the work that social scientists have done and will do, assumes implications vaster and more fearful than anything previously hinted." Also see William Kornhauser's *Scientists in Industry: Conflict and Accommodation* (1962).

10 See N. L. Faberow (1963) and Lewis A. Dextor (1958:176–82).

11 C. Wright Mills (1963:459–60) observed that "in acquiring a technical vocabulary with its terms and classifications, the thinker is acquiring, as it were, a set of colored spectacles. . . . A specialized language constitutes a veritable *a priori* form of perception and cognition. . . . Thus the observational dimensions of any verificatory model are influenced by the selected language of its users."

12 Percy Bridgman, as quoted by Pitirim Sorokin (1956:296). The sociologist might do well to be aware of the sophistication with which the theologian has come to treat "the word"—from Karl Barth's early recognition that God was "in-conceive-able"—that the God behind the God of religion would be reduced to the reification of one's epistemological presuppositions if one did anything less than simply open oneself to the miracle of His self-disclosure; through the divorce of the revelation of nature from that of history in response to an awareness of the disparity in constructs and logics of the two epistemologies; to an exceedingly contemporary view, rooted in the late Heidegger, that in language one finds the number one existential. The most recent version of the latter has come to focus upon the task identified by the term "her-

meneutics" (from "Hermes," the *messenger* of the Gods), the study of the principles underlying the interpretation of the Word. See, for instance, Gerhard Ebeling, *Word and Faith* (1963).

13 Reinhard Bendix and Bennett Berger (1959:97, 112, 113) observe that "sociologists tend to choose their theoretical equipment in accord with how well it suits the kind of substantive problems which interest them, and these, in turn, are intimately connected with their 'sense of the real'." The latter "embodies each theorist's image of society and . . . is the source of each theory's utility and unique blindness." They also state that "such terms as culture-pattern, subculture, social role, and folkways, communication, human relations, and many, many others are employed in such a way that individuals appear to act as group influences dictate. Unwittingly perhaps, this vocabulary has often had the cumulative effect of suggesting that the individual merely does what is expected of him—in the literal sense in which the actor on the medieval stage reads his text from the rolled script in his hands."

14 Wilbert Moore (1959:716) was able to observe a few years ago that "one remarkable feature of the contemporary state of sociology is its overwhelming adherence to one doctrine. That doctrine is the 'structural-functional' approach."

15 Quoted by Frank Manuel (1962:297). See also Alfred McClung Lee (1965).

16 "Logic, History of," *Encyclopaedia Britannica*, 1961, Vol. 14, p. 332b: ". . . no set of postulates, finite in number or enumerably infinite, expressible in the notation of a single applied functional calculus of first order, can be adequate for arithmetic in the sense of characterizing completely the system of negative integers."

17 *Ibid.*, 332b.

18 Michael Polanyi (1958:269). For the original, see A. Tarski (1944:341–76).

19 "Although they are very sensitive to assumptions about what might be called their 'real world,' social scientists are prone to be insensitive to assumptions in the statistical systems into which they embed their data. The measurement or statistical systems into which data are mapped constitute an integral part of theory and assumptions about the real world" (Keith Smith, 1953:536). R. B. Braithwaite (1953:174) observes that "the peculiarity of statistical reasoning is that it pre-supposes also at an early stage of the argument judgments as to what sort of a future we want. In considering the rationale of such

thinking we cannot avoid ethics' breaking into inductive logic."

20 Among them have been Harold Anderson (1959), Howard Gruber (1962), R. Taton (1962), Arthur Koestler (1959 and 1964), W. J. J. Gordon (1961), C. W. Taylor and Frank Baron (1963), and George Schwartz and Philip Bishop (1958).

21 According to a summary of the results of a 6-year study of the "creative person" conducted by the Institute of Personality Assessment and Research at Berkeley, as reported in the *New York Times*, October 22, 1961.

22 ". . . theory—at least some rudimentary theory or expectation—is always in the lead; . . . it always precedes observation; . . . the fundamental role of observations and experimental tests is to show that some of our theories are false . . ." (Popper, 1963:23).

23 "In practice three levels are commonly used: 1%, 5%, and 0.3%. There is nothing sacred about these three values; they have become established in practice without any rigid theoretical justification . . . the size of the critical region (one selects) is related to the risk one wants to accept in testing a statistical hypothesis, . . ." (p. 435); and, in speaking of the choice one must make between the likelihood of rejecting a hypothesis when actually true as over against accepting one when it is actually false, he says, "which of these two errors is most important to avoid [it being necessary to make such a decision in order to accept or reject the given hypothesis] is a subjective matter . . ." (Rosander, 1951:262).

24 Richard Rudner (1953:2), C. West Churchman (1948), and R. B. Braithwaite (1953) take similar positions.

25 Skipper, Guenther, and Nass (1967: 16–18). See also Hanan Selvin (1957:519–27), David Gold (1958), and Leslie Kish (1959:328–38).

26 Doby (1954:18).

27 Charles Schulz's Linus put the case rather baldly to Charlie Brown one day by observing, "When I grow up, I'd like to study about people. . . . People interest me. . . . I'd like to go to some big university and study all about people." Charlie Brown comments in return, "I see . . . you want to learn about people so that with your knowledge you will be equipped to help them. . . ." Linus' response is simple: "No, I'm just nosy."

28 Bertrand Russell (1962:115)—one who has never hesitated to kick over a too primly set tea table—has written recently that "it is impossible in the modern world for a man of science to say with any honesty, 'My business is to provide

knowledge, and what use is made of the knowledge is not my business.' " The considerably more conventional Whitehead (Merton, 1961:669) went at least as far as to say that "science is a river with two sources, the practical source and the theoretical source. . . . I cannot see why it is nobler to strive to understand than to busy oneself with the right ordering of one's actions. Both have their bad sides; there are evil ends directing actions, and there are ignoble curiosities of the understanding." Malinowski (1944:19–20) was led at one point to the roots of his commitment toward anthropology by claiming that "when one of us raises his voice to affirm such values as 'freedom,' 'justice,' and 'democracy,' he does it at the risk of the academically unpardonable sin of 'value-judgments' or 'suffering from a moral purpose'. . . . The student of society and of human culture has (however) . . . the duty to draw practical conclusions, to commit himself to views and decisions referring to problems of planning, and to translate his conclusions into definite propositions of statesmanship."

29 Walter Lequeur (1958:3) may have illustrated the issue of context in a review of Daniel Lerner's *The Passing of Traditional Society: The Middle East in Transition* (1958), when he noted that "Western sociologists have tried to penetrate the innermost thoughts of Anatolian peasants, Amman drivers and Damascus tailors. The Soviets, on the other hand, do not unduly bother about their present ideas, whatever these may be, but try, with considerable success, to provide new ones. Paraphrasing the late Karl Marx they appear to say: Western sociologists have only interpreted the Middle East in various ways—we shall change it. The Western authors could answer that they are social scientists, not politicians. It would be an obvious reply, and yet somewhat unsatisfactory at this late hour."

30 Robert Lynd (1949:115) was among those few who were not caught up in the corporate illusion. In reviewing what has come to be looked upon as one of the classic products of the new "scientific" sociology—"The American Soldier" studies—he observed: "These volumes depict science being used with great skill to sort out and to control men for purposes not of their own willing. It is a significant measure of the importance of liberal democracy that it must increasingly use its social sciences not directly on democracy's own problems, but tangentially and indirectly; it must pick up the crumbs from private business research on such problems as how to

gauge audience reaction so as to put together synthetic radio programs and movies, or, as in the present case, from Army research on how to turn frightened draftees into tough soldiers who will fight a war whose purposes they do not understand. With such socially extraneous purposes controlling the use of social science, each advance in its use tends to make it an instrument of mass control, and thereby a further threat to democracy."

31 Bernard Barber (1962:55) is more right than he realizes when he concludes that "the old illusion of a 'pure science' is no longer tenable."

8 The Commitments of Social Research

1 Abraham Kaplan (1964: 8, 12, 13, 27) writes that "Logicians have properly dreaded . . . a confusion between how we do think and how we ought to think. . . . Logic is normative. . . . Fortunately, there is a growing recognition—even among philosophers—of the importance for methodology of a study of the history of science, as well as a study of the timeless structure of an idealized 'language of science.' " A logic—he would prefer the term "methodology"—is to be "justified," not merely described; "Logic . . . deals with what scientists do when they are doing *well* as scientists." That he is on dangerous ground when he repeats Bridgman's unfortunate remark—one which would fail to differentiate the scientific from any other calling—that "the scientist has no other method than doing his damndest," is a pity, but should not undermine the value of his overall contribution.

2 As Ernest Nagel (1961:452) notes, "every branch of inquiry aiming at reliable general laws concerning empirical subject matter must employ a procedure that, if it is not strictly controlled experimentation, has the essential logical functions of experiment in inquiry." This is a position taken earlier by John Stuart Mill and by John Dewey, although Mill felt it wasn't feasible to strive for general laws in the social sciences.

3 M. H. Pappworth's recent *Human Guinea Pigs: Experimentation on Man* (1968) reflects the medical profession's growing concern, as well as the fact that medical journals are beginning to reject papers that appear to have involved "unethical" human experimentation.

4 As John Dewey (1929:86) put it: "all experimentation involves *overt* doing, the making of definite changes in our environment or in our relationship to it . . . experiment is not a random activity but is directed by ideas . . . the outcome of the directed activity is the construction

of *a new empirical situation.*" H. A. Shepard (1956:53), in turn, has indicated an awareness of what this implies: He notes that "if experiments are themselves interventions in the life of the non-scientific community, they cannot be kept within the system of pure science, and will have effects extending beyond that system."

5 Perhaps the best discussion available to date of this general issue is offered by Edward Shils (1959:114–57). Shils's overall stance is suggested by his statement (p. 127) that "the indispensable detachment of the social research worker from his subject matter must be combined with membership in the same moral realm with the subject matter." The sociologist, in other words, is not and should not be in a position of ethical neutrality *vis-à-vis* the subjects of his research.

6 As quoted by Alfred Stern (1956:281–95).

7 Quoted by Obler and Estrin (1962:13). Karl Mannheim (1936) may have been the first sociologist to perceive its analogical bearing on social research. See also Richard Lichtman (1967:139–50) and J. A. Barnes (1963:118–34).

8 Karl Popper (1957:14) sees it as one of the central factors leading to "the poverty of historicism." R. G. Collingwood (1946:248) views it as contributing to the richness and humane features of history as a discipline (". . . the historian himself, together with the here-and-now which forms the total evidence available to him, is a part of the process which he is studying. . . ."

9 Talcott Parsons, *et al.* (1953:96). "The observer of a system of action, as scientist, must himself in some sense be conceived of as an actor" (Parsons, 1961:325).

10 For Parsons' re-reading of Weber, see Talcott Parsons "Evaluation and Objectivity in Social Science: An Interpretation of Max Weber's Contributions" (1965).

11 Mortimer A. Sullivan, Jr., Stuart A. Queen, and Ralph C. Patrick, Jr. (1958:660).

12 Lewis Coser (1959:397). Fred Davis (1961:365), in commenting critically in another context on the use of disguised participant observers in research upon the inner dynamics of Alcoholics Anonymous, plunges headlong into the question of responsibility: ". . . in field situations in which the sociologist (or anthropologist) openly represents himself to his subjects for what he is (i.e., a person whose interest in them is professional rather than personal) he unavoidably, and properly, I would hold, invites unto himself the classic dilemma of compromising involvement in the lives of others. . . . There then follows for many a field worker the unsettling recognition that,

within very broad limits, it is precisely when his subjects palpably relate to him in his 'out of research role' . . . they tell and 'give away' more, they supply connections and insights which he would otherwise have never grasped. (One is tempted to conceive of this moral paradox as sociologists' original sin. . . .) It is in large measure due to this ineluctable transmutation of role postures in field situations that, when he later reports, the sociologist often experiences a certain guilt, a sense of having betrayed, a stench of disreputability about himself. . . . I would hold that it is just and fitting that he be made to squirm so, because in having exploited his non-scientific self (either deliberately or non-wittingly) for ends other than those immediately apprehended by his subjects he has in some significant sense violated the collective conscience of the community, if not that of the profession . . . such actions strike me as less than human, and hence unworthy of a discipline which, whatever else it represents itself as, also calls itself by that name."

13 Eugene J. Webb, Donald T. Campbell, Richard D. Schwartz, and Lee Sechrest (1966).

14 Except insofar as the act of *observation* (in contrast to the *recognition* or *deduction of order* that may follow) interferes with the route the phenomena might have taken in its absence—as illustrated by the Heisenberg principle.

15 Nagel (1961:469–70). Abraham Edel (1959:167–95) supports Nagel's reasoning, offering as a physical analogy to the "self-fulfilling" prophecy the case of a man creating an avalanche by shouting that such an avalanche would occur. There is no doubt that such unlikely examples of unintended (or, indeed, intended) "feed-back" may be imagined within the context of the physical and biological sciences. The point is, however, that *knowledge* of previous regularities *alone* would be insufficient to the task—yet it would be sufficient in the social or behavioral sciences.

16 Isidor Chein (1962:1–35) argues against the cavalier manner in which computer-wired "feed-back" mechanisms have been offered as models of man's cognitive capacities from a different perspective. Cognition is not simply a molecular process in man but molar as well. It involves a nested hierarchy of actions related intimately to the fact that man's behavior is conditioned by *gestalts* which spring from molar levels of organization far beyond the patterns to which the computer is limited by the relatively molecular nature of its mechanical and electronic fabrication. The "poverty" that Karl Popper discovered in "historicism" might be seen as an extrapolation of the

thesis I project, even though Popper (1957: ix, x) himself chooses to defend his thesis in a somewhat different fashion. He begins with what he feels to be the self-evident fact that science is unable to predict its own predictions. Then, since it is clear that knowledge—to which science is making an increasingly important contribution—has a perceptible effect upon history, history itself is unpredictable. I do not find the logic incorrect, simply more crude than it need be. For if one includes the impact of what we have come to call the social and behavioral sciences among those factors that impinge upon the direction taken by history, one introduces a function which—as we have seen—acts in principle to inhibit the projection of past order into the future of the historicist.

17 V. I. Lenin, *Materialism and Empirio-Criticism*, Foreign Languages Publishing House, Moscow, no date, pp. 130, 270. The total corpus of Marxist-Leninism, however, appears broad enough to provide the possibility that a more flexible posture in this regard might someday appear. It is in fact already suggested by the following statement from *Pravda*: "Weismannite-Morganist idealist teaching is pseudo-scientific because it is founded on the notion of the divine origin of the world and assumes eternal and unalterable scientific laws." *Pravda*, No. 240, p. 664, as quoted by John Langdon-Davies (1949).

18 As John McKinny (1954:572) has noted, "Mead . . . rejects the mechanistic assumption that . . . every effect can . . . be reduced to its causal conditions. He contends that the appearance of the effect constitutes an emergence and that the emergent itself affects an environment which, therefore, could not be known before its emergence."

19 ". . . prediction in the social sciences finds its inevitable limitation in the fact that, knowing the predicted course of events, man can alter that course, thereby nullifying the prediction itself" (Werkmeister, 1959:490).

20 "Yet because of these two different consequences of predictions themselves (self-fulfilling and suicidal prophecies), we do better to make continual short-range predictions in social life. Only thus can we constantly assess the new situations which exist because of the interaction not only of the previously existing factors but now, also, of the predictions themselves" (Barber, 1962:292).

21 Barrington Moore, *Political Power and Social Theory: Six Studies* (1958), a section of which was reprinted as "Strategy in Social Science," in Maurice Stein and Arthur Vidich (eds.), *Sociology on Trial* (1963: 66–95). The quotation is from p. 92. Robert Lane (1966:649–62) edges toward a

similar position when he concludes that "ideology is declining as a *necessary* ingredient in change, partly because . . . knowledge sets up a powerful kind of attitudinal disequilibrium all its own."

22 This, in fact, is the analogy that informs John Seeley's analysis in *The Americanization of the Unconscious*. Richard LaPiere (1959) would argue, however, that the very opposite has occurred—that the acceptance in America of Freud's image of man is an example of a "self-fulfilling" prophecy.

23 "His [Weber's] view of history is as a successive process of secularization, formalization, and bureaucratization, and—he is aware—his analysis, being a product of the end-stage of this process, is a sort of turning back of the process on itself" (Runciman, 1963:55).

24 Comparable pressure *against* the communication of "social scientific" materials may also be engendered, as illustrated by a resolution introduced at a meeting of the Oriental Society in the mid-fifties which sought to exclude articles of "the social science type" from the group's official publication.

25 "I was aware that there would be a reaction in the town when the book was published. While writing the book, however, it did not occur to us to anticipate what these reactions might be, nor did it occur to us to use such anticipations of reactions as a basis for selecting the data of carrying out the analysis. . . . One can't gear social science writing to the expected reactions of any audience, and, if one does, the writing quickly degenerates into dishonesty, all objectivity in the sense that one can speak of objectivity in the social sciences is lost." As quoted in the Editorial, *Human Organization* (1958:2).

26 Talcott Parsons, *Religious Perspectives of College Teaching in Sociology and Social Psychology*, Hazen Foundation (no date: 5, 6, 43).

9 The Presumptive Faith of Science

1 If one were to distinguish between the two in the manner suggested, the term "presupposition" would have to be used almost exclusively, for the typical scientist receives no explicit education regarding them and may complete a career of fruitful research with no awareness of their presence.

2 See René Dubos (1961:166): "What the experimenter does, and consequently what he finds, is determined to a large extent by his assumptions. Thus, in practice, the facts revealed to the experimenter are . . . distorted by

the very dreams of his reason." Or, with E. A. Burtt (1962:259): ". . . our zealous endeavor to create a 'value-free' science . . . has meant simply that the values dominating our thinking have retired to the arena of our underlying presuppositions, where they can maintain themselves against critical appraisal by being so completely taken for granted that no one's questioning attention is focused upon them."

3 "No science," Weber (Gerth and Mills, 1958:153) cautioned, "is absolutely free from presuppositions, and no science can prove its fundamental value to the man who rejects these presuppositions." He (Shils and Finch, 1949:4) also noted that "a chaos of existential judgments about countless individual events would be the only result of a serious attempt to analyze reality 'without presuppositions'. . . . Order is brought into this chaos only on the condition that in every case only a part of concrete reality is interesting and *significant* to us, because only it is related to the cultural values with which we approach reality."

4 Karl Mannheim (1936:80) states: "A clear and explicit avowal of the implicit metaphysical presuppositions which underlie and make possible empirical knowledge will do more for the clarification and advancement of research than a verbal denial of the existence of these presuppositions accompanied by their surreptitious admission through the back door."

5 "I do not believe that there is in social or any other science a rigid line between science and philosophy. . . . Thus for my scientific purposes it is essential to be a philosopher at least in a negative sense—it is necessary to uncover and criticize on philosophical grounds the assumptions which block the way to doing justice to the empirical facts as I see them. Beyond that it is necessary to be clear about the philosophical implications of one's own positive concepts" (Parsons, 1935:315).

6 Reinhard Bendix (1951:192) notes that ". . . it is less our opinions in day-to-day problems and more our major underlying assumptions that call for explicit acknowledgement." Martin Martel (1959:59) adds: "All scientific choices are based on some at least implicit strategy rules. . . . This is one sense in which scientific work may be said to proceed necessarily 'in faith'." Fred Katz, in "Theory and Practice in Sociology: A Sociological Essay on a Dilemma in Sociology," a paper delivered before the American Sociological Association, 1963, concludes: ". . . the conversion of philosophical systems into

structural components of roles means that these perspectives are systematically incorporated into the role of scientist and became silent partners in his professional efforts. This is likely to introduce emphases and biases on a large scale."

7 Will Herberg (1959: 111), astute student of philosophy and the sociology of religion, followed the thread of sociology to its ultimate skein, observing: "The most empirical society, as the best sociologists themselves are beginning to recognize, cannot operate without presuppositions—presuppositions about reality, about man and human life—which are quite philosophical, and like it or not, even theological. . . ."

8 Talcott Parsons (1961: 29).

9 Albert Einstein in a lecture at Princeton in 1939, published later as *Symposium on Science, Philosophy, and Religion* by the Conference on Science, Philosophy, and Religion in Their Relation to the Democratic Way of Life, Inc., N.Y., 1941.

10 As Benjamin Ginzburg (1936: Vol. 13: 592) put it in his strategic article in "Science" in the *Encyclopaedia of the Social Sciences*: "Science thereby becomes defined simply as rules which govern our expectation of future experience."

11 Karl Pearson was sufficiently moved by a similar awareness to add an elaborate footnote to this effect in *The Grammar of Science* (1957: 394).

12 Richard von Mises (1956: 139) writes that "traces of this idea can be found already in the work of August Comte."

13 Max Weber (1947: 88).

14 Nicholas S. Timasheff (1961: 180).

15 Anselm Strauss (1956: x) paraphrases his view in the following way: "Intelligent activity does not seek to know the world but 'undertakes to tell us what we may expect to happen when we act in such and such a fashion' . . . the past—historical or otherwise—is significant not in itself but only in relation to present and future action."

16 "The characteristic outlook of the selected group of sciences is not merely the quest for knowledge in any sense of the term but the quest for a certain type of knowledge. These sciences, or this science, may be said to look for knowledge in terms of which man may envisage the future course of phenomena unrolling themselves . . ." (Ginzburg, 1936: Vol. 13: 592). Bernard Barber (1962: 12), who writes from the dual perspective of science in general and sociology in particular, also speaks of the criterion of parsimony when he seeks to characterize the ends of theory construction, adding that "the ideal conceptual scheme at

any given time is that which has the greatest generality, that is, the one in which the number of conceptual categories or variables in terms of which abstract general propositions are stated is very small." See also Howard Becker (1950:97).

17 David Hume in *Enquiry Concerning Human Understanding*, as quoted by A. J. Ayer (1959:10).

18 Carl Michalson (1963:98). Or, to use Schrödinger's phrase, an "hypothesis of objectification" restrains those who wish to play the scientific game.

19 As John Macmurray (1961:31–2) puts it, "*any* personal activity must have a motive, and all motives are, in the larger sense, emotional. . . . The attitude of a scientist pursuing his vocation is, therefore, an emotional state." He goes on to point out, in fact, that "strangely enough, the 'objective' activity is the activity of the logical mind—of *the self as subject;* while it is the activity of the *objective* (or empirical) *self* which is called 'subjective.'" Kurt Wolff (1946:545–53), confronted by the variety of meanings that have been—and can be—read into the term "objectivity," would have us investigate the implications that they severally have for the socio-culturally selective character of the term.

20 Emile Benoit-Smullyan (1948:501) paraphrases Durkheim by observing that through the latter's eyes a social fact is "an entity which can be known only through 'external' observation . . . and not by introspection."

21 Max Weber (1947:97) acknowledges this when he writes: "Verification of subjective interpretation by comparison with the concrete course of events is, as in the case of all hypotheses, indispensable."

22 John McKinney (1954:566) has written that "the realm of science, in the view of Mead, is composed of that which is common to various observers, the world of common, necessarily social, experience, symbolically formulated."

23 Robert Bierstedt (1960:7). Kaspar Naegele (1961:10) says very much the same: "In sociology, as one confronts the world through science, the emphasis, as in the rest of science, is . . . with formulating claims by routes that others can travel . . . (through) propositions that can be disproved and shared, that are impersonal and public. . . ."

24 The "policeman" analogy was drawn by Merton in the context of a public discussion at the Eastern Sociological Society meetings in the spring of 1963. See also Robert K. Merton (1949:553).

25 See John Locke, *An Essay Concerning Human Understanding*, Book IV, Chapter II.

26 John Stuart Mill, *System of Logic*, Book VI, p. 18, as quoted by Peter Winch (1958:67–68).

27 "Carlyle has somewhere said something like this: 'Nothing but facts are of importance. John Lackland passed by here. Here is something that is admirable. Here is reality for which I would give all the theories in the world.' Carlyle was a fellow countryman of Bacon; but Bacon would not have said that. That is the language of the historian. The physicist would say rather: 'John Lackland passed by here; that makes no difference to me, for he will never pass this way again' " (Henri Poincaré, 1913:128). "Without this belief [that every detailed occurrence can be correlated with its antecedents in a perfectly definite manner, exemplifying general principles] the incredible labors of scientists would be without hope," observed Whitehead (1926:15). Like observations clutter the halls of science and its philosophy: Jacob Burckhardt's contention that "we pay attention to the repeatable, the constant, the typical as that which appeals to us and can be understood"; Russell's (1935:147), "If there is any region where there are no causal laws, that region is inaccessible to science"; Eddington's (1939:113) characterization of science as "the habit of thought which regards variety always as a challenge to further analysis, so that the ultimate end-products of analysis can always be sameness"; Weizsacker's (Michalson, 1963:41) comment that "science . . . believes in the regularity of nature . . . as firmly as religious belief is rooted in a system of religion"; and Einstein's (Laurence, 1958:6) confession, in registering a disclaimer *vis-à-vis* the implications some had drawn from Heisenberg's uncertainty principle, that "I cannot believe that God plays dice with the universe . . . the Lord may be subtle but He is not capricious."

28 As Alfred Stern (1956:295–96) has put it, even "the *demonstration of the invalidity of the law of causality necessarily presupposes its validity*."

29 As Robert Oppenheimer (1958:72) has observed, "no physicist of the nineteenth century would have contemplated in a serious way the proposition that he could not find out how the die would fall if he took the trouble. Nor should we today. Here chance appears, in other words, as a practical notion . . . as a limitation of what is profitable, sensible, appropriate, to do." Ernest Nagel (1962:628–29) has spoken to the entire issue with consummate skill: ". . . classical science is *deterministic*—in the sense that it attempts to discover the precise conditions for the occurrence of phenomena, without benefit of final causes and

without invoking experimentally unidentifiable causal agents. . . . There is, however, nothing in modern research which requires the abandonment of the generic ideal of classical science: to find the determining conditions for the occurrence of phenomena, expressible in terms of empirical control. Thus, even modern quantum-theory—although it employs technical modes of specifying the character of physical systems which are different from those used in classical mechanics—is deterministic or mechanical [in the loose sense] insofar as it rigorously specifies the unique physical conditions under which certain types of changes will occur. Similarly, modern genetics is no less deterministic than the Darwinian theory, since the former even more completely than the latter has succeeded in disclosing the mechanisms or structures involved in the transmission of characteristics from one generation to another. It is therefore simply not true that recent advances in knowledge have demonstrated the untenability of the logical canons of classical science."

30 "The proof that the reality of collective tendencies is no less than that of cosmic forces is that this reality is demonstrated in the same way, by the uniformity of effect" (Emile Durkheim, 1956:399).

31 Werkmeister (1959:494) writes: ". . . the social scientist must and does proceed on the assumption that there are typical and recurrent situations and patterns at the social level which are the result of typical and recurrent processes or functional interdependencies. His concern is and must be the discovery of laws governing what is typical and recurrent. . . ."

32 "Science is not concerned with the inner nature of any of the terms used, but only with their mutual relations. . . . The truth of the relations does not depend on the reality of the *relata*" (William C. Dampier, 1949:xii).

33 As Richard von Mises (1956:342) has noted, ". . . scientific research, toward whatever objects it may be directed, can always only determine relations or connections between groups of phenomena."

34 ". . . as long as we see only relational determinabilities in the whole realm of empirical knowledge, the formulation of an 'as such' sphere has no consequence whatsoever for the process of knowing" (Mannheim, 1936:275). Also see Mannheim's *Essays on Sociology and Social Psychology* (1953: 15–41).

35 Comparable observations by recent American sociologists have included George Lundberg's declaration (1954:9) that "the aim of all scientific investigations is to arrive at

statements about the relationships between things . . . "; John McKinney's comment (1954:565) that "scientific procedure . . . always implies a system of some sort . . . "; and Roy Francis' conclusion (Doby, 1954:9) that "science tends toward a system."

36 "Science . . . represents the most sophisticated attempt to deal with the relational image. Even here, however, relational images arise through strong filtering of messages through the value structure of the scientific subculture" (Boulding, 1961:50).

37 ". . . the object of science was still the same—the quest for a set of *relations* whose materials could be supplied in the present and which could be relied upon to predict the character of future experiences" (Ginzburg, 1936: Vol. 13:601).

10 Sociological Man as Natural Man

1 W. D. Lamont (1955) has in recent years offered a "principle of economy" as "the ultimate ground of the comparative value judgement." It would appear relatively innocuous in his hands, however, and certainly has had no visible effect upon sociology *per se*.

2 See, for instance, an unpublished paper by Charles Estus entitled "An Analysis of the Social Thought of Talcott Parsons." The whole enterprise of contemporary system design is seen by Robert Boguslaw (1965) as centered about a substitution of the value of efficiency for more humanistic ideals.

3 See K. S. Lashley in L. A. Jeffress (1951:112), and John G. Kemeny (1959), as quoted by Philip P. Wiener (1959:31).

4 An observation made during a meeting of the New York Academy of Sciences on "Human Decisions in Complex Systems," as quoted in the *New York Times*, May 21, 1960, p. 27. For a more elaborate excursion into the visions conjured up by such a mentality, see Olaf Johannesson (1968). A more serious examination may be found in Harold Sackman (1967).

5 As Werner Heisenberg (Davenport, 1955:218) has pointed out, "As facts and knowledge accumulate, the claim of the scientist to an understanding of the world in a certain sense diminishes;" one must renounce "the aim of bringing the phenomena of nature to our thinking in an immediate and living way."

6 Parsons saves his larger posture from the criticism of "reductionism," however, by allowing "personality" a status equivalent to that of "society." Neither of the latter,

he makes quite clear, may be ultimately reduced to the other.

7 T. V. Smith (1931:384) student of Mead, saw in Mead's pragmatism an implicit romanticism; C. W. Morris (1934:549–64 and 1938:109–27) identified it in turn as a species of realism.

8 ". . . with respect to the most general differentiation of social sciences from the philosophical matrix in which it had earlier been embedded, we may speak of a religious, a philosophical, and a more generally scientific aspect of this matrix. The relative predominance of these aspects partly corresponds with principal phases of Western intellectual history" (1959:548). The pat Comtean version is far from dead, as evidenced, for instance, in the unconditional support granted it by such a figure as Pierre Auger (1955:74–76) while director of the Natural Sciences Department of UNESCO. Even the conditional buttressing of the position such as that offered by Parsons contributes to the reification of our methodological postulates rather than to rhetorical sophistication.

9 The first three generalized conditions of equilibrium or laws offered by Parsons and Bales were (1) *The Principle of Inertia*: A given process of action will continue unchanged in rate and direction unless impeded or deflected by opposing motivational forces; (2) *The Principle of Action and Reaction*: If, in a system of action, there is a change in the direction of a process, it will tend to be balanced by a complementary change which is equal in motivational force and opposite in direction; (3) *The Principle of Effort*: Any change in the rate of an action process is directly proportional to the magnitude of the motivational force applied or withdrawn. Lundberg's conclusion (1956:24) is simple: that "Parsons and his associates have in effect returned to the cradle of positivism [for] August Comte in his *Positive Philosophy* (1859) asserted that Newton's three laws of motion applied to social phenomena." Indeed, he notes that Stuart Dodd had as early as 1934 specifically paraphrased Newton's laws in sociological terms, repeating them in a volume published in 1942 whose title (*Dimensions of Society*) was akin to, yet even less "physicalist" than, the title of the Parsons-Bales paper—"The Dimensions of Action-Space." The fourth "law" is explicitly acknowledged, in turn, to be essentially the same as the learning psychologist's "law of effect" and the biologist's "natural selection": (4) *The Principle of System-Integration*: Any pattern element (mode of organization of components) within a system of action will tend to be

confirmed in its place within the system (extinguished) as a function of its contribution to the integrative balance of the system. This latter predisposition to view the dynamics of the social system in terms analogous to the homeostatically conscious biologist has often been noted in critiques of Parsons' works, perhaps encouraged by the knowledge that his initial interest as an undergraduate focused upon zoology. He readily admits even at the height of his career as a social theorist that cultural and social evolution, though largely out of fashion since the turn of the century, are very compelling options. The pragmatic test of survival, he tells us somewhere, is in fact the ultimate criterion he would apply to his own theoretical system.

10 ". . . the scheme developed here is in its fundamentals applicable all the way from the phenomena of 'behavior psychology' on pre-symbolic animal and infantile levels, to the analysis of the largest scale social systems" (Parsons, Bales, and Shils, 1953:106). This admission had in fact come at least as early as the publication of *Toward a General Theory of Action*, where the group joining Parsons in the initial common statement noted that "the frame of reference of the theory of action applies in principle to any . . . complex organism" (Parsons and Shils, 1951:6).

11 Tolman's extrapolation of Parsons is supported in turn by a paper by Robert Sears also included in the *Toward a General Theory* volume wherein Sears (1951:467) speaks of the focus upon action as simply an acknowledgment that the basic facts to which science addresses itself are of an *operational* nature—man's "behavior," "the things he does," "the ends he accomplishes"—whereas such concepts as "needs," "perceptions," and "traits" are but intervening constructs drawn out of the former. "Goal," "purpose," "expectation," "entelechy" are terms no longer limited to life itself: G. A. Miller, E. Galnater, and K. H. Pribram (1960:43–45) claim that teleological mechanisms may be built of metal and glass. Isidor Chein (1962:2–3) observes that "the position taken by Miller, Galanter, and Pribram [is] that, now that machines [computers] have been built that behave purposively, *purpose* has become a legitimate scientific concept . . . . [However] the issue is not simply whether behavior is purposive. One may conceive of Man as driven by powerful instinctual drives which impel him to seek particular ends; if the environment permits, the ends will be attained and, if not, a definite something else will happen. This model, commonly thought of as a purposive one, leaves Man a passive victim of the interplay between consti-

tution and environment no less than do the non-purposive S-R models. Man, as such, has nothing to do with the outcome. He does nothing; things happen to him."

12 See Charles Estus, "A Critical Analysis of Talcott Parsons' Pattern Variables," unpublished manuscript, p. 19.

13 Mach himself admits that "during the [scientific] investigation every thinker is of necessity a theoretical determinist" (Ernst Mach, *Erkenntnis und Irrtum*, 2nd Edition, pp. 282–83, as quoted by V. I. Lenin, *Materialism and Empirio-Criticism*, no date: 194).

14 Nettler's (1959:375–84) findings in the study under question, limited though they are by the devices used, do make a significant empirical contribution. Unfortunately, he has failed to interpret the results accurately. He *has* discovered that, using his scales and sample, there appears to be a significant correlation between the belief that socio-cultural factors play a relatively limited role in structuring anti-social behavior, on the one hand, and a relative preference for punishment as over against rehabilitation, on the other. What he *thinks* he has done is to demonstrate that "determinists" are less cruel than those attached to the conception of "free will." Ignoring the logical and substantive problems in equating a preference for punishment with cruelty, what is completely clear is that he has failed to identify a "determinist" stance through the scale he utilized: None of the items could be identified unambiguously with a "determinist" position; they simply identify various degrees of "free will." *Any* introduction of "freedom" denies the determinist posture. One is reminded of the male who, when questioned concerning the condition of his girl friend, indicated that she was just "a *tiny bit* pregnant." What one might discover through further empirical research is that a curvilinear relationship exists.

15 Shils, often a collaborator with Parsons, may be revealing a comparable appreciation when he suggests that the social theorist will act as social critic through theories of the middle range rather than through the larger frame of his theory (Shils, 1961:1424).

16 The impact of the reification of the "systematic" nature of science's vision is evidenced in a miscellany of ways in the behavioral sciences. The founding father of anthropology, E. B. Tylor (1871:2, 24), set the stage in that discipline when he argued as early as 1871 that ". . . the history of mankind is part and parcel of the history of nature . . . our thoughts, wills, and actions accord with laws as definite as those which govern the motion of the

waves, the combination of acids and bases, and the growth of plants. . . . If law is anywhere it is everywhere." The recently deceased dean of American anthropology, A. L. Kroeber (1952:xiv), found its essentially nomothetic posture moving on to imply an impersonal image of man as well: "We must be ready, when we get further by it, to ignore and suppress the individual, who from the angle of the understanding of culture is perhaps more often irrelevant and distracting than helpful. . . . Values, like all sociocultural manifestations, are largely superpersonal . . . values participate in what used to be called the 'collective' or 'mass' origin—what I prefer to call the 'essential anonymity' of origin. . . . Now the collective or anonymous, being everybody's, is also nobody's: there is a quality of the impersonal about it. . . . The inquirer, if his interest is really in culture, tends . . . to omit the human agents. He operates *as if* individual personalities did not have a hand in cultural events." Leslie White (1949:349, 406) carried the position through to its logical conclusion: "Philosophies possess, hold, animate, guide and direct the articulate, protoplasmic mechanisms that are men. Whether a man—an average man, typical of his group—'believes in' Christ or Buddha, Genesis or Geology, Determinism or Free Will, is not a matter of his own choosing. His philosophy is merely the response of his neuro-sensory-muscular-glandular system to the streams of cultural stimuli impinging upon him from the outside. What is called 'philosophizing' is merely the interaction of these cultural elements within his organism. His 'choice' of philosophic beliefs is merely a neurological expression of the superior strength of some of these extra-somatic cultural forces . . . scientific interpretation is *deterministic*."

Psychology is even more fully tempted by the extrapolation of epistemology in the direction of a metaphysic. B. F. Skinner (1956:104, 109), has observed that ". . . as such explanations [those of the behavioral sciences] become more and more comprehensive, the contribution which may be claimed by the individual himself appears to approach zero. Man's vaunted creative powers, his original accomplishments in art, science, and morals, his capacity to choose and our right to hold him responsible for the consequences of his choice—none of these is conspicuous in this new self-portrait."

Though some would perhaps argue that Skinner's views here are no more representative of his larger discipline than is his particular brand of learning theory,

Gordon Allport (1948:103) has seen fit to report that, in fact, "the position of *most* psychological writers is one of naïve determinism."

The impact upon the field of political science may perhaps be illustrated by noting the way in which *freedom*—a term of obviously crucial import to the entire history of political thought and action in the West—may quite literally be reduced to the figment of a non-empirical imagination. Christian Bay (1958:22–23), writing in the initial chapter of *The Structure of Freedom*—a volume which won the highest award his profession could grant—tells us, after finding it necessary to place the focal term *freedom* in quotation marks, that it does "appear proper for a social scientist to have a bias in favor of a determinist position. . . ."

17 *Logically* the unique may indeed be *prior* to the patterned: Since the total process that makes up social existence is by definition unitary, it falls by its very nature outside the criterion that scientists set by their focus upon the recurrent. An analogous predisposition is reflected in recent theology. As Buber has put it, ". . . an object, an 'It', can always be scientifically related to other objects and appear as part of a group or a series. In this manner science insists on seeing 'It'; hence, science is able to comprehend objects and events as ruled by universal laws which make their behavior under given circumstances predictable. 'Thou,' on the other hand, is unique. 'Thou' has the unprecedented, unparalleled, and unpredictable character of an individual, a presence known only insofar as it reveals itself" (Frankfort, Wilson, and Jacobsen, 1949:12). This may help us to understand why, although Weber allied himself deliberately and finally with the *order* that might be discovered within the larger mix that is experience, Ernst Troeltsch, a close associate and disciple whose sociological attention focused upon Christianity, came down ultimately on the side of a reality characterized by the notion of individuality.

18 " 'Cultural relativism' is used as a value-charged term denoting a positive, praiseworthy attitude, while 'ethnocentrism' connotes a negative value incompatible with an unbiased, objective approach" (Bidney, 1953:424).

19 "Judgments are based on experience, and experience is interpreted by each individual in terms of his own enculturation" (Herskovits, 1955:351).

20 H. Shepard (1956:48–57) takes a similar stance, predicting that the value systems of the layman and the scientist will one day converge entirely.

21 Nevitt Sanford (1965:69) argues that "in the practice of science itself research and therapy cannot be separated"; that the apparent conflict is resolved when one realized that the ethic of the community of science provides the common bond. Ayres (1962) perceives science as providing the larger society with an ethic rooted in a commitment to truth, the value of independence of thought, and the toleration of dissent, arguing that what have been termed sacred values have been proven to be relative, while the profane values of scientific rationality are absolute, the same for all mankind. Bronowski (1956:90) concludes simply that science has "humanized our values. Men have asked for freedom, justice, and respect precisely as the scientific spirit has spread among them." René Dubos (1961:160) claims that "science meets all the requirements usually associated with the concepts of culture and humanism." Also see Russell E. Bayliff (1954:27f.).

22 See, for instance, Bernard Barber (1962: Chapter 3). Parsons (1967:64), too, argues that we ". . . have vested interest in what is in some sense a 'liberal' society."

23 Joseph Fichter and William Kolb (1953:544) observe that "this ethical code [of the scientist] . . . fails to cover the problems arising from the relations between the scientist and the objects of his observation and experimentation. This may be due in part to the very conceptualization of phenomena as 'objects.' Only 'subjects' have rights which must be respected. . . ."

24 Isidore Chein (1962:7) puts the temptation confronting the behavioral scientist in the following terms: "He may try to apply it to everyone else, but he cannot apply it to himself as a basis of action. He thus professes a faith in an order of law that applies to everyone else, but, implicitly at least, he reserves to himself a special order of law. He knows that he can intervene in events, but he claims that no one else can—and this in the name of science." But it is Henry Kariel (1960:244, 248) who has spelled out its implications for behavioral science most fully: "United in their aim of constructing and testing a behavioral science, social scientists are induced to engage in operations which are unchecked, theoretically, by anything but their own power to be operative. . . [for] to control constructs themselves, to impose a check on science, is to cut into its capacity for experimental action. It is at once unnatural and suicidal, for it delimits science, accepting not its own reason, but one which professes to transcend it. . . . Thus, the purpose of science becomes a pseudo-purpose: control, not in reference to a transcending

objective, but for its own sake. Thereby science, equated with spontaneous right action, gains autonomy. . . . It becomes self-reliant and self-justifying; it is measured, not against a higher order of reality, not against standards anteceding the conventions of empirical science, but against an ideal which values the capacity to exercise power, to be effective, to flex one's instruments . . . for the control of nature, of society, and of man. Thus a genuine science is manipulative knowledge . . . science's own framework, including the rules of procedure by which it is built up, remains free. Unlike the data it orders, it is incommensurate, introduced to rid the world of what is designated as risky, provisional, or fateful . . . when consistently loyal to his position, he [the behavioral scientist] will have to fight for its incarnation, stilling whatever voices presume to resist it, aiding whatever resembles it. He must prompt men to realize their destiny, working not only as their prophet but also as their redeemer."

25 Essentially similar images of the scientific mode are seen in Max Scheler's contention that the scientist *qua* scientist has the will to master but not the will to love and in Heidegger's contrast between "Everyday Being-with"—the public and impersonal—as over against "Dasein-with Others"—the genuinely interpersonal.

26 As quoted by Ashley Montagu in a review of Theodore Kroeber, *Ishi in Two Worlds: A Biography of the Last Wild Indian in North America* (1961) in *New York Times Book Review*, December 10, p. 22. Though examinations of the scientist himself have of late shown him to be far from the coldly dispassionate creature some have stereotyped him to be, there are indications that he is, empirically viewed, relatively asocial. Once recent summary of the data (Roe, 1962:91) speaks of him as showing a "much stronger preoccupation with things and ideas than with people."

11 The Marxist Analogue

1 "In the United States," Mills noted (1962:10, 11), "the intellectual influences of Marxism are often hidden; many of those whose very categories of thought are influenced by Marx are often unaware of the source of their own methods and conceptions." "Classical Marxism has been central to the development of modern sociology." "Many," he argued (1959:48), "who reject (or more accurately, ignore) Marxist ways of thinking about human affairs are actually rejecting the classic traditions of their own disciplines."

2 "On the sociological level, Marx is one of the symbolic 'grandfathers' of the theory of action" (Parsons, 1961: 361). By this Parsons meant that through Marx's historically rooted empiricism a foundation was laid which made it possible for later social theory to avoid the traditional temptations of idealism and organicism. Or, as Peter Blau and Joan Moore (1959:167) put it about the same time in a short piece introducing the general field of sociology, "by concentrating on objective 'material' conditions instead of spiritual forces, he defines social phenomena in a way that makes their scientific study possible . . . [while] his emphasis on the relationship between social groups as central for explaining historical processes is more conducive to a sociological approach than the essentially biological concept of survival of the fittest."

3 "Marx the economist is less important today than Marx the political sociologist. As a sociologist, as an analyst of the class content of historical movement, Marx remains the master" (Feuer, 1959:xxi).

4 In comparing the approach of the two postures to religion Merton (1957:4, 39–41) observed that "the functionalists, with their emphasis on religion as a *social mechanism* for 'reinforcing the sentiments most essential to the institutional integration of the society,' may not differ materially in their analytical framework from the Marxists who, if their metaphor of 'opium of the masses' is converted into a neutral statement of social fact, also assert that religion operates as a social mechanism for reinforcing certain secular as well as sacred sentiments among its believers."

5 "If Marxist sociology does not differ methodologically from functional analysis [and he contends that it does not], it seems doubtful that *any* kind of sociology does" (Davis, 1959:769).

6 From Karl Marx's "Sixth Thesis on Feuerbach" (Selsam and Martel, 1963:317); Karl Marx (1913:268); A. G. Spirkin (1961:118); Karl Marx, in T. B. Bottomore (1964:96).

7 T. B. Bottomore and Maximilien Rubel remind us that Mead was a close student of Marx's sociological theories, pointing to his chapter on 'Karl Marx and Socialism" in M. H. Moore (1936).

8 The quotations used included "Now, if crimes observed . . . show . . . [that] 'it would be difficult to decide in respect to which of the two [the physical world and the social system] the acting causes produce their effect with

utmost regularity' is there not a necessity for deeply reflecting upon an alteration of the system that breeds these crimes?" Karl Marx, *New York Daily Tribune*, from Bottomore and Rubel (1956:235).

"The criminal . . . appears as . . . [one among] 'equilibrating forces' which establish a just balance and open up a whole perspective of 'useful' occupations" (K. Marx, "*Theorien ueber den Mehrwert*," 1, *ibid.*, 168). "The different spheres . . . constantly tend to an equilibrium . . . this constant tendency to equilibrium, of the various spheres is exercised, only in the shape of a reaction against the constant upsetting of this equilibrium" (K. Marx, 1906: 390–91). Charles Loomis recounts the episode in his presidential address before the 1967 meetings of the A.S.A. (1967:876).

9 See Michael Polanyi (1957:480) and David Thomson (1955:27).

10 ". . . the 'modern' level of sociological thinking has emerged from the intellectual 'marriage' between the utilitarian and the more collectivistic elements in the main Western traditions of social thought. . . . On the level of social systems it can be said [to have been] foreshadowed in 1848, the year in which the last great utilitarian documents—John Stuart Mill's *Principles of Political Economy*—coincided in publication with the *Communist Manifesto*. . . . It is no accident that the problem of socialism was not only politically but also intellectually so salient in the late 19th century in the West. There seems to me to be no doubt that, along with various others, Marx was perhaps the most important original 'go-between' of the marriage of the two basic traditions we are discussing" (Parsons, 1961:19–20).

11 Holland had apparently also been included, while in 1895 Engels added France. The latter in fact concluded finally that "history has shown us wrong" (Fischer, 1965:3).

12 Friedrich Engels (1947:121) and Marx and Engels (1935:234).

13 Quoted by Lenin in V. I. Lenin, *Materialism and Empirio-Criticism* (no date:259).

14 *Ibid.*, 39, 27.

15 See Howard Selsam (1963:52). Joravsky (1961:22) finds, indeed, that there is little in *Materialism and Empirio-Criticism* to commit the orthodox to one physical model rather than another.

16 It must have been out of an awareness of these portions of the Marxist scriptures that Sidney Hook (1933:6) was led to declare, in his early work on Marx, that "there is

nothing *a priori* in Marx's philosophy; it is naturalistic, historical, and empirical throughout." Though Hook may well have altered his ideological stance over the years, others equally as anti-Marxist as the present Hook have found themselves led to the same conclusion. More recently, for instance, Joravsky (1961:11) has observed that "it is possible to argue that this empirical criterion of truth was more nearly characteristic of Marx and Engels' attitude towards the natural sciences than their occasional readiness to derive theories from philosophical principles and prescribe them to specific sciences. The chief evidence for this argument would be the absence of such prescriptions from the works they published in their lifetime, and the consequent fact that their followers have never been able to agree on what specific theories of natural science, if any, are incumbent on Marxists by virtue of their philosophy." It is evidence such as this that has led Howard Selsam (1963:44–45) to conclude that Marxism-Leninism never has, and is never likely to be, formulated definitively; that its fundamental points of reference are few and entirely scientific; that it is eminently subtle and complex, having drawn from philosophic traditions which it professes to reject; and that "it is necessarily responsive, by its own inherent nature, to every development in the natural and social sciences."

17 "In spite of the elements of conflict that have appeared from time to time, Christianity and science have a very deep foundation in common—it is not by chance that Christian civilization has been the mother of science . . . the rise of social science . . . is a development which is a logical and inevitable outcome of the evolution of Christianity itself" (Parsons, *Religious Perspectives of College Teaching in Sociology and Social Psychology* (no date: 44).

18 Leopold Labedz (1962:140) makes the same point. An excellent example of the new mood may be found in Leszek Kowlakowski (1968).

19 V. I. Lenin (*op. cit.*: 177, 270, 271, 331). Russell Davenport (1955:227–28) would have us take Lenin at his word: "May it not be that the [Marxist] doctrine of Materialism, though deriving its name from matter, is nothing more or less than the doctrine of externalization—that reality can only be discovered by looking at things and experience from the outside? . . . Materialism is not, in fact, a doctrine of matter but of truth—a way of looking at things, which asserts that the human mind can only come to truth by the use of the outward-looking consciousness . . . Matter, in other words, did not create Materialism.

Externalism created matter as Marx and Engels and the whole nineteenth century conceived it. . . .

"Reality, in other words, is what we can perceive with our senses and our instruments by looking outward from ourselves while the inward consciousness is entangled in endless illusions. . . ."

20 It is interesting to note that Erich Fromm (1961:17) chooses to use the term "indispensable" rather than "determined" or "necessary" in his translation of the same passage.

21 V. I. Lenin (*op. cit.*: 125). Marxism, Polanyi suggests (1958:228), enables one to both have the cake of ruthless objectivity and to eat it with passion as well. It "conjures away the contradiction between the high moral dynamism of our age and our stern critical passion which demands that we see human affairs objectively, i.e. as a mechanistic process in the Laplacean manner."

22 "The classical values of truth, beauty and goodness depend for their meaning entirely on the existence of society and change their character with the change of that society. . . . This relativity is itself an absolute thing—the only 'absolute' there is. . . . The . . . so-called . . . scientific truths . . . are relative . . ." (Bernal, 1949:59–60).

23 As Lewis Feuer notes (1963:136), "they [Marx and Engels] left a tremendous gap in their theory of socialism by simply ruling out ethical ideas as 'modern mythology.' They made it all the easier for the Stalinist perversion of their philosophy to justify itself with appeals to technological necessity, the historical mission of hatred, and the meaninglessness of absolute justice." "Our morality," Lenin admitted, "is completely subordinate to the interests of the class struggle of the proletariat" (Fischer, 1965:3). "In Soviet practice," Fischer continued (p. 67), "this easily becomes the immorality of the leader's struggle for absolute supremacy; and when the leader is a monster somewhat mad, the result is the history of Russia from 1934 to 1953. But, as Nicolaevsky says, this attitude toward means and ends 'still determines the basic line of the Kremlin'."

24 "His [Marx's] emphasis on the *relationships* between social groups as central for explaining historical processes is conducive to a sociological approach . . ." (Blau and Moore, 1959:167).

25 "N. Bukharin was one of the first of later Marxists to develop formally the use of system analysis on a sociological level. For example, a society 'may be regarded as a whole consisting of parts [elements] related to each other;

in other words, the whole may be regarded as a system.'" Gouldner (1959:269n) quotes N. Bukharin (1925:87).

26 Nearly three-fourths acknowledged that "most sociologists merely pay lip service to the ideal," while a plurality (45%) felt that the value-free ideal "helps sociology to remain independent of outside pressures and influence" (Gouldner and Sprehe, 1965:42–44).

27 "The sociologist, in fact, is an object of history. . . . Research is a living relationship between men. . . . Indeed, the sociologist and his 'object' form a couple, each one of which is to be interpreted by the other; the *relationship* between them must be itself interpreted as a moment in history. . . . The wish to put the sociologist out of the experimental field expresses simultaneously a bourgeois 'objectivism' and the sociologist's own experience of being excluded" (Sartre, 1963:72, 71).

28 ". . . despite itself [orthodox] Marxism tends to eliminate the questioner from his investigation and to make of the questioned the object of an absolute Knowledge" (Sartre, 1963:175).

29 "Man, is, for himself and for others, a signifying being . . . one can never understand the slightest of his gestures, without going *beyond the pure present and explaining it by the future*" (Sartre, 1963:115, 116). "It was legitimate for the natural sciences to free themselves from the anthropomorphism which consists in bestowing human properties on inanimate objects. But it is perfectly absurd to assume by analogy the same scorn for anthropomorphism where anthropology [in its generic sense] is concerned. When one is studying man, what can be more exact or more rigorous than to *recognize human properties in him*? The simple inspection of the social field ought to have led to the discovery that the relation to ends is a permanent structure of human enterprises and that it is *on the basis of this relation* that real men evaluate actions, institutions, or economic constructions. It ought to have been established that our comprehension of the other is necessarily attained through ends . . . the notions of alienation and mystification have meaning only to the precise degree that they steal away the ends and disqualify them. . . . American sociologists . . . foolishly substitute(s) for the givens of experience an abstract causalism or certain . . . concepts such as motivation, attitude, or role, which have no meaning except in conjunction with a finality" (Sartre, 1963:157–58). See also *L'Etre et le Néant, Essai d'Ontologie Phénoménologique* (1950), English translation by Hazel E. Barnes, *Being and Nothingness* (1950).

30 ". . . knowing," Sartre reminds us (1963: 168), "is inevitably practical: it changes the known." See also Sartre (1962: 246), as quoted by Walter Odajnyk (1965: 29).

31 See Bottomore and Rubel (1956), Dunayevskaya (1958), Fromm (1961), and Bottomore (1964).

32 Marx's own phrasing, in translation (Fromm, 1961: 99–103) reads: "1) the relationship of the worker to the *product of labor* as an alien object which dominates him. This relationship is at the same time the relationship to the sensuous external world, to natural objects, as an alien and hostile world; 2) the relationship of labor to the *act of production* within *labour* . . . his personal life . . . as an activity which is directed against himself, independent of him and not belonging to him. This is self-alienation. . . . 3) Thus alienated labor turns the *species life of man*, and also nature as his mental species-property, into an alien being and into a *means* for *his individual existence*. It alienates from man his own body, external nature, his mental life and his *human* life. 4) A direct consequence of the alienation of man from the product of his labor, from his life activity and from his species life is that *man* is *alienated* from other men . . . [from] their labor and . . . [from] the objects of their labor."

33 See Erich Fromm (1961: vi and 1963: 194) and a quotation from Fromm in Coser and Rosenberg (1964: 519).

34 Fromm (1961: 5, 64, 68 and 1964: 191). Indeed, if one wished to build a scaffolding upon which to drape Marx as Old Testament Prophet, the materials appear on hand: rabbinic roots on both sides of the family; the parents' conversion to Christianity when Karl was six; a final examination paper at the gymnasium level entitled "The Union of the Faithful with Christ according to John 15: 1–14, Exhibited in the Ground and Essence, in Its Absolute Necessity and Its Effects"; a letter from father to son while the latter was at the University containing the observation that "a great help for morality is pure faith in God . . . there are moments in life in which even the atheist is involuntarily drawn to the adoration of the Highest" (Fulton, 1960: 53); and the dedication of his doctoral dissertation to a professor "who . . . is living proof that idealism is not imagination, but the truth." Nor could one ignore the coincidence that his break with the language traditional to the sacred coincided approximately with his father's death.

35 A Soviet spokesman for orthodox Marxism-Leninism (see Tucker, 1964: 169) has declared that the current interest in the early writings represents an "ideological

diversion. . . . Artificially emphasizing certain not yet mature thoughts of Marx, the falsifiers try to make them the center of gravity of the interpretation of Marxism as a whole." Another official Soviet statement concluded: "The question of Hegel was settled long ago. There is no reason whatsoever to pose it now" (Dunayevskaya, 1964: 39–40).

36 Quoted by Robert Tucker (1964: 173).

37 Karl Marx in a letter dated April, 1867, as noted by A. James Gregor (1962a: 101).

38 Gregor (*op. cit.*: 101). The issue of relative blame is likely to remain unresolved, for Marx's daughter destroyed a significant segment of the Marx-Engels correspondence (*Ibid.*: 101).

39 T. B. Bottomore and Maximilien Rubel (1956: v) reported as recently as 1955 that "the internal political struggles in the USSR . . . apparently resulted in the abandonment of the project . . . viz. the publication of the complete works of Marx and Engels. Of the forty-two volumes originally planned only twelve have been published."

40 A. James Gregor (1962b: 89) observes that " 'Alienation' in the *Manuscripts* is a vague concept and in the last analysis seems to be, with respect to private property, an esoteric and logically precedent act."

41 Capitalism's "manifest content," as Robert Tucker points out (1946: 165–66, 175), "is not the self but society. This fact is epitomized in Marx's statement in the *Communist Manifesto*: 'Capital is not personal power; it is a social power.' As presented in this document, the Marxian theory of history runs exclusively in abstract social and economic categories. . . . Here everything is impersonal, strictly societal . . . the inner conflict of alienated man with himself became, in Marx's mind, a social conflict between 'labour' and 'capital,' and the alienated species-self became the class-divided society."

42 T. B. Bottomore, "Karl Marx: Sociologist or Marxist?" a paper given before the American Sociological Association meeting in Chicago, September, 1965. ". . . a historical conception . . . is at odds with the idea of a positive science which seems generally to inspire Marx's mature work. We may attribute greater or lesser importance to the Hegelianism or the positivism of Marx's theory, but it is impossible to reconcile them" (*Ibid.*). In his introduction to *Karl Marx: Early Writings* (1964: xiii) he adds, "The cast of Marx's mind was fundamentally scientific."

43 "*The Economic and Philosophic Manuscripts of 1844* . . . can

best be understood in the light of Marx's mature thinking and not the other way around . . . an objective, scientific approach . . . underlines and pervades all their subsequent thought" (Selsam and Martel, 1963: 19–20). Sidney Hook (1966: 2)—responsible as Bottomore has been for the translation of a portion of Marx's writings into English—characterizes the *Manuscripts* as "juvenilia" and describes the mature Marx as a social determinist. Among others adding their voices to the growing list who find the two Marxes incommensurate one would have to include Daniel Bell (1959) and Lewis Feuer (1962: 116–34). The latter in fact sees in Marx's flirtation with the notion of alienation a romanticism with preponderantly sexual overtones.

44 Jindrich Zeleny (1968), Czech Marxist and political philosopher, indeed perceives *four* stages in Marx's intellectual development: (1) a Hegelian period evidenced by the doctoral dissertation written in 1841; (2) pre-communist phase (1842–3) in which he criticizes Hegel from the perspective of Feuerbach; (3) the interval encompassed by the economic and philosophic manuscripts of 1844 in which Marx was inspired by Moses Hess and Friedrich Engels to substitute economic alienation for the religious alienation of Feuerbach and to project the future in utopian and humanist terms; and (4) the period beginning with the *Theses on Feuerbach* and *The German Ideology* (1845) and moving on through *Capital* in which he replaces earlier utopian and humanistic elements with empirical presuppositions, transforming his posture into a scientific theory rooted in a series of socio-political and economic "laws" that point toward the inevitable transition of bourgeois capitalism into socialism and communism.

12 The Calling of Sociology

1 Thomas Luckmann is currently preparing for publication, in German, a major systematic restatement of Schütz' position that had been left unfinished at his death.

2 ". . . our conception of sociology . . . does not imply . . . that it cannot be 'value-free' " (Berger and Luckmann, 1966: 173). Berger (1963: 152–53) had spoken to the issue in a more positive manner earlier when he argued, in *Invitation to Sociology*, that there was nothing ethically reprehensible in ethical neutrality as such. That the issue may lie simply in the breadth of his image of ethical or value-neutrality, is suggested, perhaps, by his further observation that "Machiavellianism, be it political or sociological, is a way of looking, in itself ethically neutral."

3 ". . . we can help him, to give himself an account of the ultimate meaning of his own conduct . . . a teacher who succeeds in this . . . stands in the service of 'moral' forces; he fulfills the duty of bringing about self-clarification and a sense of responsibility" (Gerth and Mills, 1958: 152).

4 Peter Berger (1963:166) makes a similar observation when he notes that it is characteristic of sociology to pay "careful attention to matters that other scholars might consider pedestrian and unworthy of the dignity of being objects of scientific investigation—something one might almost call a democratic focus of interest. . . . Everything that human beings are to do, no matter how commonplace, can become significant for sociological research." H. Richard Niebuhr (1960:87) sees such catholicity analogous to the "purest" religious insight: ". . . it appears to move with the confidence that whatever is, is worthy of attention. . . . [it] seems to care for 'widows and orphans'—for bereaved and abandoned facts, for processes and experiences that have lost meaning because they did not fit into an accepted framework of interpretation." Note also Everett Hughes' observation (1963:890) in his presidential address before the American Sociological Association: [Sociology] ". . . is a detachment of deep concern and intense curiosity that turns away from no human activity."

5 "Sociological understanding cannot by itself be a school of compassion, but it can illuminate the mystifications that commonly cover up pitilessness . . . sociological understanding can be an important part of a certain sense of life that is particularly modern, that has its own genius of compassion and that can be the foundation of a genuine humanism" (Berger, 1963:161–62).

6 Feuerbach rather than George Herbert Mead may have been responsible for reimplanting such an archetypal awareness in the mind of modern man when he noted that "The individual man for himself does not have man's being in himself, either as a moral or a thinking being. Man's being is contained in community, in the unity of man with man—a unity which rests, however, only on the reality of the difference between I and Thou" (Pfeutze, 1954:28). Its archetypal quality may be illustrated by the fact that the Japanese word for man, "ningen," means—when addressed literally—"between man and man."

7 ". . . because of these . . . consequences of predictions themselves, we do better to make continual short-range predictions in social life. Only thus can we constantly assess the new situations which exist because of the inter-

action not only of the previously existing factors but now, also, of the predictions themselves" (Barber 1962:292).

8 ". . . we would contend that, taking the total output of the social sciences as a background to our thinking, it is not so much determination as ficticiousness which is the main impression. . . . The social sciences present us not so much with man the slave as with man the clown. . . . The result of a serious immersion in the social sciences is that this fictitious universe is breached, if only to the extent of a little finger stuck through a colossal zeppelin. . . . This act of consciousness is the first step into freedom. That this act is a possibility is the decisive justification of the social scientific enterprise" (Berger, 1961:65–66).

Bibliography

Adams, Bert, "Coercion and Consensus Theories: Some Unresolved Issues," *American Journal of Sociology*, 71 (May, 1966), pp. 714–17.

Advisory Committee on Government Programs in the Behavioral Sciences, "The Behavioral Sciences and the Federal Government," *American Sociologist*, 3 (November, 1968), pp. 308–11.

Ahmad, Imtiaz, "Note on Sociology in India," *American Sociologist*, 1 (February, 1966), pp. 244–47.

Alexander, Chester, "Occupational Interests of Sociology Majors," *American Sociological Review*, 13 (December, 1948), pp. 758–63.

Allport, Gordon, *Survey of College Reading Materials*, Yale, 1948.

Alpert, Harry, *Emile Durkheim and His Sociology*, Columbia, 1939.

———, "The Social Science Research Program of the National Science Foundation," *American Sociological Review*, 22 (October, 1957), pp. 582–85.

———, "The Growth of Social Research in the United States," in Daniel Lerner (ed.), *The Human Meaning of the Social Sciences*, Meridian, 1959, pp. 73–88.

———, "Attitudes Towards Federal Support of Social Sciences: 1961 Version," *American Sociological Review*, 26 (October, 1961), pp. 785–86.

———, "Some Observations on the State of Sociology," *Pacific Sociological Review*, 6 (Fall, 1963), pp. 45–58.

American Psychological Association, "Ethical Standards of Psychologists," Washington, D.C., 1953.

———, *Casebook on Ethical Standards of Psychologists*, 1967.

American Psychologist: Issues devoted to "Discussion of Ethics," 7 (August, 1952), pp. 425–55, " 'Camelot' and Psychological Testing," 21 (May, 1966), pp. 401–78;

"Role of Psychology and Psychologists in Public Affairs," 22 (March, 1967), pp. 179–233.

American Sociological Association, "Code of Ethics (First Draft)," Washington, D.C., no date.

American Sociological Review, "The A.S.A. and Public Policy: an Exchange of Letters to the Editor," 30 (February, 1965), pp. 128–31.

Anderson, Harold (ed.), *Creativity and Its Cultivation*, Harper, 1959.

Angell, Robert, *Free Society and Moral Crisis*, University of Michigan, 1958.

Arendt, Hannah, "Religion and Politics," *Confluence*, II (September, 1953), pp. 105–26.

Auger, Pierre, "Some Thoughts on the Human Values of Science," *Impact of Science on Society*, UNESCO, IV (Autumn, 1953), pp. 127–42.

———, "Who? Why? How?" *Bulletin of the Atomic Scientists*, XI (March, 1955), pp. 74–76.

Axelson, Leland J., "Differences in Productivity of Doctorates in Sociology," *Journal of Educational Sociology*, 33 (October, 1959), pp. 49–55.

———, "Graduate Schools and the Productivity of Their Graduates," *American Journal of Sociology*, 66 (December, 1960), pp. 171–75.

Ayer, A. J., *Language, Truth, and Logic*, Dover, 1946.

———, (ed.), *Logical Positivism*, Free Press, 1959.

Ayres, C. E., *Toward a Reasonable Society, The Values of Industrial Civilization*, University of Texas, 1962.

Babchuck, Nicholas and Alan P. Bates, "Professor or Producer: The Two Faces of Academic Man," *Social Forces*, 40 (March, 1962), pp. 341–48.

Baber, Ray E., "A Discussion of the Introductory Course," *Social Forces*, 9 (March, 1931), pp. 324–31.

Baier, Horst, "Soziologie zwischen Subject und Object: Zur Erkenntnistheoretischen Situation der Westdeutschen Soziologie," *Soziale Welt*, 14/3–4 (1963), pp. 276–96.

Bain, Read, "Reactions of College Students to Elementary Sociology," *Social Forces*, 5 (September, 1927), pp. 66–69.

———, "Trends in American Society," *Social Forces*, 5 (June, 1927), pp. 413–22.

———, "Social Work Material in Introductory Sociology Texts," *Social Forces*, 8 (June, 1930), pp. 498–502.

———, "Letter to the Editor," *American Sociological Review*, 27 (October, 1962), pp. 746–48.

Barber, Bernard, "Structural-Functional Analysis: Some Problems and Misunderstandings," *American Sociological Review*, 21 (April, 1956), pp. 129–35.

———, *Science and the Social Order*, Rev. ed., Collier, 1962.

———, "The Functions and Dysfunctions of 'Fashion' in Science: Some General Considerations, and a Partial Illustration with the Case of Medical Sociology," Paper read at the Annual Meeting of the American Sociological Association, 1956.

Barber, Bernard and Walter Hirsch (eds.), *The Sociology of Science*, Free Press, 1962.

Barber, Bernard and Robert K. Merton, "Brief Bibliography for the Sociology of Science," *Proceedings of the American Academy of Arts and Sciences*, 80 (May, 1952).

Baritz, Loren, *The Servants of Power: A History of the Use of Social Science in American Industry*, Wesleyan University, 1960.

Barnes, J. A., "Some Ethical Problems in Modern Fieldwork," *British Journal of Sociology*, 14 (June, 1963), pp. 118–34.

Barnes, Robert E., "Communications to the Editor," *American Sociologist*, 2 (February, 1967), pp. 22–24.

Barrett, Donald N. and Mansell J. Blair, "Undergraduate Sociology Programs in Catholic Colleges in the United States, 1942–1964," *Sociological Analysis*, 26 (Spring, 1965), pp. 45–50.

Barrett, William, *Irrational Man*, Doubleday-Anchor, 1962.

Barton, Allen, "Administrative and Critical Functions of Applied Research, *The Human Factor*, 8 (Spring, 1969), pp. 45–53.

Bates, Allan, P., "Undergraduate Sociology: A Problem for the Profession," *Sociological Quarterly*, 6 (1965), pp. 21–36.

Bay, Christian, *The Structure of Freedom*, Stanford U., 1958.

Bayliff, Russell E. *et al.*, *Values and Policy in American Society*, W. C. Brown, 1954.

Beals, Ralph, "Background Information on Problems of Anthropological Research and Ethics," *American Anthropological Association Fellow Newsletter*, 8 (January, 1967), p. 16.

Beals, Ralph L., *Politics of Social Research*, Aldine, 1969.

Becker, Howard, *Through Values to Social Interpretation*, Duke, 1950.

——, "Normative Reactions to Normlessness," *American Sociological Review*, 25 (December, 1960), pp. 803–10.

Becker, Howard and Alvin Boskoff (eds.), *Modern Sociological Theory in Continuity and Change*, Dryden, 1957.

Becker, Howard P., "Distribution of Space in the *American Journal of Sociology*, 1895–1927," *American Journal of Sociology*, 36 (May, 1930), pp. 461–66.

———, "Space Apportioned Forty-Eight Topics in the *American Journal of Sociology*, 1895–1930," *American Journal of Sociology*, 38 (July, 1932), pp. 71–78.

Bell, Daniel, "The Meaning of Alienation," *Thought*, 1959, republished in Leopold Labedz (ed.), *Revisionism: Essays on the History of Marxist Ideas*, Praeger, 1962.

———, *The End of Ideology: On the Exhaustion of Political Ideas in the Fifties*, Free Press, 1960.

Benchimol, Samuel, "Sociology in Brazil: A Comparative Study," *Sociology and Social Research*, 32 (November-December, 1947), pp. 591–99.

Bender, Annabelle *et al.*, "American Sociological Regional Societies: Social Characteristics of Presidents," *Sociological Inquiry*, 35 (1965), pp. 207–18.

Bendix, Reinhard, "The Image of Man in the Social Sciences: The Basic Assumptions of Present-Day Research," *Commentary*, 11 (1951), pp. 187–92; reprinted in Seymour Lipset and Neil Smelser (eds.), *Sociology: The Progress of a Decade*, Prentice-Hall, 1961, pp. 30–37.

Bendix, Reinhard and Bennett Berger, "Images of Society and Problems of Concept Formation," in Llewellyn Gross (ed.), *Symposium on Sociological Theory*, Row, Peterson, 1959, pp. 97–113.

Benoit-Smullyan, Emile, "The Sociologism of Emile Durkheim and His School," in Harry Elmer Barnes (ed.), *An Introduction to the History of Sociology*, University of Chicago, 1948, pp. 499–537.

Bensman, Joseph and Bernard Rosenberg, *Mass, Class, and Bureacracy*, Prentice-Hall, 1963.

Berger, Bennett M., "Sociology and the Intellectuals: An Analysis of a Stereotype," *Antioch Review*, 17 (1957), pp. 275–89; reprinted in Seymour Lipset and Neil Smelser (eds.), *Sociology: The Progress of a Decade*, Prentice-Hall, 1961, pp. 37–45.

———, "Model of a Man Engagé," review of C. Wright Mills, *Power, Politics and People*, Oxford, 1963, in *New York Times Book Review*, April, 28, 1963, pp. 3, 50.

Berger, Peter, *The Noise of Solemn Assemblies*, Doubleday, 1961.

———, *The Precarious Vision*, Doubleday, 1961.

———, *Invitation to Sociology: A Humanistic Perspective*, Doubleday-Anchor, 1963.

———, *The Sacred Canopy*, Doubleday, 1967.

———, *Rumor of Angels*, Doubleday, 1968.

Berger, Peter and Thomas Luckmann, "Sociology of Religion and Sociology of Knowledge," *Sociology and Social Research*, 47 (July, 1963), pp. 417–27.

———, "Social Mobility and Personal Identity," *European Journal of Sociology*, V (1964), pp. 331–34.

———, *The Social Construction of Reality*, Doubleday, 1966.

Berger, Peter and Stanley Pullberg, "Reification and the Sociological Critique of Consciousness," *History and Theory* IV (1965), pp. 196–211.

Berghe, Pierre L. van den, "Dialectic and Functionalism: Toward a Theoretical Synthesis," *American Sociological Review*, 28 (October, 1963), pp. 695–705.

———, "An African Camelot?" *Trans-Action* (March, 1967), pp. 63–64.

Bernal, J. D., *The Freedom of Necessity*, Routledge and Kegan Paul, 1949.

———, *Marx and Science*, International, 1952.

Bernard, Jessie, "Some Current Conceptualizations in the Field of Conflict," *American Journal of Sociology*, 70 (January, 1965), pp. 442–54.

Bernard, Luther L., "The Teaching of Sociology in the United States," *American Journal of Sociology*, 15 (September, 1909), pp. 164–213.

———, "The Teaching of Sociology in Southern Colleges and Universities," *American Journal of Sociology*, 23 (January, 1918), pp. 491–515.

———, "The Teaching of Sociology in the United States in the Last Fifty Years," *American Journal of Sociology*, 50 (May, 1945), pp. 534–48.

———, "Sociological Trends in the South," *Social Forces*, 27 (October, 1948), pp. 12–19.

Bidney, David, "The Concept of Value in Modern Anthropology," in A. L. Kroeber (ed.), *Anthropology Today*, University of Chicago, 1953, pp. 682–99.

———, *Theoretical Anthropology*, Columbia, 1953.

Bierstedt, Robert, "Sociology and Humane Learning," *American Sociological Review*, 25 (February, 1960), pp. 3–9.

Birnbaum, Norman, "Conflicting Interpretations of the Rise of Capitalism: Marx and Weber," *British Journal of Sociology*, IV/2 (1953).

———, "Monarchs and Sociologists: A Reply to Professor Shils and Mr. Yound," *Sociological Review*, III/1 (1955).

———, "Science, Ideology and Dialogue: The Amsterdam Sociological Congress," *Commentary*, XXII/6 (1956).

———, "Marxism and Social Change in the 20th Century," *Transactions of the Third World Congress of Sociology*, Vol. III, 1957.

———, "The Sociological Analysis of Ideologies (1940–1960): A Trend Report and Bibliography," *Current Sociology*, IX/2 (1960).

———, "David Riesman's Image of Political Process," in Seymour Lipset and Leo Lowenthal (eds.), *Culture and Social Character: the Work of David Riesman*, Free Press, 1961, pp. 207–25.

———, "Introduction," German Edition, C. Wright Mills, *The Sociological Imagination*, Neuwied, 1963.

———, "The Crisis in Marxist Sociology," *Social Research*, 35 (Summer, 1968), pp. 348–80.

———, "Conservative Sociology," *Berkeley Journal of Sociology*, XIII (1968), pp. 97–103.

———, "On the Idea of a Political Avant-Garde in Industrial Society: the Intellectuals and the Technical Intelligentsia," *Praxis*, 1968.

———, *The Crisis of Industrial Society*, Oxford, 1969.

Black, Max (ed.), *The Social Theories of Talcott Parsons*, Prentice-Hall, 1961.

Blau, Peter, *Exchange and Power in Social Life*, Wiley, 1964.

Blau, Peter and Joan Moore, "Sociology," in B. F. Hoselitz (ed.), *A Reader's Guide to the Social Sciences*, Free Press, 1959, pp. 158–87.

Boalt, Gunnar, *The Sociology of Research*, Southern Illinois University, 1969.

Bogardus, Emory S., "Obtaining a Position in Sociology," *Sociology and Social Research*, 38 (September–October, 1953), pp. 38–45.

———, "Teaching Problems of Young Sociologists," *Sociology and Social Research*, 38 (January–February, 1954), pp. 174–82.

———, "Special Problems of Young Sociologists," *Sociology and Social Research*, 38 (March–April, 1954), pp. 242–52.

———, "Functions of a Sociology Honor Society," *Sociology and Social Research*, 39 (January–February, 1955), pp. 184–86.

———, "Forty Years of Sociology and Social Research," *Sociology and Social Research*, 40 (July, 1956), pp. 426–32.

Borgatta, Edgar R., "Sociologists and Sociologically Trained Practitioners," *American Sociological Review*, 24 (October, 1959), pp. 695–97.

Borko, Harold (ed.), *Computer Applications in the Behavioral Sciences*, Prentice-Hall, 1962.

Bosserman, Phillip, *Dialectical Sociology*, Porter Sargent, 1968.

Bottomore, T. B. (ed.), *Karl Marx: Early Writings*, translated by T. B. Bottomore, McGraw-Hill, 1964.

———, "Karl Marx: Sociologist or Marxist?" a paper delivered before the American Sociological Association, Chicago, August, 1965.

Bottomore, T. B. and Maximilien Rubel (eds.), *Karl Marx: Selected Writings in Sociology and Social Philosophy*, translated by T. B. Bottomore, London: C. A. Watts, 1956 (McGraw-Hill Paperback Edition, 1964).

Boulding, Kenneth, *The Image*, University of Michigan, 1961.

———, "General Systems as a Point of View," unpublished paper given at the Second Systems Symposium, Case Institute of Technology, Cleveland, April 4, 1963.

Bowers, Raymond V., "Occupational Roles of Sociologists," *American Sociological Review*, 23 (October, 1958), pp. 583–84.

Bowman, Claude C., "Is Sociology Too Detached?" *American Sociological Review*, 21 (October, 1956), pp. 563–68.

Braithwaite, R. B., *Scientific Explanation*, Cambridge University, 1953.

Bramson, Leon, *The Political Context of Sociology*, Princeton, 1961.

Braude, Lee, "Ethical Neutrality and the Perspective of the Sociologist," *Sociological Quarterly*, 5 (Autumn, 1964), pp. 396–99.

Braybrooke, David (ed.), *Philosophical Problems of the Social Sciences*, Macmillan, 1965.

Bredemeier, Harry, "The Methodology of Functionalism," *American Sociological Review*, 20 (April, 1955), pp. 173–80.

Bressler, Marvin, "The Conventional Wisdom of Education and Sociology," in Charles H. Page (ed.), *Sociology and Contemporary Education*, Random House, 1964, pp. 76–114.

Bridgman, Percy, "Remarks on Niels Bohr's Talk," *Daedalus* (Spring 1958), pp. 175–77.

———, "Quo Vadis?" *Daedalus* (Winter, 1958), pp. 85–93.

Broadus, Robert N., "A Citation Study for Sociology," *American Sociologist*, 2 (February, 1967), pp. 19–20.

Bronowski, Jacob, *Science and Human Values*, Messner, 1956.

———, "The Creative Process," *Scientific American* (September, 1958), pp. 62–63.

———, "The Values of Science," in Abraham Maslow (ed.), *New Knowledge in Human Values*, Harper & Row, 1959.

Brookover, Wilbur B. and William V. D'Antonio, "Problems for Research in Teaching Sociology," *Sociology and Social Research*, 42 (July–August, 1958), pp. 410–14.

Brooks, Lee M., "Some Regional Implications of Sociological Instruction," *Social Forces*, 24 (October, 1945), pp. 74–79.

———, "Some Postwar Challenges to Sociology," *Sociology and Social Research*, 31 (March–April, 1947), pp. 268–72.

Brown, Robert, *Explanation in Social Science*, Aldine, 1963.

Bruyn, Severyn T., *The Human Perspective in Sociology*, Prentice-Hall, 1966.

Buckley, Walter, "Social Stratification and the Functional Theory of Social Differentiation," *American Sociological Review*, 23 (August, 1958), pp. 369–75.

Bukharin, N., *Historical Materialism: A System of Sociology*, International Publishers, 1925.

Burchard, Waldo W., "Lawyers, Political Scientists, Sociologists—And Concealed Microphones," *American Sociological Review*, 23 (December, 1958), pp. 686–91.

Burckhardt, Jacob, *Weltgeschichte Betrachtungen*, Leipzig, 2nd ed. 1935.

Burma, John H., "Advantages of a Small Sociology Department," *Sociology and Social Research*, 35 (May–June, 1951), pp. 346–48.

Burtt, E. A., *Metaphysical Foundations of Modern Physical Science*, Humanities Press, 1932.

———, "The Value Presuppositions of Science," in Paul C. Obler and Herman Estrin (eds.), *The New Scientists*, Doubleday-Anchor, 1962 (reprinted from *Bulletin of the Atomic Scientists*, 13 [March, 1957]).

Bynder, Herbert, "Sociology in a Hospital: A Case Study in Frustration," in Arthur B. Shostak (ed.), *Sociology in Action*, Dorsey, 1966.

Cahnman, J. and Alvin Boskoff (eds.), *Sociology and History*, Free Press, 1964.

Cancian, Francesca, "Functional Analysis of Change," *American Sociological Review*, 25 (December, 1960), pp. 818–27.

Cantor, Nathaniel, "The Teaching and Learning of Sociology," *American Journal of Sociology*, 55 (July, 1949), pp. 18–24.

Caplow, Theodore and Reece McGee, *The Academic Marketplace*, Basic Books, 1958.

Carey, Alex, "The Hawthorne Studies: A Radical Criticism," *American Sociological Review*, 32 (June, 1967), pp. 403–16.

Carney, Richard E., "A Reply to Isidor Chein on Images of Man," distributed in printed form by the Society for the Psychological Study of Social Issues, 1959.

Carter, Hugh, "Research Interests of American Sociologists." *Social Forces*, 6 (November, 1927), pp. 209–12.

Catlin, G. E. G., *The Rules of Sociological Method*, University of Chicago, 1938.

Chapin, F. Stuart, "Report on the Questionnaire of the Committee on Teaching," *American Journal of Sociology*, 16 (May, 1911), pp. 774–85.

———, "Sociologists and Sociology," *Journal of Applied Sociology*, 10 (May–June, 1926), pp. 416–17.

———, "The Present State of the Profession," *American Journal of Sociology*, 39 (January, 1934), pp. 506–08.

Charlety, Sebastien, *Histoire du Saint-Simonisme*, Paris: Paul Hartmann, 1931.

Chein, Isidor, "Towards a Science of Morality," *Journal of Social Psychology*, 25 (1947), pp. 235–38.

———, "The Image of Man," *Journal of Social Issues*, 18 (1962), pp. 1–35.

Childe, V. G., *What Happened in History*, Pelican, 1950.

Chinoy, Eli, "Popular Sociology," in Charles H. Page (ed.), *Sociology and Contemporary Education*, Random House, 1964, pp. 115–34.

Churchman, C. West, *Theory of Experimental Inference*, Macmillan, 1948.

Clark, Carroll D., "Research Funds and the Publicly Employed Sociologist," *Social Problems*, 1 (January, 1954), pp. 98–99.

Clark, Terry, N., William Kornblum, Harold Bloom, and Susan Tobias, "Discipline, Method, Community Structure, and Decision-Making: The Role and Limitations of the Sociology of Knowledge," *American Sociologist*, 3 (August, 1968), pp. 214–17.

Clinard, Marshall C., "The Sociologist and Social Change in Underdeveloped Countries," *Social Problems*, 10 (Winter, 1963), pp. 207–19.

———, (ed.), *Anomie and Deviant Behavior*, Free Press, 1964.

Clinard, M. C. and J. W. Elder, "Sociology in India: A Study in the Sociology of Knowledge," *American Sociological Review*, 30 (August, 1965), pp. 581–87.

Clow, F. R., "Sociology in Normal Schools: The Report of a

Committee," *American Journal of Sociology*, 25 (March, 1920), pp. 584–636.

Cloward, Richard, "Illegitimate Means, Anomie, and Deviant Behavior," *American Sociological Review*, 24 (April, 1959), pp. 164–76.

Cohen, Albert K., "The Sociology of the Deviant Act: Anomie Theory and Beyond," *American Sociological Review*, 30 (February, 1965), pp. 5–14.

Cohen, Morris R., "The Social Sciences and the Natural Sciences," in W. F. Ogburn and Alexander Goldenweiser (eds.), *The Social Sciences and Their Inter-Relations*, Houghton Mifflin, 1927.

Collingwood, R. G., *The Idea of History*, Oxford, 1946.

Committee on Research of the American Sociological Society, "Report of the Committee on Research," *American Sociological Review*, 20 (February, 1955), pp. 97–100.

Committee on the Teaching of Sociology of the Southern Sociological Society, "Education for Marriage and Family Relations in Southern Colleges," *Social Forces*, 32 (October, 1953), pp. 61–65.

Commoner, Barry, The Social Responsibility of the Scientist," *Oberlin Alumni Magazine*, February, 1962, pp. 4–9.

Conant, James, *Science and Common Sense*, Yale, 1951.

———, *Modern Science and Modern Men*, Columbia, 1952.

Conyers, James E., "Negro Doctorates in Sociology," Paper presented at the Annual Meeting of the American Sociological Association, 1966.

Coogan, John Edward, S. J., "Free Will and the Academic Criminologist," *Federal Probation*, 20 (June, 1956), pp. 48–54.

Coser, Lewis A., "The Functions of Small Group Research," *Social Problems*, 3 (July, 1955), pp. 1–6.

———, *The Functions of Social Conflict*, Free Press, 1956.

———, "Georg Simmel's Style of Work: A Contribution to the Sociology of the Sociologist," *American Journal of Sociology*, 63 (May, 1958), pp. 635–40.

———, "A Question of Professional Ethics?" *American Sociological Review*, 24 (June, 1959), pp. 397–98.

———, *Continuities in the Study of Social Conflict*, Free Press, 1967.

Coser, Lewis A. and Bernard Rosenberg (eds.), *Social Theory*, Macmillan, 2nd ed., 1964.

Couch, W. T., "Objectivity and Social Science," in Helmut Schoek and J. W. Wiggins (eds.), *Scientism and Values*, Van Nostrand, 1960.

Crane, Diana, "Scientists at Major and Minor Universities: A Study of Productivity and Recognition," *American Sociological Review*, 30 (October, 1965), pp. 699–714.

———, "The Gatekeepers of Science: Some Factors Affecting the Selection of Articles for Scientific Journals," *American Sociologist*, 2 (November, 1967), pp. 195–201.

Crawford, Elisabeth T. and Albert D. Biderman (eds.), *Social Scientists and International Affairs*, Wiley, 1969.

Crawford, W. Rex, "International Relations and Sociology," *American Sociological Review*, 13 (June, 1948), pp. 263–68.

Crispi, Leo, "Social Science—a Stepchild," *American Association of University Professors Bulletin*, 31 (Summer, 1945), pp. 189–96.

Cuber, John F., "The Effect of an Introductory Sociology Course Upon Students' Verbalized Attitudes," *Social Forces*, 17 (May, 1939), pp. 490–94.

Dahrendorf, Ralf, "Out of Utopia: Toward a Reorientation of Sociological Analysis," *American Journal of Sociology*, 64 (1958), pp. 115–27.

Daire, Maurice, "Chicago Versus the Rest of Us," *American Sociological Review*, 27 (August, 1962), p. 592.

Dalby, Louise E., "Man and the Higher Order of the Machine," *Liberal Education*, 48 (October, 1962), pp. 340–41.

Dampier, William C., *A History of Science*, Macmillan, 1949.

Davenport, Russell, *The Dignity of Man*, Harper, 1955.

Davis, Arthur K., "Review of Robert A. Nisbet, *Quest for Community*," *American Sociological Review*, 18 (August, 1953), p. 443.

Davis, F. James, "Courses Preferred for Admission to Graduate Departments of Sociology," *American Sociological Review*, 25 (February, 1960), pp. 102–07.

Davis, Fred, "Comment on 'Initial Interaction of Newcomers in Alcoholics Anonymous,' " *Social Problems*, 8 (Spring, 1961), p. 365.

Davis, Jerome, "The Sociologist and Social Action," *American Sociological Review*, 5 (April, 1950), pp. 171–76.

Davis, Kingsley, *Human Society*, Macmillan, 1949.

———, "The Myth of Functional Analysis as a Special Method in Sociology and Anthropology," *American Sociological Review*, 24 (December, 1959), pp. 757–72.

Davis, Kingsley and W. E. Moore, "Some Principles of Stratification," *American Sociological Review*, 10 (April, 1945), pp. 242–49.

Davis, Kingsley *et al.*, *Modern American Society*, Rinehart, 1949.

Day, George M., "History of the Pacific Sociological Society," *Sociology and Social Research*, 40 (July–August, 1956).

De Graff, Harmon O., "The Teaching of Urban Sociology," *Social Forces*, 5 (December, 1926), pp. 248–54.

DeGrange, McQuilkin, *The Nature and Elements of Sociology*, Yale, 1953.

Demerath, N. J., III and Richard A. Peterson (eds.), *System, Change, and Conflict*, Free Press, 1967.

Dent, Carle E., "The Status of Introductory Sociology on the Pacific Coast," *Sociology and Society Research*, 21 (March–April, 1937), pp. 356–60.

Desan, Wilfred, *The Marxism of Jean-Paul Sartre*, Doubleday, 1965.

Descartes, René, *Discourse on Method*, Great Books Foundation, 1952.

Detweiler, Frederick G., "The Teaching of Sociology," *Social Forces*, 4 (September, 1925), pp. 69–70.

Deutscher, Irwin, "On Social Science and the Sociology of Knowledge," Letter to the Editor, *American Sociologist*, 3 (November, 1968), pp. 291–92.

Dewey, John, *The Quest for Certainty*, Balch, 1929.

Dexter, Lewis A., "A Note in Selective Inattention in Social Science," *Social Problems*, 6 (Fall, 1958), pp. 176–82.

Dilthey, Wilhelm, *Einleitung in die Geistewissenschaften*, Leipzig and Berlin, 2nd ed., 1923.

Doby, John *et al.*, *An Introduction to Social Research*, Stackpole, 1954.

Dodd, Stuart C., "Raising Research-to-Teaching Ratios," *Social Forces*, 35 (December, 1956), pp. 103–11.

Dore, Ronald, "Function and Cause," *American Sociological Review*, 26 (December, 1961), pp. 843–53.

Dostoevsky, Fyodor, *Notes From the Underground and The Grand Inquisitor*, Dutton, 1960.

Douglas, Jack D., *The Relevance of Sociology*, Appleton-Century-Crofts, 1969.

———, *The Impact of the Social Sciences*, Appleton-Century-Crofts, 1969.

Douglas, William O., *Freedom of the Mind*, Public Affairs Pamphlets, 1962.

Dubin, Robert, "Deviant Behavior and Social Structure: Continuities in Social Theory," *American Sociological Review*, 24 (April, 1959), pp. 147–64.

Dubos, René, *The Dreams of Reason: Science and Utopia*, Columbia University, 1961.

Dunayevskaya, Raya, *Marxism and Freedom*, Bookman, 1958.

Duncan, H. D. and W. L. Duncan, "Shifts of Interest of American Sociologists," *Social Forces*, 12 (1933), pp. 209–12.

———, "Research Interests in Sociology," *Sociology and Social Research*, 19 (1935), pp. 442–46.

Durkheim, Emile, *The Rules of Sociological Method*, translated by S. A. Solovay and J. H. Mueller, ed. by G. E. G. Catlin, University of Chicago, 1938.

———, *Suicide: A Study in Sociology*, translated by George Simpson, Free Press, 1951.

———, *Sociology and Philosophy*, Free Press, 1953.

———, *Elementary Forms of the Religious Life*, Free Press, 1954.

———, *Pragmatisme et Sociologie*, Paris: Librarie Philosophique J. Vrin, 1955.

———, "The External Reality of Society," in Edgar F. Borgetta and Henry J. Meyer (eds.), *Sociological Theory: Present Day Sociology from the Past*, Knopf, 1956; reprinted

from Emile Durkheim, *Suicide*, translated by George Simpson, Free Press, 1951, pp. 399–403.
Durkheim,, Emile, *Socialism and Saint Simon*, Alvin Gouldner (ed.), Antioch Press, 1958.
Dushkind, Donald S., "Physical, Psychological, Cultural, and Social Forces Affecting Sociological Research," *Journal of Educational Sociology*, 27 (October, 1963), pp. 80–90.
Ebeling, Gerhard, *Word and Faith*, Fortress, 1963.
Eddington, Sir Arthur, *The Philosophy of Physical Science*, Cambridge University, 1939.
Einstein, Albert, Lecture at Princeton in 1939, published as *Symposium on Science, Philosophy, and Religion*, Conference on Science, Philosophy, and Religion in Their Relation to the Democratic Way of Life, Inc., N.Y., 1941.
———, "Science and Religion," *Science News Letter*, September 21, 1940, p. 181.
———, "The Fundamentals of Theoretical Physics," *Science*, 91 (1940), pp. 487–92; reprinted in Herbert Feigl and May Brodbeck (eds.), *Readings in the Philosophy of Science*, Appleton-Century-Crofts, 1953, pp. 253–61.
Einstein, Albert and L. Infeld, *The Evolution of Physics*, Simon and Schuster, 1942.
Einstein, Albert and M. Planck, *Where Is Science Going?*, Norton, 1932.
Eisenstadt, S. N., "Institutionalization and Change," *American Sociological Review*, 29 (April, 1964), pp. 235–47.
———, "Social Change, Differentiation and Evolution," *American Sociological Review*, 29 (June, 1964), pp. 375–86.
Eister, Allan W., "Values, Sociology and the Sociologists," *Sociological Analysis*, 25 (1964), pp. 108–12.
Elliot, Mabel A., "Pressures upon Research and Publication in Sociology," *Social Problems*, 1 (January, 1954), pp. 94–97.
Emmett, Dorothy M., *Function, Purpose, and Powers*, London: Macmillan, 1958.
———, *Rules, Roles, and Relations*, St. Martin's Press, 1966.
Encyclopaedia Britannica, "Logic, History of," 1961, Vol. 14, p. 332 ff.
Engels, Friedrich, *Socialism, Utopian and Scientific*, C. H. Kerr, 1918.
———, *Dialectics of Nature*, translated by C. Dutt, International Publishers, 1940.
———, *Herr Eugen Dühring's Revolution in Science* (Anti-Dühring), Foreign Languages Publishing House, Moscow, 1962.
Erikson, Kai T., "A Comment on Disguised Observation in Sociology," *Social Problems*, 14 (1967), pp. 366–73.
Estus, Charles, "An Analysis of the Social Thought of Talcott Parsons," unpublished manuscript.
———, "A Critical Analysis of Talcott Parsons' Pattern Variables," unpublished manuscript.

Etzioni, Amitai, "Social Analysis as a Sociological Vocation," *American Journal of Sociology*, 70 (March, 1965), pp. 613–25.

———, *The Active Society*, Free Press, 1968.

———, "On Public Affairs Statements of Professional Associations," *American Sociologist*, 3 (November, 1968), pp. 279–80.

Evans-Pritchard, E. E., *Nuer Religion*, Oxford, 1956.

Executive Office of the President, Office of Science and Technology, *Privacy and Behavioral Research*, U.S. Government Printing Office, February, 1967.

Faberow, N. L. (ed.), *Taboo Topics*, Atherton, 1963.

Fallding, Harold, "Towards a Reconciliation of Mills with Parsons," *American Sociological Review*, 26 (October, 1961), pp. 778–80.

———, "Functional Analysis in Sociology," *American Sociological Review*, 28 (February, 1963), pp. 5–13.

———, *The Sociological Task*, Prentice-Hall, 1968.

Faris, Ellsworth, "Too Many Ph.D's?" *American Journal of Sociology*, 39 (January, 1934), pp. 509–12.

Faris, Robert E. L., *Chicago Sociology, 1920–1932*, Chandler, 1967.

Farnsworth, Dana L., "Rules Governing the Participation of Healthy Human Beings as Subjects in Research," Harvard University Health Services, adopted by the President and the Fellows, April 1, 1963.

Fasola-Bologna, Alfredo, "The Inevitable Radicalization of Liberal Sociologists," *The Human Factor*, 8 (Spring, 1969), pp. 19–30.

Fava, Sylvia F., "Status of Women in Professional Sociology," *American Sociological Review*, 25 (April, 1960), pp. 271–76.

Feigl, Herbert, "The Scientific Outlook: Naturalism and Humanism," *American Quarterly*, I (1949), p. 11.

Fellows, Erwin W., "Science and Values: A Survey of Current Points of View," *Scientific Monthly*, 73 (August, 1951), pp. 111–13.

———, "The Sociologist and Social Planning," *Sociology and Social Research*, 36 (March–April, 1952), pp. 220–36.

Ferriss, Abbott L., "Introductory Sociology in the Southeastern States: 1950," *Social Forces*, 29 (March, 1951), pp. 295–301.

———, "Sociological Manpower," *American Sociological Review*, 29 (February, 1964), pp. 103–14.

———, "Educational Interrelations Among Social Sciences," *American Sociologist*, 1 (February, 1965), pp. 15–23.

———, "Predicting Graduate Student Migration," *Social Forces*, 43 (1965), pp. 310–19.

———, "Sociological Manpower, Corrections," communication to the editor, *American Sociological Review*, 30 (February, 1965), p. 112.

———, "Educational Specialization of Southern Sociologists with the Doctorate," *Social Forces*, 44 (June, 1966), pp. 569–73.

Ferriss, Abbot, L., "Forecasting Supply and Demand of Sociologists," *American Sociologist*, 3 (August, 1968), pp. 225–34.

Festinger, Leon and Daniel Katz, *Research Methods in the Behavioral Sciences*, Dryden, 1953.

Feuer, Lewis, "What is Alienation? The Career of a Concept," in Maurice Stein and Arthur Vidich (eds.), *Sociology on Trial*, Prentice-Hall, 1963, pp. 127–47.

——— (ed.), *Marx and Engels: Basic Writings on Politics and Philosophy*, Doubleday, 1959.

———, *The Scientific Intellectual: the Psychological and Sociological Origins of Modern Science*, Basic Books, 1963.

Fichter, Joseph H. and William L. Kolb, "Ethical Limitations on Sociological Reporting," *American Sociological Review*, 18 (October, 1953), pp. 544–50.

Firth, Raymond, "Function," in Sol Tax (ed.), *Current Anthropology*, University of Chicago, 1955, pp. 247–51.

Fischer, George, "Current Soviet Work in Sociology: A Note on the Sociology of Knowledge," *American Sociologist*, 1 (May, 1966), pp. 127–32.

———, *Science and Ideology in Soviet Society*, Atherton, 1967.

Fischer, Louis, "A Good Long Look Inside," Review of Boris Nicolaevsky and Janet D. Zagnoria (eds.), *Power and the Soviet Elite*, Praeger, 1965, *New York Times Book Review*, November 21, 1965, p. 3.

Fitch, Robert E., "The Scientist as Priest and Savior," *Christian Century*, 75 (March 26, 1958).

Fleron, Frederic J., *Communist Studies and the Social Studies*, Rand McNally, 1969.

Foreman, Paul B., "An Analysis of Content in Introductory Sociology Courses," *Social Forces*, 17 (December, 1938), pp. 211–19.

Forsyth, F. Howard, "Relevance and the Academic Bias," *American Sociological Review*, 11 (February, 1946), pp. 26–31.

Frank, Philipp, *Einstein: His Life and Times*, translated by George Rosen, Knopf, 1947.

———, "Contemporary Science and the Contemporary World View," *Daedalus* (Winter, 1958), pp. 65–76.

———, *Modern Science and Its Philosophy*, Collier, 1961.

Frankfort, H. and H. A., John A. Wilson, and Thorkild Jacobsen, *Before Philosophy, The Intellectual Adventure of Ancient Man*, Penguin, 1949.

Friedrichs, Robert W., "Sociological Man: An Inquiry into Assumptions," *University College Quarterly*, 6 (May, 1961), pp. 23–30.

———, "Objectivity *versus* Value Neutrality?" *Faculty Forum*, (December, 1964), pp. 1–2.

———, "The Limits of 'Objectivity' in Social Research," a paper delivered at the Sixth World Congress of Sociology, Evian, France, September, 1966.

———, "The Dialectical Nature of Behavioral Science," a paper delivered at the 1967 Annual Meeting of the American Sociological Association.
———, "Choice and Commitment in Social Research," *American Sociologist*, 3 (February, 1968), pp. 8–11.
———, "Phenomenology as a General Theory of Social Action," *Journal of Value Inquiry*, 2 (Spring, 1968), pp. 1–8.
———, "The Presumptive Faith of Science," a paper delivered at the 1968 Annual Meeting of the American Association for the Advancement of Science.
Friestadt, Hans, "Modern Marxism and Scientific Knowledge: Any Common Ground?" *Studies on the Left*, 1/3 (1960), pp. 62–69.
Fromm, Erich, *The Sane Society*, Rinehart, 1955.
———, *Marx's Concept of Man*, Ungar, 1961.
———, *The Dogma of Christ and Other Essays on Religion*, Holt, Rinehart, and Winston, 1963.
———, "Problems of Interpreting Marx," in Irving Horowitz (ed.), *The New Sociology*, Oxford, 1964, pp. 188–95.
Fulton, Robert, *Original Marxism—Estranged Offspring*, Christopher, 1960.
Furfey, Paul H., "The Sociologist and Scientific Objectivity," *American Catholic Sociological Review*, 6 (March, 1945), pp. 3–12.
———, "The Social Philosophy of Social Pathologists," *Social Problems*, 2 (1954), pp. 71–75.
———, "Sociological Science and the Problem of Values," in Llewellyn Gross (ed.), *Symposium on Sociological Theory*, Row, Peterson. 1959, pp. 509–30.
Gamson, William A., "Sociology's Children of Affluence," *American Sociologist*, 3 (November, 1968), pp. 286–89.
Garfinkel, Harold, *Studies in Ethno-methodology*, Prentice-Hall 1967.
Gee, Wilson, *Social Science Research Organization in American Universities and Colleges*, Appleton-Century, 1934.
Gellner, Ernest, "Concepts and Society," *Transactions of the Fifth World Congress of Sociology*, International Sociological Association, 1962, Vol. 1.
Gerth, Hans and C. Wright Mills (eds.), *From Max Weber: Essays in Sociology*, Oxford, 1946.
Gewirth, Alan, "Can Man Change Laws of Social Science?" *Philosophy of Science*, 21 (July, 1954), pp. 229–41.
Gibson, Morgan, "Review of Fritz Pappenheim's *The Alienation of Modern Man*," in *Studies on the Left*, 1/3 (1960), pp. 121–24.
Gibson, Quentin, *The Logic of Social Inquiry*, Routledge and Kegan Paul, 1960.
Ginzburg, Benjamin, "Science," *Encyclopaedia of the Social Sciences*, Macmillan, 1937, Vol. 13, pp. 591–602.
Glass, Bentley, "The Academic Scientist: 1940–1960,"

American Association of University Professors Bulletin, 49 (Summer, 1960), pp. 149–55.

Glass, Ruth, "Detachment and Attachment," *Transactions of the Second World Congress in Sociology*, II (London: International Sociological Association, 1954), pp. 220–25.

Glazer, Nathan, "Government by Manipulation: The Social Scientist Reports for Service," *Commentary* (July, 1946), pp. 81–86.

———, "Notes Toward a Sociocultural Interpretation of American Sociology," *American Sociological Review* (October, 1946), pp. 545–53.

Goffman, Erving, *The Presentation of Self in Everyday Life*, Doubleday, 1959.

Gold, David, "Comment on 'A Critique of Tests of Significance,'" *American Sociological Review*, 23 (February, 1958), pp. 85–86.

———, "Statistical Tests and Substantive Significance," *American Sociologist*, 4 (February, 1969), pp. 42–46.

Gold, Raymond L., "Roles in Sociological Field Observation," *Social Forces*, 36 (March, 1958), pp. 217–23.

Goldschmidt, Walter, "Anthropology and the Modern World," in Walter Goldschmidt (ed.), *Exploring the Ways of Mankind*, Dryden, 1962.

Goode, William, "Community within a Community: The Professions," *American Sociological Review*, 22 (April, 1957), pp. 194–200.

———, "Encroachment, Charlatanism, and the Emerging Profession: Psychology, Sociology, and Medicine," *American Sociological Review*, 25 (December, 1960), pp. 902–14.

———, "In Memoriam: C. Wright Mills (1916–1962)," *American Sociological Review*, 27 (August, 1962), pp. 579–80.

Goodrich, Doris W., "An Analysis of Manuscripts Received by the Editors of the *American Sociological Review* from May 1, 1944 to September 1, 1945," *American Sociological Review*, 10 (December, 1945), pp. 716–25.

Gordon, W. J. J., *Synectics: The Development of Creativity*, Harper, 1961.

Gouldner, Alvin W., "Reciprocity and Autonomy," in Llewellyn Gross (ed.), *Symposium on Sociological Theory*, Row, Peterson, 1969, pp. 241–70.

———, "The Norm of Reciprocity: A Preliminary Statement," *American Sociological Review*, 25 (April, 1960), pp. 161–78.

———, "Anti-Minotaur: The Myth of a Value-Free Sociology," *Social Problems*, 9 (Winter, 1962), pp. 199–213.

———, "The Sociologist as Partisan: Sociology and the Welfare State," *American Sociologist* 3 (May, 1968), pp. 103–16.

Gouldner, Alvin W. and J. Timothy Sprehe, "The Study of

Man, 4: Sociologists Look at Themselves," *Trans-Action*, 2 (May and June, 1965), pp. 42–44.

Greer, Scott, *The Logic of Social Inquiry*, Aldine, 1969.

Gregor, James A., "Review of Erich Fromm's *Marx's Concept of Man*," *Studies on the Left*, 3/1 (1962), pp. 85–92.

———, "Review of Robert Tucker's *Philosophy and Myth in Karl Marx*," *Studies on the Left*, 2/3 (1962), pp. 95–102.

Gross, Edward, "Social Science Techniques: a Problem of Power and Responsibility," *Scientific Monthly*, 83 (November, 1956), pp. 242–47.

———, "An Epistemological View of Sociological Theory," *American Journal of Sociology*, 65 (March, 1960), pp. 441–48.

Gross, Llewellyn, *Symposium on Sociological Theory*, Row, Peterson, 1959.

———, "Preface to a Metatheoretical Framework for Sociology," *American Journal of Sociology*, 67 (September, 1961), pp. 125–43.

——— (ed.), *Sociological Theory: Inquiries and Paradigms*, Harper and Row, 1967.

Gruber, Terrell and M. Wertheimer (eds.), *Contemporary Approaches to Creative Thinking*, Atherton, 1962.

Grunbaum, Adolf, "Historical Determinism, Social Activism, and Prediction in the Social Sciences," *British Journal for the Philosophy of Science*, 7 (1956), pp. 236–40.

Gurvitch, Georges, *Dialectique et Sociologie*, Paris: Flammarion, 1962.

Habenstein, Robert W., "Critique of 'Profession' as a Sociological Category," *Sociological Quarterly*, 4 (1963), pp. 291–300.

Haller, Archibald and Edgar F. Borgatta, *Rural Sociology in 1967*, *American Sociologist*, 3 (November, 1968), pp. 289–90.

Halsted, George, *The Foundations of Science*, Science Press, 1913.

Hamilton, C. Horace, "Some Current Problems in the Development of Rural Sociology," *Rural Sociology*, 15 (December, 1950), pp. 315–21.

Hammond, Philip (ed.), *Sociologists at Work*, Free Press, 1964.

Handy, Rollo, "Personality Factors and Intellectual Production," *Philosophy of Science*, 23 (October, 1956), pp. 325–32.

Hannaford, Robert V., "Ethical Values in Scientific Method," *Liberal Education* (March, 1962), pp. 26–31.

Harris, Thomas L., "Functions of a Sociology Department in a State University," *American Journal of Sociology*, 28 (November, 1922), pp. 326–31.

Hart, Hornell, "The History of Social Thought: A Consensus of American Opinion," *Social Forces*, 6 (December, 1927), pp. 190–96.

———, "Value Judgments in Sociology," *American Sociological Review*, 3 (December, 1938), pp. 862–67.

Hart, Hornell, "The Pre-War Upsurge in Social Science," *American Sociological Review*, 14 (October, 1949), pp. 599–607.

Harte, Thomas J., "Catholics as Sociologists," *American Catholic Sociological Review*, 13 (March, 1952), pp. 2–9.

Hartt, Julian, "The Realities of the Human Situation," *The Christian Scholar*, 13 (Fall, 1960), pp. 231–36.

Hatt, Howard E., *Cybernetics and the Image of Man*, Abingdon, 1968.

Hawley, Claude E. and Lewis A. Dexter, "Some Data for Studying the Supply of Sociologists," *American Sociological Review*, 17 (February, 1952), pp. 96–97.

Heaton, E. W., *The Old Testament Prophets*, Penguin, 1961.

Heim, Karl, *The Transformation of the Scientific World View*, SCM Press, 1953.

Helbrich, Margaret L., "Occupations of Sociology Majors: A Selected Group," *Sociology and Social Research*, 43 (March–April, 1959), pp. 276–78.

Hempel, Carl, "The Logic of Functional Analysis," in Llewellyn Gross (ed.), *Symposium on Sociological Theory*, Row, Peterson, 1959, pp. 132–37.

Herberg, Will, *Judaism and Modern Man*, Farrar, Straus and Young, 1951.

———, "Theological Presuppositions of Social Philosophy," *Drew Gateway*, 29 (Winter, 1959), pp. 94–113.

Herring, Pendleton, "On Trends and Tendencies," in C. E. Boewe and R. F. Nichols (eds.), *Both Humanities and Humane: The Humanities and Social Science in Graduate Education*, University of Pennsylvania, 1960, pp. 169–81.

Herskovits, Melville J., "Tender and Tough-Minded Anthropology and the Study of Values in Culture," *Southwestern Journal of Anthropology*, 7 (1951), pp. 24–29.

———, *Cultural Anthropology*, Knopf, 1955.

Hertzler, Joyce O., "American Regionalism and the Regional Sociological Society," *American Sociological Review*, 3 (December, 1958), pp. 738–48.

Heschel, Abraham J., *The Prophets*, Harper, 1962.

Hield, Wayne, "The Study of Change in Social Science," *British Journal of Sociology*, 5 (March, 1954), pp. 1–11.

Higbie, Charles E. and Phillip E. Hammond, "A Mildly Sociological View of the Press Coverage of a Sociological Convention," *American Sociologist*, 1 (May, 1966), pp. 145–47.

Hilgard, Ernest R., *Theories of Learning*, Appleton-Century-Crofts, 1956.

Himes, Joseph S., Jr., "The Teacher of Sociology in the Negro College," *Social Forces*, 29 (March, 1951), pp. 302–05.

Hinkle, Roscoe C. and Gisela J. Hinkle, *The Development of Modern Sociology*, Doubleday, 1954.

Hobbs, A. H., *The Claims of Sociology: A Critique of Textbooks*, Telegraph Press, 1951.

Hoffer, Charles R., "The Development of Rural Sociology," *Rural Sociology*, 26 (March, 1961), pp. 1–14.

Hoffer, F. W., "Five Years of Ph.D. Research in Economics and Sociology," *Social Forces*, 4 (1925), pp. 74–77.

Holzner, Burkart, *Reality Construction in Society*, Schenckman, 1968.

Homans, George, "Schlesinger on Humanism and Empirical Research," *American Sociological Review*, 28 (February, 1963), pp. 97–100.

———, "Commentary," *Sociological Inquiry* (Spring, 1964), p. 225.

———, "Bringing Men Back In," *American Sociological Review*, 29 (December, 1969), pp. 809–18.

———, *The Nature of Social Science*, Harcourt, Brace, 1967.

Hook, Sidney, *Towards the Understanding of Karl Marx*, John Day, 1933.

———, "Karl Marx's Second Coming," in *New York Times Book Review*, May 22, 1966, p. 2.

Hopper, Janice A., "Sociologists in the 1964 National Register of Scientific and Technical Personnel," *American Sociologist*, 1 (February, 1966), pp. 71–78.

———, "Preliminary Report on Salaries and Selected Characteristics of Sociologists in the 1966 National Science Foundation Register of Scientific and Technical Personnel," *American Sociologist*, 2 (August, 1967), pp. 151–54.

Horowitz, Irving L., "Social Science Objectivity and Value Neutrality: Historical Problems and Projections," *Diogenes*, 39 (Fall, 1962), pp. 17–44.

———, "Establishment Sociology: The Value of Being Value-Free," *Inquiry*, 6 (Spring, 1963), pp. 129–39.

———, "Max Weber and the Spirit of American Sociology," *Sociological Quarterly*, 5 (1964), pp. 344–54.

——— (ed.), *The New Sociology*, Oxford, 1964.

———, "Professionalism and Disciplinarianism: Two Styles of Sociological Performances," *Philosophy of Science*, 31 (1964), pp. 275–81.

———, "The Life and Death of Camelot," *Trans-Action*, 3 (November–December, 1965), pp. 3–7, 44–47.

———, "Mainliners and Marginals: the Human Shape of Sociological Theory," in Llewellyn Gross (ed.), *Sociological Theory: Inquiries and Paradigms*, Harper & Row, 1967, pp. 358–83.

———, *The Rise and Fall of Project Camelot*, M.I.T., 1967.

———, *Professing Sociology: Studies in the Life Cycle of Social Science*, Aldine, 1968.

——— (ed.), "Sociological Self Images: A Collective Portrait," special issue of *American Behavioral Scientist*, 12 (September–October, 1969).

Horton, John, "Order and Conflict Theories of Social Problems as Competing Ideologies," *American Journal of Sociology* 71 (1966), pp. 701–13.

Hoult, Thomas, ". . . Who Shall Prepare Himself to the Battle?", *American Sociologist*, 3 (February, 1968), pp. 3–7.

Howells, William, *The Heathens: Primitive Man and His Religions*, Doubleday, 1956.

Howerth, Ira W., "Present Condition of Sociology in the United States," *Annals of the American Academy of Political and Social Sciences*, 5 (September, 1894), pp. 260–69.

Hughes, Everett C., "Professional and Career Problems of Sociology," *Transactions of the Second World Congress of Sociology*, II: *The Training, Professional Activities and Responsibilities of Sociologists* (London: International Sociological Association, 1954), pp. 178–85.

———, "Sociologists and the Public," *Transactions of the Fifth World Congress in Sociology*, I, Louvain, Belgium: International Sociological Association, 1962, pp. 77–86.

———, "Race Relations and the Sociological Imagination," *American Sociological Review*, 28 (December, 1963), pp. 879–90.

Hughes, H. Stuart, *Consciousness and Society*, Knopf, 1958.

Hughes, John E., "Catholic, Scientist, and Sociologist," *American Catholic Sociological Review*, 24 (Winter, 1963), pp. 285–301.

Human Organization, "Code of Ethics of the Society for Applied Anthropology," 10 (Summer, 1951), p. 32.

———, "Research—Business or Scholarship?—An Editorial," 11 (Fall, 1952), pp. 3–4; 11 (Winter, 1952), p. 4; 12 (Summer, 1953), pp. 3–4.

———, Editorial, 17 (Summer, 1958).

Hunt, Morton, "How Does it Come to Be So?", *The New Yorker*, January 28, 1961.

Husserl, Edmund, *Ideas: General Introduction to Pure Phenomenology*, Macmillan, 1931.

Huxley, Julian, *Knowledge, Morality, and Destiny*, Mentor, 1960.

Inkeles, Alex, *What Is Sociology?*, Englewood Cliffs, New Jersey: Prentice-Hall, 1964, Chapter 8.

Jay, Martin, "The *Institut für Sozialforschung* and the Origins of Critical Sociology," *The Human Factor*, 8 (Spring, 1969), pp. 6–18.

Jedrzejewski, Clement S., "Towards A Sociology of Civilization," multilith by author, 1966.

Jeffress, L. A. (ed.), *Cerebral Mechanism in Behavior, The Hixon Symposium*, London, 1951.

Jeffrey, R. C., "Valuation and Acceptance of Scientific Hypotheses," *Philosophy of Science*, 23 (July, 1956), pp. 237–46.

Johannesson, Olaf, *The Tale of the Big Computer: A Vision*, Coward-McCann, 1968.

John, M. E., "Rural Sociology in the Years Ahead," *Rural Sociology*, 27 (June, 1962), pp. 109–15.

Joravsky, David, *Soviet Marxism and Natural Science, 1917–1932*, Columbia University, 1961.

Jordon, Millard L., "Leisure Time Activities of Sociologists, Attorneys, Physicists, and People at Large from Greater Cleveland," *Sociology and Social Research*, 47 (April, 1963), pp. 290–97.

Kane, John J., "Are Catholic Sociologists a Minority Group?", *American Catholic Sociological Review*, 14 (March, 1953), pp. 2–12.

Kantor, J. R., *The Logic of Modern Science*, Principia, 1953.

Kaplan, Abraham, *The Conduct of Inquiry: Methodology for Behavioral Science*, Chandler, 1964.

Kaplan, Bernice, "Contrasts between Anthropologists and Sociologists at Annual Conventions," a paper delivered before the 1967 meeting of the American Anthropological Association.

Kaplan, Max, "Sociology and the President's Bold New Plan: The Role of Sociologists in Analyzing World Problems," *Social Forces*, 28 (March, 1950), pp. 285–89.

Kariel, Henry S., "Social Science as Autonomous Activity," *Scientism and Values*, Van Nostrand, 1960.

Karpf, M. J., "The Relation Between Sociology and Social Work," *Journal of Social Forces*, 3 (January, 1925), pp. 419–27.

Kassof, Allen, "American Sociology through Soviet Eyes," *American Sociological Review*, 30 (February, 1965), pp. 114–21.

Katz, Fred E., "Theory and Practice in Sociology: A Sociological Essay on a Dilemma in Sociology," a paper delivered before the American Sociological Association, 1963.

———, "Analytic and Applied Sociologists: A Sociological Essay on a Dilemma in Sociology," *Sociology and Social Research*, 48 (July, 1964), pp. 440–47.

Katzenback, Edward Jr., "Ideas: A New Defense Industry," *The Reporter*, March 7, 1961, pp. 17–21.

Kaufmann, Felix, *Methodology of the Social Sciences*, Oxford, 1944.

Kazin, Alfred, "With a Love for the Passing Ideal," a review of *The Letters of George Santayana*, Daniel Cory (ed.), Scribner's, 1955, in *New York Times Book Review*, November 13, 1955, p. 6.

Keller, Charles R., Address before the annual meeting of the New Jersey Council for the Social Studies as reported by the *New York Times*, January 15, 1961, p. E, 11.

Kelman, Herbert C., "Deception in Social Research," *Trans-action* (July–August, 1967), 20–24.

Kelsen, Hans, *The Political Theory of Bolshevism*, University of California, Berkeley, 1948.

Kemeny, John G., *A Philosopher Looks at Science*, Van Nostrand, 1959.

Kennedy, Raymond and Ruby Jo Reeves Kennedy, "Sociology

in American Colleges," *American Sociological Review*, 7 (October, 1942), pp. 661–75.

Kirk, Russell, "Is Social Science Scientific?", *New York Times Magazine*, June 25, 1961, pp. 11, 15–16, 18.

Kiser, C. V. *et al.*, "Symposium on the Use of Official Statistics for Thesis Topics in the Field of Sociology," *Milbank Memorial Fund Quarterly*, 43 (1965), pp. 7–41.

Kish, Leslie, "Some Statistical Problems in Research Design," *American Sociologist*, 24 (June, 1959), pp. 328–38.

Klausner, Samuel Z., "On Some Differences in Modes of Research Among Psychologists and Sociologists," *Transactions of the Fifth World Congress of Sociology*, IV, Louvain, Belgium: International Sociological Association, 1964, pp. 209–35.

———, "An Empirical Study of 'Ethical Neutrality' Among Behavioral Scientists," *Sociological Analysis*, 27 (Winter, 1966), pp. 223–38.

Klaw, Spencer, *The New Brahmins: Scientific Life in America*, Morrow, 1968.

Kluckhohn, Clyde and Dorothy Leighton, *The Navaho*, Harvard, 1946.

Knudsen, Dean D. and Ted R. Vaughan, "Quality in Graduate Education: A Re-evaluation of the Rankings of Sociology Departments in the Carter Report," *American Sociologist*, 4 (February, 1969), pp. 12–19.

Koenig, Daniel J., " 'Catholic Sociology' in the *American Catholic Sociological Review*," *Sociological Analysis*, 25 (Fall, 1964), pp. 174–76.

Koestler, Arthur, *The Sleepwalkers*, Macmillan, 1959.

———, *The Act of Creation*, Macmillan, 1964.

Kolaja, Jiri, "Sociology in Romania," *American Sociologist*, 3 (August, 1968), pp. 241–43.

Kolakowski, Leszek, *Toward a Marxist Humanism: Essays on the Left Today*, Grove, 1968.

———, *The Alienation of Reason: A History of Positivist Thought*, Doubleday-Anchor, 1969.

Kolb, William L., "Values, Positivism, and the Functional Theory of Religion: the Growth of a Moral Dilemma," *Social Forces* (May, 1953), pp. 305–11; reprinted in J. Milton Yinger, *Religion, Society and the Individual*, Macmillan, 1957, pp. 599–609.

———, "The Changing Prominence of Values in Modern Sociological Theory," in Howard Becker and Alvin Boskoff (eds.), *Modern Sociological Theory*, Dryden, 1957, pp. 93–132.

———, "The Place of Values in Urban Social Theory: The Clarification of a Theoretical Issue," *Alpha Kappa Deltan*, 28 (1958), pp. 37–41.

———, "Values, Politics, and Sociology," Review article in *American Sociological Review*, 25 (December, 1960), pp. 966–69.

———, "Review of *The Human Meaning of the Social Sciences*," Daniel Lerner (ed.), Meridian, 1959, in *American Sociological Review*, 25 (February, 1960), pp. 117–18.

———, "Review of Gunnar Myrdal, *Value in Social Theory*," Harper, 1959, in *American Sociological Review*, 25 (August, 1960), p. 582.

———, "Values, Politics, and Images of Man in American Sociology," *Christian Scholar*, 44 (Winter, 1961), pp. 319–31.

———, "Images of Man and the Sociology of Religion," *Journal for the Scientific Study of Religion*, 1 (October, 1961), pp. 5–22.

———, "Rejoinder to Comment of Talcott Parsons," *Journal for the Scientific Study of Religion*, 1 (Spring, 1962), pp. 214–17.

———, "Freedom and Theoretical Models in Social Science," in Bartlett H. Stoodley (ed.), *Society and Self*, Free Press, 1962.

———, "Christian Faith and Social Institutions," *Faculty Forum*, 20 (March, 1962), pp. 1–2.

———, "Review of Peter Berger, *The Precarious Vision* and *The Noise of Solemn Assemblies*, both Doubleday, 1961, in *Journal for the Scientific Study of Religion*, 2 (Fall, 1962), pp. 136–37.

Komarovsky, Mirra, "Teaching College Sociology," *Social Forces*, 30 (December, 1951), pp. 252–56.

Kornhauser, William, *Scientists in Industry: Conflict and Accommodation*, University of California, Berkeley, 1962.

Kourvetavis, George A. and Charles C. Moskos, Jr., "A Report on Sociology in Greece," *American Sociologist*, 3 (August, 1968), pp. 243–45.

Kroeber, A. L., *The Nature of Culture*, University of Chicago, 1952.

Kubie, Lawrence S., "Some Unresolved Problems of the Scientific Career," *American Scientist*, 41 (October, 1958), pp. 596–98.

Kuhn, Thomas S., *The Structure of Scientific Revolutions*, University of Chicago, 1962.

Kuhne, Otto, *Allgemeine Soziologie*, Berlin, 1958.

Kulp, Daniel L., "Preparing Sociology Teachers," *Sociology and Social Research*, 15 (November–December, 1930), pp. 135–44.

Kurtz, Richard A. and John R. Maiolo, "Surgery for Sociology: The Need for Introductory Text Opening Chapterectomy," *American Sociologist*, 3 (February, 1968), pp. 39–41.

Kutak, Robert I., "The Sociological Curriculum in the Southeastern States," *Social Forces*, 24 (October, 1945), pp. 56–66.

Labedz, Leopold, "How Free is Soviet Science? Technology under Totalitarianism," in Bernard Barber and Walter Hirsch (eds.), *The Sociology of Science*, Free Press, 1962, pp. 129–41.

Labovitz, Sanford, "Criteria for Selecting a Significance Level: A Note on the Sacredness of .05." *American Sociologist*, 3 (August, 1968), pp. 220–22.

Ladd, Everett C., Jr., "Professors and Political Petitions," *Science*, 163 (March 28, 1969), pp. 1425–30.

Laing, James T., "The Folkways of Regional Sociological Societies," *Sociology and Social Research*, 32 (July–August, 1948).

Lamont, W. D., *The Value Judgement*, Edinburgh University, 1955.

Landis, Judson T., "Rural Sociology in the Teacher's Colleges of the United States," *Rural Sociology*, 10 (September, 1945), pp. 313–16.

———, "The Sociology Curriculum and Teacher Training," *American Sociological Review*, 12 (February, 1947), pp. 113–16.

Lane, Robert "The Decline of Politics and Ideology in a Knowledgeable Society," *American Sociological Review*, 31 (October, 1966), pp. 649–62.

Langdon-Davies, John, *Russia Turns the Clock Back*, Longmans, 1949.

LaPiere, Richard, *The Freudian Ethic*, Duell, Sloan & Pearce, 1959.

de Laplace, Pierre Simon, *Traité de Probabilité*, Academy of Science, Paris, 1886.

Lapp, Ralph E., *The New Priesthood*, Harper and Row, 1965.

Larrabee, Eric, *The Self-Conscious Society*, Doubleday, 1960.

Larson, Olaf F., "The Role of Rural Sociology in a Changing Society," *Rural Sociology*, 24 (March, 1959), pp. 1–10.

Lastrucci, Carlo, *The Scientific Approach: Basic Principles of the Scientific Method*, Schenkman, 1963.

Laurence, William L., "The Manner of Matter," *New York Times Book Review*, (August 17, 1958), p. 6.

Lazarsfeld, Paul F., "What is Sociology?" *Universitets Studentkontor*, Skrivemaskinstua, Oslo, September, 1948 (mimeographed).

———, "The Sociology of Empirical Social Research," *American Sociological Review*, 27 (December, 1962), pp. 757–67.

Lazarsfeld, Paul F. and Ruth Leeds, "International Sociology as a Sociological Problem," *American Sociological Review*, 27 (October, 1962), pp. 732–41.

Lee, Alfred M., "Individual and Organizational Research in Sociology," *American Sociological Review*, 16 (October, 1951), pp. 701–07.

———, "Subsidies for Sociological Research," in A. M. Lee (ed.), *Readings in Sociology*, Barnes and Noble, 1951, pp. 407–11.

———, "Responsibilities and Privileges in Sociological Research," *Sociology and Social Research*, 37 (July, 1952–1953), pp. 367–74.

———, "Sociologists in an Integrating Society: Significance and Satisfaction in Sociological Work," *Social Problems*, 2 (October, 1954), pp. 57–66.

———, "Annual Report for 1962–63 of the Society for the Study of Social Problems Representative to the American Sociological Association Council," *Social Problems*, 11 (Winter, 1964), pp. 319–21.

———, "Annual Report for 1963–64 of the Society for the Study of Social Problems Representative to the American Sociological Association Council," *Social Problems*, 12 (Winter, 1965), pp. 356–60.

———, "The Concept of System," *Social Research*, 32 (Autumn, 1965).

———, *Multivalent Man*, Braziller, 1966.

Lenin, V. I., *Materialism and Empirio-Criticism*, Moscow: Foreign Languages Publishing House, no date.

———, *Imperialist War*, *Collected Works*, Vol. 18, International Publishers, 1930.

Lerner, Daniel (ed.), *The Human Meaning of the Social Sciences*, Meridian, 1959.

Levy, Marion J., Jr., "Some Problems for a Unified Theory of Human Nature," in Edward A. Tiryakian (ed.), *Sociological Theory, Values, and Sociocultural Change*, Free Press, 1963, pp. 9–32.

Lichman, Richard, "Indeterminacy in the Social Sciences," *Inquiry*, 10 (Summer, 1967), pp. 139–50.

Lindesmith, Alfred R., "Social Problems and Sociological Theory," *Social Problems*, 8 (Fall, 1960), pp. 98–102.

Lipset, Seymour and Neil Smelser, "The Setting of Sociology in the 1950's," in Seymour Lipset and Neil Smelser (eds.), *Sociology: the Progress of a Decade*, Prentice-Hall, 1961, pp. 1–13.

Locke, John, *An Essay Concerning Human Understanding*, Book IV, Chapter 11.

Lockwood, David, "Some Reflections on 'The Social System,'" *British Journal of Sociology*, 7 (June, 1956), pp. 134–46.

Loomis, Charles P., "In Praise of Conflict and Its Resolution," *American Sociological Review*, 32 (December, 1967), pp. 875–90.

Lowry, Ritchie P., "Influencing Leadership in Community Studies: Moral and Political Roles of the Social Scientist," in Arthur B. Shostak (ed.), *Sociology in Action*, Dorsey, 1966, pp. 100–07.

Luckmann, Thomas, "On Religion in Modern Society: Individual Consciousness, World View, Institution," *Journal for the Scientific Study of Religion*, 2 (Spring, 1963), pp. 147–62.

———, *The Invisible Religion*, Macmillan, 1967.

Luecke, Richard, "Ghosts Walk Again," *Christian Century*, October 5, 1960, pp. 1151–52.

Lundberg, George A., "The Interests of Members of the American Sociological Society, 1930," *American Journal of Sociology*, 37 (May, 1930), pp. 458–60.

———, "The Future of the Social Sciences," *Scientific Monthly*, 53 (October, 1941), pp. 346–59.

———, "Sociologists and the Peace," *American Sociological Review*, 9 (February, 1944), pp. 1–13.

———, "The Proximate Future of American Sociology: The Growth of the Scientific Method, *American Journal of Sociology*, 50 (May, 1945), pp. 501–13.

———, *Can Science Save Us?*, Longmans, Green, 1947.

———, "The Senate Ponders Social Science," *The Scientific Monthly*, 64 (May, 1947), pp. 397–411.

———, "Some Convergences in Sociological Theory," *American Journal of Sociology*, 62 (July, 1956), pp. 21–27.

———, *et al.*, *Sociology*, Harper, 1954.

———, *et al.*, *Sociology*, Harper, 2nd ed., 1958.

Lynd, Robert S., *Knowledge for What?*, Princeton, 1939.

———, "The Science of Inhuman Relations," *The New Republic*, August 27, 1949, pp. 22–25.

McCartney, James L., "The Effects of Financial Support on Trends in Sociological Theory," Unpublished paper, Department of Sociology, University of Missouri, no date (mineo).

———, "The Support of Sociological Research Trends and Consequences," Unpublished Ph.D. dissertation, University of Minnesota, 1965.

McClosky, Herbert and John H. Schaar, "Psychological Dimensions of Anomy," *American Sociological Review*, 30 (February, 1965), pp. 14–40.

McEwen, William P., *The Problem of Social-Scientific Knowledge*, Bedminster, 1963.

McKinney, John C., "Methodological Convergence of Mead, Lundberg, and Parsons," *American Journal of Sociology*, 59 (May, 1954), pp. 565–74.

McNeil, Elton B. (ed.), *The Nature of Human Conflict*, Prentice-Hall, 1965.

Mack, Raymond W., "Ego, Energy, and the Education of a Sociologist," *American Behavioral Scientist*, 12 (1968), pp. 37–40.

Macmurray, John, *The Self as Agent*, Faber and Faber, 1957.

———, *Persons in Relation*, Faber and Faber, 1961.

Malinowski, Bronislaw, *Freedom and Civilization*, Roy, 1944.

———, *Magic, Science and Religion*, Doubleday-Anchor, 1955.

Manis, Jerome G., "Situational and Personal Factors Associated with the Publication Productivity of Social Scientists after Entrance into the Academic Field," Unpublished M.A. thesis, University of Chicago, 1949.

Mannheim, Karl, *Ideology and Utopia*, Harcourt Brace, 1936.

———, *Freedom, Power, and Democratic Planning*, Oxford, 1950.

———, *Essays on Sociology and Social Psychology*, Oxford, 1953.

Manuel, Frank E., *The Prophets of Paris*, Harvard, 1962.
Marcuse, Herbert, *One Dimensional Man*, Beacon Press, 1964.
———, *Eros and Civilization*, Vintage, 1968.
———, *Reason and Revolution*, Beacon Press, 1968.
Marsh, Robert M., "Training for Comparative Research in Sociology," *American Sociological Review*, 27 (February, 1962), pp. 147–49.
Martel, Martin, "Some Controversial Assumptions in Parsons' Approach to Social Systems Theory, *Alpha Kappa Deltan*, 29 (Winter, 1959).
Martindale, Don, "Social Disorganization: The Conflict of Normative and Empirical Approaches," in Howard Becker and Alvin Boskoff (eds.), *Modern Sociological Theory in Continuity and Change*, Dryden, 1957, pp. 340–67.
———, "The Roles of Humanism and Scientism in the Evolution of Sociology," in G. K. Zollschan and Walter Hirsch (eds.), *Explorations in Social Change*, Houghton Mifflin, 1964, pp. 452–90.
———, "Limits of and Alternatives to Functionalism in Sociology," in Don Martindale (ed.), *Functionalism in the Social Sciences: The Strengths and Limits of Functionalism in Anthropology, Economics, Political Science, and Sociology*, American Academy of Political and Social Science, Monograph 5 (February, 1965), pp. 144–62.
Marx, Karl, Letter dated April, 1867 (890), in *Der Briefwechsel zwischen Friedrich Engels und Karl Marx, 1844–1883*, Stuttgart: Dietz, 1913.
———, *Capital*, 3 Vols., translated by E. Unterman, Kerr, 1906–09.
———, *Critique of Political Economy*, Kerr, 1913.
———, Selected Essays, International, 1926.
———, *Selected Works*, Cooperative Publishing Society, Moscow, 1935, Vol. I.
———, *The German Ideology*, International, 1939.
———, *Letters to Americans, 1848–1895*, International, 1953.
———, "Preface to Contribution to a Critique of Political Economy," in Karl Marx and Friedrich Engels, *Selected Works*, Vol. I, Moscow: Foreign Languages Publishing House, 1955.
———, *The Holy Family*, Moscow: Foreign Language Press, 1956.
———, *Economic and Philosophic Manuscripts*, Moscow: Foreign Languages Press, 1959.
———, *Economic and Philosophic Manuscripts of 1844*, Dirk J. Struik, (ed.), International, 1963.
———, "Sixth Thesis on Feuerbach," in Howard Selsam and Harry Martel (eds.), *Reader in Marxist Philosophy*, International, 1963.
———, "Bruno Bauer, 'Die Fahigkeit der Hentigen Juden und Christen, Frei zu Werden'," in T. B. Bottomore

(ed.), *Karl Marx: Early Writings*, McGraw-Hill, 1964, pp. 32–40.

Marks, Karl, "Theorien ueber den Mehrwert," in T. B. Bottomore and Maximilien Rubel (eds.), *Karl Marx: Selected Writings*, McGraw-Hill, 1964, pp. 157–60.

Marx, Karl and Friedrich Engels, *A Handbook of Marxism*, Emile Burns (ed.), Random House, 1935.

———, *Selected Correspondence, 1846–1895*, International, 1942.

Maslow, A. H. (ed.), *New Knowledge in Human Values*, Harper, 1959.

Mazur, Allan, "The Littlest Science," *American Sociologist*, 3 (August, 1968), pp. 195–200.

Mead, George Herbert, "National-Mindedness and International-Mindedness," *International Journal of Ethics*, 39 (1929), pp. 395–407.

Mead, Margaret, "Research with Human Beings: A Model Derived from Anthropological Field Practice," *Daedalus*, 98 (Spring, 1969), pp. 361–86.

Meadows, Paul, "Towards the New Human Image," *Noetics*, 1/1 (1964).

Medalia, Nahum Z. and Ward S. Mason, "Position and Prospects of Sociologists in Federal Employment," *American Sociological Review*, 28 (April, 1963), pp. 280–87.

Meltzer, Bernard N., "The Productivity of Social Scientists," *American Journal of Sociology*, 55 (July, 1947), pp. 25–29.

Meltzer, Leo, "Scientific Productivity in Organizational Settings," *Journal of Social Issues*, 12 (1956), pp. 32–40.

Mercer, Blaine E. and Judson B. Pearson, "The Ethics of Academic Status-Striving," *Sociology and Social Research*, 47 (October, 1962), pp. 51–56.

Mercer, Blaine E. and Judson B. Pearson, "Personal and Institutional Characteristics of Academic Sociologists," *Sociology and Social Research*, 46 (April, 1962), pp. 259–70.

Merrill, Francis E., "Social Selves and Social Problems," *Sociology and Social Research*, 49 (July, 1965), pp. 389–400.

Merton, Robert K., "Science, Technology and Society in Seventeenth Century England," *Osiris*, IV, Part 2, Bruges, 1938.

———, "Social Structure and Anomie," *American Sociological Review*, 3 (October, 1938), pp. 677–82.

———, "The Role of the Intellectual in Public Bureaucracy," *Social Forces*, 23 (May, 1945), pp. 405–15.

———, *Social Theory and Social Structure*, Free Press, 1949.

———, *Social Theory and Social Structure*, Free Press, Rev. ed., 1957.

———, "Notes on Problem-Finding in Sociology," in Robert Merton, Leonard Broom, and Leonard Cottrell, Jr., *Sociology Today*, Basic Books, 1959, pp. ix–xxxiv.

———, "Now the Case *for* Sociology," *New York Times Magazine*, July 16, 1961, pp. 14, 19–21.

———, "Social Conflict over Styles of Sociological Work,"

Transactions of the Fourth World Congress of Sociology, III, Louvain, Belgium: International Sociological Association, 1961, pp. 21–44.

———, "Science and the Social Order," in Bernard Barber and Walter Hirsch (eds.), *The Sociology of Science*, Free Press, 1962, pp. 16–28.

Merton, Robert and Robert A. Nisbet, *Contemporary Social Problems*, Harcourt, Brace, 1961.

Michalson, Carl, *The Rationality of Faith*, Scribners, 1963.

Miller, G. A., E. Galanter, and K. H. Pribram, *Plans and the Structure of Behavior*, Holt, 1960.

Mills, C. Wright, "The Professional Ideology of Social Pathologists," *American Journal of Sociology*, 49 (September, 1943), pp. 165–80.

———, "Two Styles of Research in Current Social Studies," *Philosophy of Science*, 20 (1953), pp. 266–75.

———, *The Sociological Imagination*, Oxford, 1959.

———, *The Marxists*, Dell, 1962.

———, *Power, Politics, and People*, Oxford, 1963.

Millsap, Mary Ann, "The Spatial Mobility of American Doctoral Social Scientists: A Cohort Analysis," Paper presented at the Annual Meeting of the American Sociological Association, 1967.

Mintz, Geraldine R., "Some Observations on the Function of Women Sociologists at Sociology Conventions," *American Sociologist*, 2 (August, 1967), pp. 158–59.

"Minutes of the First Meeting of the 1964 Council, Montreal, August 30, 1964," *American Sociological Review*, 29 (December, 1964), 890–91.

Mizruchi, E. H., *Success and Opportunity: A Study of Anomie*, Free Press, 1964.

Modrzhinskaia, E. D., "Progressionye iavlenie v sovremennor amerikansor sotsiologii," ("Progressive Phenomena in Contemporary American Sociology"), *Voprosy filosofi*, November, 1962, pp. 3–18.

Montagu, Ashley, "Review of Theodora Kroeber, *Ishi in Two Worlds: A Biography of the Last Wild Indian in North America*," University of California, Los Angeles, 1961, *New York Times Book Review*, December 10, 1961, pp. 20, 22.

Moore, Barrington, Jr., *Political Power and Social Theory*, Harvard, 1958.

———, "Revolution in America?" *New York Review of Books*, January 30, 1969, pp. 6–12.

Moore, Wilbert E., "The Whole State of Sociology," *American Sociological Review*, 24 (October, 1959), pp. 715–18.

———, "A Reconsideration of Theories of Social Change," *American Sociological Review*, 25 (December, 1960), pp. 810–18.

———, *Social Change*, Prentice-Hall, 1963.

Moore, Wilbert, E. "Predicting Discontinuities in Social Change," *American Sociological Review*, 29 (June, 1964), pp. 331–38.

———, "The Utility of Utopia's," *American Sociological Review*, 31 (December, 1966), pp. 765–72.

———, *Order and Change: Essays in Comparative Sociology*, Wiley, 1967.

Moreno, J. L., "Psychiatric Encounter in Soviet Russia," an undated pamphlet reprinted with some alterations, from *Progress in Psychotherapy*, Grune and Stratton, 1960, Vol. 5, pp. 1–24.

Morris, C. W., "Pragmatism and Metaphysics," *Philosophical Review*, 43 (November, 1934), pp. 549–64.

———, "Pierce, Mead, and Pragmatism," *Philosophical Review*, 47 (March, 1938), pp. 109–27.

Motz, Anabelle B., Wayne C. Rohrer, and Patricia Dagilaitis, "American Sociological Regional Societies: Social Characteristics of Presidents," *Sociological Inquiry*, 35 (Spring, 1965), pp. 207–18.

Murray, Henry A. and C. D. Morgan, "A Clinical Study of Sentiments," *Genetic Psychology Monographs*, 32 (1945).

Myrdal, Gunnar, *An American Dilemma*, Harper & Row, 1955.

———, *Value in Social Theory*, Harper & Row, 1959.

Naegele, Kasper D., "Some Observations on the Scope of Sociological Analysis," in Talcott Parsons *et al.*, *Theories of Society*, Vol. 1, Free Press, 1961, pp. 3–29.

Nagel, Ernest, "The Concept Levels in Social Theory," in Llewellyn Gross (ed.), *Symposium on Sociological Theory*, Row, Peterson, 1959, pp. 167–95.

———, "The Place of Science in a Liberal Education, *Daedalus*, 8 (Winter, 1959), pp. 56–74.

———, *The Structure of Science*, Princeton, 1961.

———, "Malicious Philosophies of Science," in Bernard Barber and Walter Hirsch (eds.), *The Sociology of Science*, Free Press, 1962, pp. 623–39.

Natanson, Maurice (ed.), *Philosophy of the Social Sciences: A Reader*, Random House, 1963.

"National Support for Behavioral Science," pamphlet dated February, 1958, Washington, D.C.

Nettler, Gwynne, "Toward a Definition of the Sociologist," *American Sociological Review*, 12 (October, 1947), pp. 553–60.

———, "Should Small Departments Have Majors in Sociology?" *Sociology and Social Research*, 35 (March–April, 1951), pp. 349–50.

———, "Cruelty, Dignity, and Determinism," *American Sociological Review*, 24 (June, 1959), pp. 375–84.

———, "On Cruelty, Dignity and Determinism, *American Sociological Review*, 24 (October, 1959), pp. 692–93.

———, "Using Our Heads," *American Sociologist*, 3 (August, 1968), pp. 200–07.

Neurath, Otto, *Empirische Soziologie*, Vienna: Springer, 1931.

Niebuhr, H. Richard, *Radical Monotheism and Western Culture*, Harper, 1960.

Nilsson, Nils Ake, "Pasternak: 'We are the Guests of Existence," *Reporter*, (November 27, 1958), pp. 34–35.

Nisbet, Robert, "Sociology as an Art Form," in Maurice Stein and Arthur Vidich (eds.), *Sociology on Trial*, Prentice-Hall, 1963.

———, *The Sociological Tradition*, Basic Books, 1966.

———, *Tradition and Revolt*, Random House, 1968.

Northrop, F. S. C., "Ethics and the Integration of Natural Knowledge," *The Nature of Concepts, Their Inter-relation and Role in Social Structure*, Proceedings of the Stillwater Conference, Stillwater, Oklahoma, June, 1950.

———, "Cultural Values," in A. L. Kroeber (ed.), *Anthropology Today*, University of Chicago, 1953, pp. 668–81.

———, "Values," in Sol Tax (ed.), *An Appraisal of Anthropology Today*, University of Chicago, 1953, pp. 322–41.

———, *The Logic of the Sciences and the Humanities*, Meridian, 1959.

Novack, George (ed.), *Existentialism versus Marxism*, Delta, 1966.

O'Brien, Robert W., Clarence C. Schrag, and Walter T. Martin (eds.), *Readings in General Sociology*, Houghton Mifflin, 2nd ed., 1957.

——— (eds.), *Readings in General Sociology*, Houghton Mifflin, 3rd ed., 1964.

O'Neill, William L., "Divorce and the Professionalization of the Social Scientist," *Journal of the History of the Behavioral Sciences*, 2 (October, 1966), pp. 291–302.

Obler, Paul C. and Herman Estrin (eds.), *The New Scientist*, Doubleday-Anchor, 1962.

Odum, Howard W., *American Sociology: The Story of Sociology in the United States through 1950*, Longmans, Green, 1951.

Odajnk, Walter, *Marxism and Existentialism*, Doubleday-Anchor, 1965.

Oppenheimer, Robert, "The Growth of Science and the Structure of Culture," *Daedalus* (Winter, 1958), pp. 67–76.

Orzack, Louis H., "Report on Sociology Courses and Sociology Teachers in Massachusetts Colleges and Universities," *American Sociologist*, 1 (November, 1966), pp. 257–58.

Ostwald, Wilhelm, *Vorlesungen uber Naturphilosophie*, Leipzig, 1905, (available in English translation as *Natural Philosophy*, New York, 1910).

Page, Charles, "Sociology as a Teaching Enterprise," in Robert K. Merton *et al.* (eds.), *Sociology Today*, Basic Books, 1959, pp. 579–600.

Palmore, Erdman, "Sociologists' Class Origins and Political Ideologies," *Sociology and Social Research*, 47 (October, 1962), pp. 45–50.

Pappenheim, Fritz, *The Alienation of Modern Man*, Monthly Review Press, 1959.

Pappworth, M. H., *Human Guinea Pigs: Experimentation on Man*, Beacon Press, 1968.

Park, Peter, "The Cretan Dictum: A Functional Analysis of Sociology," *American Sociologist*, 2 (August, 1967), pp. 155–57.

Parker, Douglas A, "On Values and Value Judgments in Sociology," Communications to the Editor, *American Sociological Review*, 32 (June, 1967), 463–66.

Parsons, Talcott, "The Place of Ultimate Values in Sociological Theory," *Ethics* (April, 1935), pp. 282–316.

———, *The Structure of Social Action*, McGraw-Hill, 1937.

———, "The Professions and Social Structure," *Social Forces*, 17 (1939), pp. 457–67.

———, "The Present Position and Prospects of Systematic Theory in Sociology," in Georges Gurvitch and Wilbert E. Moore (eds.), *Twentieth-Century Sociology*, Philosophical Library, 1945.

———, "Preface to the Second Edition," *The Structure of Social Action*, 2nd ed., Free Press, 1949.

———, *The Social System*, Free Press, 1951.

———, "Man in his Social Environment—as Viewed by Modern Social Science," *Centennial Review*, 1 (Winter, 1957).

———, "Some Problems Confronting Sociology as a Profession," *American Sociological Review*, 24 (August, 1959), pp. 547–59.

———, "Report of the Committee on the Profession, *American Sociological Review*, 25 (December, 1960), p. 945.

———, "Pattern Variables Revisited: A Response to Robert Dubin," *American Sociological Review*, 25 (August, 1960), pp. 467–83.

———, "Comment," *Journal for the Scientific Study of Religion*, 1 (October, 1961), pp. 22–29.

———, "An Outline of the Social System," in Talcott Parsons, *et al.*, *Theories of Society*, Vol. 1, Free Press, 1961, pp. 30–79.

———, "The Point of View of the Author," in Max Black (ed.), *The Social Theories of Talcott Parsons*, Prentice-Hall, 1961.

———, "Some Aspects of the Relation between Social Science and Ethics," in Bernard Barber and Walter Hirsch (eds.), *The Sociology of Science*, Free Press, 1962, pp. 590–95.

———, "Evolutionary Universals in Society," *American Sociological Review*, 29 (June, 1964), pp. 339–57.

———, "The Sibley Report on Training in Sociology," *American Sociological Review*, 29 (June 1964), pp. 747–48.

———, "Evaluation and Objectivity in Social Science: An Interpretation of Max Weber's Contributions," in the Proceedings of the German Sociological Association," *Deutsche Gessellschaft für Sociologie* and *Journal of Social Sciences*, Vol. 17, No. 1, 1965; reprinted in Talcott

Parsons, *Sociological Theory and Modern Society*, Free Press, 1967, pp. 79–101.

———, "The Editor's Column," *American Sociologist*, 1 (May, 1966), pp. 124–26.

———, *Societies: Evolutionary and Comparative Perspectives*, Prentice-Hall, 1966.

———, "The Editor's Column," *American Sociologist*, 2 (May, 1967), p. 64.

———, "Introduction to the Paperback Edition," *The Structure of Social Action*, Free Press, 1968.

———, "Research with Human Subjects and the 'Professional Complex,'" *Daedalus*, 98 (Spring, 1969), pp. 325–60.

———, *Religious Perspectives of College Teaching in Sociology and Social Psychology*, Hazen Foundation, no date.

Parsons, Talcott and R. F. Bales, *Family, Socialization and Interaction Process*, Free Press, 1955.

Parsons, Talcott, R. F. Bales, and E. A. Shils, *Working Papers in the Theory of Action*, Free Press, 1953.

Parsons, Talcott, *et al.*, *Toward a General Theory of Action*, Harvard University, 1951.

Parsons, Talcott and Edward Shils, "Values, Motives, and Systems of Action," in Talcott Parsons and E. Shils (eds.), *Toward a General Theory of Action*, Harvard University, 1951, pp. 47–233.

Parsons, Talcott and Neil J. Smelser, *Economy and Society*, Free Press, 1959.

Pazhitnov, L., "Uistokov revoliutsionnogo perevorota v filosofii," *Kommunist*, 2 (February, 1958), p. 88.

Pearson, Karl, *The Grammar of Science*, Meridian, 1957.

Petras, James F. and Michael Shute, "Berkeley '65," *Partisan Review*, 32 (Spring, 1965), pp. 314–23.

Pfuetze, Paul E., *Self, Society, Existence*, Harper, 1954.

Podell, Lawrence, Martin Vogelfanger, and Roberta Rogers, "Sociology in American Colleges: Fifteen Years Later," *American Sociological Review*, 24 (February, 1959), pp. 87–95.

Poincaré, Henri, *Science and Hypotheses*, London: Walter Scott, 1907.

———, *Dernières Pensées*, Paris: Ernest Flammarion, 1913, as translated and adapted in Kingsley Davis, *et al.* (eds.), *Modern American Society*, Rinehart, 1949, pp. 3–17.

Polanyi, Michael, "Scientific Outlook: Its Sickness and Cure," *Science*, 125:3246 (March 15, 1957), pp. 480–84.

———, *Personal Knowledge: Toward a Post-Critical Philosophy*, University of Chicago, 1958.

———, "The Republic of Science," *Minerva*, 1 (Autumn, 1962), pp. 49–61.

Pollard, William, *Chance and Providence*, Scribners, 1958.

Popovich, Mihailo, "What American Sociologists Think About Their Science and Its Problems," *American Sociologist*, 1 (May, 1966), pp. 133–35.

Popper, Karl, *The Poverty of Historicism*, Beacon, 1957.

———, "Problems of Scientific Knowledge," *Bulletin of the International House of Japan*, 12 (October, 1963).

Pravda, 240, p. 664, as quoted by John Langdon-Davies, *Russia Turns the Clock Back*, Longmans, 1949.

Price, Derek, *Little Science, Big Science*, Columbia University, 1963.

Queen, Stuart A., "Sociologists in the Present Crisis," *Social Forces*, 20 (October, 1941), pp. 1–7.

———, "Can Sociologists Face Reality?" *American Sociological Review*, 7 (February, 1942), pp. 1–12.

"Questions for Sociology: An Informal Round Table Symposium," *Social Forces*, 13 (December, 1934), pp. 165–223.

Radcliffe-Brown, A. R., *Taboo*, Cambridge University, 1939.

Rapoport, Anatol, "Uses and Limitations of Mathematical Models in Social Science," in Llewellyn Gross (ed.), *Symposium on Sociological Theory*, Row, Peterson, 1959.

Rapoport, Robert N., "Notes on the Disparagement of 'Sociologizing' in Collaborative Research," *Human Organization*, 16 (Spring, 1957), pp. 14–15.

Reckless, Walter C., "Minimum Standards of Training in Research Techniques: Papers from a Round Table," *Sociology and Social Research*, 18 (January–February, 1934), pp. 203–22.

Record, Wilson, "Some Reflections on Bureaucratic Trends in Sociological Research," *American Sociological Review*, 25 (June, 1960), pp. 411–14.

———, "Foundation Support of Social Science in the U.S.A.: A Critique," *Sociologia Internationalis*, 1 (Summer, 1963).

Reid, L. A. "Religion, Science, and Other Modes of Knowledge," *Hibbert Journal*, 54 (October, 1955), pp. 2–14.

Remming, Gunter W., *Road to Suspicion: A Study of Modern Mentality and the Sociology of Knowledge*, Appleton-Century-Crofts, 1967.

———, "The Age of Suspicion: A History of the Sociology of Knowledge in Two Countries," mineographed, undated.

"Reports on the Introductory Course in Sociology in American Colleges and Universities," *Journal of Educational Sociology*, 7 (September, 1933), entire issue.

Rickert, Heinrich, *Die Grenzen der Naturwissenschaftlichen Begriffbildung*, Tubingen, 2nd ed., 1913.

Rieff, Philip, *Freud: The Mind of the Moralist*, Viking, 1959.

Riley, Matilda White, "Membership of the American Sociological Association, 1950–59," *American Sociological Review*, 25 (December, 1960), pp. 914–26.

Rjazanov, D. and V. Adoratski (eds.), *Historisch-Kritische Gesamtausgabe*, Berlin: Marx-Engels Verlag, 1932.

Robbins, Richard, "Sociology and Congressional Lawmaking," in Arthur B. Shostak (ed.), *Sociology in Action*, Dorsey, 1966, pp. 188–200.

Roe, Anne, "The Psychology of the Scientist," *Science*, 134 (August 18, 1961), pp. 456–59; reprinted in Paul C. Obler and Herman A. Estrin (eds.), *The New Scientist*, Doubleday-Anchor, 1962, pp. 84–92.

Rogers, Everett M. and John P. Clark, "Social Change and Introductory Rural Sociology Courses," *Rural Sociology*, 24 (September, 1959), pp. 267–71.

Rohrer, Wayne C. and A. B. Motz, "The Presidency of Three Learned Societies: Social Characteristics of the Presidents and Modes of Accession to Office," *Sociology and Social Research*, 46 (April, 1962), pp. 271–81.

Roman, Paul and Philip Taietz, "Academic Structure and Disengagement: The Emeritus Professor," Paper presented at the Annual Meeting of the American Sociological Association, 1966.

Rosander, A. C., *Elementary Principles of Statistics*, Van Nostrand, 1951.

Rose, Arnold M., *Theory and Method in the Social Sciences*, University of Minnesota, 1954.

Ross, E. A., "The Sociologist in the Role of Prophet," *American Sociological Review*, 8 (February, 1943), pp. 10–14.

Roth, Julius, "Dangerous and Difficult Enterprise?" *American Sociological Review*, 24 (June, 1959), p. 398.

Rothbard, Murray N., "The Mantle of Science," in Helmut Schoek and J. W. Wiggins, (eds.), *Scientism and Values*, Van Nostrand, 1960, pp. 159–80.

Rudner, Richard, "The Scientist as Scientist Makes Value Judgments," *Philosophy of Science*, 20 (January, 1953), pp. 1–6.

———, "Can Science Provide an Ethical Code?" *The Humanist* (September–October, 1958), pp. 35–47.

Ruebhausen, Oscar M. and Orville G. Brim, Jr., "Privacy and Behavioral Research," Paper presented at the Rockefeller Institute Conference on Law and the Social Role of Science, April 8, 1965.

Rumney, Jay and Joseph Maier, *Sociology: The Science of Society*, Henry Schuman, 1953.

Runciman, W. G., *Social Science and Political Theory*, Cambridge University, 1963.

Russell, Bertrand, *The Problems of Philosophy*, Holt, 1912.

———, *Religion and Science*, Home University Library, 1935.

———, "The Social Responsibilities of Scientists," in Paul C. Obler and Herman Estrin (eds.), *The New Scientist*, Doubleday-Anchor, 1962; reprinted from *Science*, 131: 3378 (February 12, 1960).

Sackman, Harold, *Computers, System Science and Evolving Society: The Challenge of Man-Machine Digital Systems*, Wiley, 1967.

Safilios-Rothschild, Constantina, "The Present Status of Sociology in Greece," *American Sociologist*, 3 (November, 1968), pp. 280–84.

Salomon, Albert, *The Tyranny of Progress*, Noonday, 1955.

Sanford, Nevitt, "Social Science and Social Reform," *Journal of Social Issues*, 21 (April, 1965), pp. 54–70.

Saran, A. K., "Some Aspects of Positivism in Sociology," *Transactions of the Fifth World Congress of Sociology*, International Sociological Association, 1962, pp. 220–23.

Sartre, Jean-Paul, *L'Être et le Néant, Essai d'Ontologie Phénoménologique*, Paris: Gallimard, 1950. English translation by Hazel E. Barnes as *Being and Nothingness*, Philosophical Library, 1950.

———, *Critique de la raison dialectique, précédé de Question de méthode*, Paris: Gallimard, 1960.

———, "Materialism and Revolution," in Jean-Paul Sartre, *Literary and Philosophic Essays*, New York, 1962.

———, *Search for a Method: the Sartrian Approach to the Sociology and Philosophy of History*, translated by Hazel Barnes, Knopf, 1963.

Saveth, Edward N. (ed.), *American History and the Social Sciences*, Free Press, 1964.

Scheler, Max, *The Eternal in Man*, Harper, 1961.

Schilling, Harold K., "Concerning the Nature of Science and Religion: A Study of Presuppositions," pamphlet, State University of Iowa, 1958.

Schlesinger, Arthur M., Jr., "A Humanist Looks at Empirical Social Research," *American Sociological Review*, 27 (December, 1962), pp. 768–71.

Schmid, Calvin F. and Mildred Giblin, "Needs and Standards in Training Sociologists," *Sociology and Social Research*, 39 (May–June, 1955).

Schloeck, Helmut and J. W. Wiggins (eds.), *Scientism and Values*, Van Nostrand, 1960.

Schuler, Edgar A., "The Role of the Sociologist as Advisor Overseas," *American Sociologist*, 1 (May, 1966), pp. 149–42.

Schütz, Alfred, *Collected Papers I: The Problem of Social Reality*, Maurice Natanson (ed.), The Hague: Martinus Nijhoff, 1962.

———, *Collected Papers II: Studies in Social Theory*, Arird Brodersen (ed.), The Hague: Martinus Nijhoff, 1965.

———, *Collected Papers III: Studies in Phenomenological Philosophy*, I. Schütz (ed.), The Hague: Martinus Nijhoff, 1966.

———, *The Phenomenology of the Social World*, Northwestern University, 1967.

Schwartz, George and Philip Bishop, *Moments of Discovery*, Basic Books, 1958.

Scott, John Finley, "The Changing Foundations of the Parsonian Action Scheme," *American Sociological Review*, 28 (October, 1963), pp. 716–35.

Sears, Robert R., "Social Behavior and Personality Development," in Talcott Parsons *et al.* (eds.), *Toward a General Theory of Action*, Harvard University, 1951, pp. 465–77.

Seeley, John R., "Social Science? Some Probative Problems,"

in Maurice Stein and Arthur Vidich (eds.), *Sociology on Trial*, Prentice-Hall, 1963.
———, *The Americanization of the Unconscious*, International Science Press, 1967.
Segerstedt, Torgny T., *The Nature of Social Reality, An Essay in the Epistemology of Empirical Sociology*, Bedminster, 1966.
Selsam, Howard, "Some Comments on Lenin's Philosophical Notebooks," *Studies on the Left*, 3/2 (1963).
Selsam, Howard and Harry Martel (eds.), *Reader in Marxist Philosophy*, International Publishers, 1963.
Selvin, Hanan, "A Critique of Tests of Significance in Survey Research," *American Sociologist*, 22 (October, 1957), pp. 519–27.
———, "Education of Sociologists," *British Journal of Sociology*, 15 (1964), pp. 262–66.
Selznick, Philip, "Review of *Invitation to Sociology*," *American Sociological Review*, 29 (April, 1964), pp. 285–86.
Sewell, William H., "Rural Sociological Research, 1936–1965," *Rural Sociology*, 30 (December, 1965), pp. 428–51.
Shanas, Ethel, "The *A.J.S.* Through Fifty Years," *American Journal of Sociology*, 50 (May, 1945), pp. 522–33.
Sheldon, Henry D., Jr., "Analysis of the 1941 Census of Research," *American Sociological Review*, 6 (October, 1941), pp. 531–42.
———, "Analysis of the 1962 Census of Research," *American Sociological Review*, 7 (October, 1942), pp. 534–37.
Shepards, H., "Basic Research and the Social System of Pure Science," *Philosophy of Science*, 23 (October, 1956), pp. 48–57.
Shibutani, Tamotsu, *Society and Personality: an Interactionist Approach to Social Psychology*, Prentice-Hall, 1961.
Shils, Edward, "Social Inquiry and the Autonomy of the Individual," in Daniel Lerner (ed.), *The Human Meaning of the Social Sciences*, Meridian, 1959, pp. 114–57.
———, "The Calling of Sociology," in Talcott Parsons *et al.*, *Theories of Society*, Vol. 2, Free Press, 1961, pp. 1405–50.
Sibley, Elbridge, "Professional Activities and Responsibilities of Sociologists in the United States," *Transaction of the Second World Congress of Sociology*, II, London: International Sociological Association, 1954, pp. 216–19.
———, "The Objectives of Sociological Training," *American Sociological Review*, 25 (August, 1960), pp. 571–75.
———, *The Education of Sociologists in the United States*, Russell Sage Foundation, 1963.
Siekevitz, Philip, "A New Ethics for Science," *The Nation*, March 15, 1958.
Silvert, Kalman K., "American Academic Ethics and Social Research Abroad," *American Universities Field Staff Reports Service*, West Coast South America Series, Vol. XII, No. 3, 1965.
Simey, Lord, "Weber's Sociological Theory, and the Modern

Dilemma of Value and Belief in the Social Sciences," in Joan Brothers (ed.), *Readings in the Sociology of Religion*, Pergamon, 1967, pp. 89–114.

Simpson, George E., *Suicide: A Study in Sociology*, Free Press, 1951.

———, *Sociologist Abroad*, The Hague: Martinus Nijhoff, 1959.

Simpson, George E. and J. Milton Yinger, *Racial and Cultural Minorities*, Harper, Rev. ed., 1958.

Simpson, Richard L., "A Modification of the Functional Theory of Stratification," *Social Forces*, 35 (December, 1956), pp. 132–37.

———, "Expanding and Declining Fields in American Sociology," *American Sociological Review*, 26 (June, 1961), pp. 458–66.

Sjoberg, Gideon, "Science and Changing Publication Patterns," *Philosophy of Science*, 23 (1956), pp. 90–96.

———, (ed.), *Politics, Ethics, and Social Research*, Schenkman, 1968.

Skinner, B. F., "Freedom and the Control of Men," *Perspectives USA*, New Directions, 15 (1956).

Skipper, James K., Jr., Anthony L. Guenther, and Gilbert Nass, "The Sacredness of .05: A Note Concerning the Uses of Statistical Levels in Social Science," *American Sociologist*, 2 (February, 1967), pp. 16–18.

Sletto, Raymond F., "Role of Sociologists in Public Affairs," *Social Forces*, 28 (December, 1949), pp. 233–34.

Small, Albion W., "What is a Sociologist?" *American Journal of Sociology*, 8 (January, 1903), pp. 468–77.

———, "Fifty Years of Sociology in the United States: 1865–1915," *American Journal of Sociology*, 21 (May, 1916), pp. 721–864.

Smith, Keith, "Distribution-free Statistical Methods and the Concept of Power Efficiency," in Leon Festinger and Daniel Katz (eds.), *Research Methods in the Behavioral Sciences*, Dryden, 1953.

Smith, T. V., "The Social Philosophy of George Herbert Mead," *American Journal of Sociology*, 37 (January, 1931), pp. 368–85.

———, "Peirce, Mead, and Pragmatism," *Philosophical Review*, 47 (March, 1938), pp. 109–27.

Smith, T. V., and C. W. Morris, "Pragmatism and Metaphysics," *Philosophical Review*, 43 (November, 1934), pp. 549–64.

Smith, William C., "Difficulties of the Small Sociology Department," *Sociology and Social Research*, 35 (March–April, 1951), pp. 273–76.

Benoit-Smullyan, Emile, "The Sociologism of Emile Durkheim," in Harry Elmer Barnes (ed.), *An Introduction to the History of Sociology*, University of Chicago, 1948.

Snell, Putney and Russell Middleton, "Ethical Relativism and Anomia," *American Journal of Sociology*, 67 (1962), pp. 430–38.

Snow, C. P., "The Moral Un-Neutrality of Science," in Paul Obler and Herman Estrin (eds.), *The New Scientist*, Doubleday-Anchor, 1962.

Sorokin, Pitirim A., *Fads and Foibles in Modern Sociology*, Regnery, 1956.

———, "Sociology of Yesterday, Today, and Tomorrow," *American Sociological Review*, 30 (December, 1965), pp. 833–43.

Spirkin, A. G., "On the Nature of Consciousness," *Voprosy Filosofic*, XV/6 (June, 1961).

Srole, Leo, "Social Integration and Certain Corollaries: An Exploratory Study," *American Sociological Review*, 21 (December, 1956), pp. 709–16.

Struening, E. L. and A. H. Richardson, "A Factor Analytic Exploration of the Alienation, Anomia and Authoritarian Domain," *American Sociological Review*, 30 (October, 1965), pp. 768–76.

"Statement on Professional Ethics," *AAUP Bulletin*, Autumn, 1966, pp. 290–91.

Stein, Maurice and Arthur Vidich (eds,), *Sociology on Trial*, Prentice-Hall, 1963.

Stern, Alfred, "Science and the Philosopher," *American Scientist*, 44 (July, 1956), pp. 281–95; reprinted in Paul C. Obler and Herman Estrin (eds.), *The New Scientist*, Doubleday-Anchor, 1962, pp. 280–301.

Stewart, William H., "Clarification of Procedure on Clinical Research and Investigation Involving Human Subjects," *American Sociologist*, 2 (February, 1967), p. 21.

Storer, Norman W., "The Literature of Science and the Publication Explosion," paper read at the Annual Meeting of the American Sociological Association, 1964.

Straus, Murray A. and David J. Radel, "Eminence, Productivity, and Power of Sociologists in Various Regions," *American Sociologist*, 4 (February, 1969), pp. 1–4.

Strauss, Anselm, *The Social Psychology of George Herbert Mead*, University of Chicago, 1956.

Street, Paul, "Introduction," in Gunnar Myrdal, *Value in Social Theory*, Harper, 1959, pp. ix–xlvi.

Sullivan, Mortimer A., Jr., Stuart A. Queen, and Ralph C. Patrick, Jr., "Participant Observation as Employed in the Study of a Military Training Program," *American Sociological Review*, 23 (December, 1958), pp. 660–67.

Sussman, Marvin B., "The Social Problems of the Sociologist," *Social Problems* II (Winter, 1964), pp. 215–25.

———, "The Sociologist as a Tool of Action," in Arthur B. Shostak (ed.), *Sociology in Action*, Dorsey, 1966, pp. 3–12.

Taft, Donald, *Criminology*, Rev. ed., Macmillan, 1950.

Tarski, A. "The Semantic Conception of Truth and the Foundations of Semantics," *Philosophy and Phenomenological Research*, 4 (1944), pp. 341–76.

Taton, R., *Reason and Chance in Scientific Discovery*, Basic Books, 1962.

Taylor, Carl C., "Sociology on the Spot," *Rural Sociology*, 2 (December, 1937), pp. 373–81.

———, "Participation of Sociologists in National Affairs," *American Sociological Review*, 7 (April, 1942), pp. 157–59.

———, "The Sociologist's Part in Planning the Columbia Basin," *American Sociological Review*, 11 (June, 1946), pp. 321–30.

Taylor, C. W. and Frank Baron (eds.), *Scientific Creativity, Its Recognition and Development*, Wiley, 1963.

Taylor, John F. A., "The Masks of Society: the Grounds for Obligation in the Scientific Enterprise," *Journal of Philosophy*, 15 (June, 1958).

———, *The Masks of Society*, Appleton-Century-Cofts, 1966.

Taylor, K. W., "Rules of Evidence," Letter to the Editor, *American Sociologist*, 3 (November, 1968), pp. 301–03.

Tax, Sol (ed.), *An Appraisal of Anthropology Today*, University of Chicago, 1953.

Thomson, David, "Scientific Thought and Revolutionary Movements," *Impact of Science on Society*, 6 (March, 1955).

Tibbitts, Helen G., "Research in the Development of Sociology: A Pilot Study in Methodology," *American Sociological Review*, 27 (December, 1962), pp. 892–901.

Timasheff, Nicholas S., *Sociological Theory: Its Nature and Growth*, Random House, Rev. ed., 1961.

Tiryakian, Edward A., *Sociologism and Existentialism*, Prentice-Hall, 1962.

———, "Existential Phenomenology and the Sociological Tradition," *American Sociological Review*, 30 (October, 1965), pp. 674–88.

——, "A Problem for the Sociology of Knowledge: The Mutual Unawareness of Emile Durkheim and Max Weber," *European Journal of Sociology*, 7 (1966), pp. 330–36.

"Tiryakian-Berger Exchange," *American Sociological Review*, 32 (April, 1966), pp. 259–64.

Tolman, Edward C., "A Psychological Model," in Talcott Parsons *et al.* (eds.), *Toward a General Theory of Action*, Harvard University, 1951, pp. 279–359.

Tucker, Robert, *Philosophy and Myth in Karl Marx*, Cambridge University, 1946.

Tumin, Melvin, "The Functionalist Approach to Social Problems," *Social Problems*, 12 (Spring, 1965), pp. 379–88.

Turner, Henry A., *et al.*, "Political Orientations of Academically Affiliated Sociologists," *Sociology and Social Research*, 46 (April, 1962), pp. 273–89.

Tylor, E. B., *Primitive Culture*, 5th ed., London, 1871.

Underwood, Richard, *The Possibility of the World in "Time of the World-Picture": Prolegomena to a Study of the Depth Psychology of C. G. Jung in Relation to Contemporary Theologi-*

cal Interpretation, unpublished doctoral dissertation, Drew University, 1961.

The University Community and Overseas Research: Guidelines for the Future, A Public Policy Statement from the Board of Trustees of Education and World Affairs, March 29, 1967.

Vaughan, Ted R. and Larry T. Reynolds, "The Sociology of Symbolic Interactionism," *American Sociologist*, 3 (August, 1968), pp. 208–14.

Vincent, Melvin, "Trends and Emphases in Sociology," *Sociology and Social Research*, 33 (April, 1949), pp. 255–62.

Vogt, Edvard, "Objectivity in Research in the Sociology of Religion," in Joan Brothers (ed.), *Readings in the Sociology of Religion*, Pergamon, 1967, pp. 115–25.

von Mises, Richard, *Positivism*, George Braziller, 1956.

Waddington, C. H., *The Scientific Attitude*, Pelican, 1941.

Walter, Paul F., "A Philosophy for Sociologists," *Sociology and Social Research*, 31 (March–April, 1947), pp. 262–67.

Wanderer, Jules J., "Academic Origins of Contributors to the *A.S.R.*, 1955–65," *American Sociologist*, 1 (November, 1966), pp. 241–43.

Ward, Lester, *Dynamic Sociology*, New York, 1883.

———, *Pure Sociology*, New York, 1903.

Warner, W. Lloyd, *American Life, Dream and Reality*, University of Chicago, 1953.

Watson, James D., *The Double Helix: A Personal Account of the Discovery of DNA*, Atheneum, 1968.

Watts, Alan W., *The Joyous Cosmology: Adventures in the Chemistry of Consciousness*, Pantheon, 1962.

Waxman, Chaim I. (ed.), *The End of Ideology Debate*, Funk and Wagnalls, 1969.

Webb, Eugene J., Donald T. Campbell, Richard D. Schwartz, and Lee Sechrest, *Unobtrusive Measures, Nonreactive Research in the Social Sciences*, Rand McNally, 1966.

Weber, Max, "Wissenschaft als Beruf," *Gesammelte Aufsaetze zur Wissenschaftslehre*, Tübingen, 1922; translated and published as "Science as a Vocation," in Hans Gerth and C. Wright Mills (eds.), *From Max Weber: Essays in Sociology*, Oxford, 1958, pp. 129–56.

———, *The Theory of Social and Economic Organization*, translated by Talcott Parsons, Oxford, 1947.

———, *The Methodology of the Social Sciences*, translated and edited by Edward A. Shils and Henry A. Finch, Free Press, 1949.

Werkmeister, W. H., "Theory Construction and the Problem of Objectivity," in Llewellyn Gross (ed.), *Symposium on Sociological Theory*, Row, Peterson, 1959, pp. 483–508.

White, Leslie, *The Science of Culture*, Grove, 1949.

White, William Foote, "The Role of the U.S. Professor in Developing Countries," *American Sociologist*, 4 (February, 1969), pp. 19–28.

Whitehead, Alfred North, *Science and the Modern World*, Cambridge University, 1926.

———, *Aims of Education*, Macmillan, 1938.

Wiener, Norbert, "A Rebellious Scientist After Two Years," *Bulletin of the Atomic Scientists*, 4 (November, 1948), pp. 338–39.

———, *The Human Use of Human Beings: Cybernetics and Society*, Houghton Mifflin, 1950.

Wiener, Philip P., "Raising Some Fundamental Questions," *New York Times Book Review*, April 19, 1959, p. 31.

Willhelm, Sidney, "Scientific Unaccountability and Moral Accountability," in Irving L. Horowitz (ed.), *The New Sociology*, Oxford, 1964, pp. 181–87.

Williams, Robin, "Some Further Comments on Chronic Controversies," *American Journal of Sociology*, 71 (May, 1966), pp. 717–21.

Wilson, Everett K., *Sociology: Rules, Roles, and Relationships*, Dorsey, 1966.

Wilson, Logan, *The Academic Man: Sociology of a Profession*, Oxford, 1958.

Winch, Peter, *The Idea of a Social Science and Its Relation to Philosophy*, Routledge and Kegan Paul, 1958.

Windelband, Wilhelm, *Geschichte und Naturwissenschaft*, Strassburg, 1894.

Winter, Gibson, *Elements For a Social Ethic: Scientific and Ethical Perspectives on Social Process*, Macmillan, 1966.

Wolff, Kurt, "Notes Toward a Socio-cultural Interpretation of American Sociology," *American Sociological Review*, 11 (October, 1946), pp. 545–53.

———, "The Sociology of Knowledge and Sociological Theory," in Llewellyn Gross (ed.), *Symposium on Sociological Theory*, Row, Peterson, 1959.

Wolff, Kurt and Barrington Moore, Jr., *The Critical Spirit: Essays in Honor of Herbert Marcuse*, Beacon Press, 1968.

Wolff, Robert P., Barrington Moore, and Herbert Marcuse, *A Critique of Pure Tolerance*, Beacon Press, 1968.

Woods, Sister Frances Jerome, "The Image of the American Catholic Sociologist," *American Catholic Sociological Review*, 23 (Fall, 1962), pp. 195–206.

Woodward, C. Vann, "Our Past Isn't What It Used to Be," *New York Times Book Review*, July 28, 1963, pp. 1, 24, 25.

Wrong, Dennis, "The Failure of American Sociology," *Commentary* (November, 1959), pp. 375–80.

———, "The Oversocialized Conception of Man in Modern Sociology," *American Sociological Review*, 26 (April, 1961), pp. 183–93.

———, "Human Nature and the Perspective of Sociology," *Social Research*, 30 (Autumn, 1963), pp. 300–18.

Young, Donald, "Sociology and the Practicing Professions," *American Sociological Review*, 20 (December, 1955), pp. 641–48.

Youngblood, Bonney, "The Status of Rural Sociological Research in the State Agricultural Experiment Stations," *Rural Sociology*, 14 (June, 1949), pp. 111–15.
Zelený, Jindřich, *Die Wissenschaftslogik bei Marx und "Das Kapital,"* Akademie-Verlag, Berlin, 1968.
Zeleny, Leslie D., "Introductory Sociology in State Teachers Colleges," *Sociology and Social Research*, 23 (July–August, 1939), pp. 555–61.
Zetterberg, Hans, *Sociology in the United States of America, 1945–1955*, UNESCO, 1956.
———, *Social Theory and Social Practice*, Bedminster, 1962.
Znaniecki, Florian, *The Social Role of the Man of Knowledge*, Columbia University, 1940.
Zuurdeeg, Willem F., *An Analytical Philosophy of Religion*, Abingdon, 1958.

Bibliography for Foreword

[English translations given when available]

Adorno, Theodor, and Walter Dirks (Editors), *Soziologische Exkurse*. Institut fuer Sozialforschung. Frankfurt: Europaische Verlagsanstalt, 1956.
Aron, Raymond, *Marxism and the Existentialists*. New York: Harper & Row, 1969.
Bourdieu, Pierre, and Jean-Claude Passeron, "Sociology and Philosophy in France Since 1945—Death and Resurrection of a Philosophy Without Subject." *Social Research*, Vol. 34, No. 1, Spring, 1967, pp. 162–212.
Bourdieu, Pierre, Jean-Claude Chamboredon, Jean-Claude Passeron, *Le Métier de Sociologue*, I. Paris: Mouton/Bordas, 1968.
Dahrendorf, Ralf, *Essays in the Theory of Society*. Stanford: Stanford University Press, 1968.
Desroche, Henri, *Socialismes et Sociologie Religieuse*. Paris: Éditions Cujas, 1965.
Ginsburg, Morris, *Essays in Sociology and Social Philosophy*, I, II. London: Heinemann, 1956.
Gurvitch, Georges, *Determinismes sociaux et Liberté Humaine*. Paris: Presses Universitaires de France (2nd Edition), 1963.
Gurvitch, Georges, *La Vocation Actuelle de la Sociologie*, I. Paris: Presses Universitaires de France (Third Edition), 1963.
Habermas, Jürgen, "Zur Logik der Sozialwissenschaften," *Philosophische Rundschau*, Bieheft 5. Tubingen: Mohr (Siebeck), 1967.
Habermas, Jürgen, *Erkenntnis und Interesse*. Frankfurt: Suhrkamp, 1968.
Horkheimer, Max, *Kritische Theorie*, I, Ii, Frankfurt: Suhrkamp, 1968.

Lefebvre, Henri, "Forme, Fonction, Structure dans *Le Capital*," *L'Homme et la Société*, No. 7, Janvier-Fevrier, 1968, pp. 69–82.

Schelsky, Helmut, *Ortsbestimmung der deutschen Soziologie.* Düsseldorf-Köln: Diederichs, 1965.

Schelsky, Helmut, *Auf der Suche nach Wirklichkeit: Gesammelte Aufsatze.* Düsseldorf-Köln: Diederichs, 1965.

Touraine, Alain, *Sociologie de l'Action.* Paris: Seuil, 1965.

Index